STEVE BACON

Hammers in Focus

A PHOTOGRAPHIC HISTORY OVER THREE DECADES

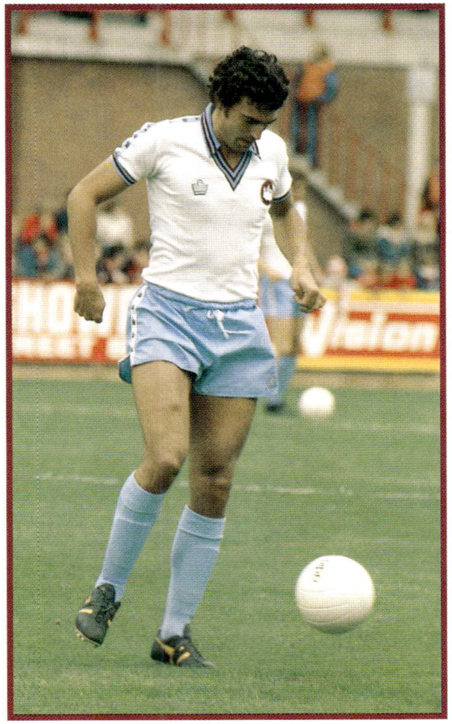

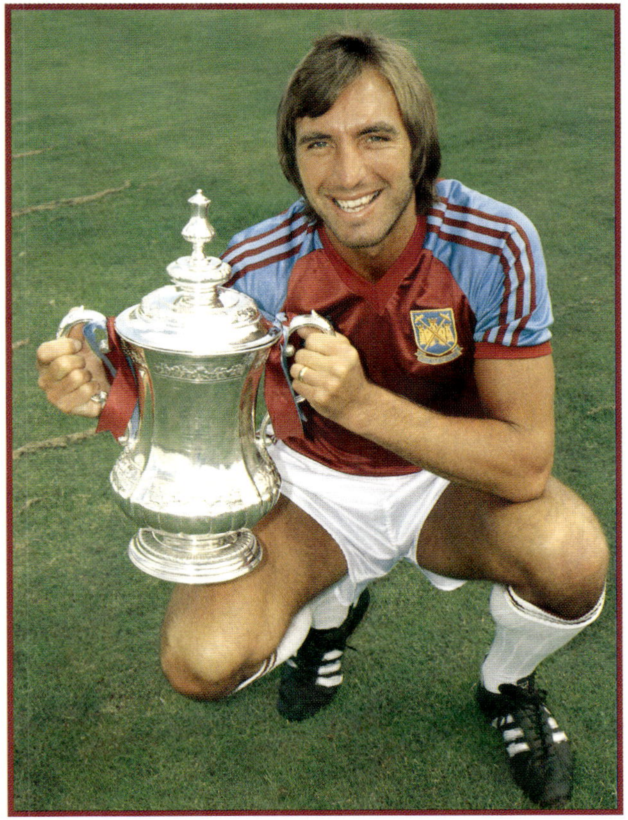

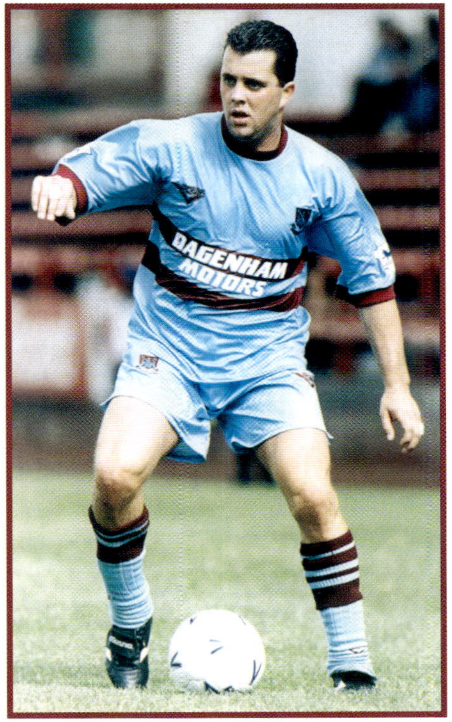

The Hallamshire Press 1998

Published by The Hallamshire Press

The Hallamshire Press is an imprint of
Interleaf Productions Limited
Broom Hall
Sheffield S10 2DR
England

Typeset by Interleaf Productions Limited
Printed in Singapore

British Library Cataloguing in Publication Data:

Bacon, Steve
Hammers in focus : a photographic history over three decades
1. West Ham United - History 2. West Ham United - Pictorial works
I. Title
796.3'34'0942176

ISBN 1 874718 47 4

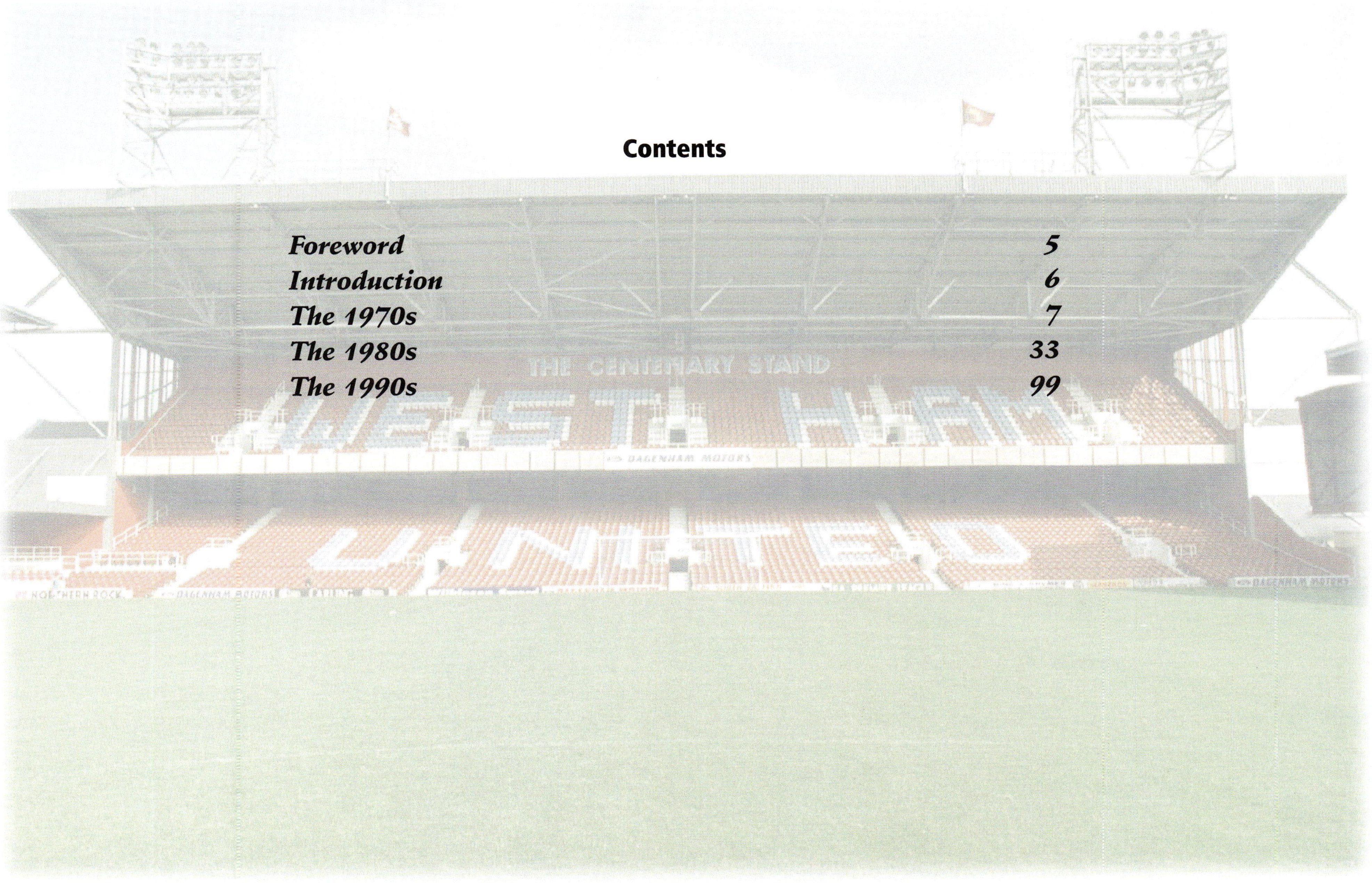

Contents

This book is dedicated to my mother, Eileen, and my late father, Thomas, who put up with my many and varied fads as a youngster. Over thirty years ago mum dubbed my venture into photography another 'five-minutes' wonder'. I proved you wrong on that one at least, didn't I?

I would like to thank the following people for their help in compiling this book: my brother, Martin (what he doesn't know about West Ham United just isn't worth knowing); Nicky Hayes of *The Sun* for taking the fine photographs of myself; and Clive Leatherdale, whose book *West Ham United: From Greenwood to Redknapp Match by Match* was a great help in matching some of the pictures to their correct games when memory failed.

Foreword

If a stranger was introduced to Steve Bacon and asked to guess his likely occupation, I doubt very much whether the answer 'West Ham United's official photographer' would spring immediately to mind!

This certainly passed through my mind when Steve first showed up at our Chadwell Heath training ground more than twenty years ago. Since then he has become a popular figure with both players and supporters alike: a real character whom the crowd immediately associate now as part of the overall 'team'. He has lasted the course longer than most of the players—including myself—and that in itself is testimony to his own particular brand of skills.

I can assure you that it takes a very special individual to survive at one club for as long as Steve has. Footballers are such diverse personalities and the first priority of any photographer is to gain their trust. Whenever someone from the media is around, players will initially show a certain wariness. The fact that Steve first contacted the club while working for the local newspaper obviously helped break down that initial barrier and, gradually, as he became our regular 'snapper', the lads would automatically include him in the general banter and mickey-taking.

With such a long association with the club, Steve is bound to have witnessed a few controversies behind the scenes but, then again, he has never sought to benefit from his privileged position and remains continually loyal to West Ham. He has always been only too pleased to help players out with additional 'shots' from matches and has earned their respect for the quality and professionalism of his work.

A still photograph can often capture the raw emotion and passion of a game even better than a moving image; a single expression of joy or anguish may encapsulate the mood and atmosphere of an entire match. Steve has accumulated a superb back catalogue of just such images, providing a fascinating insight into the highs and lows of West Ham's recent history.

All Hammers' fans know the unpredictable nature of their team, but few clubs can boast the really exceptional affinity and loyalty that seems to unite all of those associated with the club, at whatever level. Steve continues to bring to life the excitement of being part of that culture and, with West Ham currently constructing their strongest squad for many years, I am sure that some memorable moments are beckoning in the not-too-distant future.

Trevor Brooking, MBE

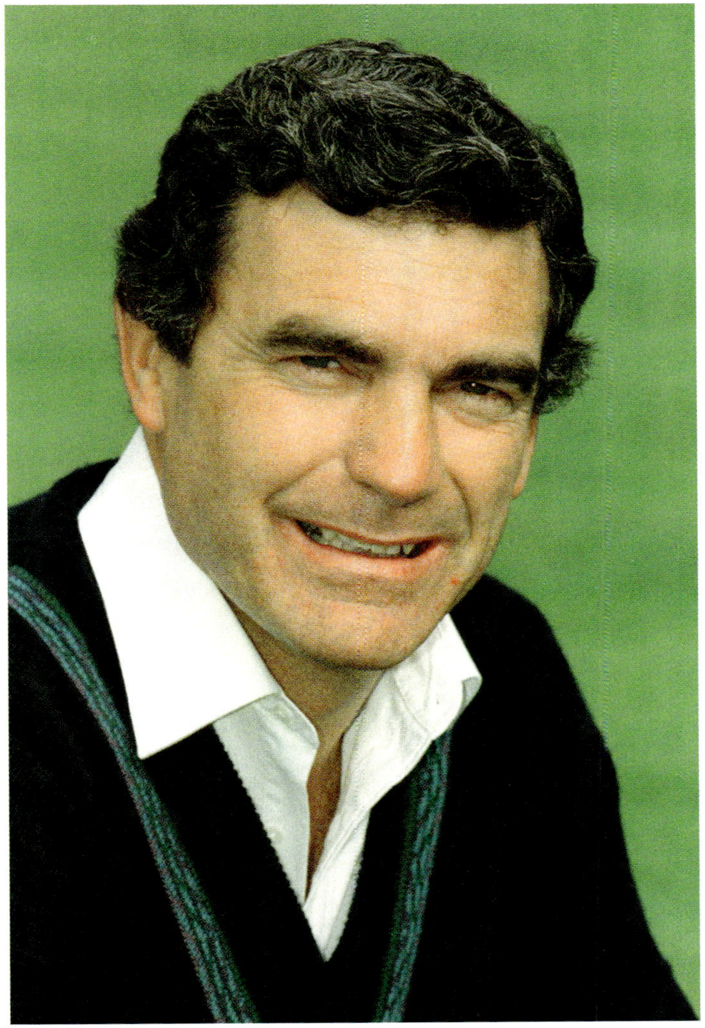

Introduction

Steve Bacon has been an unmissable figure at football grounds the length and breadth of the country for over twenty years. Wherever West Ham United are playing you will find him photographing the action from the touchlines.

Steve, the son of a Billingsgate fish porter, is proud of his East End roots and still lives just a long free-kick from the Boleyn Ground where he has covered matches for both the Newham Recorder *and the club programme since 1976.*

'Having supported the Hammers since I was a youngster,' says Steve, 'it was a dream come true to be asked to photograph their matches, and since 1976 I've missed only a handful of games.'

Steve left East Ham Grammar School in 1968 keen to find a job in photography but, with no success in that direction, took a job as a clerical assistant in the Civil Service, a position that would last all of six months.

'I couldn't cope with the nine-to-five regime,' he says, 'so I was always looking through the job adverts in the newspapers. I found a job in a photographic studio in the City where I gained a good basic training, but it still wasn't what I wanted.'

A series of good-fortuned contacts finally led Steve to a meeting with Arthur Edwards, now the much-respected Sun *royal photographer. 'Arthur was rapidly becoming more and more involved at the* Sun *and needed somebody to handle his local agency work around the East End,' explains Steve.*

'One thing led to another and, after serving my "apprenticeship" covering non-league football and then the likes of Orient and Millwall, I progressed to covering the Hammers on a permanent basis.'

Becoming a regular and respected face on the West Ham scene, Steve was soon invited to become the club's official photographer. 'John Lyall asked me if I could take the job on, and I jumped at the chance,' says Steve. 'My first official team group was for the 1980–81 season with the newly-won FA Cup proudly on display.'

Since then Steve has supplied all of the club's photographic needs, supplying shots for the programme, Hammers' Shop and commercial department. His job has taken him all over the world, including the Centenary Tour to Australia in the summer of 1995.

'I can never thank the directors of the club enough for inviting me on that tour — truly the trip of a lifetime. But then that's the way it is at West Ham: they have the reputation of being a family club and I have been privileged to be part of that family for so many years.'

This collection of over 200 photographs, selected and captioned by Steve himself, is testament to the skill and versatility of one of football's most colourful characters, recognised by both players and supporters alike at football grounds all over the country.

Steve is also well respected by his fellow professionals in what is, sometimes, a cut-throat business. His good-humoured approach to his trade has won him many friends and it shows in the photographs he produces.

It's been my good fortune to work closely with Steve for many years now. The value of having someone who thinks along the same lines is literally beyond measure. Steve also puts doing a proper job before personal convenience which, since this often means the pair of us working some very odd hours, has made a similar sense of humour perhaps the most important aspect of the relationship!

Trevor Smith
Recorder Newspapers
July 1998

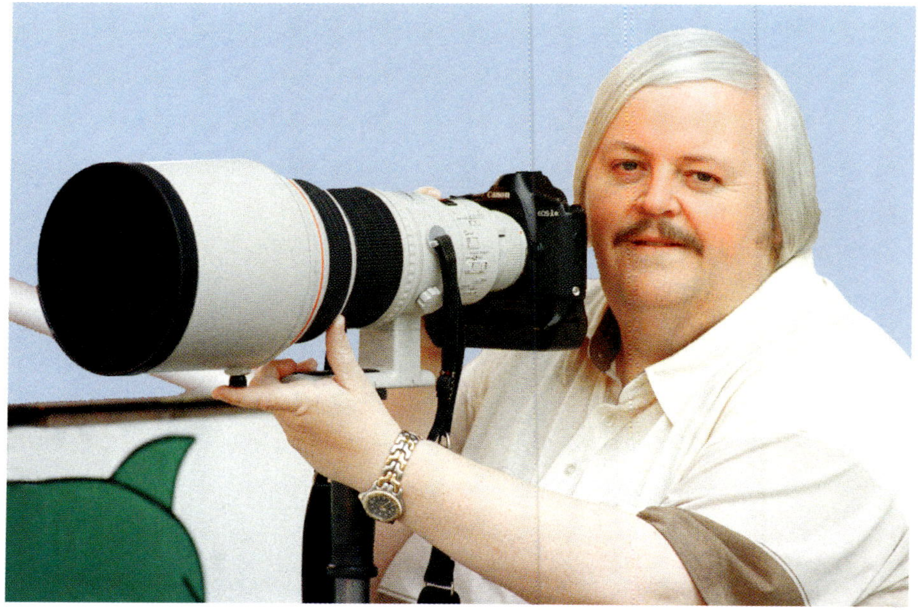

Steve Bacon

The 1970s

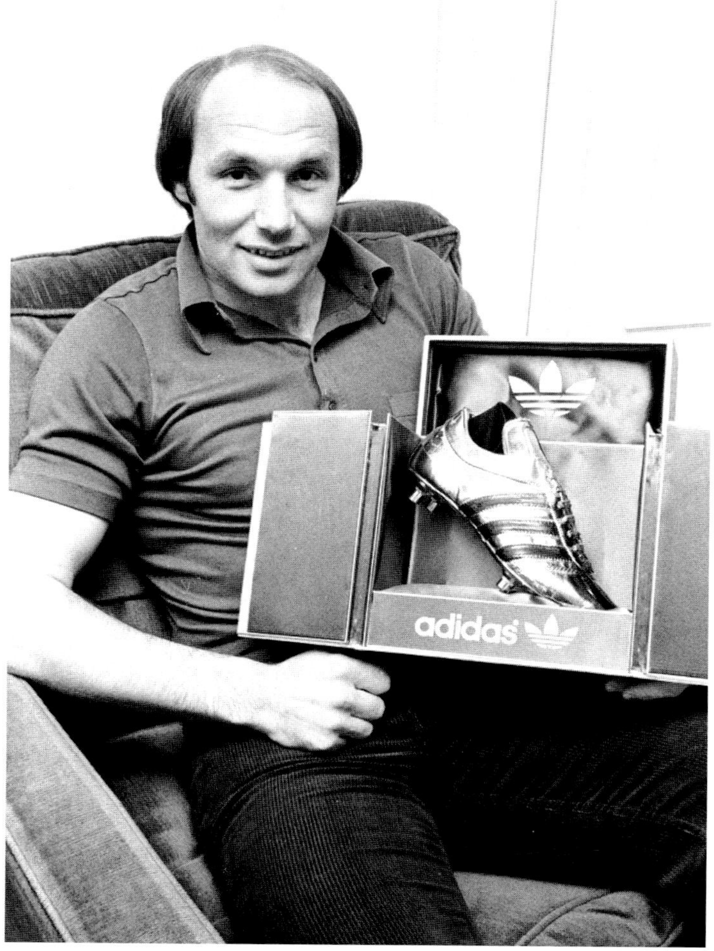

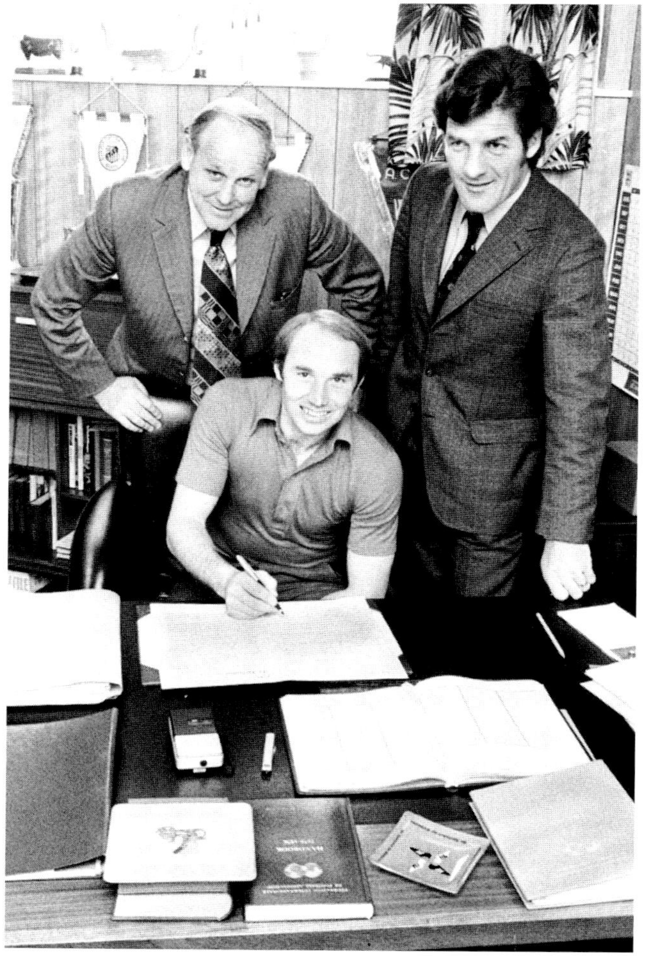

Golden boy. Bryan Robson proudly poses with his Adidas Golden Boot award at his Woodford Green home in May 1979. Pop won the award for scoring 26 league and cup goals.

Second time around. Bryan Robson rejoins the Hammers in October 1976, signing up in front of a delighted Ron Greenwood and John Lyall.

Mine host. Pop Robson, Pat Holland, Bill Green and Tommy Taylor toast Frank Lampard at the opening of his Plaistow pub, The Britannia. Keith Robson pulls himself another pint in the background.

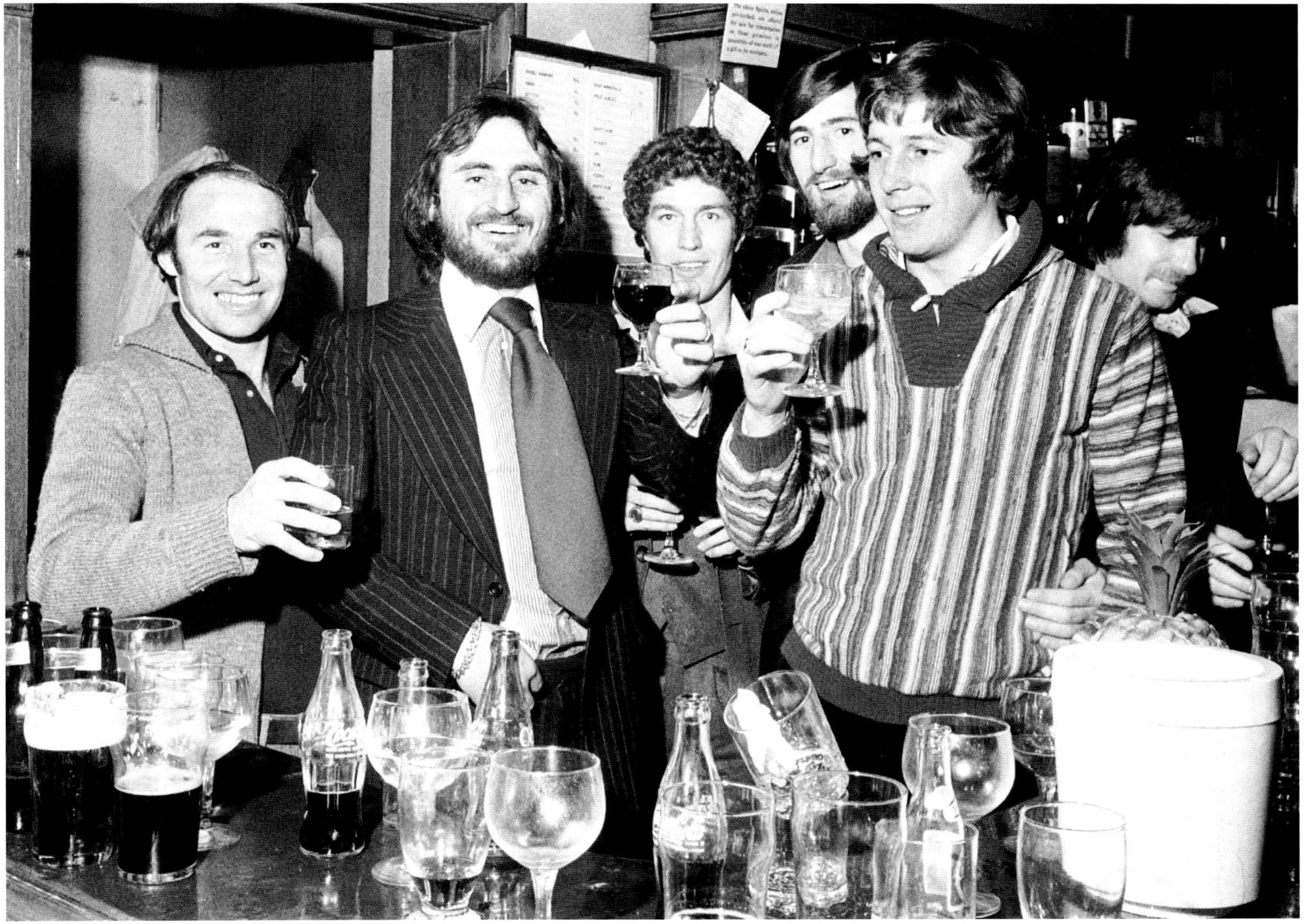

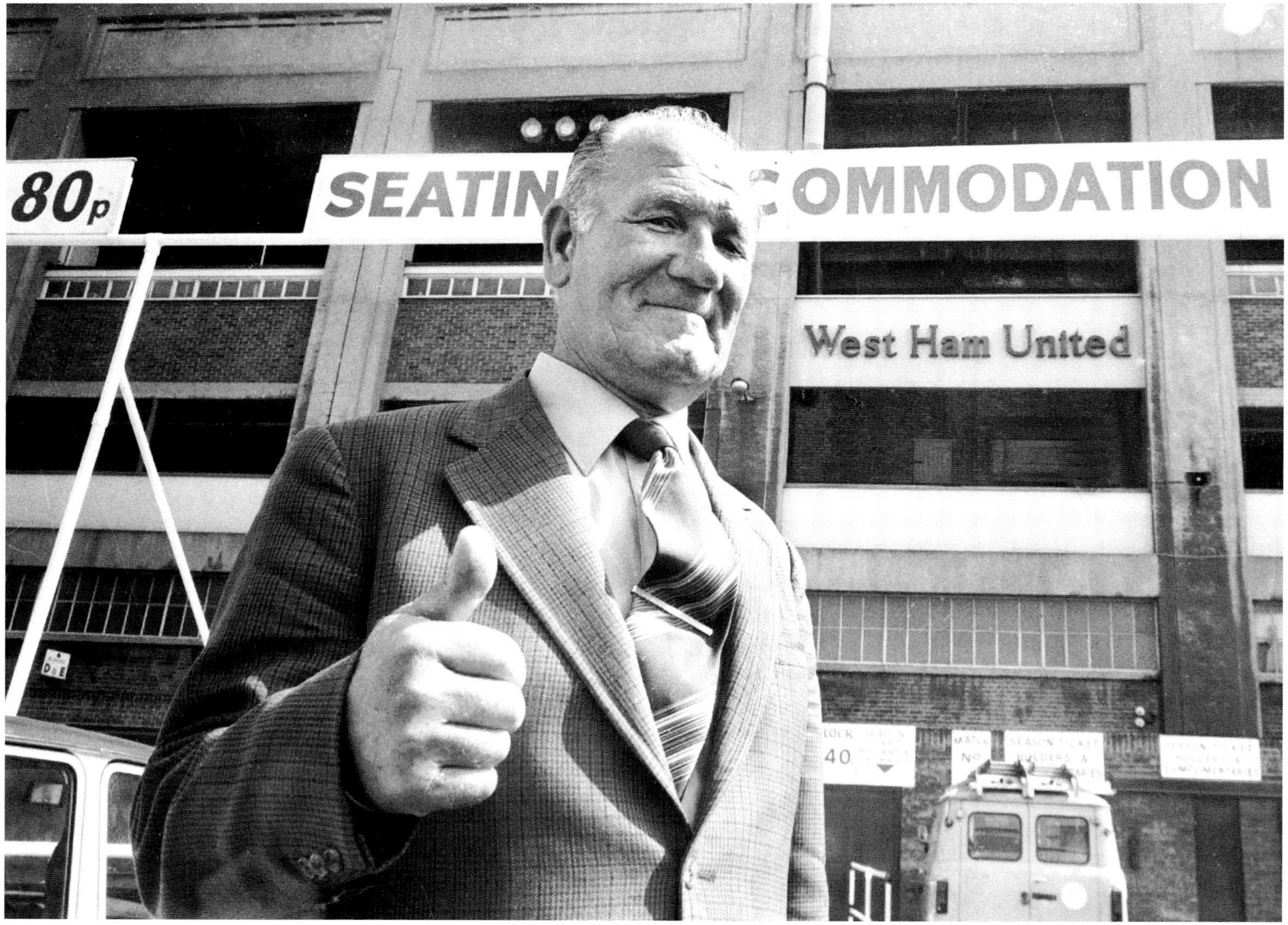
80p
SEATIN
COMMODATION
West Ham United

All the best. Chief scout Wally St Pier calls it a day and leaves Upton Park with a smile and a thumbs-up in August 1976.

Dog-gone it. This mutt got all done up like a dog's dinner to show the world who his favourite football team of the seventies were.

Smile please. Paul Brush was the only ever-present during the 1978–79 season — except of course for yours truly. The Newham Recorder *thought it would be a good idea to get Paul to put me in the frame for once. Don't we look young!*

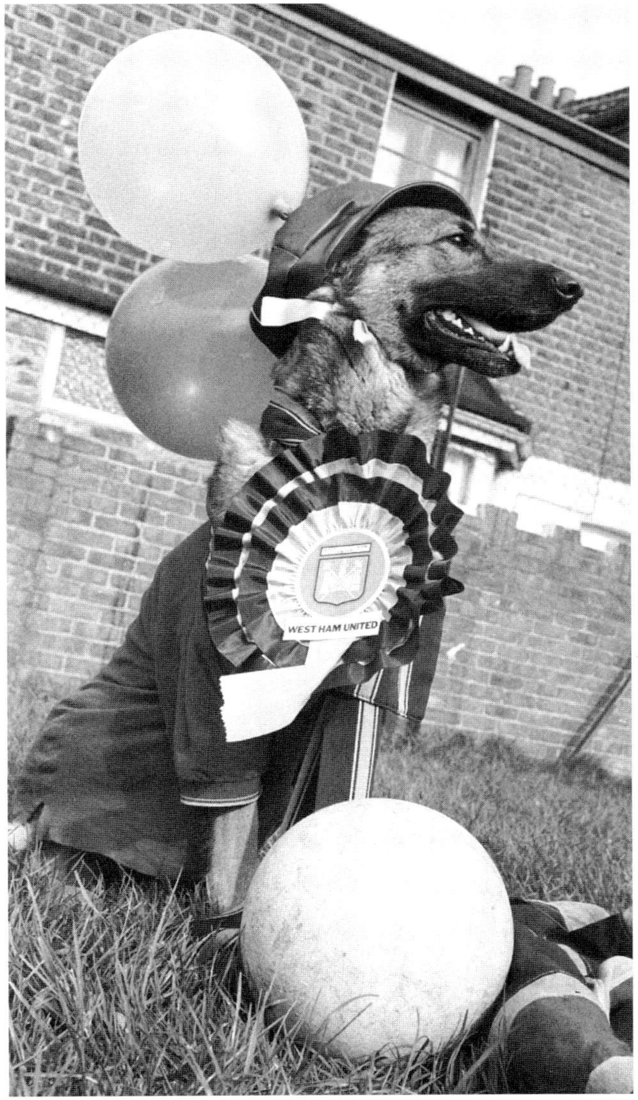

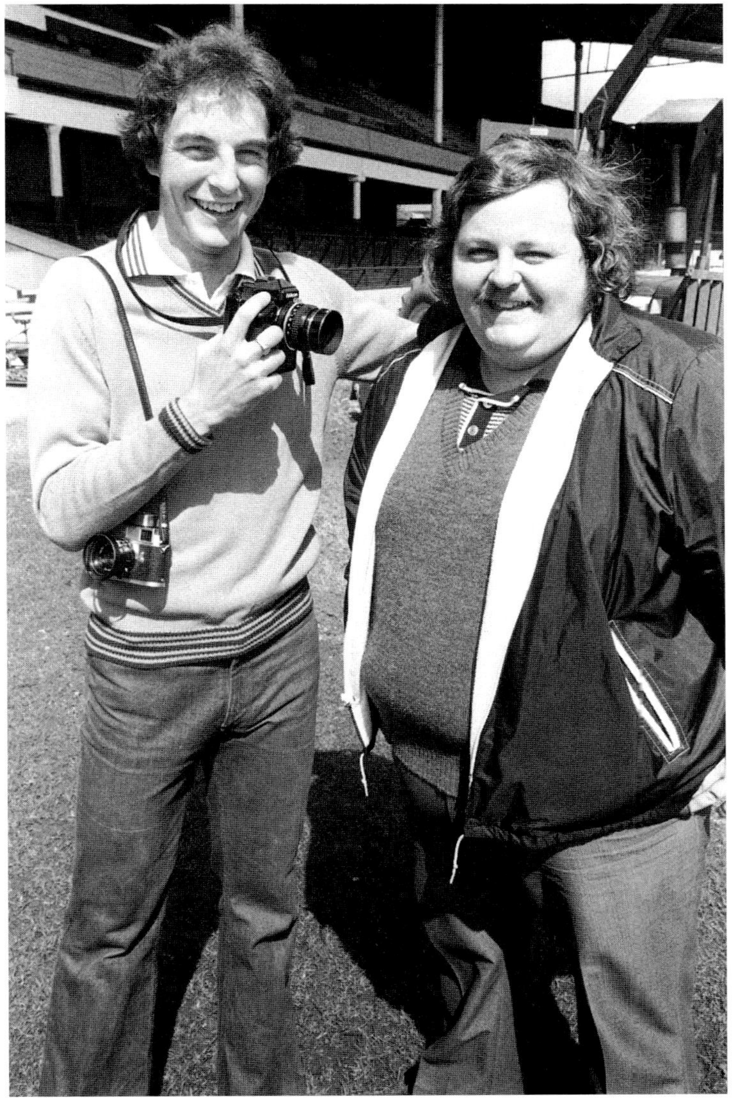

One for the future. Youth team coach Tony Carr puts a group of young hopefuls through a training session in May 1977. Watching intently, tracksuited with a foot on the ball, is a young Paul Allen who is destined to make the big time with West Ham.

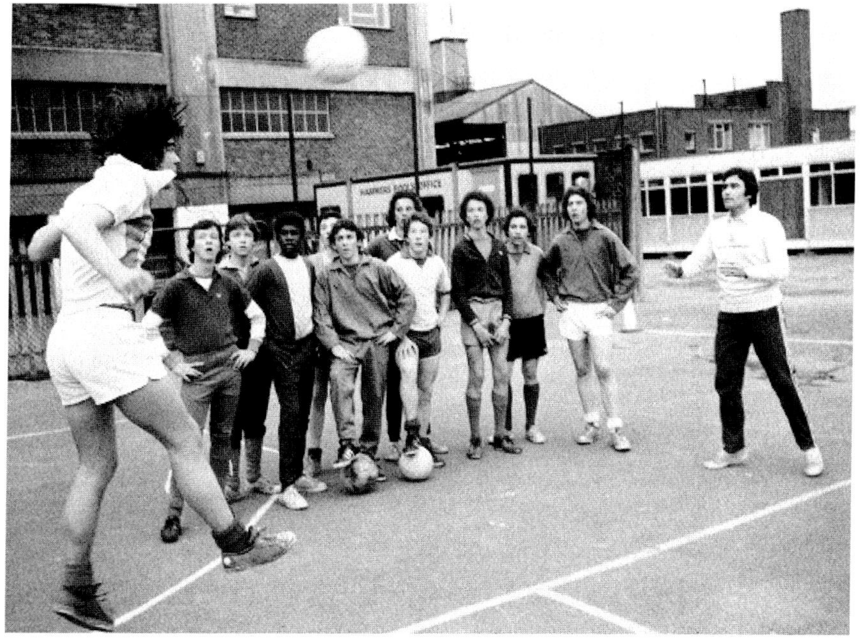

The bad old days. Police face up to angry Millwall fans on the South Bank in October 1978 as Hammers win 3–0 thanks to a Pop Robson hat-trick. I don't like the way that the dog on the left is looking at me — I think he's just spotted lunch!

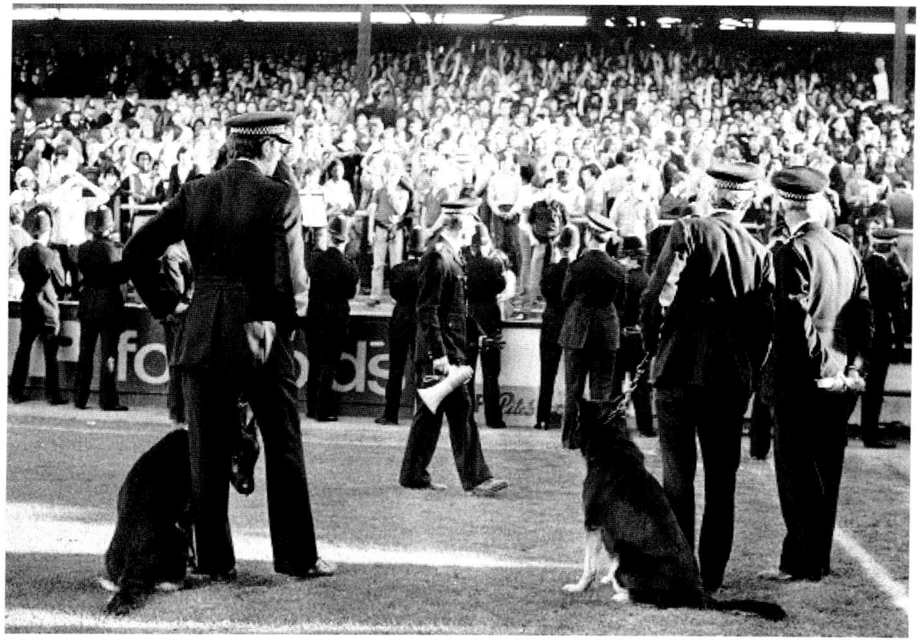

Pop goes the 'keeper. 'Keeper Paul Bradshaw's expression says it all as Pop Robson scores Hammers' second goal in a 2–2 draw at Molineux in October 1977.

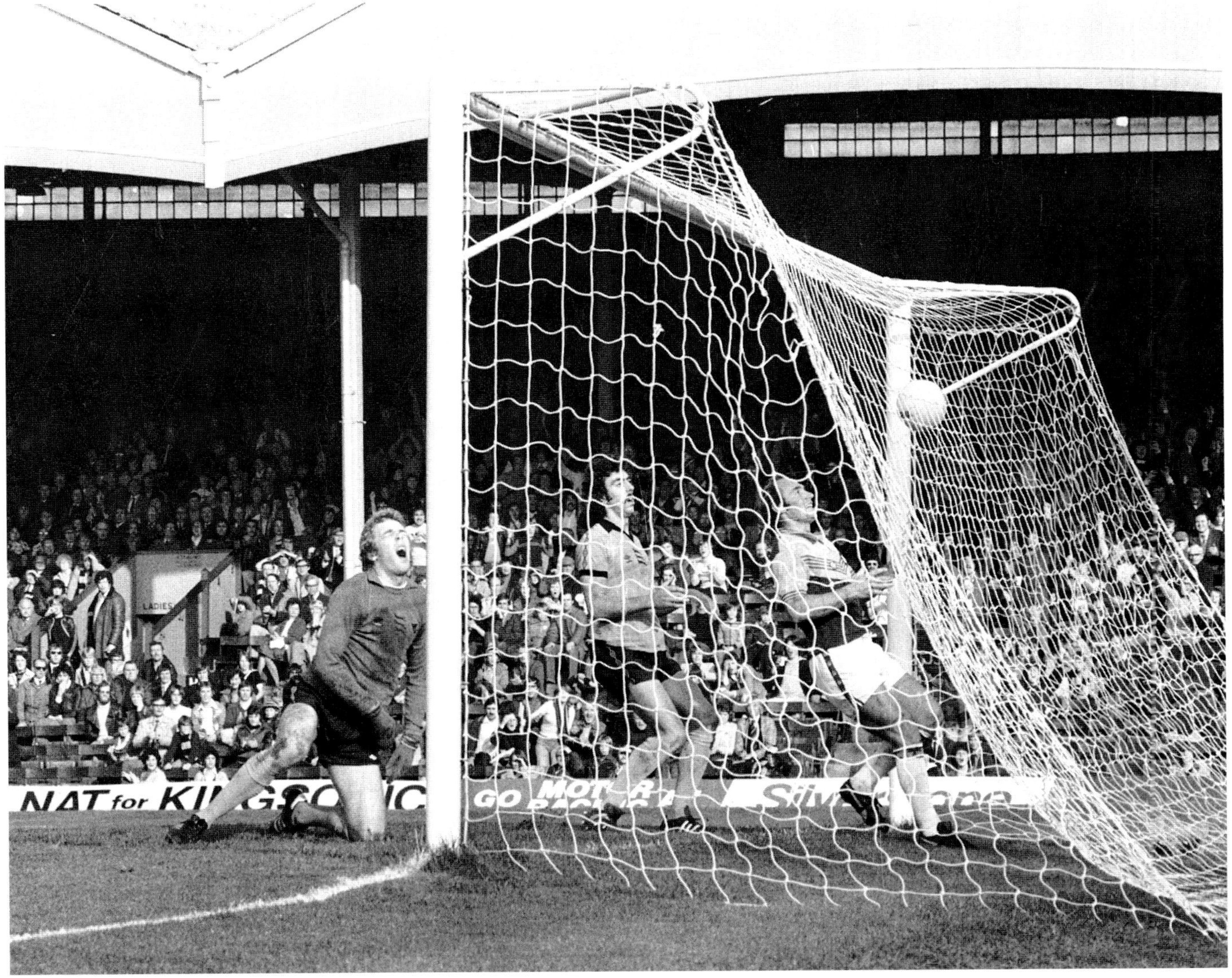

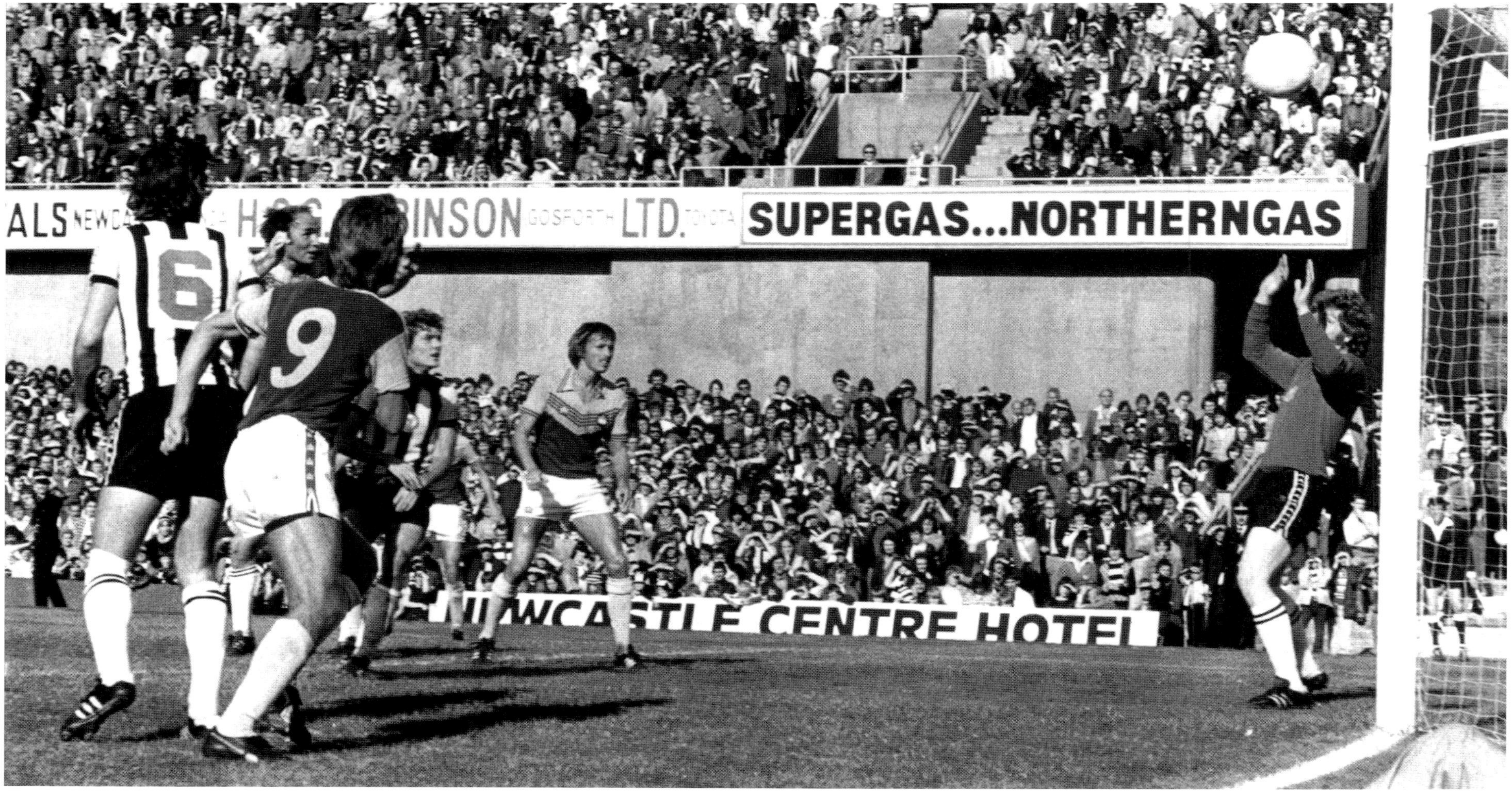
SUPERGAS...NORTHERNGAS
GOSFORTH
LTD.

Back home. Pop Robson returned to his native north-east to help Hammers gain their first win of the 1977–78 season against Newcastle on September 3rd. This header gave the Londoners a 3–2 victory after trailing 2–0 at one stage.

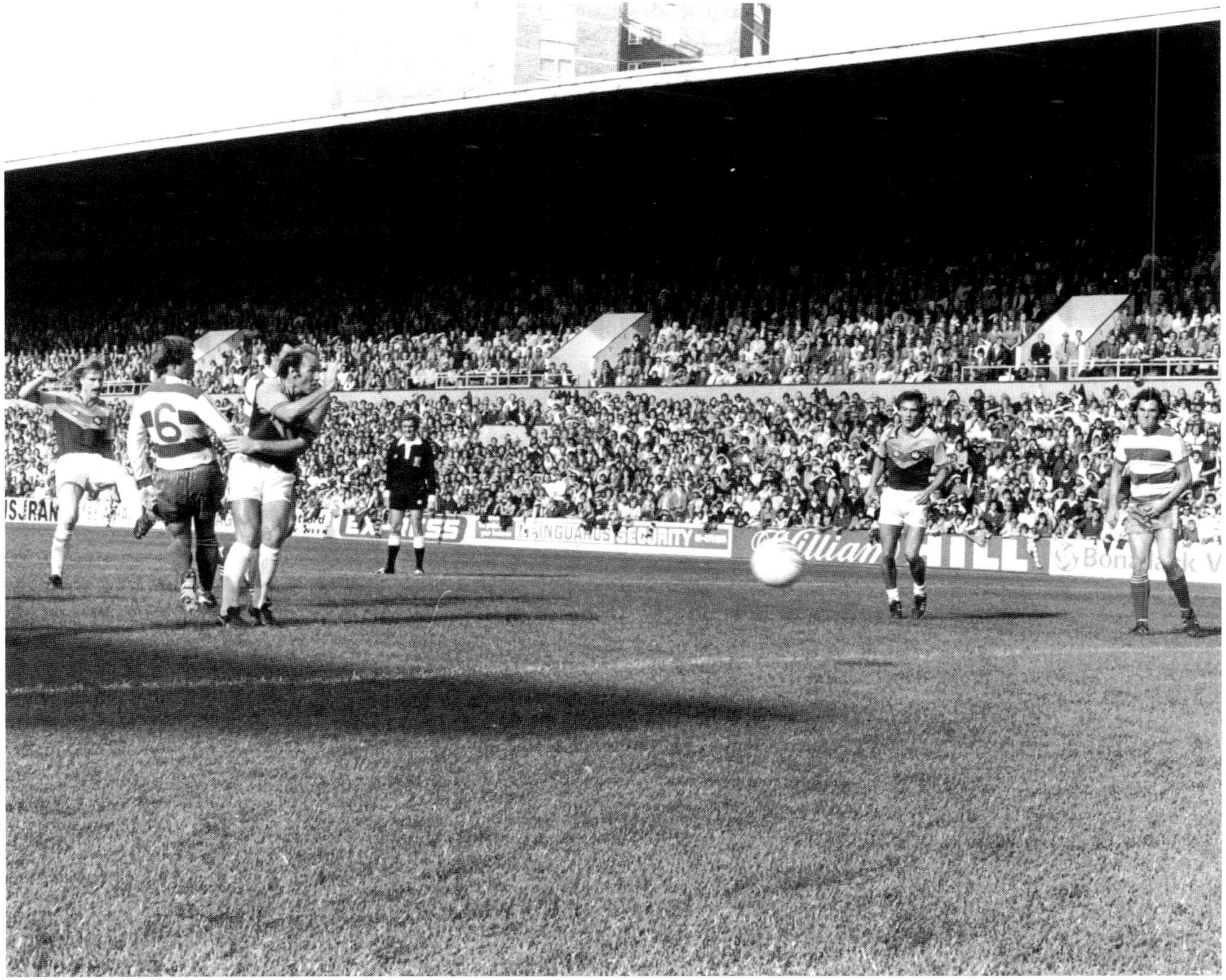

Making amends. Kevin Lock hammers home the equaliser in the 2–2 draw against QPR at Upton Park in September 1977. Kevin had scored an own-goal in the thirteenth minute to put Rangers ahead.

High flyer. Alan Taylor gets head and shoulders above Terry Darracott but heads the ball inches wide of the post in a 1–1 draw against Everton in the 1977–78 season.

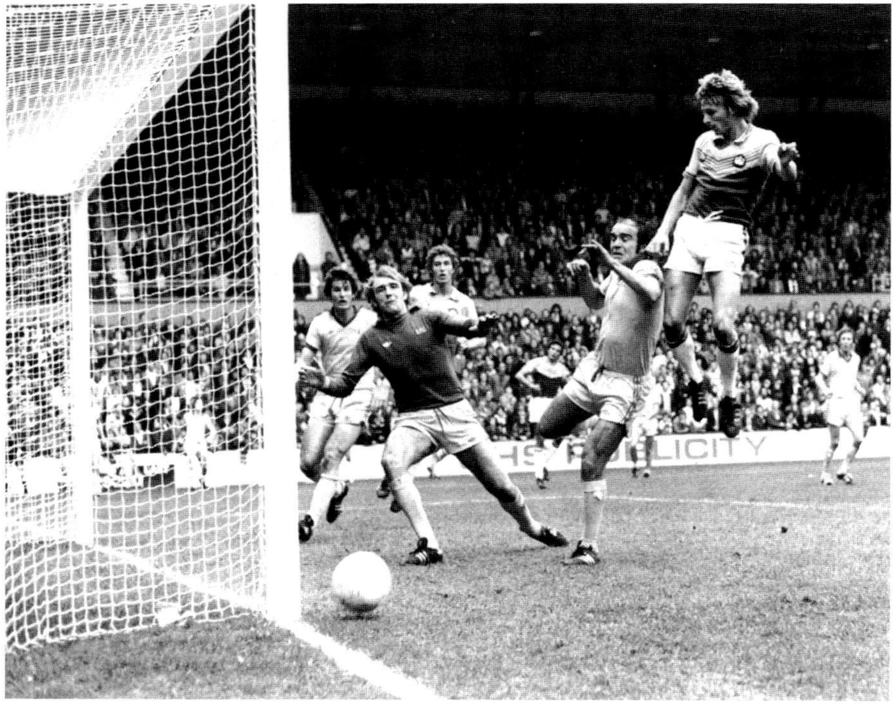

Four-pointer. Derek Hales scores the vital only goal against fellow relegation strugglers Newcastle United in January 1978.

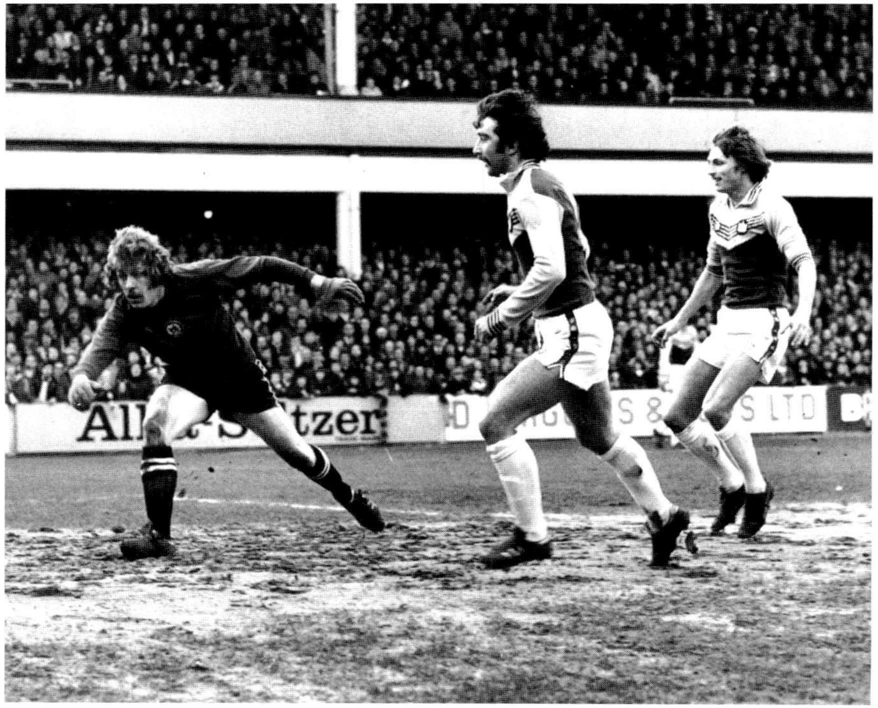

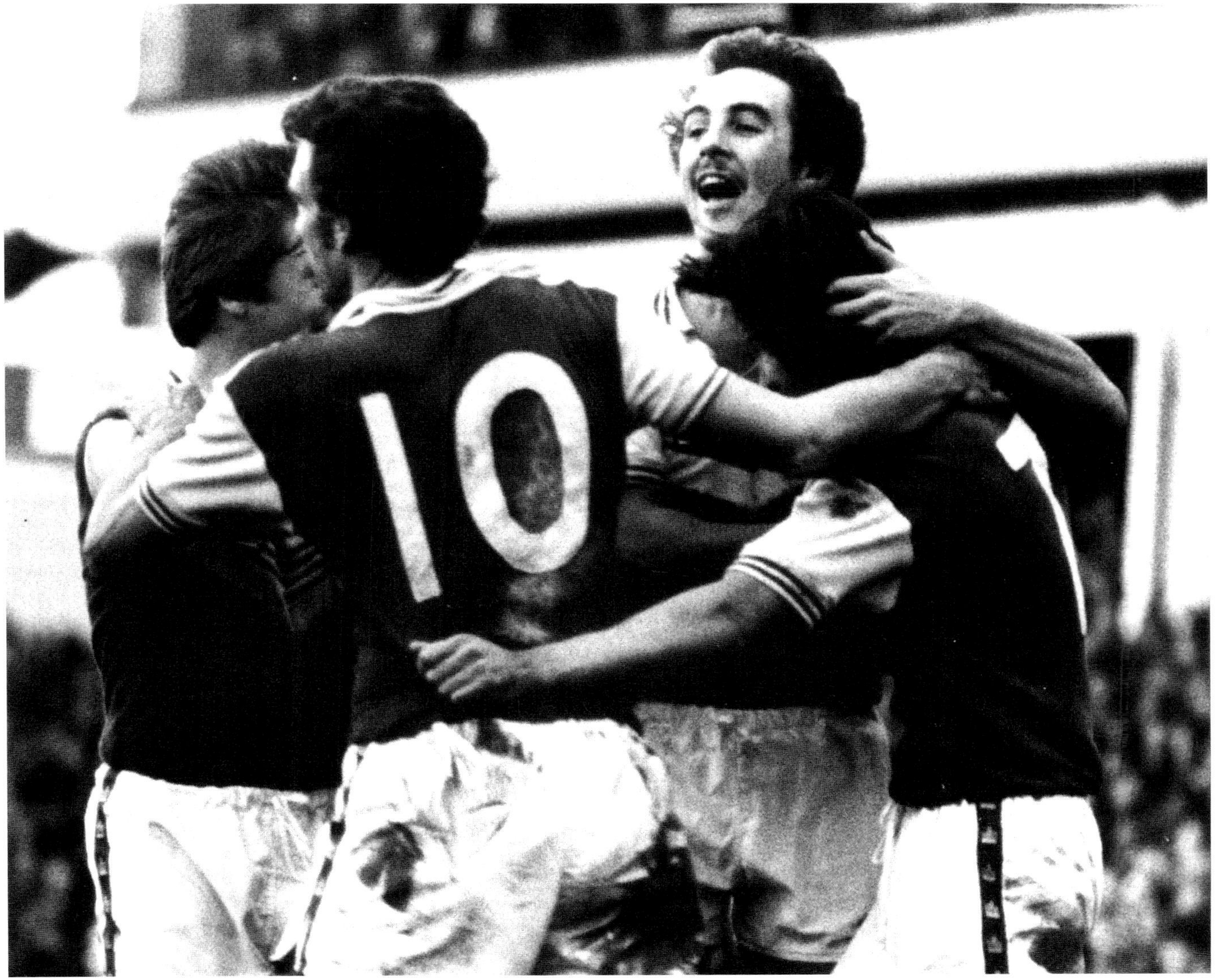

Dev's delight. Alan Devonshire is mobbed by his team-mates after the first of his two goals in the 3–3 draw with West Bromwich Albion at Upton Park in 1977.

Nearly. Derek Hales beats QPR 'keeper Phil Parkes, but his effort in this 1978 FA Cup fourth round clash at Upton Park was ruled offside and the match ended in a 1–1 draw.

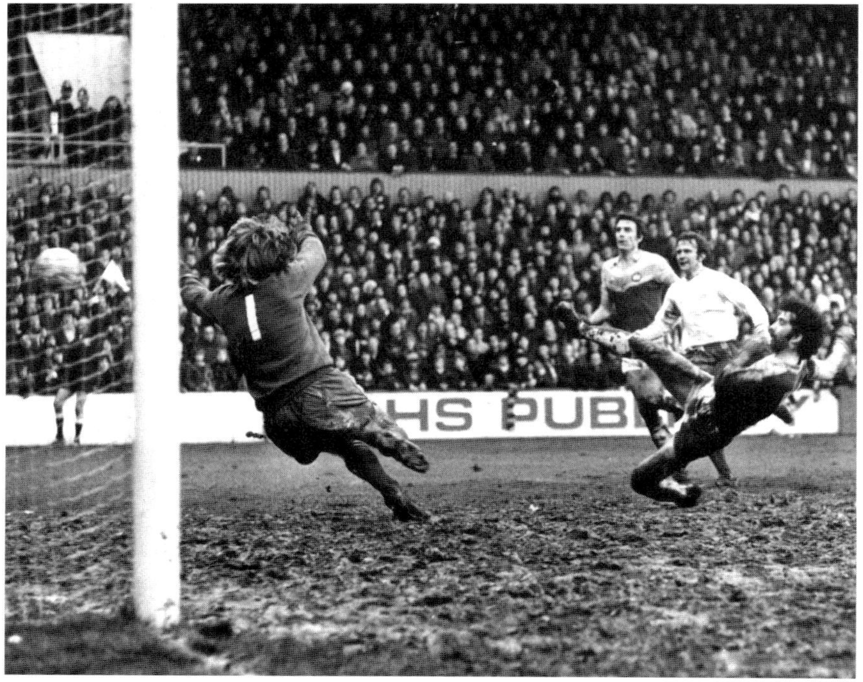

False hopes. Pop Robson puts the ball wide of QPR's Phil Parkes to give West Ham the lead in the 1978 FA Cup fourth round replay at Loftus Road. Hammers were destroyed in the second period as Rangers went on to win 6–1.

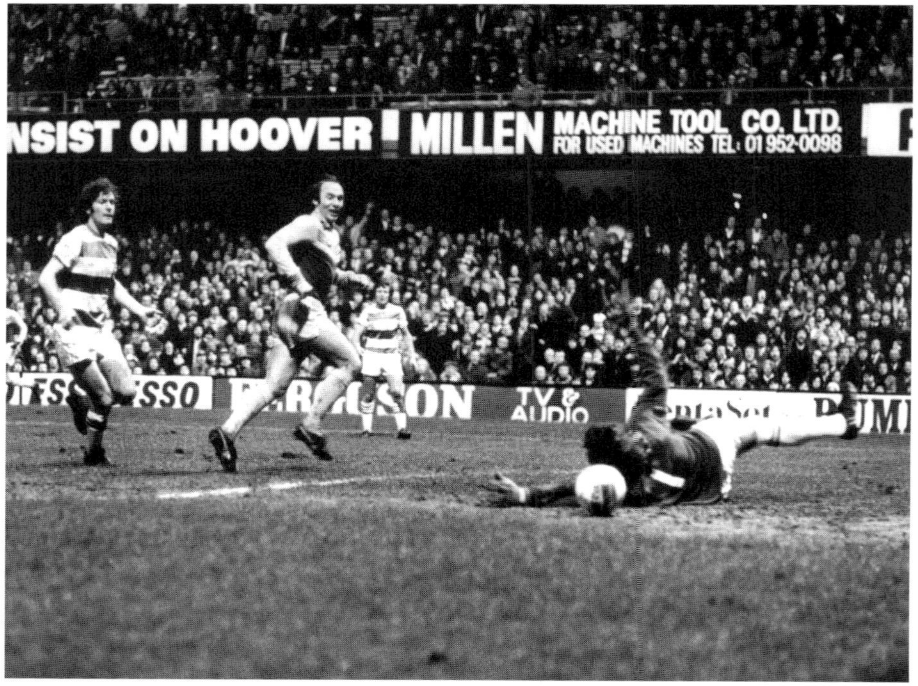

Going Dutch. The grounded Pat Holland scores Hammers' second goal in a 2–1 victory over Coventry City at Upton Park in 1978. Tommy Taylor had given the home side the lead after twenty minutes.

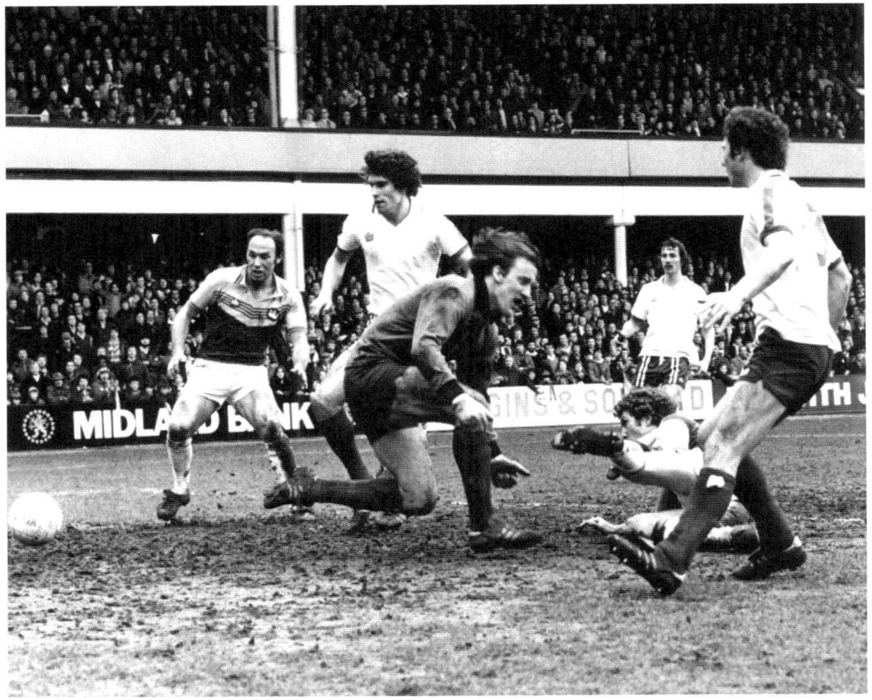

No happy return. David Cross signed for West Ham for a club record fee of £180,000 on 9th December 1977, and made his debut a week later against his old club West Bromwich Albion at the Hawthorns. A bloody Cross looks dejected as his former team-mates celebrate a 1–0 victory in the background.

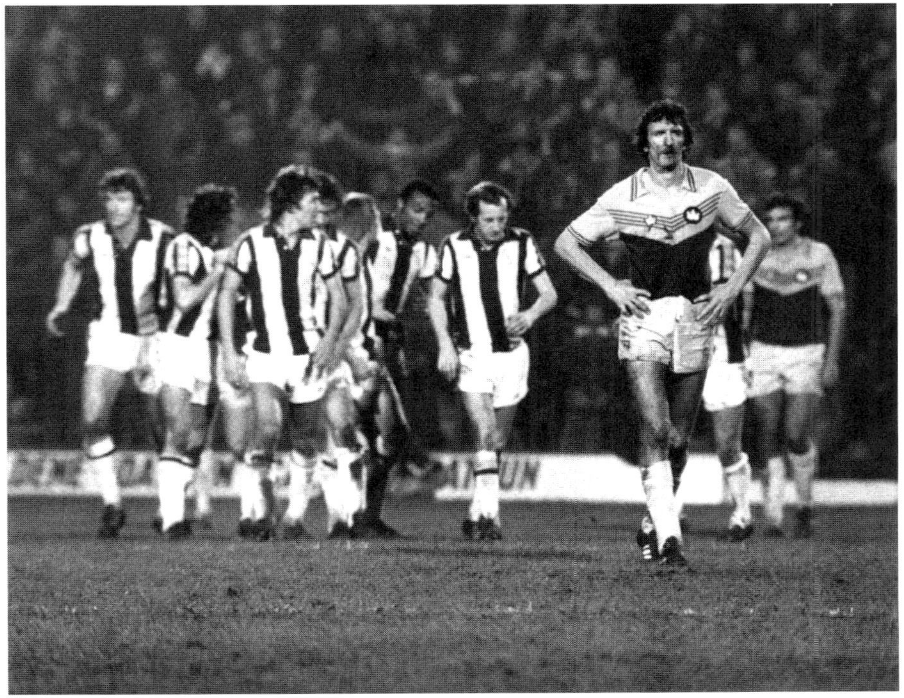

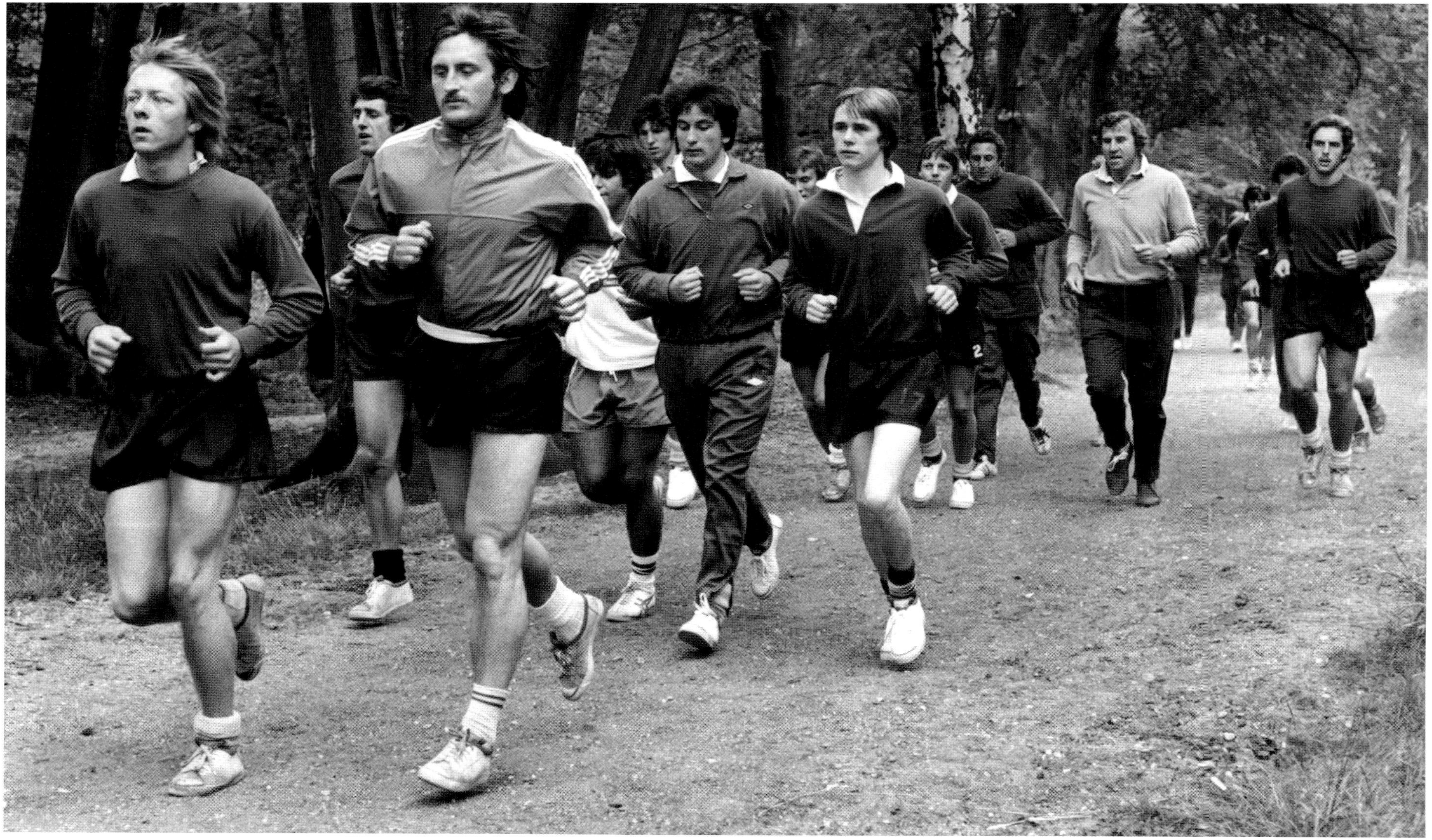

Leaders of the pack. Alan Curbishley and Frank Lampard head this late 1970s pre-season run through the forest with other notables such as Bobby Ferguson, George Cowie, Alvin Martin, John Radford and Paul Brush following close behind.

Hair we are. Mick McGiven relaxes at home in Woodford Green shortly after signing for West Ham in 1973. I shot a feature for the Newham Recorder, *and remain good friends with Mick to this day.*

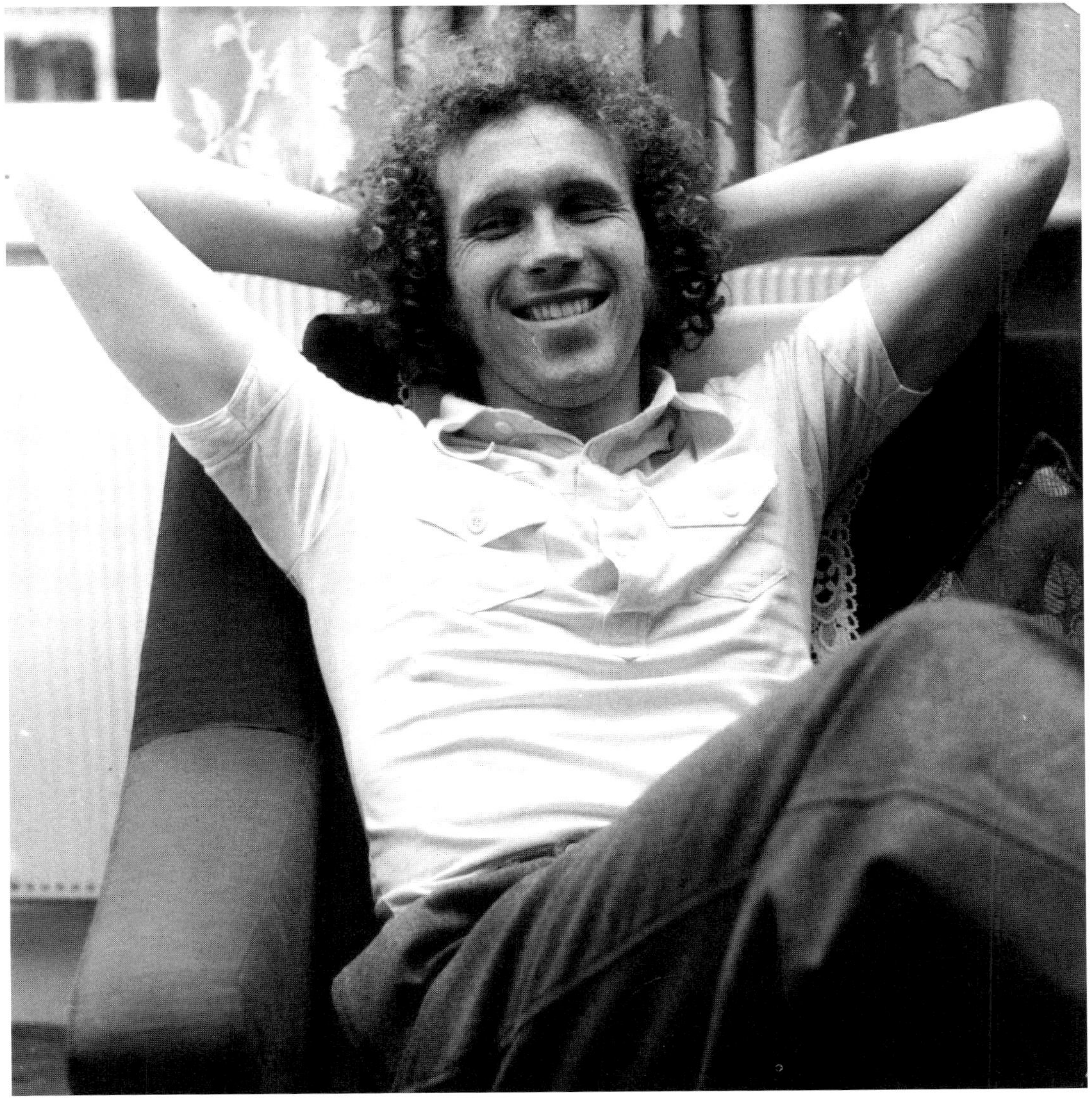

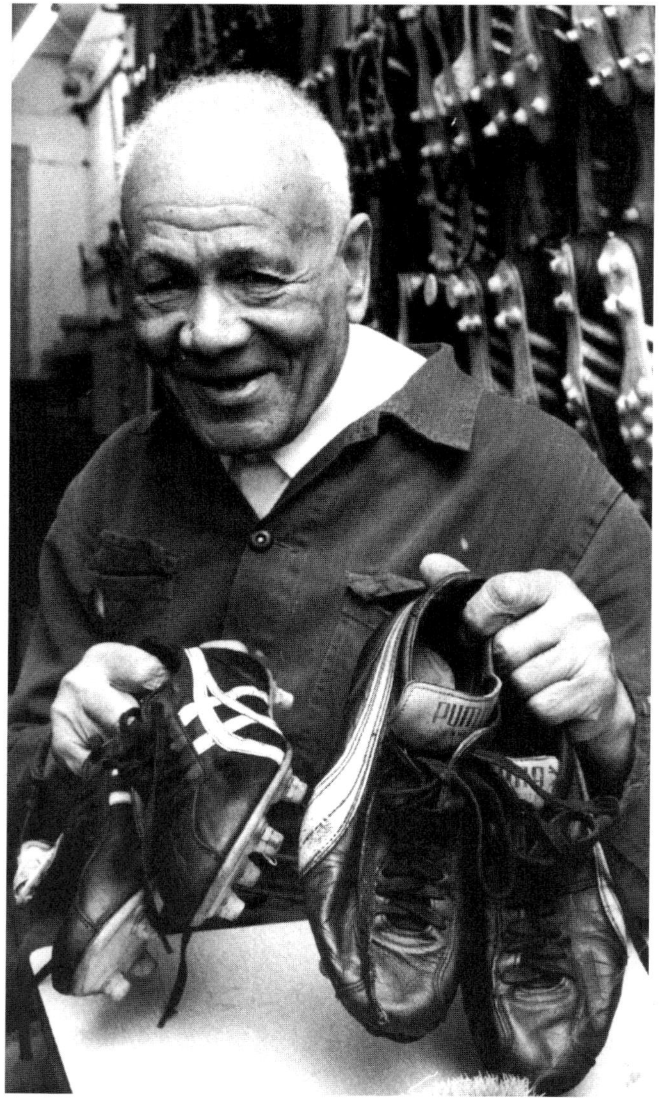

Brown boots. Jack Leslie was an old pro footballer who looked after the players' footwear in the '70s. He was never in a bad mood, as I think this picture shows.

If the cap fits. Pop superstar Elton John sports some natty headgear as he watches his beloved Watford in a third round FA Cup tie at Upton Park in January 1978. Hammers won this, the first meeting of the two sides since their old Southern League days in the early part of the century, thanks to a Pop Robson goal in the 80th minute.

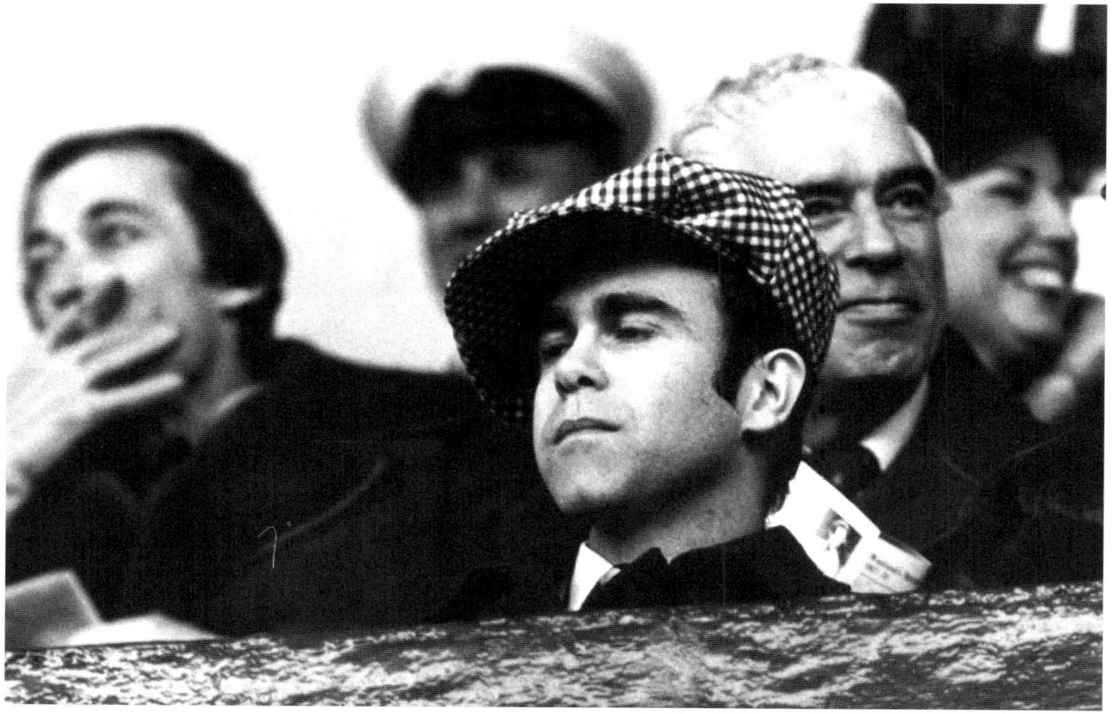

Chilly Willy. On a bitterly cold December night, the Friday before Christmas 1979, one brave supporter streaked on to the field trouserless. Billy Bonds can't believe his eyes as the teams take to the field after the interval.

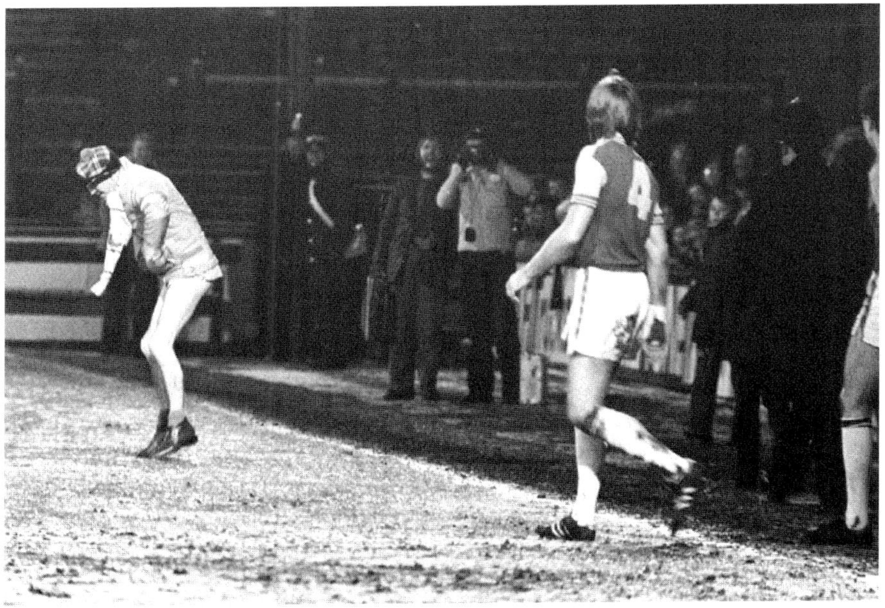

Funny guy. David Cross signed for West Ham in December 1977, for a then club record fee of £180,000, watched here by manager John Lyall. Crossie was, without doubt, one of the funniest men I've ever met and trips with him were never dull!

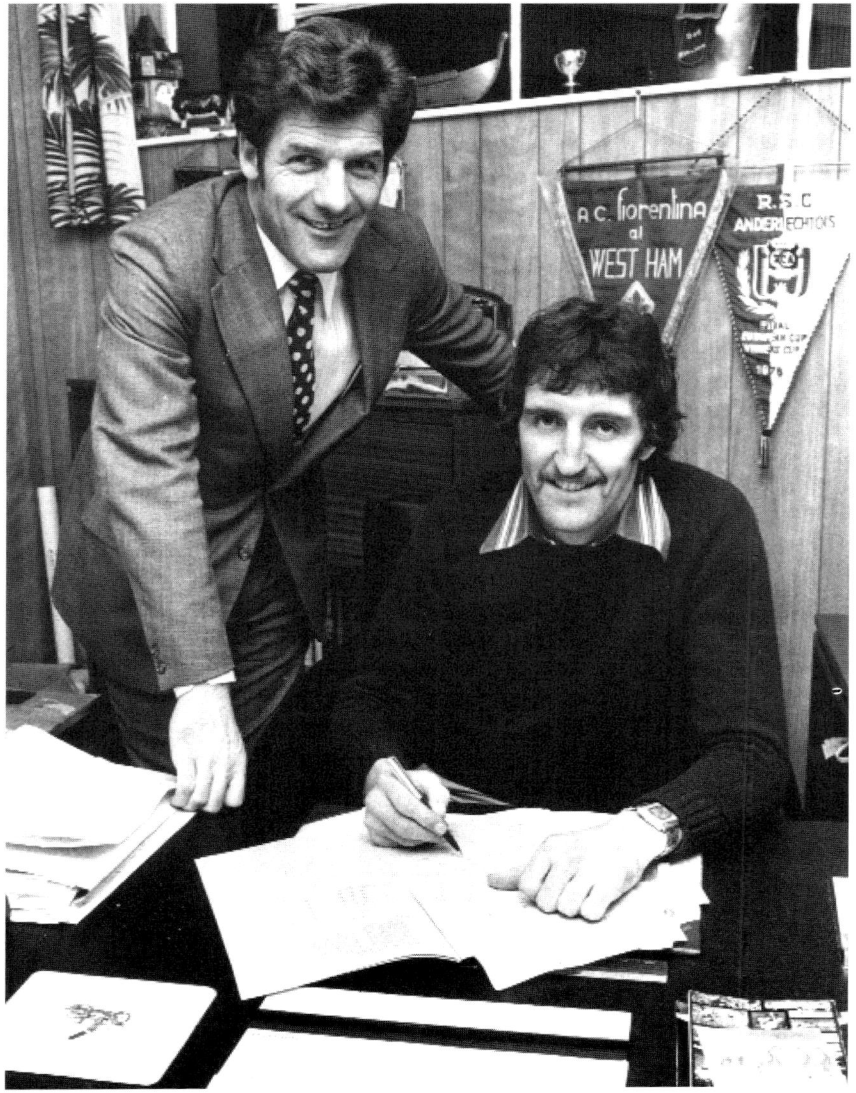

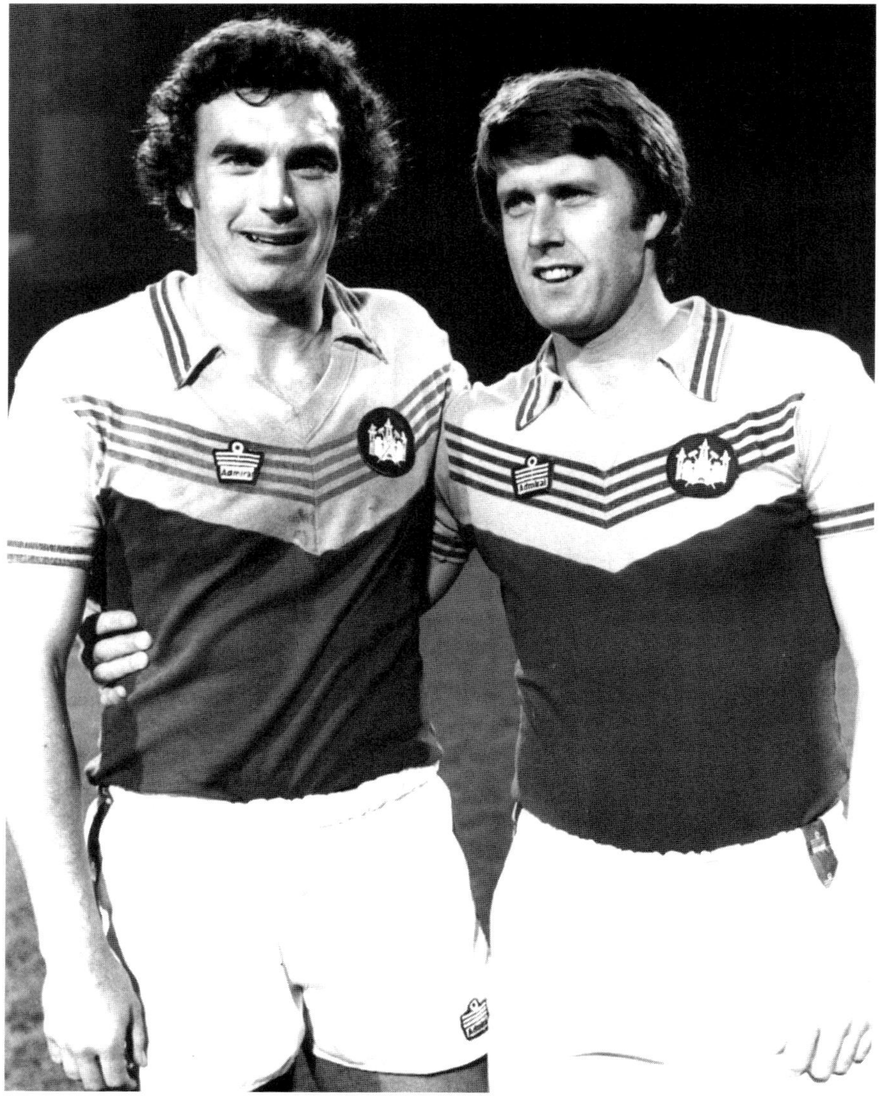

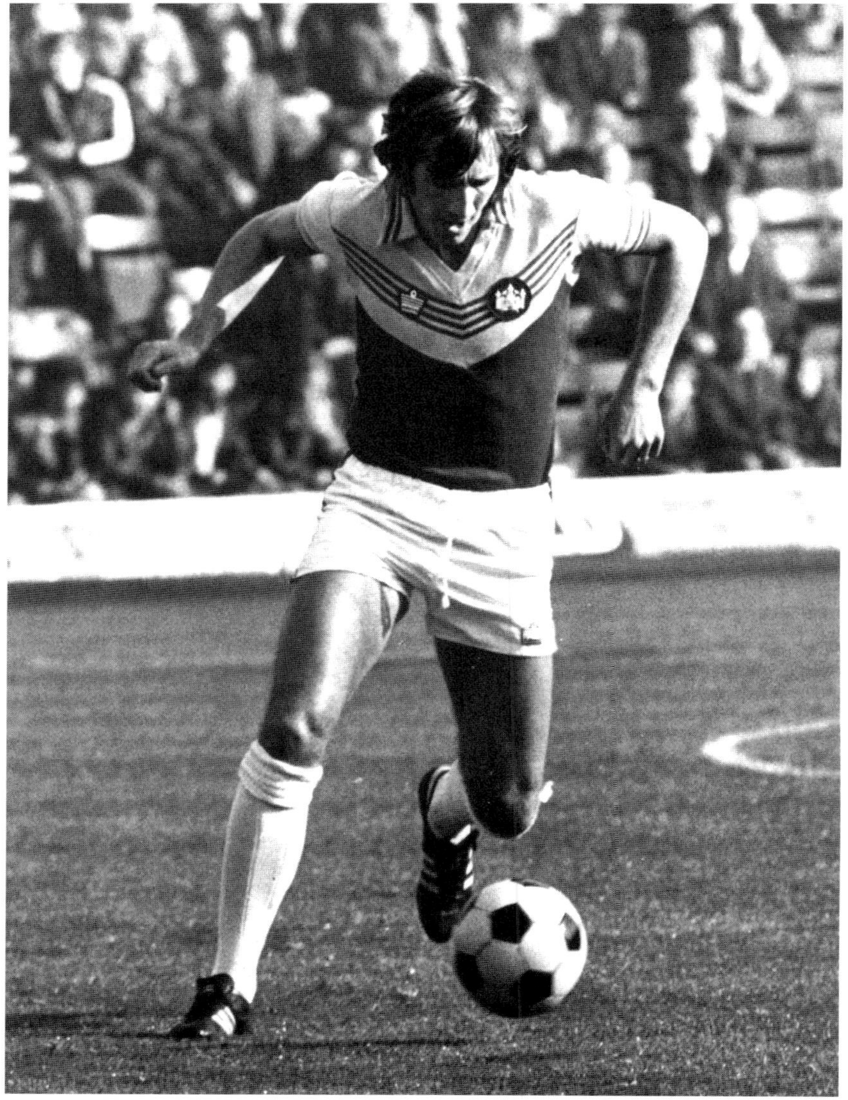

Hammers' heroes. World Cup hero Geoff Hurst turned out for his former team-mate Trevor Brooking's testimonial in 1977. I don't know who got the biggest cheer on the night.

My hero. OK, I admit it, Billy Bonds is a personal hero of mine — and of thousands of other West Ham fans too. I like this shot of Bonzo in typical action pose.

Tricky Trev. Arsenal's Peter Simpson finds Trevor Brooking as slippery as one of those East End eels as he tries to contain him in a 1977 London derby at Highbury.

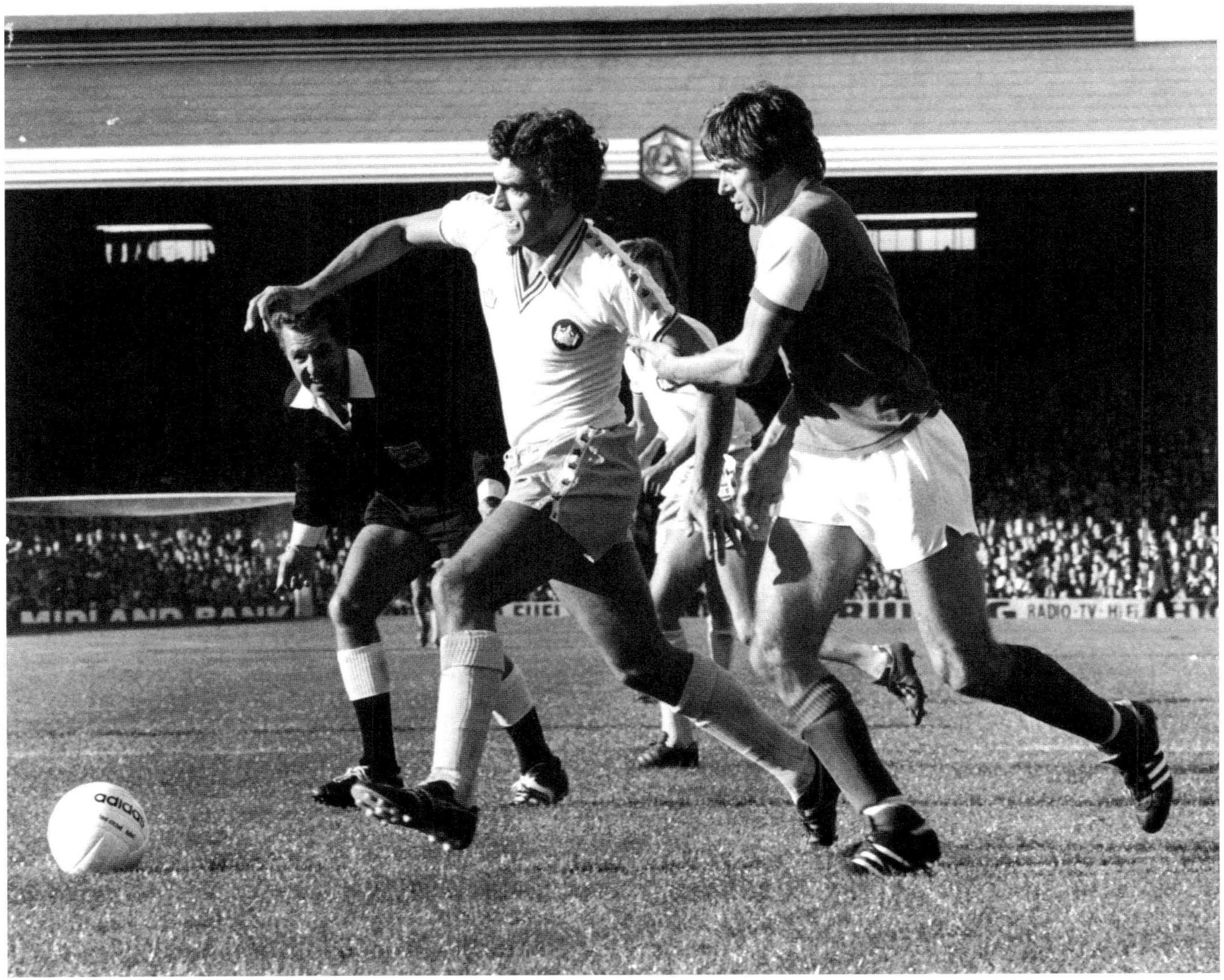

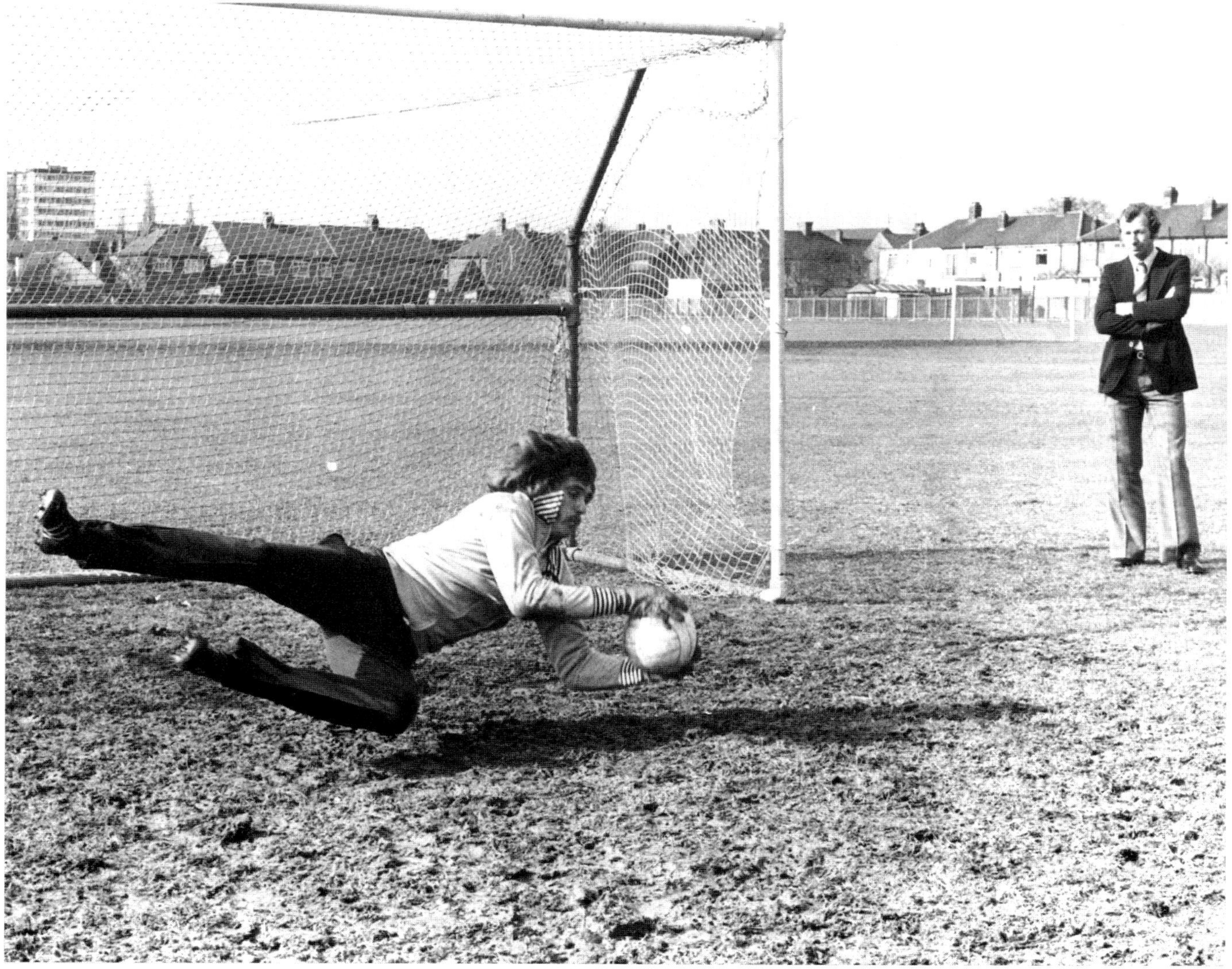

Record-breaker. When Phil Parkes joined West Ham in February 1979 for £565,000, it was a world record fee for a goalkeeper. Few, if any, would argue that it was anything other than money well spent. Parksie's mentor Bob Wilson, the former Arsenal and Scotland 'keeper, watches the big man go through his first training session at Chadwell Heath.

Tee-time. PFA golf champions and their spoils. Tommy Taylor, Mervyn Day, Bobby Ferguson, Pop Robson and Trevor Brooking parade the silverware.

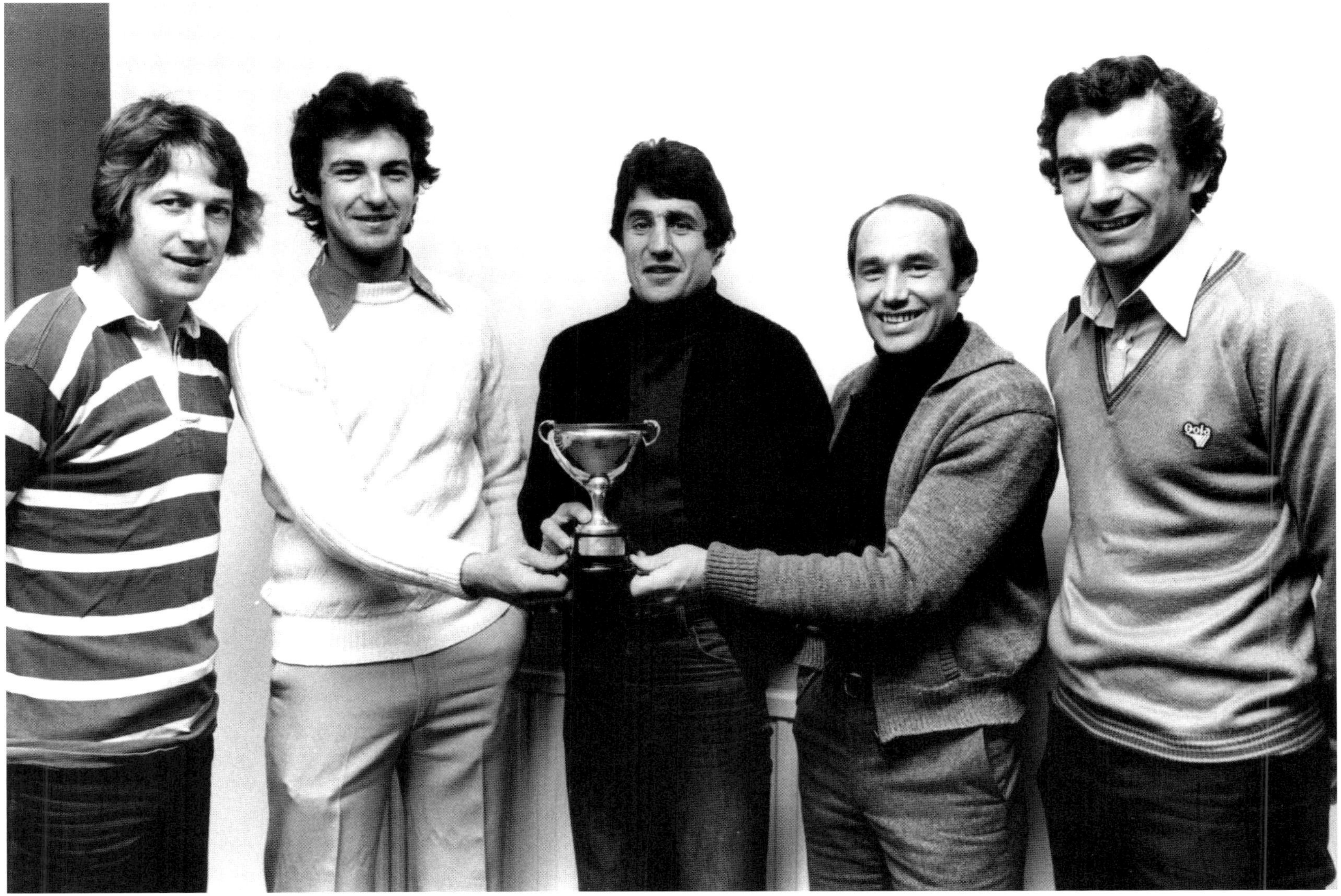

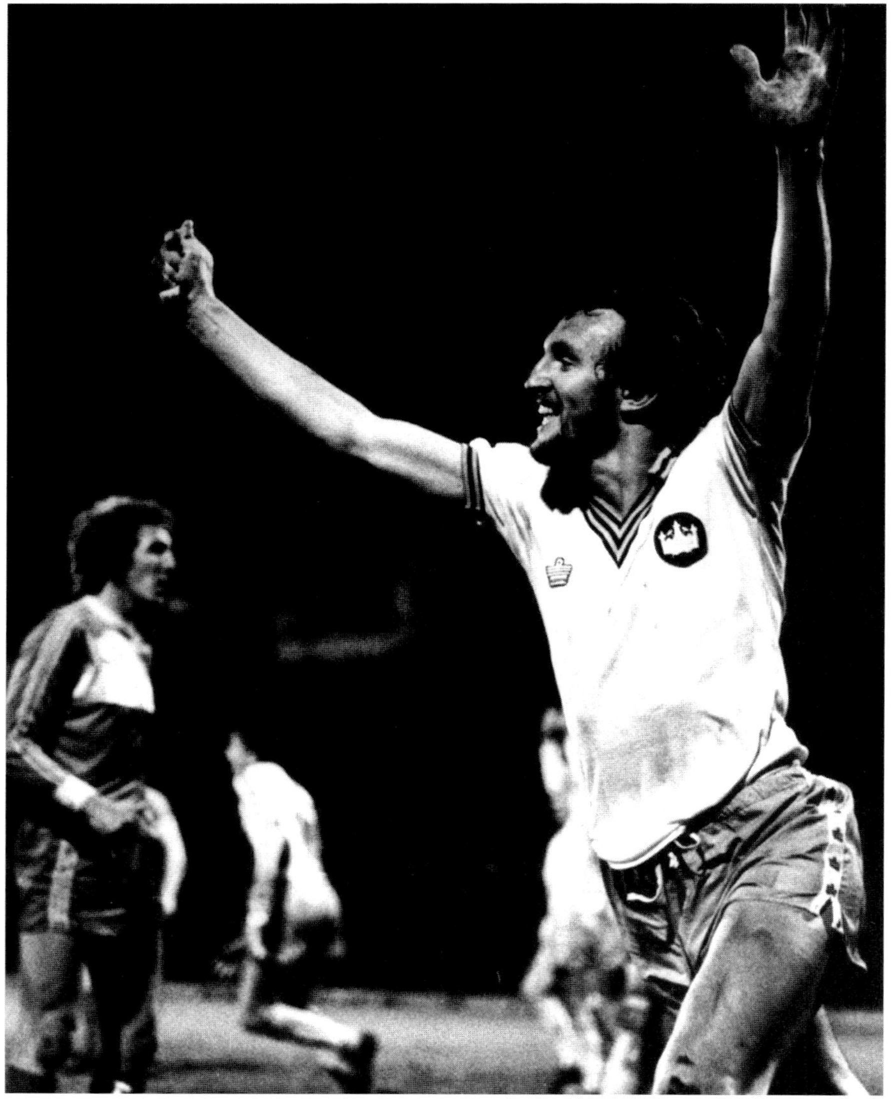

Dave the rave. David Cross salutes yet another goal for the Hammers — and there were quite a few in his career.

Best seats in the house. Team attendant Albert Walker, manager John Lyall, director Brian Cearns and caterer Pat Doran watch from the directors' box. Brian Cearns was a real gentleman and good company on away trips. Pat Doran catered on our trip to Russia, where I ate better than at home!

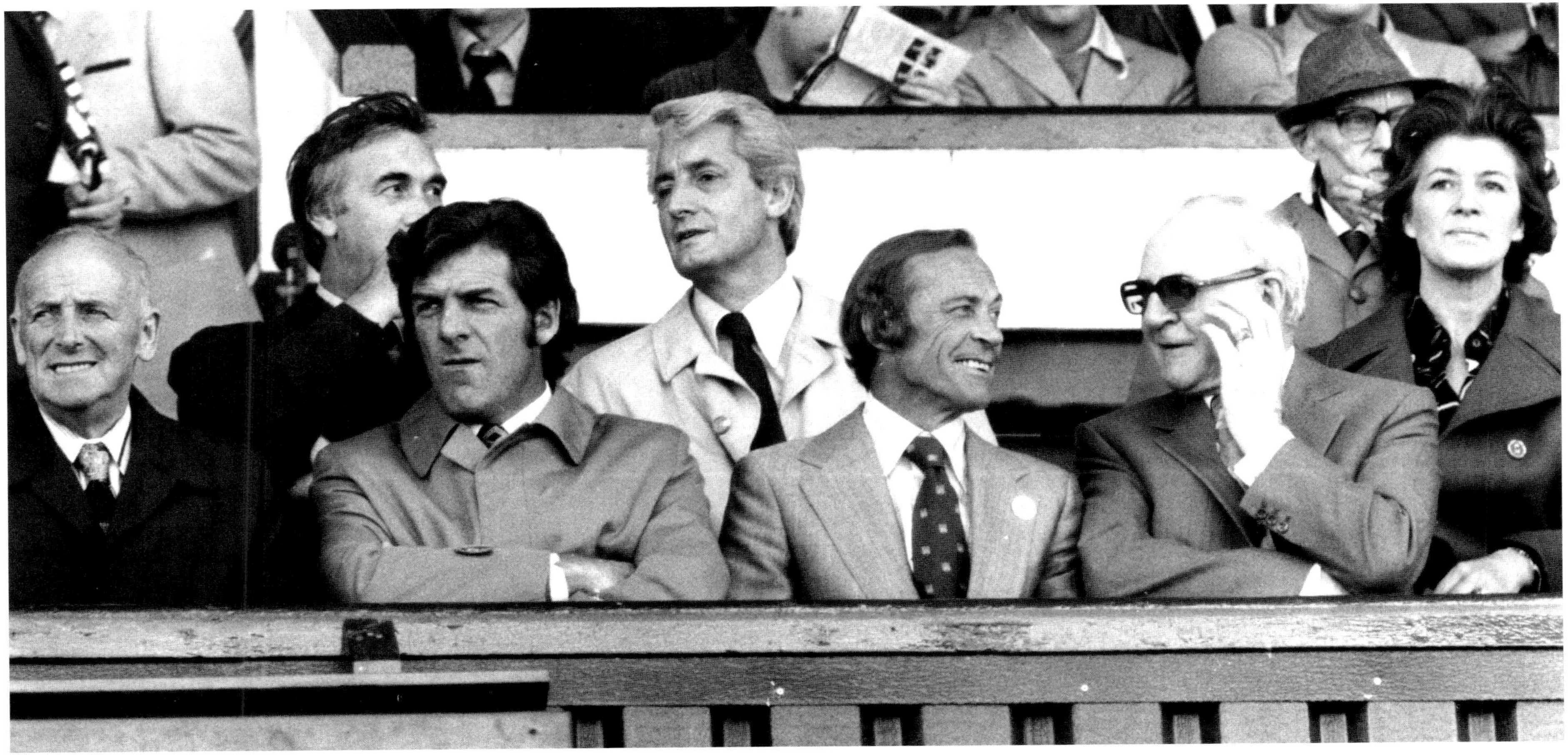

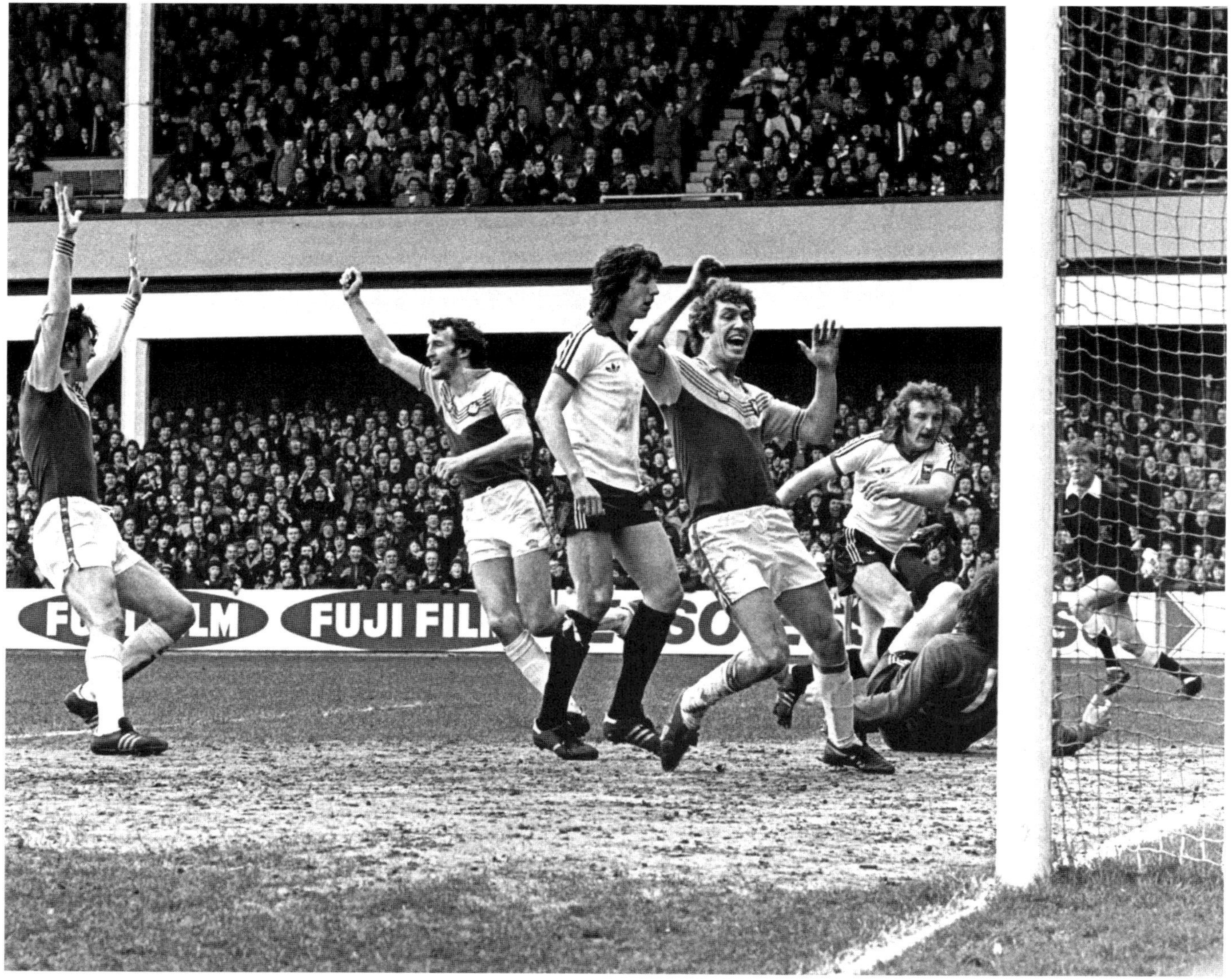

Strike three. Pat Holland and Bill Green join David Cross in celebrating his hat-trick against Ipswich Town at Upton Park in March 1978.

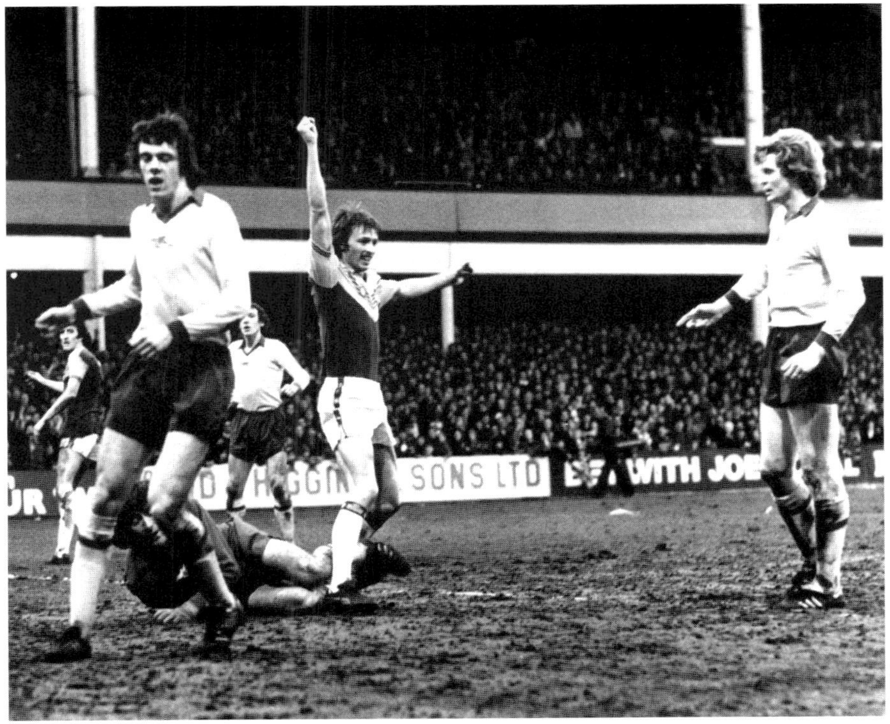

Tinker Taylor. Alan Taylor celebrates beating Arsenal's Pat Jennings in a 1978 2–2 draw at Upton Park. David Cross saved a point with his 89th-minute leveller.

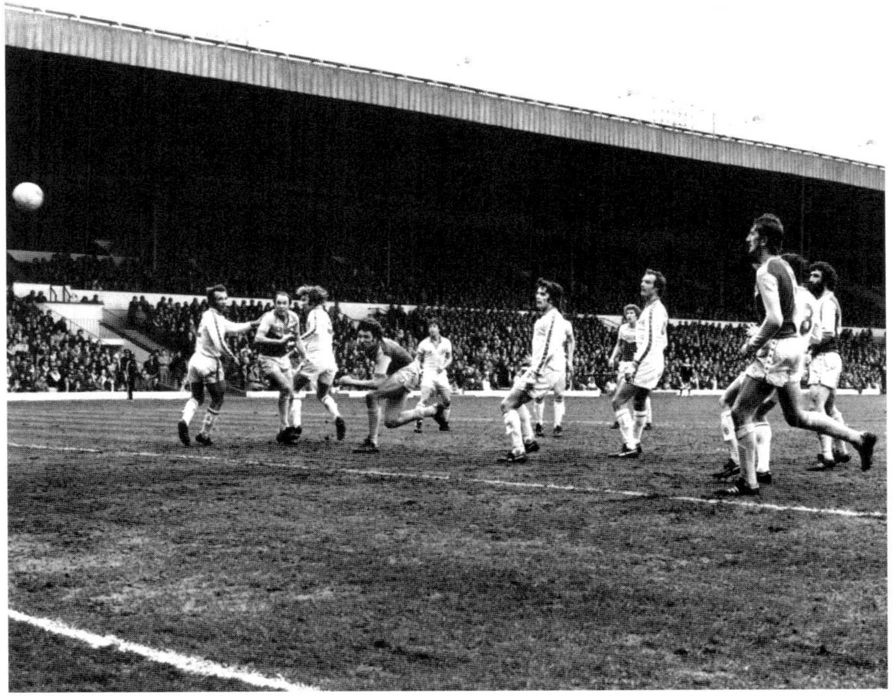

Dream debut. Alvin Martin scores with a header in his first full game for Hammers at Elland Road in April 1978. West Ham went on to win the game 2–1 with Derek Hales scoring the other goal. It was the Londoners' first win there in the top flight for 48 years.

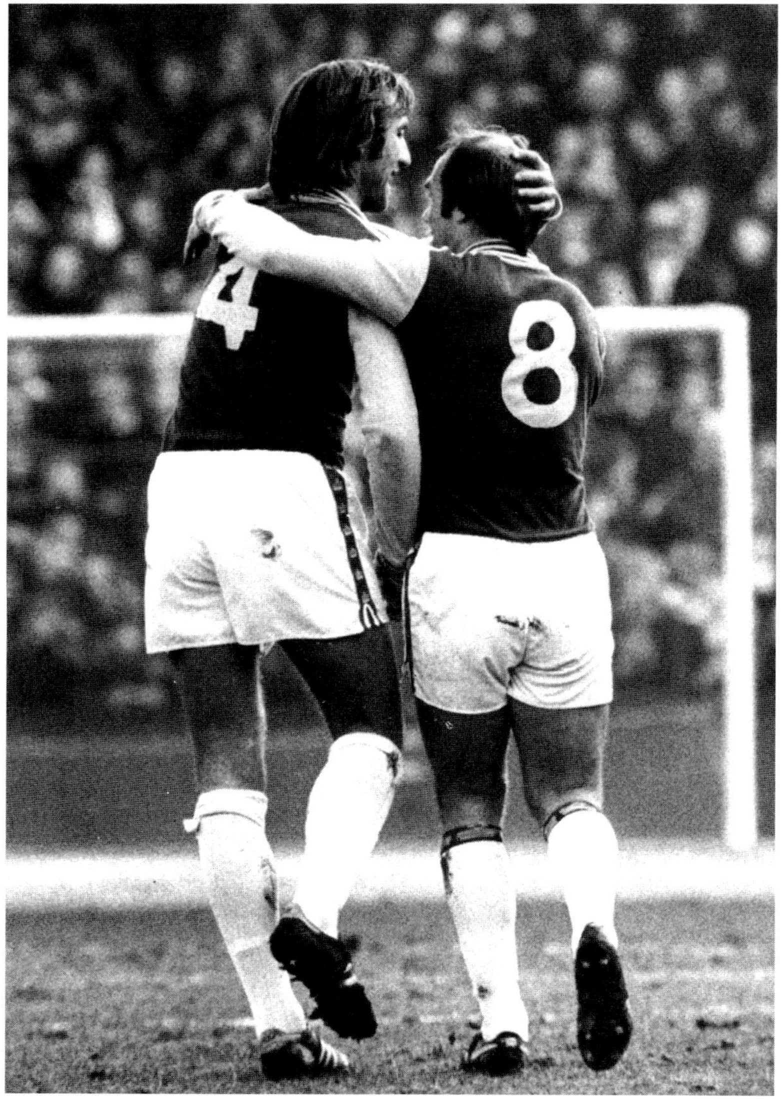

Dear old pals. There's just something about this picture that I really like. Billy Bonds and Pop Robson were great buddies off the pitch, and I think that fact comes through in this goal celebration shot.

The 1980s

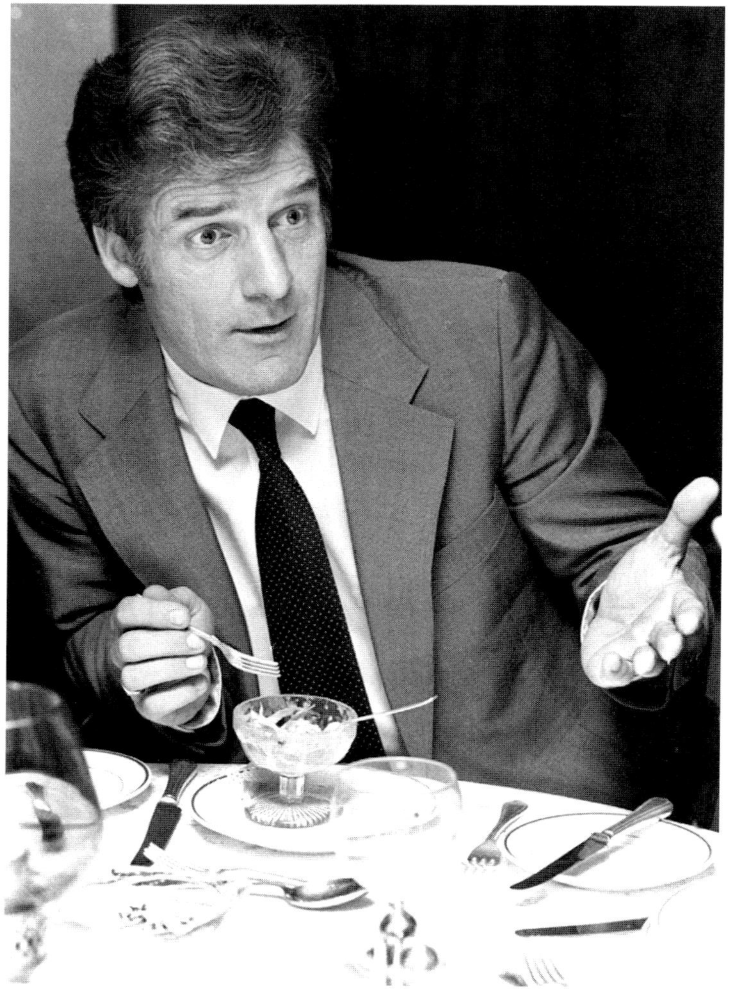

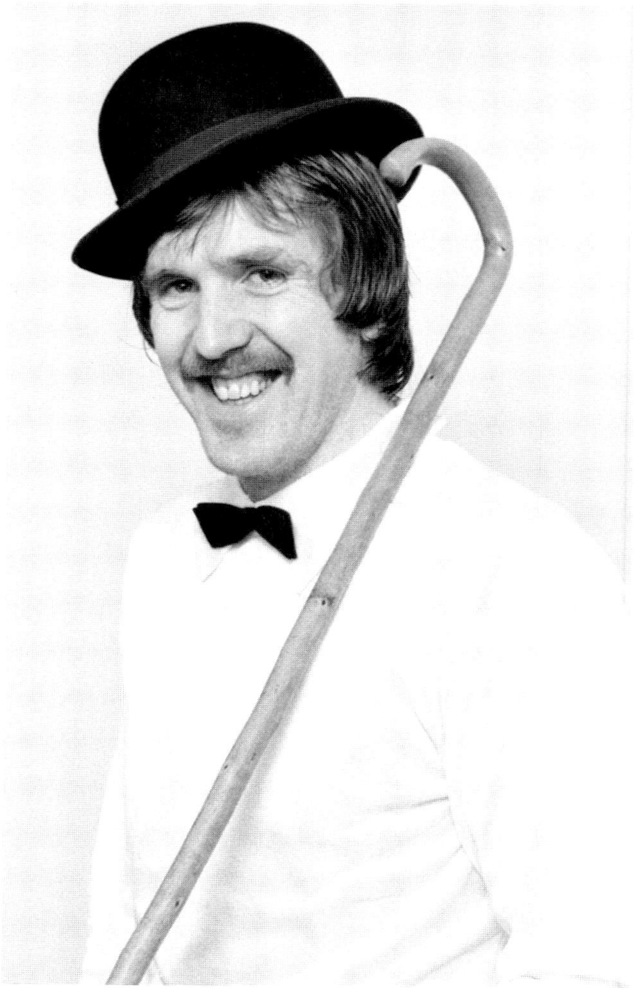

Lyall at lunch. West Ham manager John Lyall is in expressive mood as he holds court at a luncheon given by a Dutch journalist at White Hart Lane. Ex-Tottenham boss Bill Nicholson was also a guest and held me spellbound with some of his tales of times gone by.

Dressed to thrill. Phil Parkes dons a white jersey for the visit of Arsenal and their green and purple away strip that was the vogue for a time in the '80s. Unable to wear his usual green top, which would have clashed with his opponents, Phil opted for the white — with matching accessories, of course.

The moustache gives him away. England Cricket captain and life-long Hammers' fan Graham Gooch joins in a training session at Chadwell Heath in an effort to gain extra fitness for a forthcoming cricket tour. Goochie always kept in touch with his team's results wherever in the world he travelled.

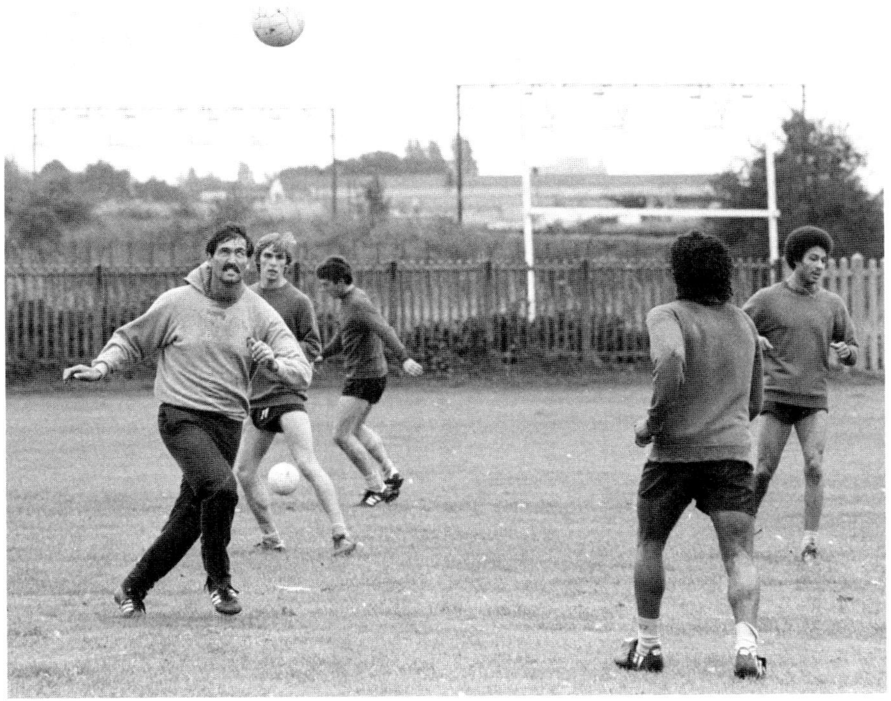

The photograph that still haunts me after all of these years. Hammers' youngster Gerhard Ampofo lies screaming in agony on the Upton Park pitch, his leg shattered and twisted. Physio Dave Gladstone summons immediate medical assistance as Gerhard's brother, Chris, clutches his head in horror as he sees his brother's injury. I was physically sick that night!

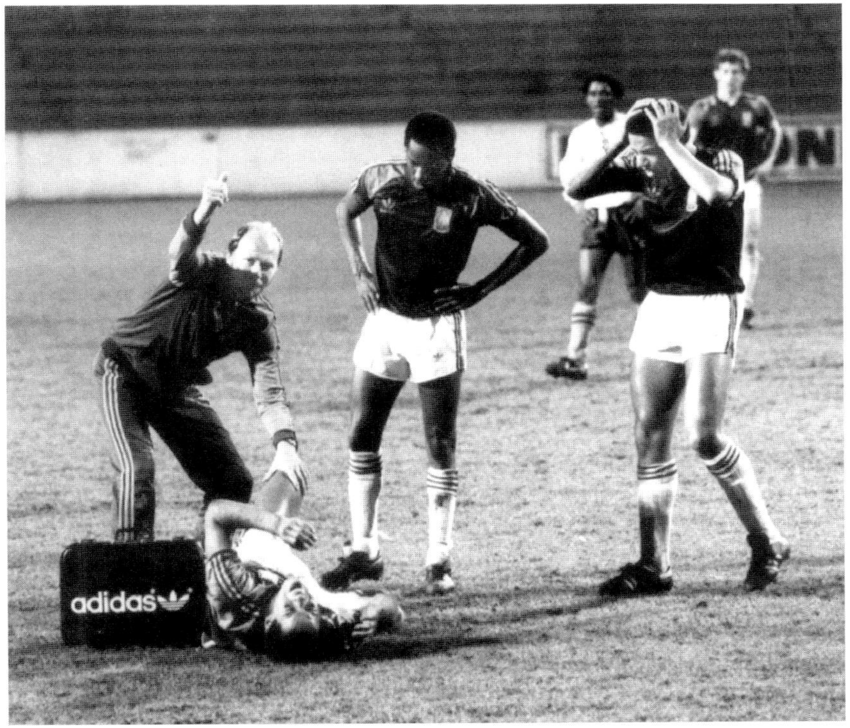

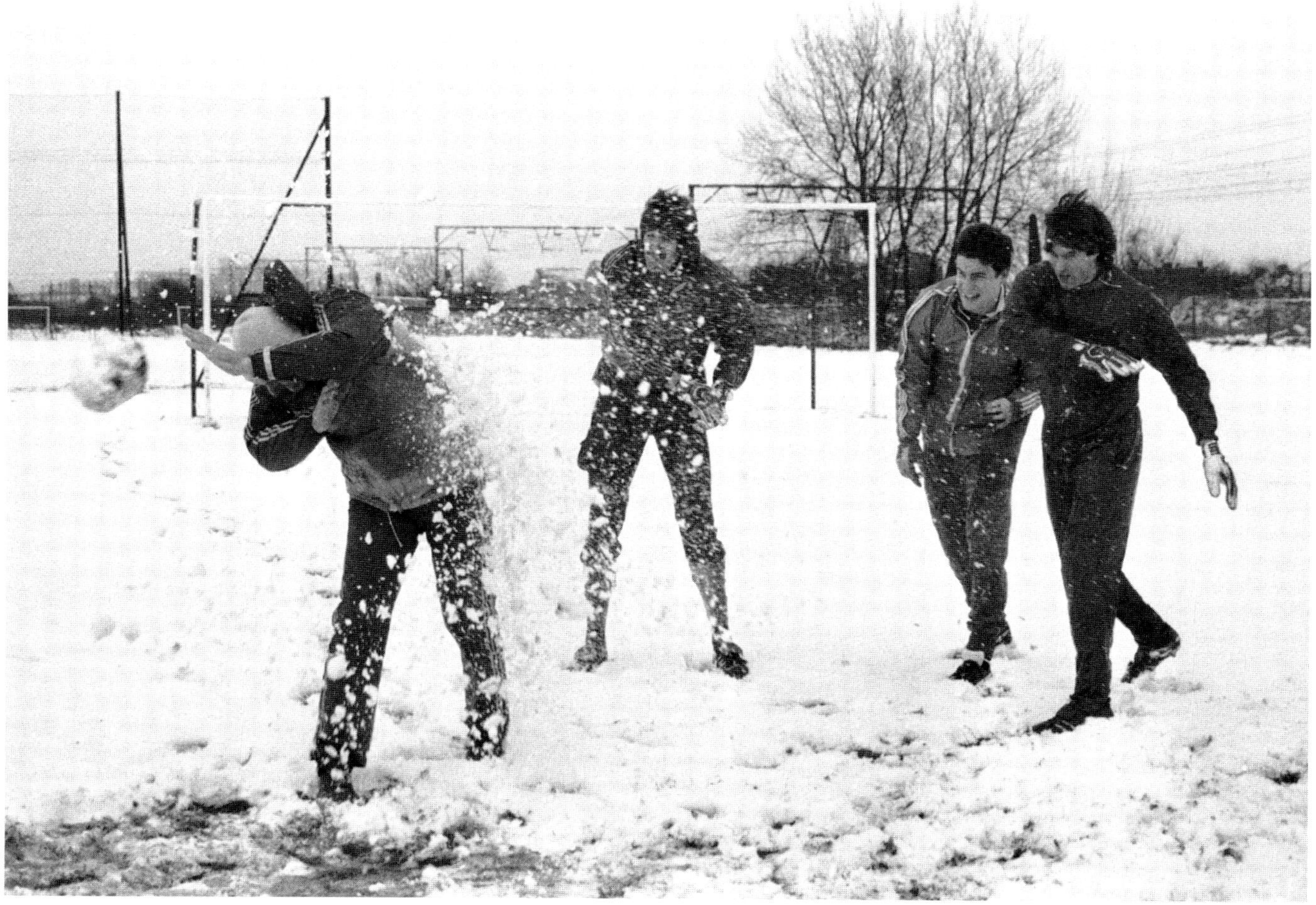

Snow joke. Hammers' goalkeeping coach Ernie Gregory comes under fire as Phil Parkes, John Vaughan and Tom McAlister take a break from training on a snow-covered pitch.

Fantastic. West Ham parade the FA Cup the day after beating Arsenal 1–0 in the final. The huge crowds lined the route for miles and, at the famous Boleyn Tavern, next to the Upton Park ground, the coach could barely make its way through the throng.

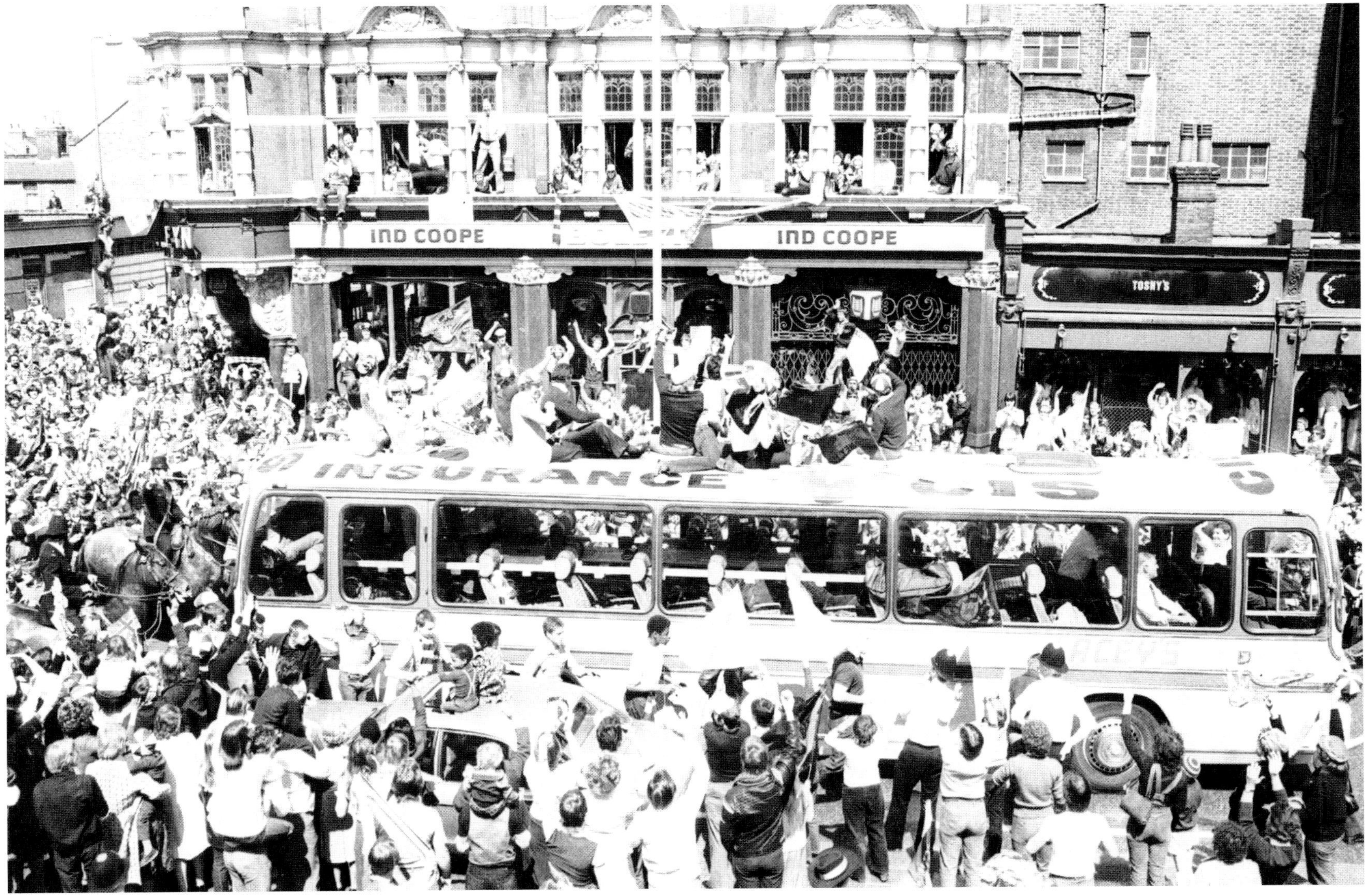
IND COOPE
IND COOPE
TOSHY'S
INSURANCE
CIS

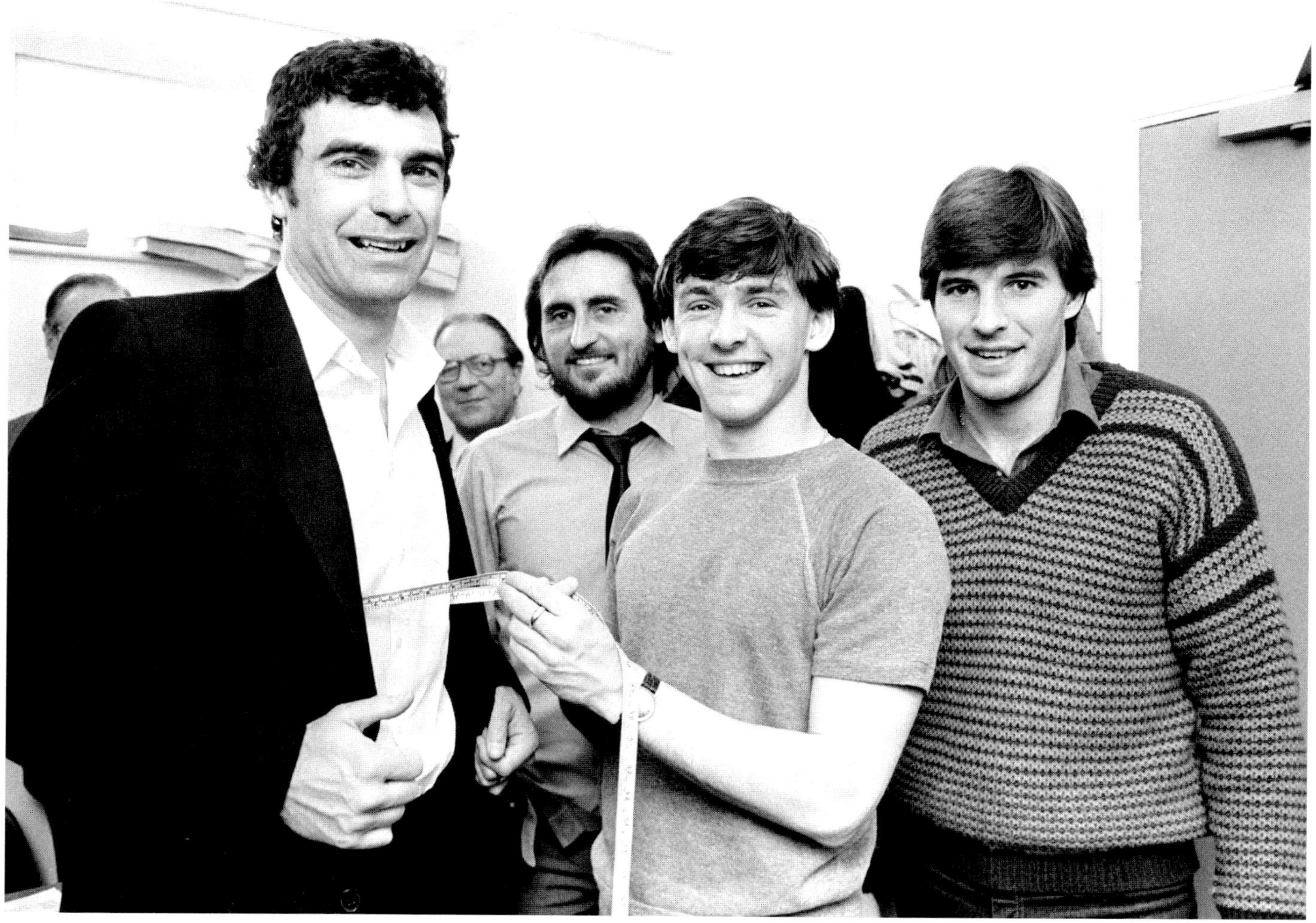

Suits you sir. Paul Allen gets the measure of Trevor Brooking as the players are fitted for their new club suits. Nicky Morgan waits his turn.

Local heroes. the victorious cup-winning squad meet the Mayor of Newham in his parlour at a civic reception given to celebrate the 1980 win over Arsenal.

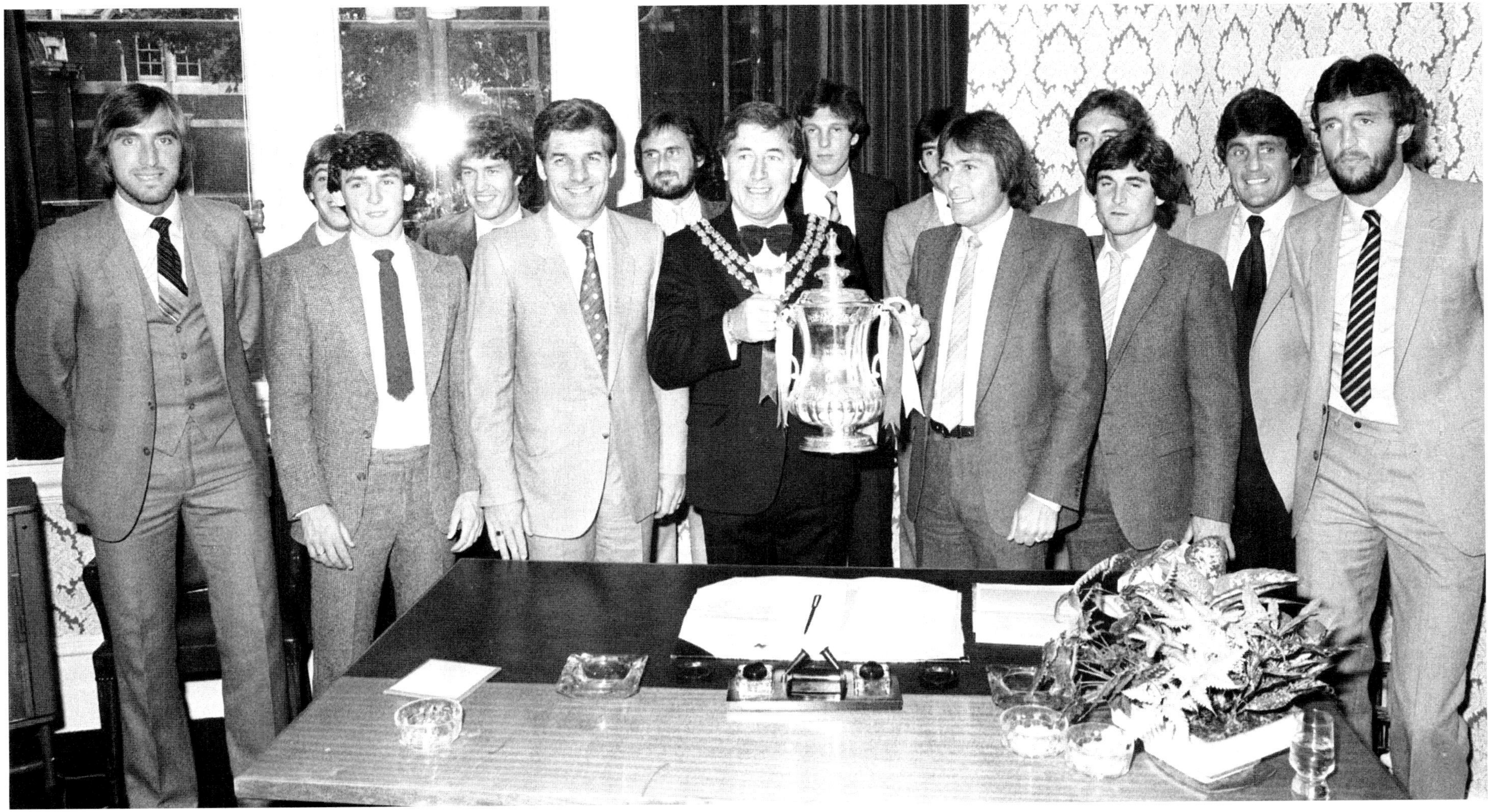

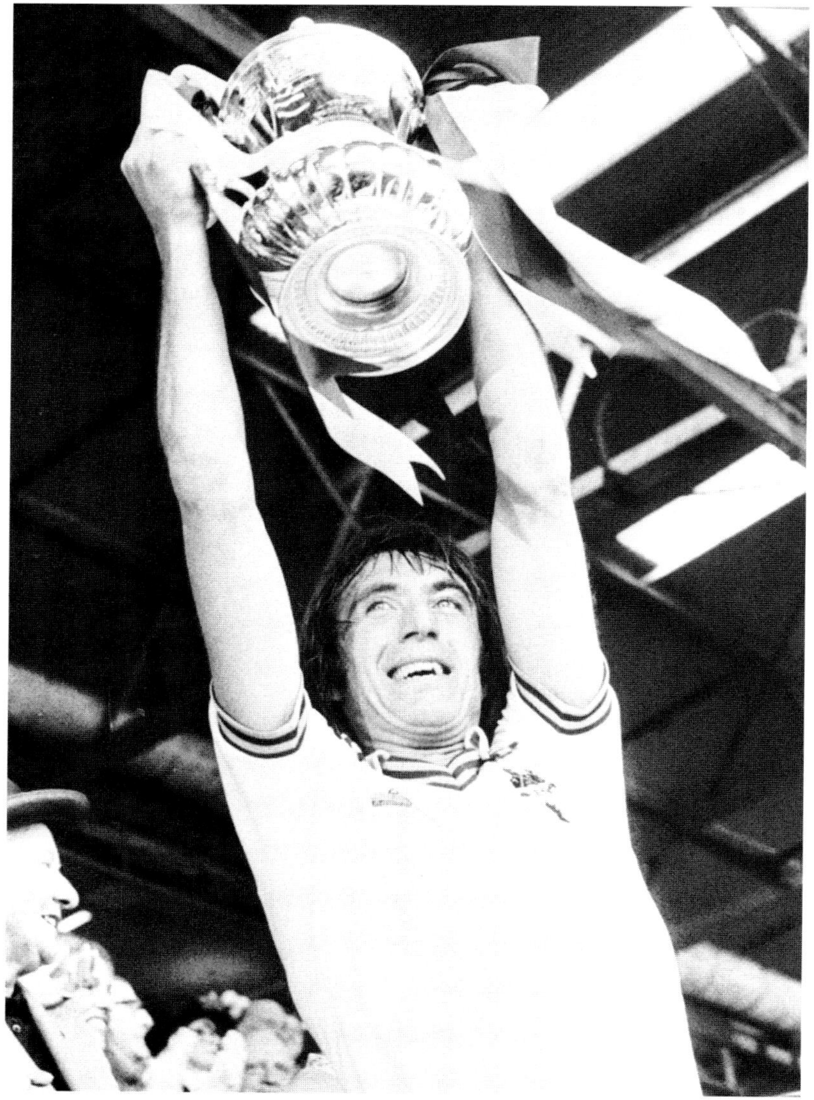

Captain Fantastic. Billy Bonds raises the FA Cup to the delighted Hammers' fans at Wembley on that glorious May day in 1980.

Champions. Billy Bonds raises the second division championship trophy above his head after receiving it from Matt Busby. Hammers ran away with the league in 1980–81 with a total of 66 points.

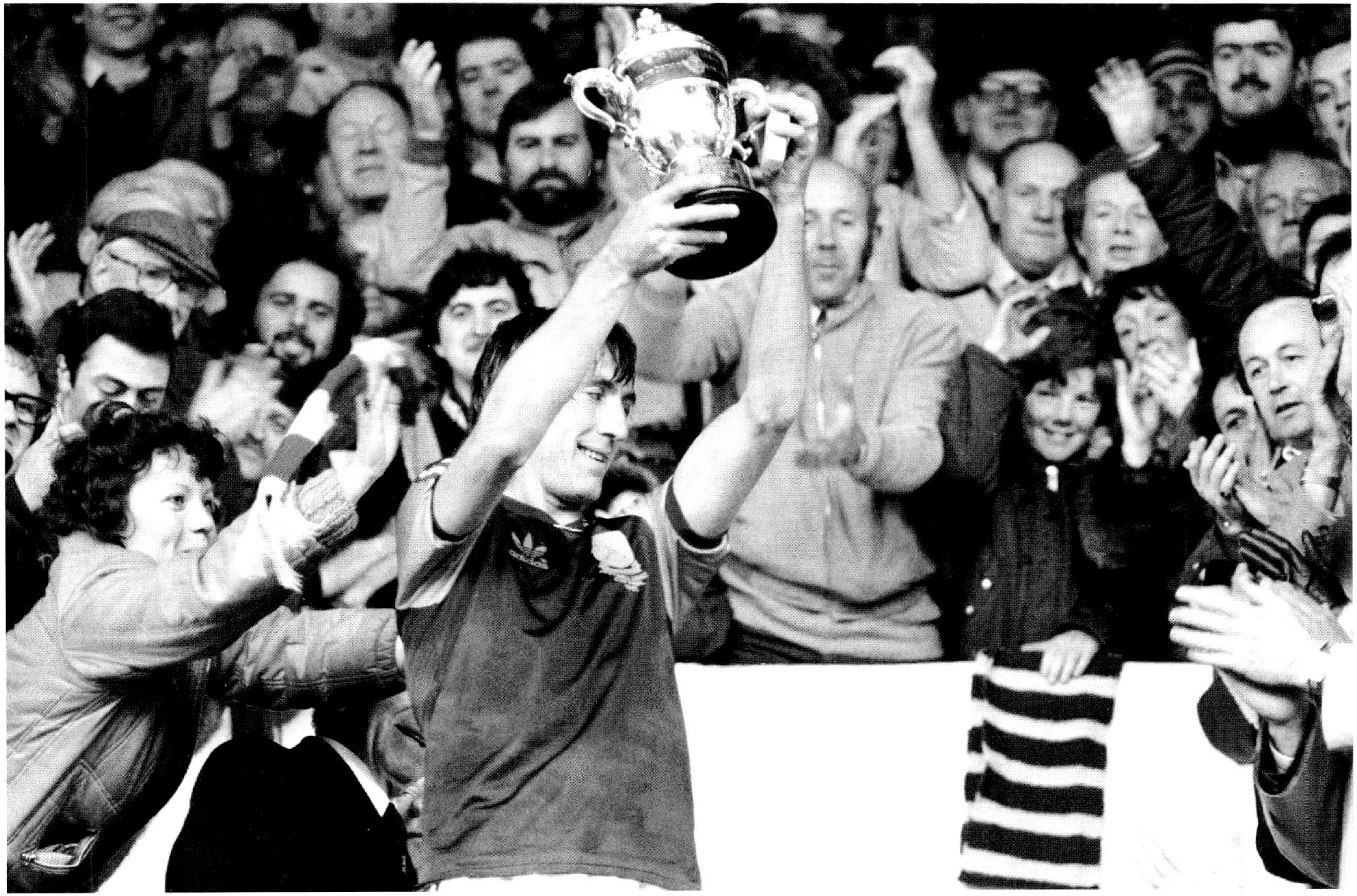
adidas

Legs eleven: no problem persuading the players to pose for a picture this time. Ray Stewart, Alvin Martin, Alan Devonshire and Phil Parkes take part in a publicity photo shoot at the training ground with a selection of scantily clad ladies.

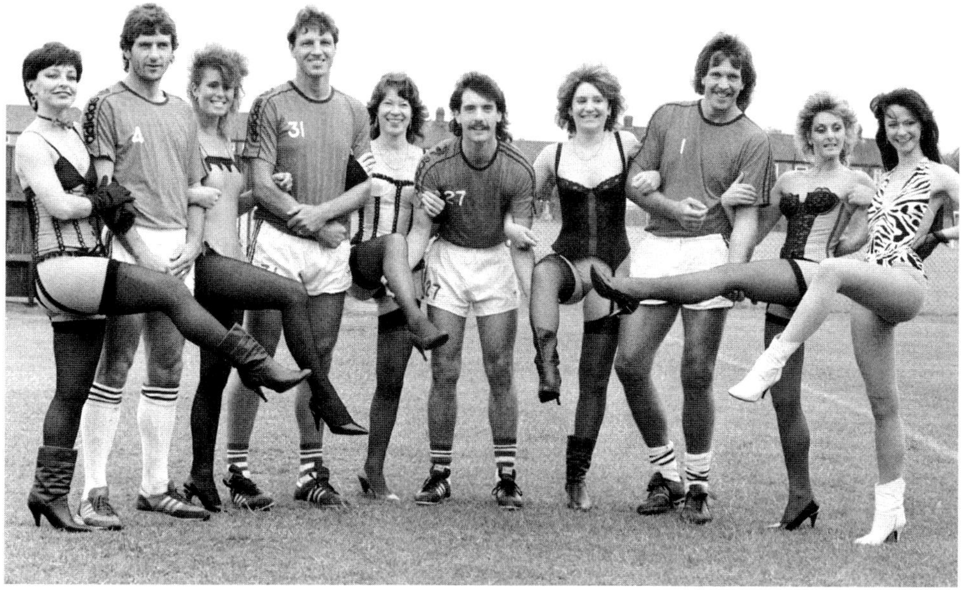

Lovely bubbly. Paul Allen and Paul Brush crack open the champagne on the team bus as the happy Hammers travel home after booking their place in the 1980 FA Cup final with a 2–1 victory over Everton in the Elland Road replay.

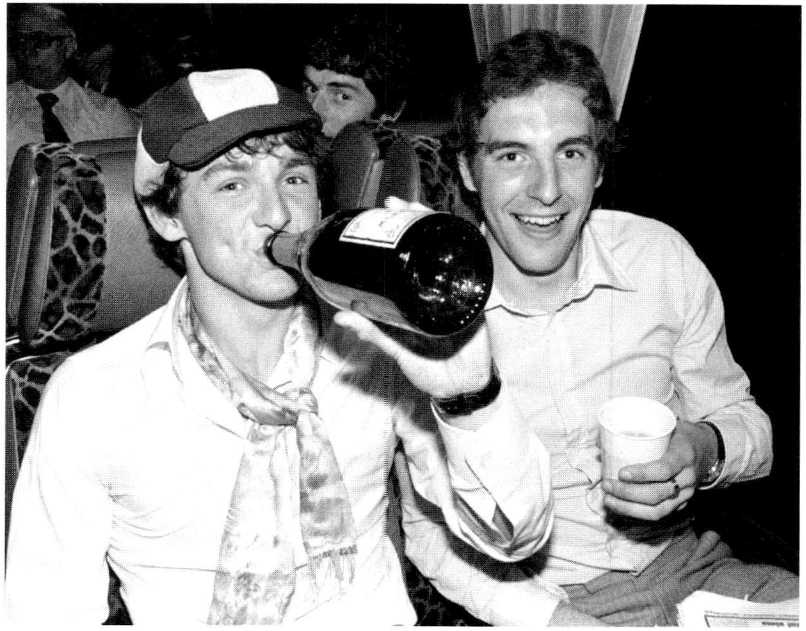

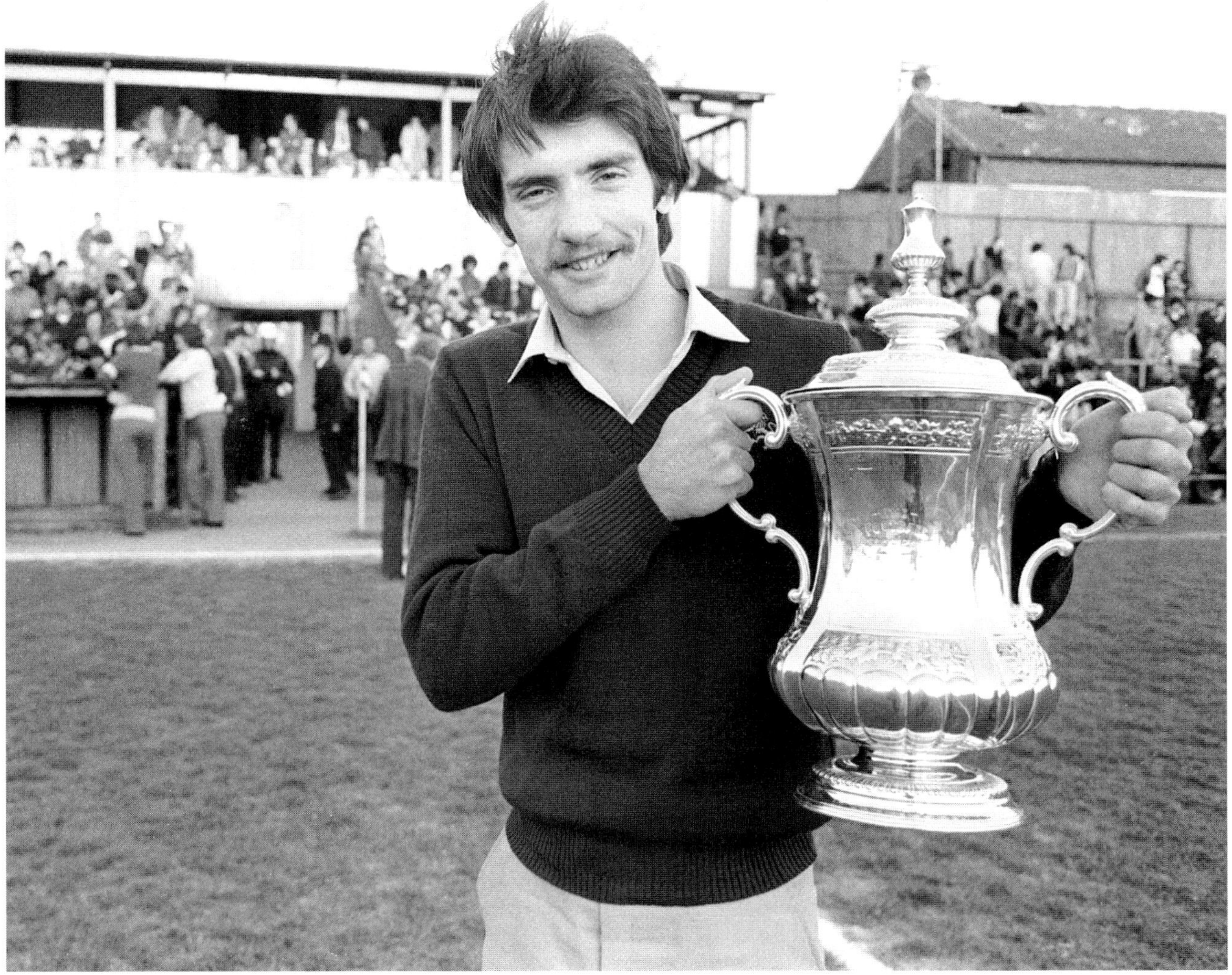

Back to his roots. Alan Devonshire proudly shows off the FA Cup on the Southall pitch when West Ham played a charity match at his old club shortly after their 1980 Wembley win. Dev cost Hammers just £5,000 in 1976 — not bad, eh?

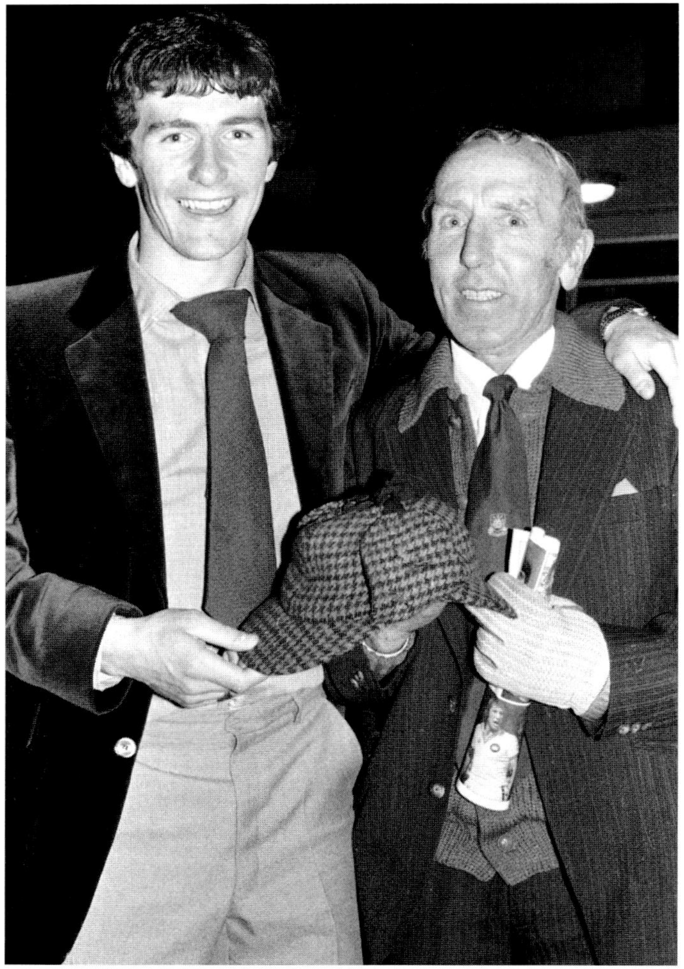

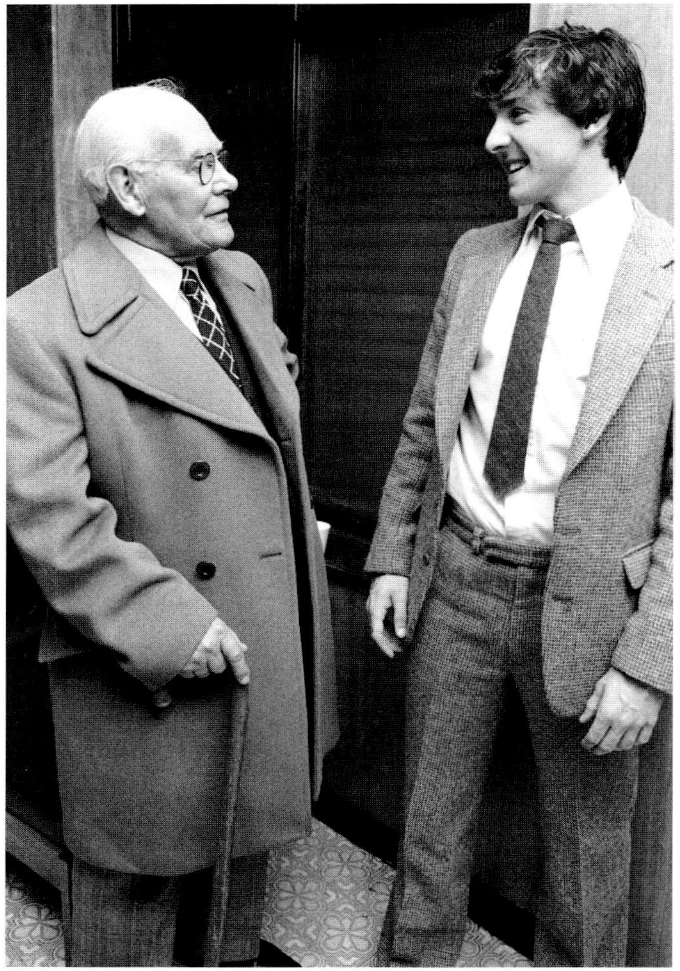

Wee Archie. it's funny how some things stick in your mind. After beating Everton in the 1980 FA Cup replay, this picture of a youthful looking Ray Stewart celebrating after the match with his dad, Archie, still remains one of my most vivid memories of the night.

The old and the new. Soon to become the youngest player to take part in an FA Cup final, Paul Allen had the honour of meeting Jimmy Ruffell in 1980. Jimmy was the oldest surviving member of West Ham's 1923 cup final team who played in the first-ever final at Wembley Stadium.

Name one famous Belgian. François van der Elst is welcomed to his first West Ham training session by Frank Lampard, Trevor Brooking and Billy Bonds in January 1982. François had been a major influence in Hammers' European Cup Winners' Cup final defeat by Anderlecht in 1976, scoring two goals.

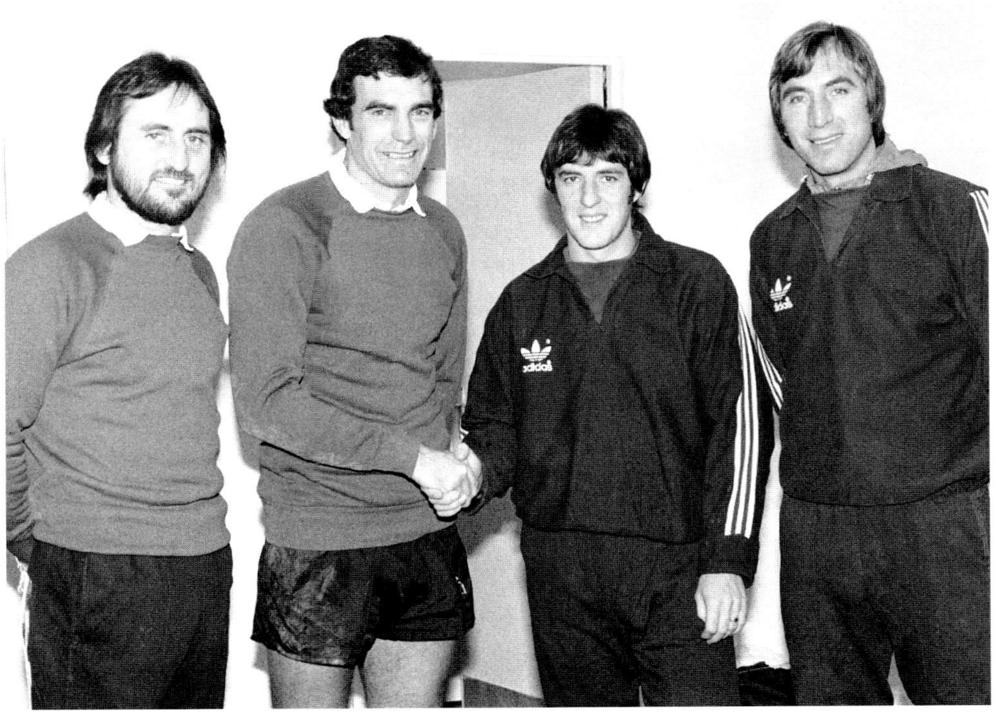

Penalty hero. Ray Stewart reflects on his 89th-minute penalty kick against Aston Villa in Hammers' 1980 FA Cup quarter-final tie at Upton Park. Ray's late winner set up a semi-final meeting with Everton en route to their Wembley success against Arsenal.

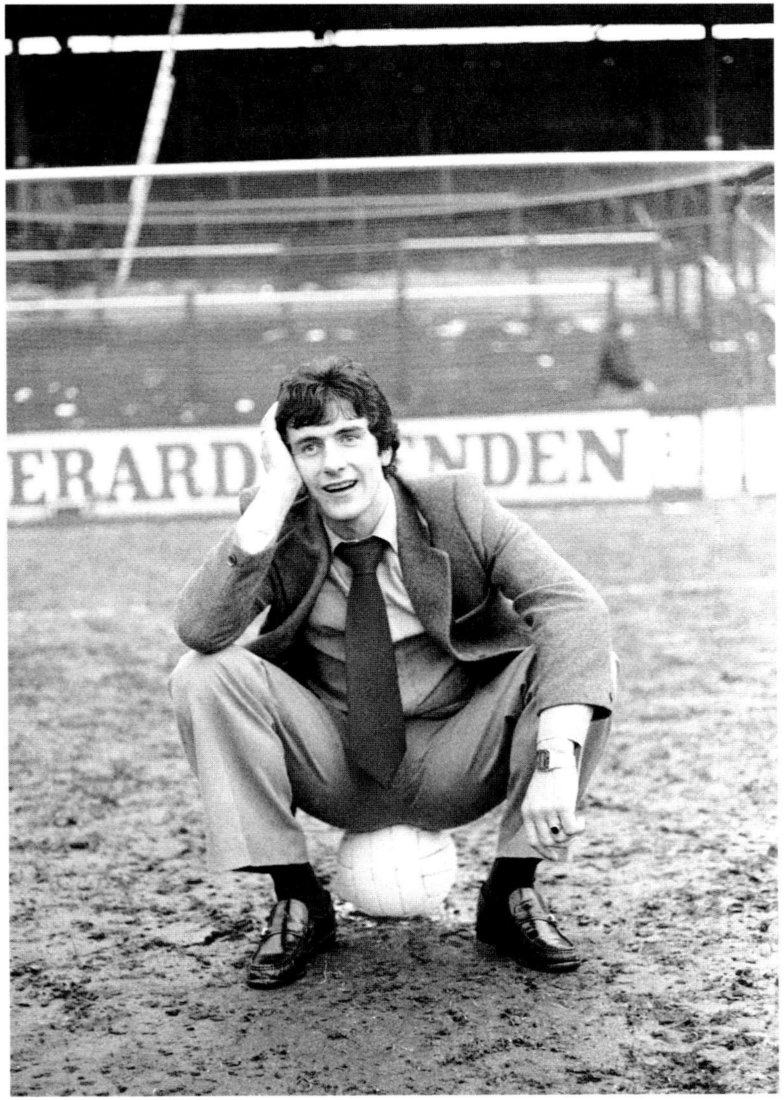

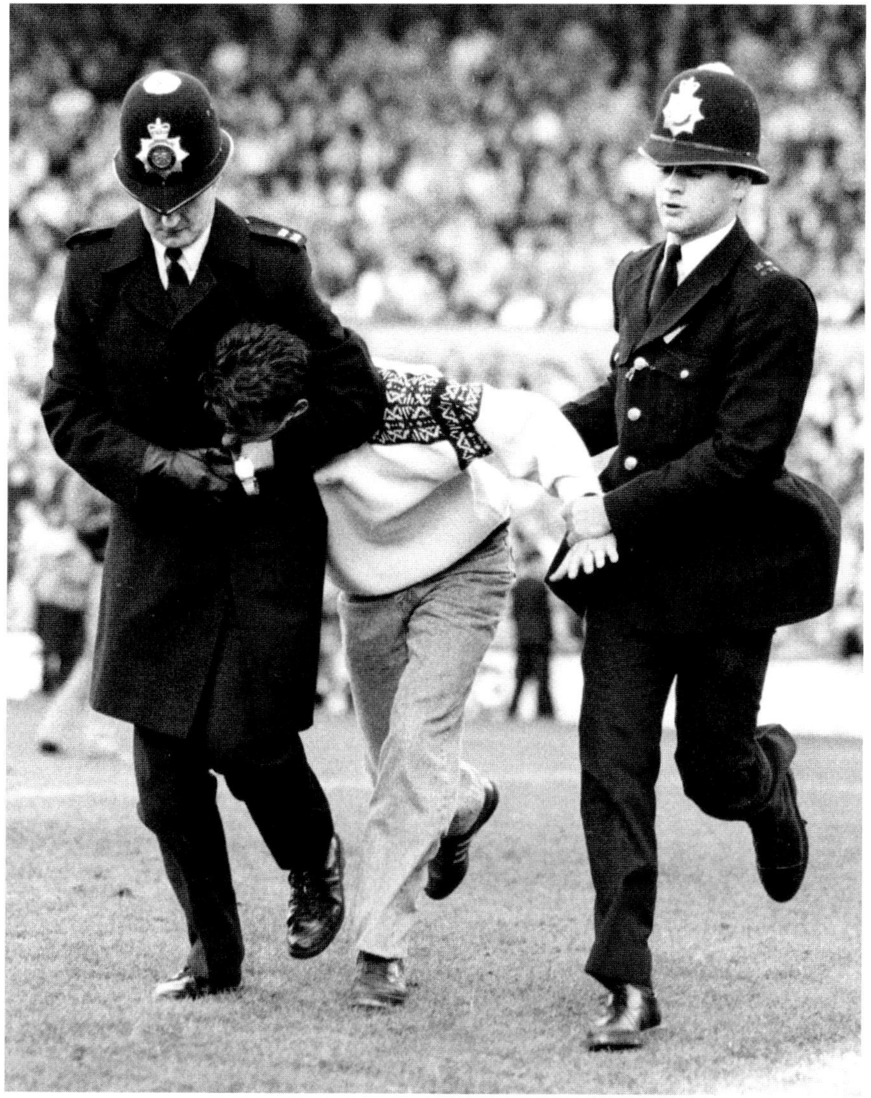

You're nicked: a home league match with Newcastle United and the inevitable crowd problems that blighted much of the 1980s. These policemen, thankfully, did not stand on ceremony and persuaded this 'fan' to leave.

Yes Minister. Former Prime Minister and local MP James Callaghan is introduced to the players at Ninian Park before Hammers' game with Cardiff City in April 1980. Former West Ham 'keeper Peter Grotier's mistake gave the visitors a 1–0 win.

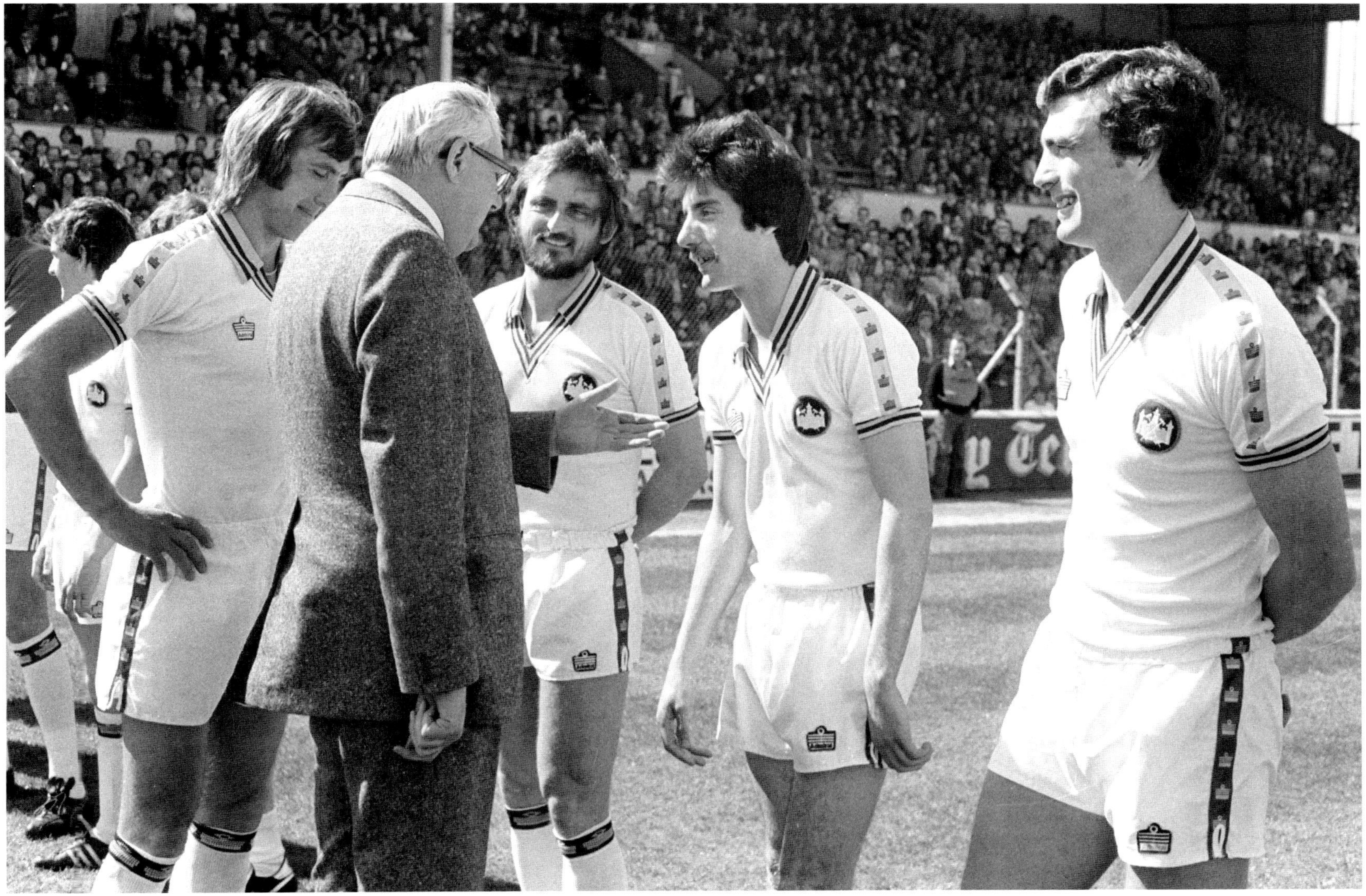

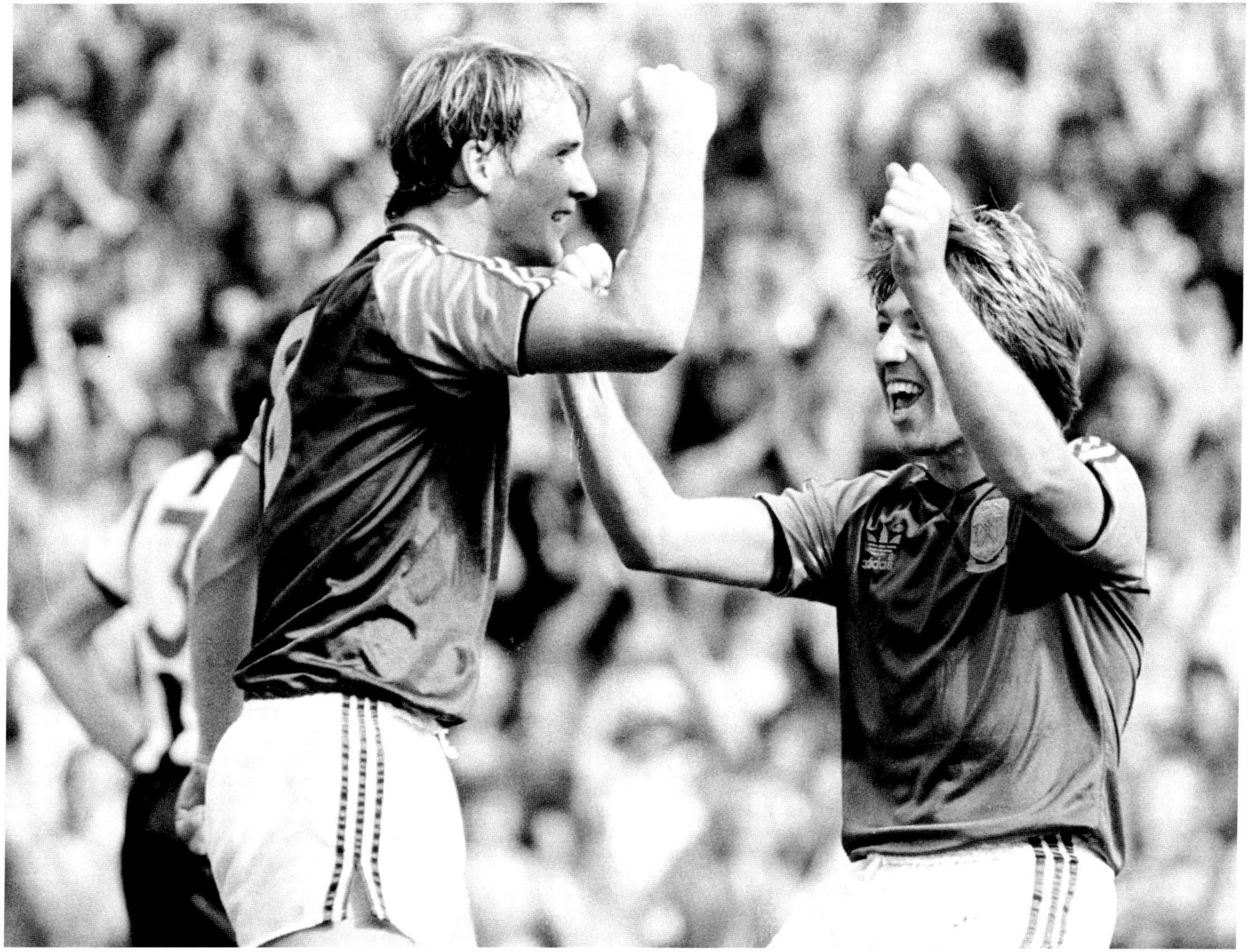

First of many. Paul Goddard celebrates his first-ever goal for West Ham against Notts County at Upton Park in August 1980. Geoff Pike is first on the scene to congratulate the striker who scored a second, later in the game, as Hammers went on to win 4–0.

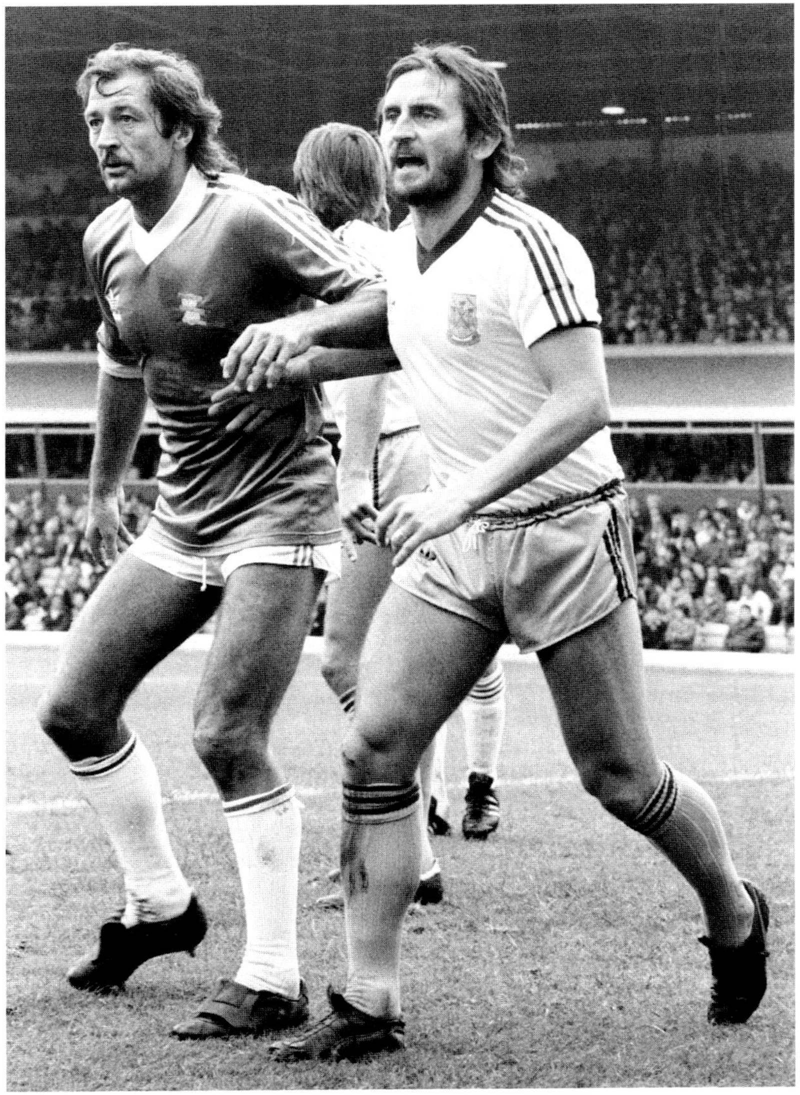

Let's be Frank. Frank Lampard and Frank Worthington indulge in a bit of argy-bargy as they wait for a corner to be taken at St Andrew's, Birmingham, in a 2–2 draw in October 1981.

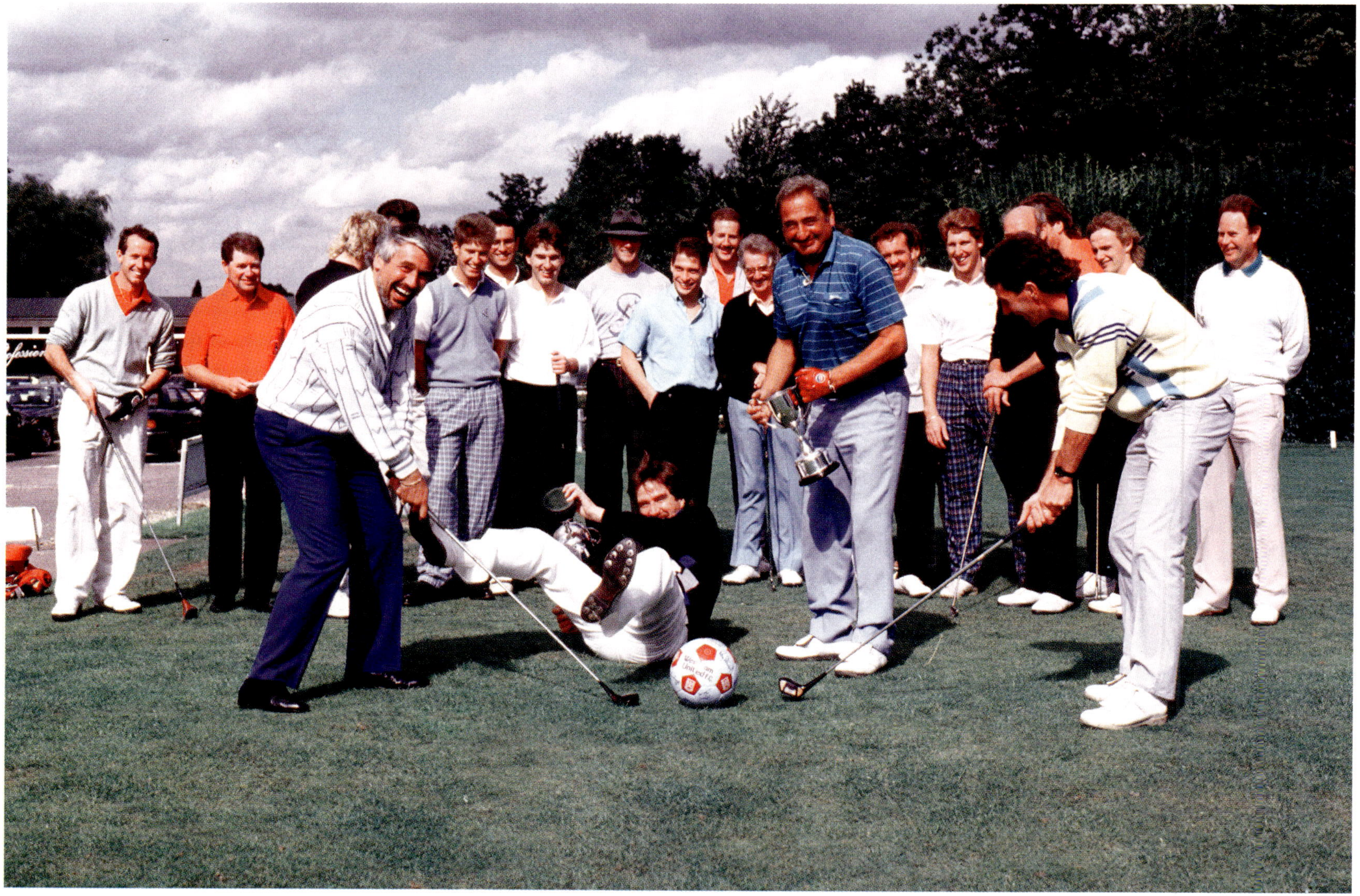

Fall guy. The occasion was a charity golf day at Southend organised by Ray Stewart (who else?). The late Bernie Winters headed the line-up of celebrities, but it was snooker player Cliff Thorburn who stole the show as he ended all ends up during the photo session.

Bath night. The jubilant West Ham youngsters celebrate Southern Junior Floodlit Cup victory in the Upton Park bath after the final. Future first-teamers Steve Potts, George Parris and Tony Cottee enjoy success early in their careers.

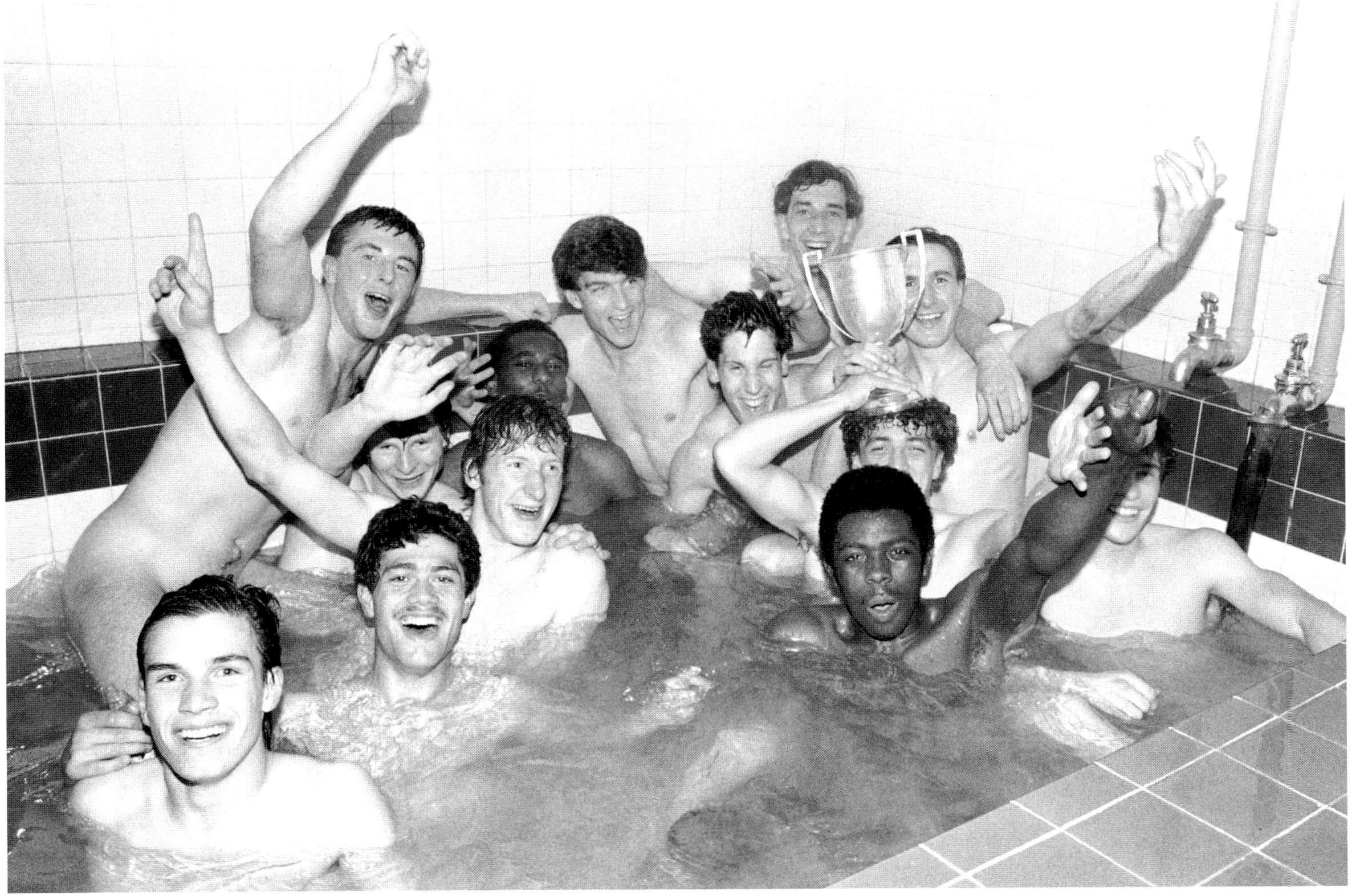

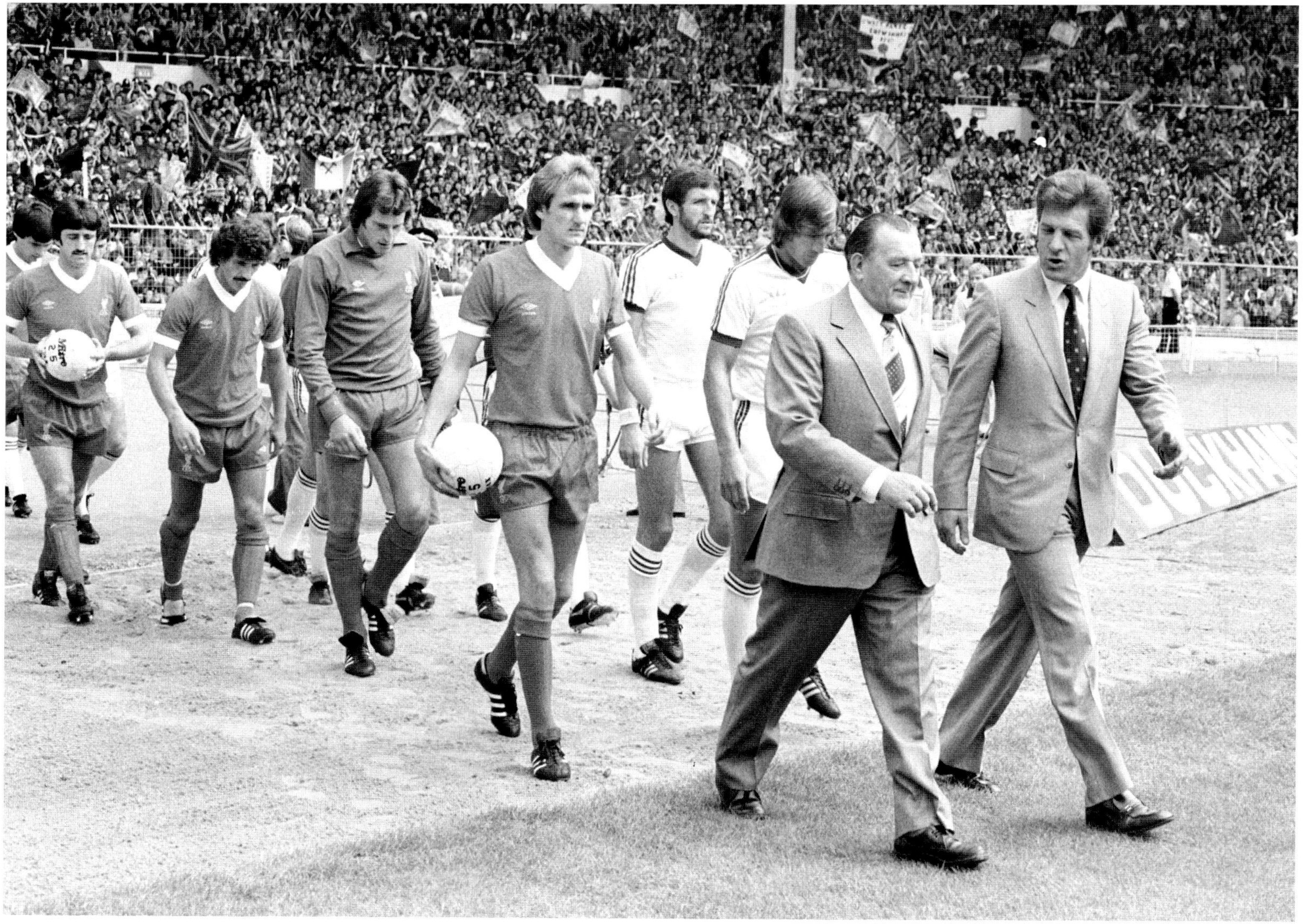

Managing well. John Lyall and his Liverpool counterpart Bob Paisley proudly lead out their sides for the Charity Shield at Wembley as the 1980–81 season gets under way. Liverpool won the match thanks to a Terry McDermott 18th-minute goal.

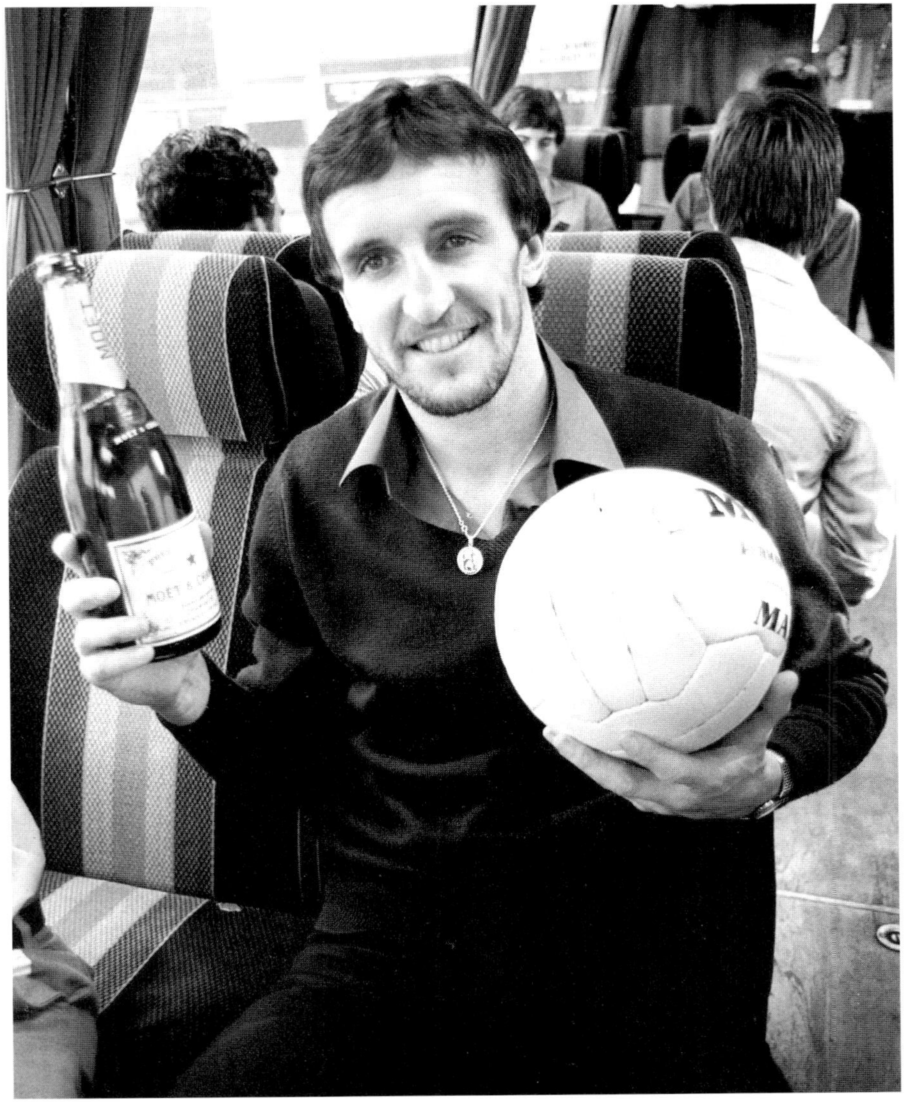

A good day's work. David Cross celebrates on the team bus home after Hammers had clinched promotion back to the first division with a 5–1 win at Grimsby Town in April 1981. Crossie scored four times to take the match ball and a well-earned bottle of bubbly.

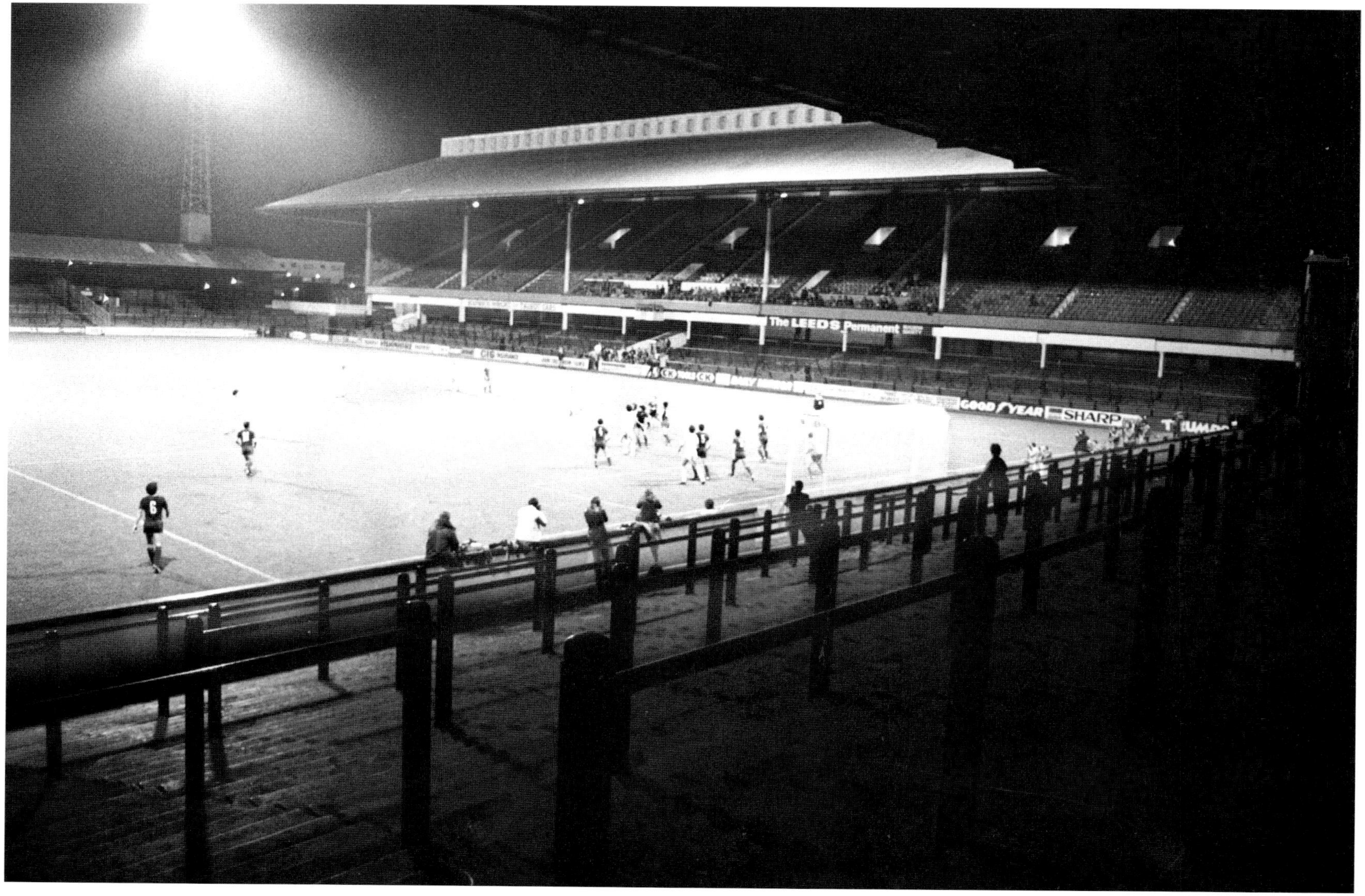
The LEEDS Permanent
GOODYEAR
SHARP

A night to remember. This was the eerie scene at Upton Park in October 1980 for West Ham's European Cup Winners' Cup first round, second leg tie against Castilla. Crowd trouble in the Bernabeu Stadium during Hammers' first-leg 3–1 defeat led UEFA to instruct that the second leg be played behind closed doors. The strange atmosphere must have suited West Ham who won 5–1 to go through to the next round 6–4 on aggregate.

Ouch. Paul Allen is hacked down during a vicious game against Politecnica Timisoara in Romania in November 1980. West Ham had won the first leg of their Cup Winners' Cup second round tie 4–0 but lost the away leg to a Paltinisanu goal. It was the most dismal place on God's earth and we were all delighted to fly out as soon as the match was over.

From Russia with style. David Cross scores Hammers' only goal of the night as they go down 1–4 to a superior Dynamo Tbilisi side in the first leg of their third round European Cup Winners' Cup tie at Upton Park in March 1981. The 34,957 crowd applauded the Georgian side off of the pitch at the end of the game.

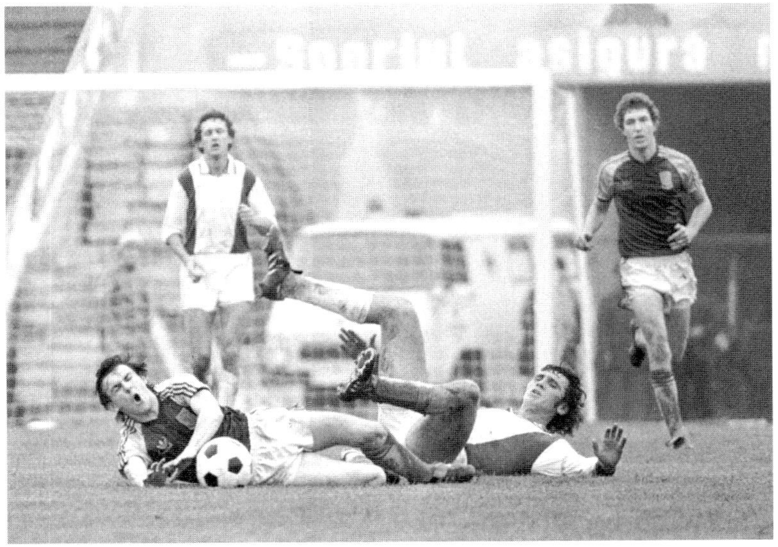

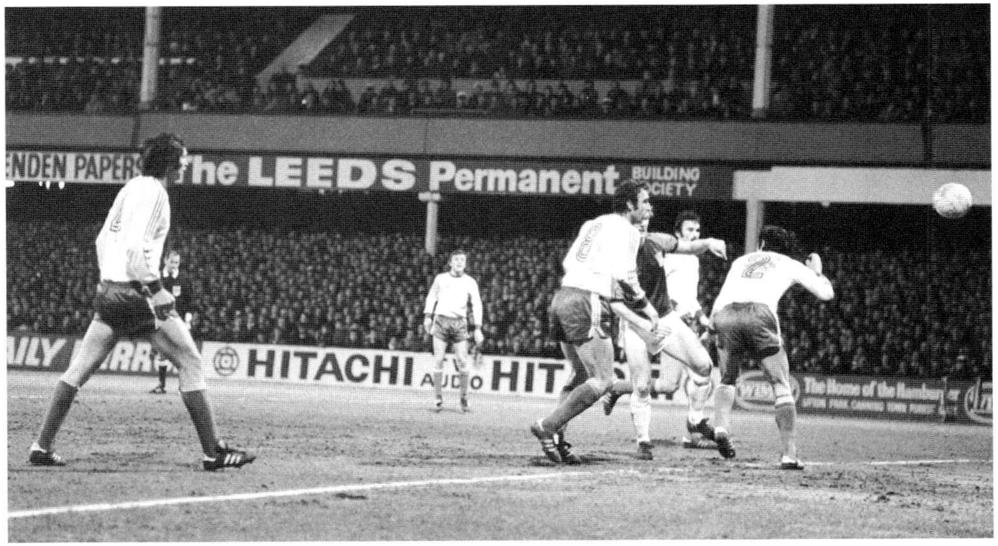

Crossfire. David Cross scores Hammers' only goal as they go down 3–1 to Castilla in the Bernabeu Stadium in Madrid at the start of their European Cup Winners' Cup adventure.

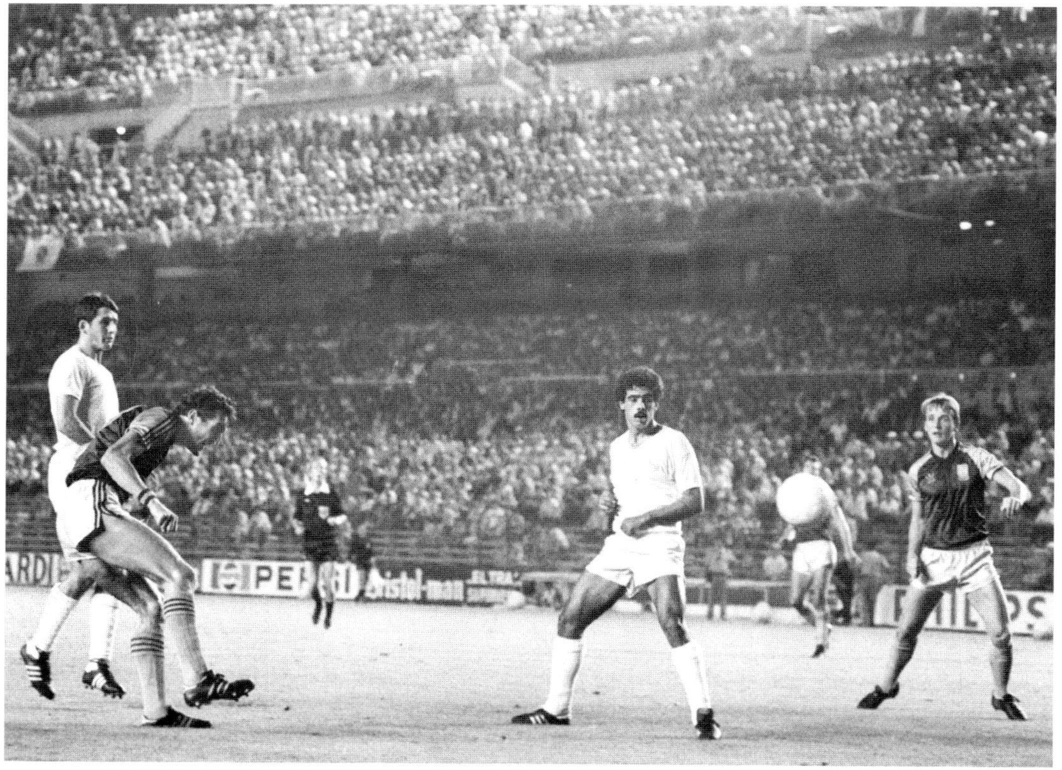

All clear now. Stuart Pearson has just put West Ham ahead in the 88th minute against Dynamo Tbilisi in Georgia — but then you can see that by the scoreboard, can't you? Hammers bowed out of the 1980–81 Cup Winners' Cup competition 4–2 on aggregate.

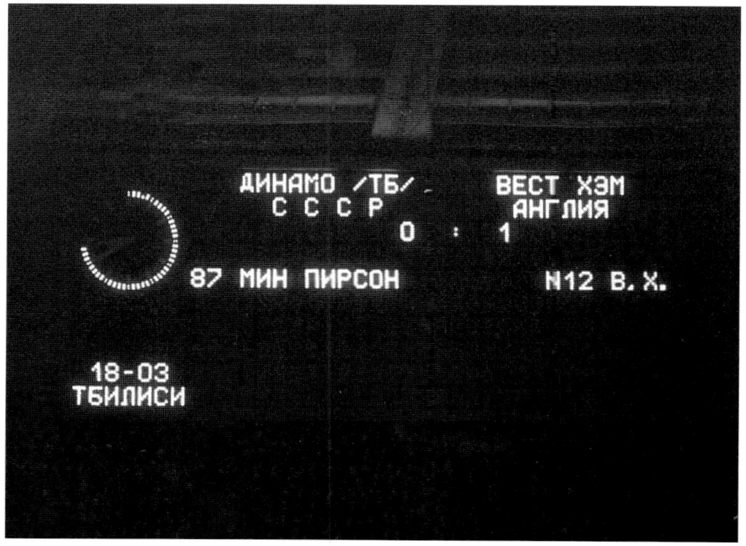

We know a song about that. Frank Lampard dives to head his now legendary goal against Everton in the 1980 FA Cup semi-final replay against Everton at Elland Road. Hammers went on to win the trophy that year and the fans still sing about the goal to this very day.

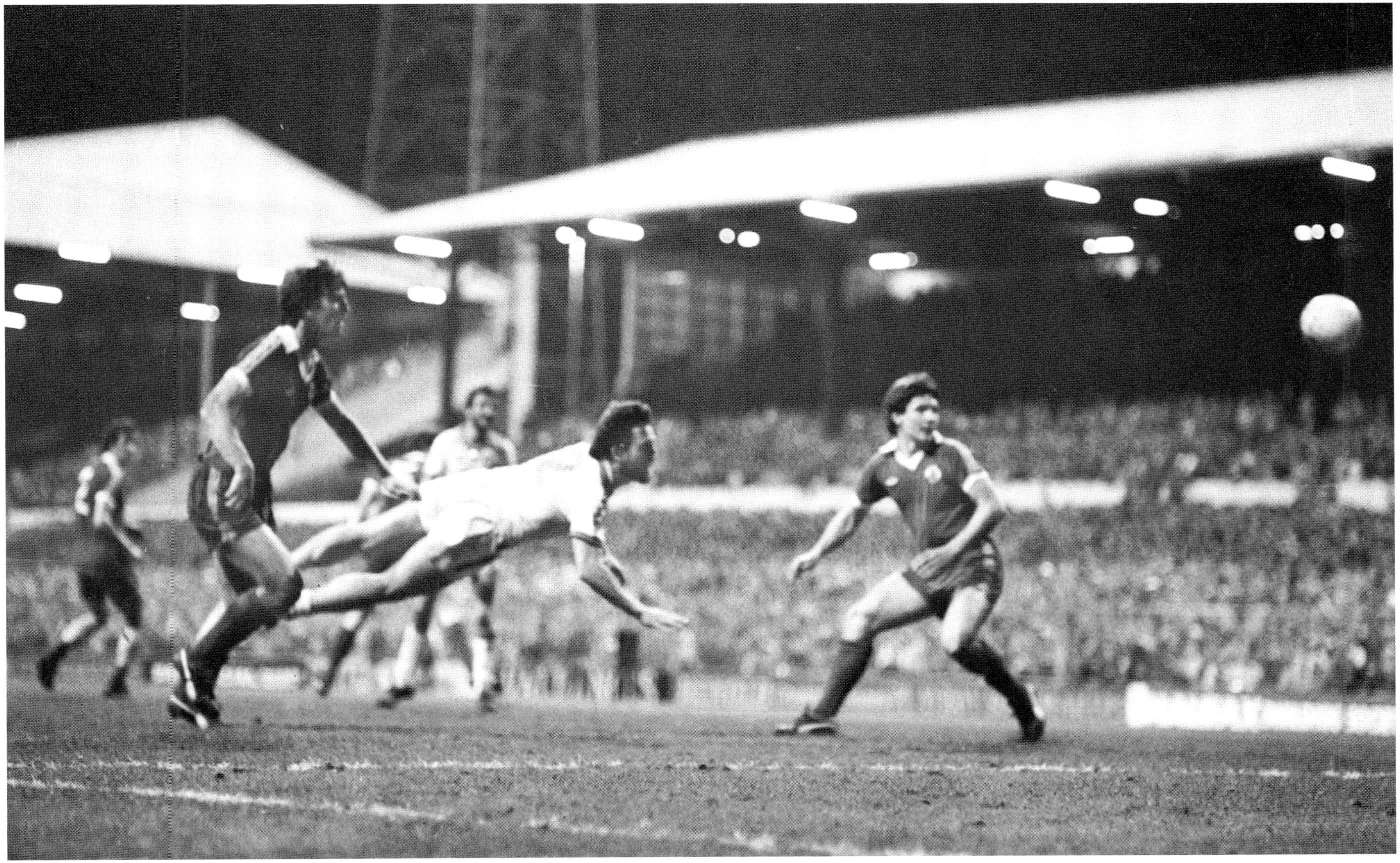

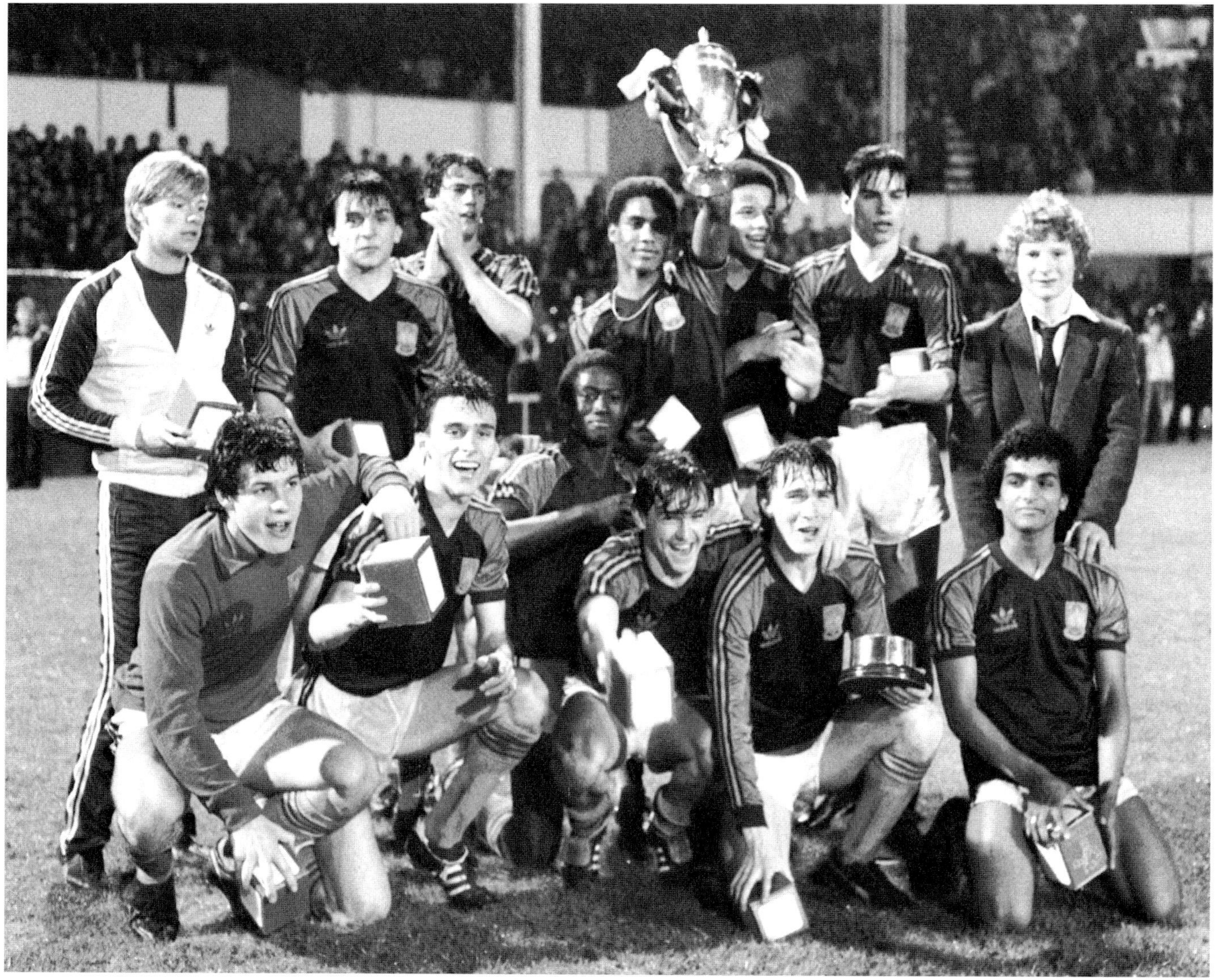

Young guns. Hammers' FA Youth Cup winners parade the trophy after the second leg of the 1980–81 final against Tottenham Hotspur at White Hart Lane. West Ham lost 1–0 on the night but, with a 2–0 lead from the first leg, won the tie 2–1 on aggregate.

Sporting gesture. Sheffield Wednesday players applaud league champions West Ham onto the Hillsborough pitch for the final game of the 1980–81 season. A Nicky Morgan goal in the 64th minute gave the Hammers a 1–0 victory and a total points tally of 66 for the season — breaking Middlesbrough's record by one point.

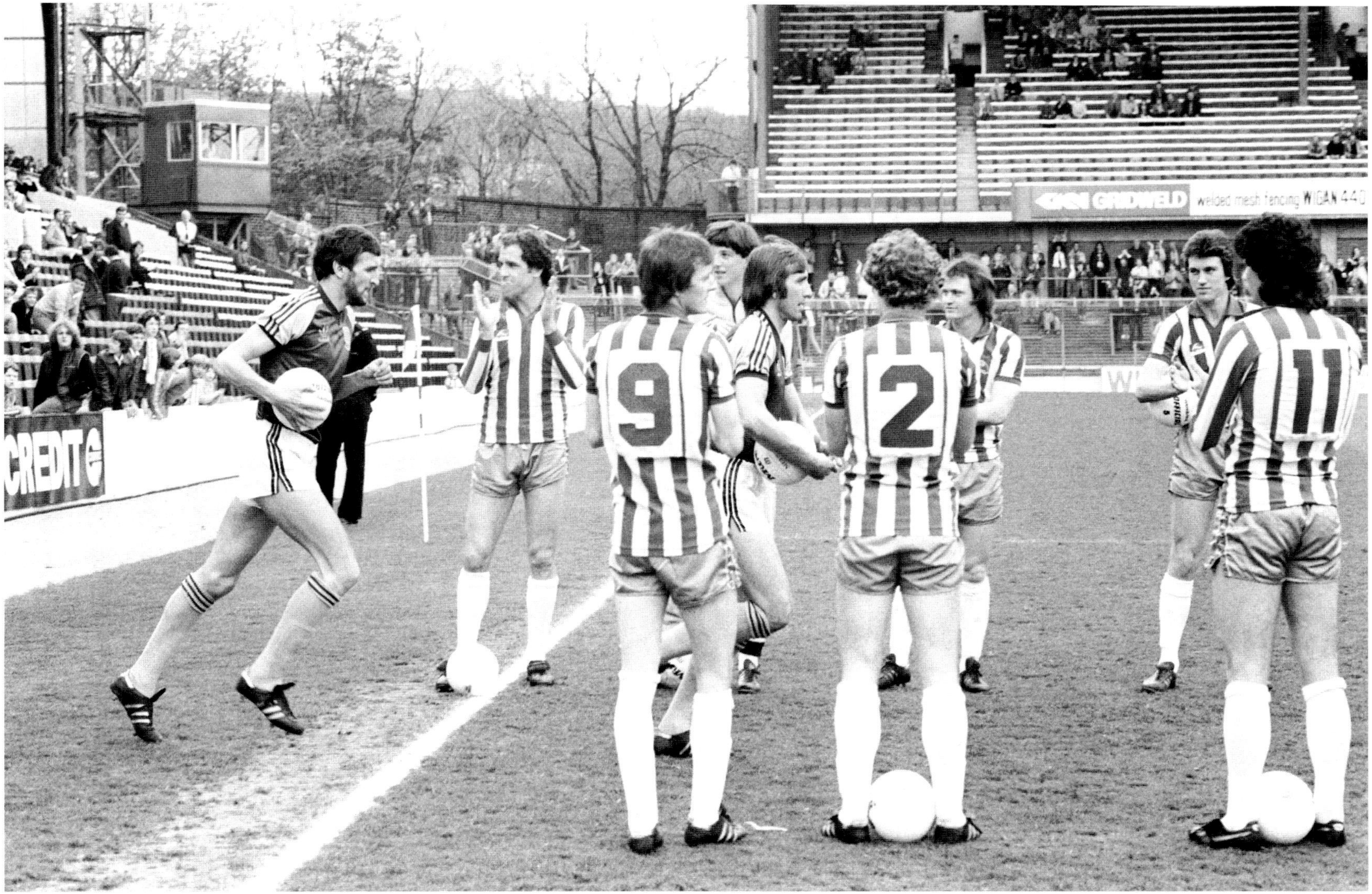
CREDIT
GRIDWELD
welded mesh fencing WIGAN 440

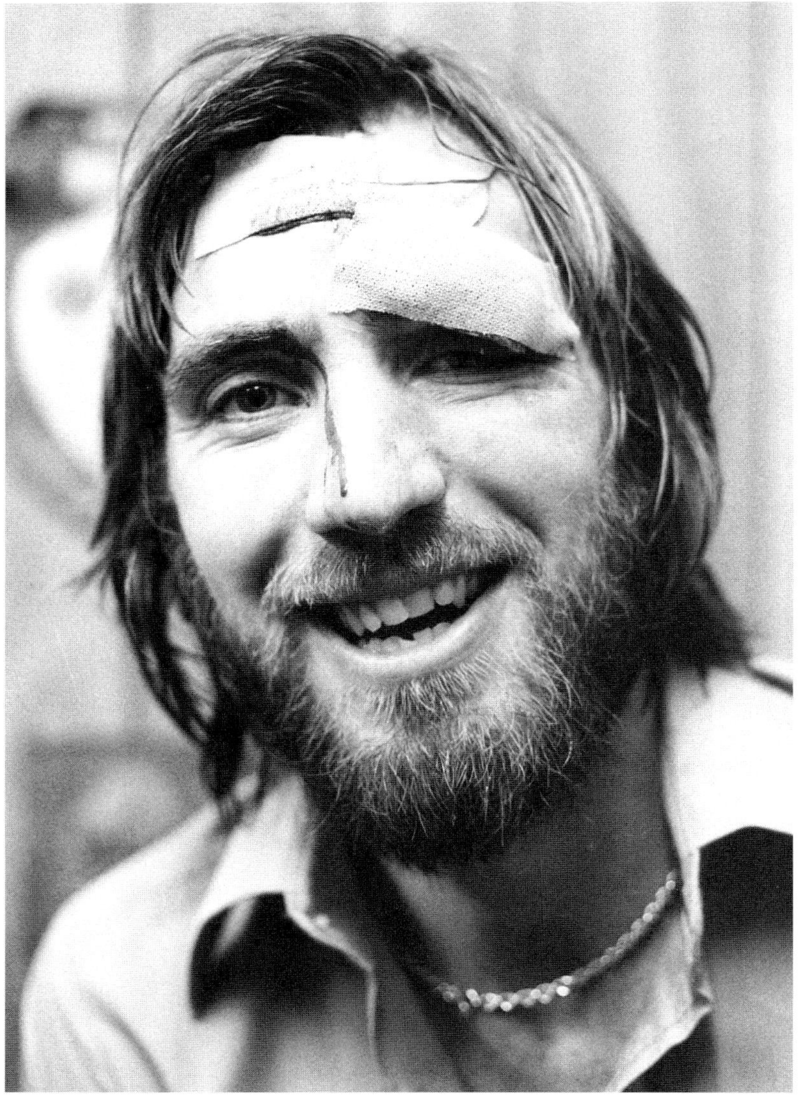

Captain courageous. Billy Bonds tried to make his usual quick getaway from Upton Park but, after his clash of heads with team-mate Alvin Martin, I ambushed him in the dressing-room corridor and persuaded him to let me get a picture of the damage. He even managed a smile for me.

Author-author. Billy Bonds lends his support to his old mate Trevor Brooking who was launching his autobiography at a City wine bar.

If I had a hammer. The day after the cup final victory over Arsenal, the Hammers toured the streets in an open-topped coach ending up at a reception at East Ham Town Hall. I caught up with David Cross trying to make off with this super memento — I don't think that he managed to hold on to it, though.

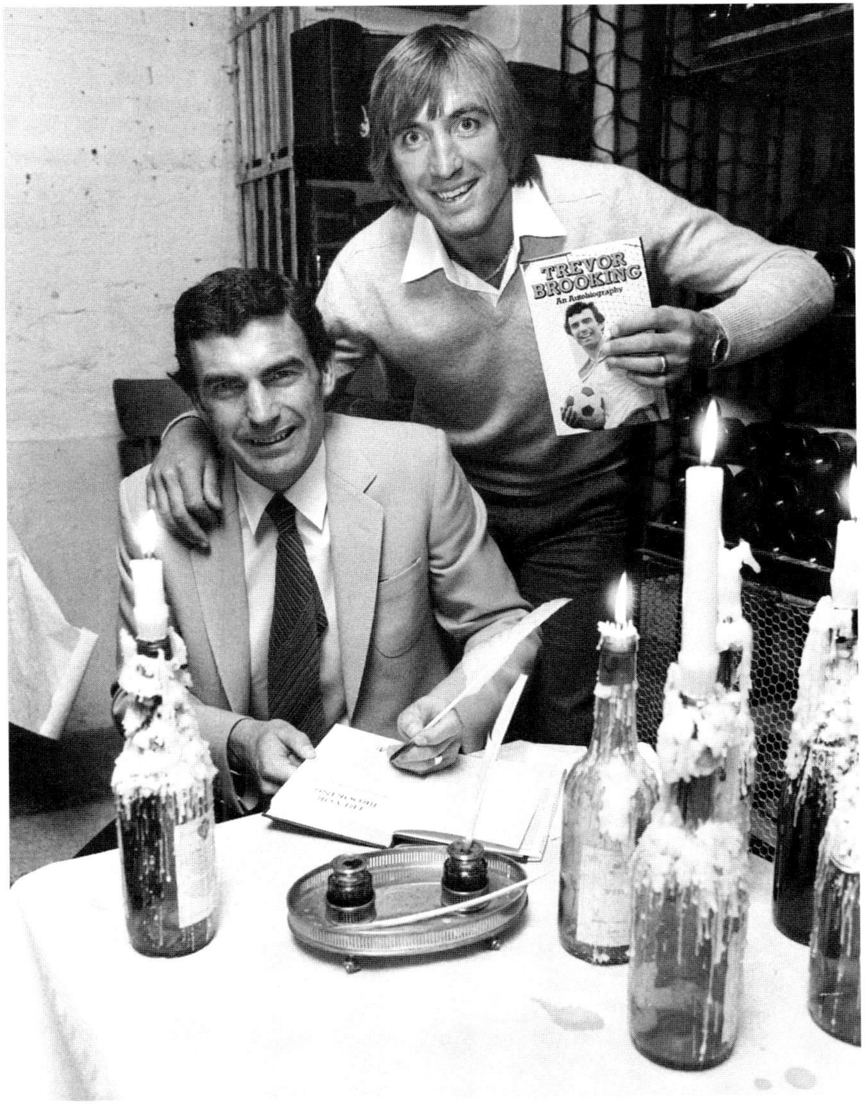
TREVOR
BROOKING
An Autobiography

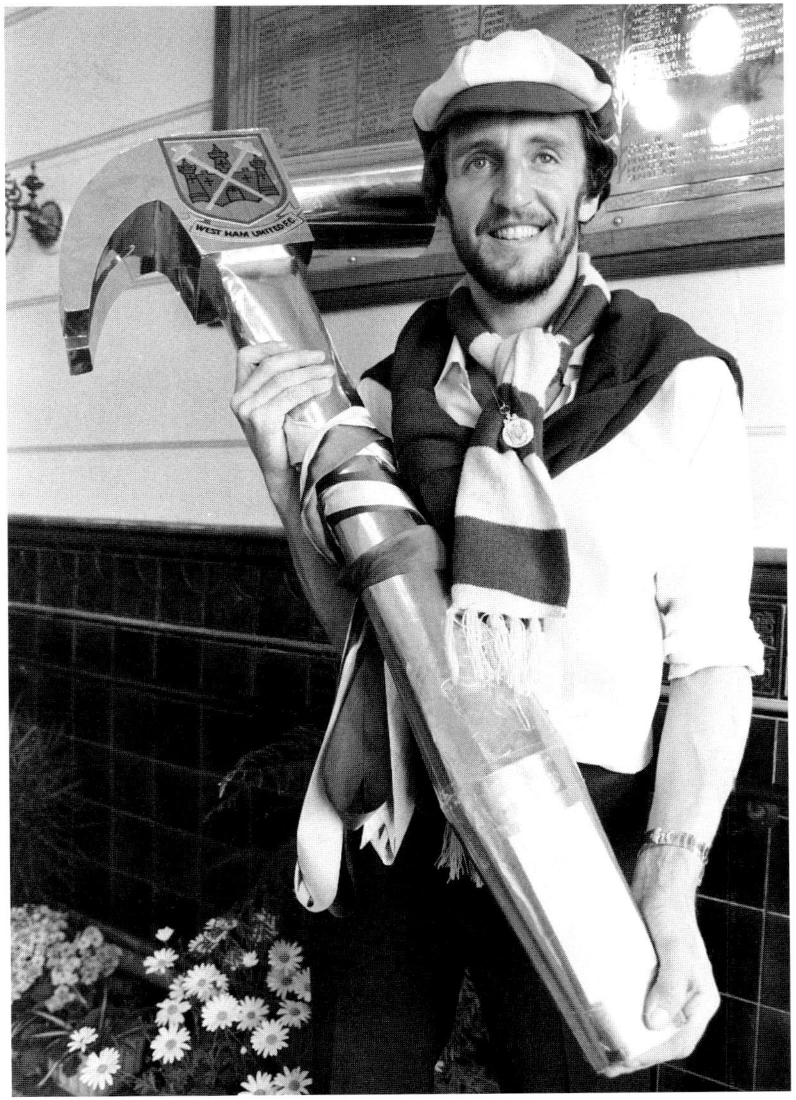
WEST HAM UNITED F.C.

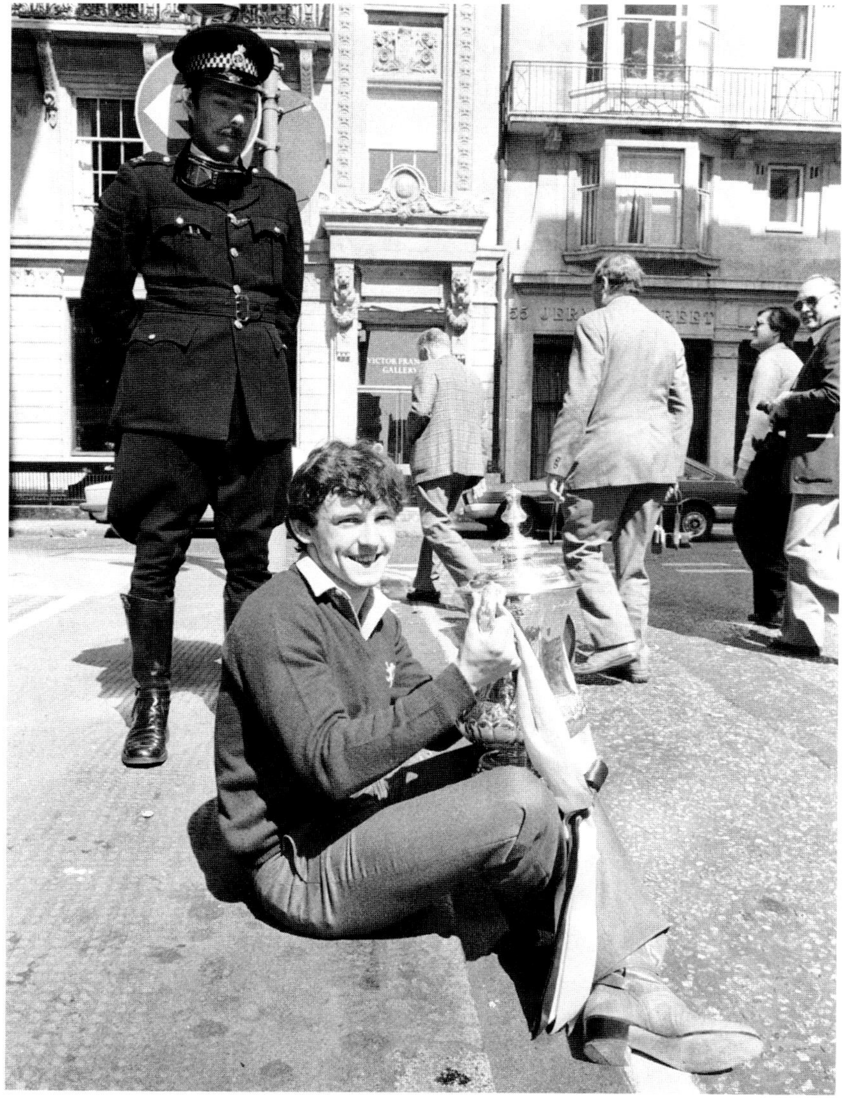

'Ello-'ello. This motorcycle cop keeps a watchful eye on Paul Allen and the FA Cup outside the team's West End hotel on the Sunday morning after the cup victory. We had spent the previous night at Quaglino's, so there were a few sore heads that morning.

Gangway. The police do a fine job of clearing the way for the players' convoy as they arrive at a swamped East Ham Town Hall after the street procession with the FA Cup.

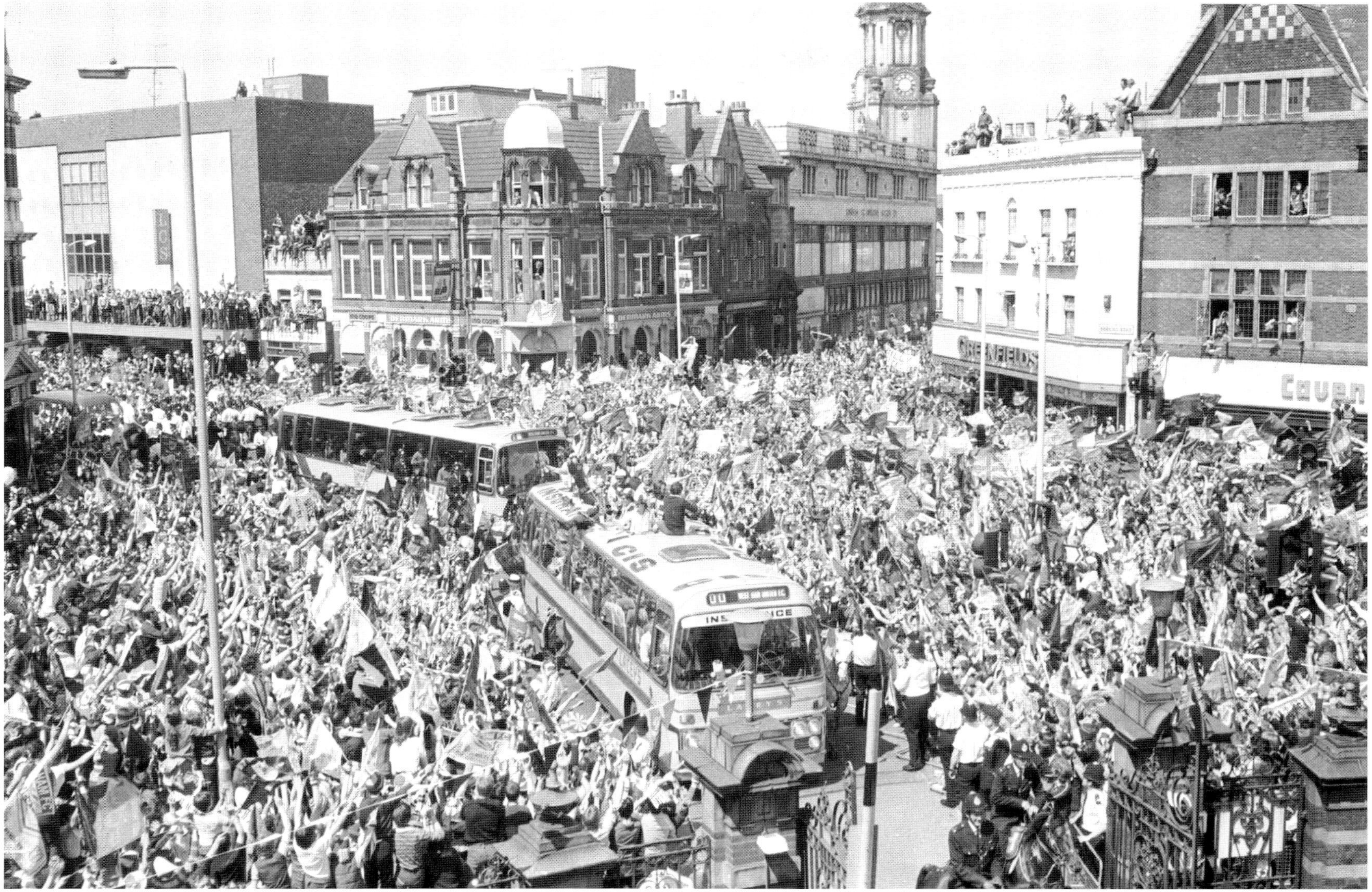
GREENFIELDS

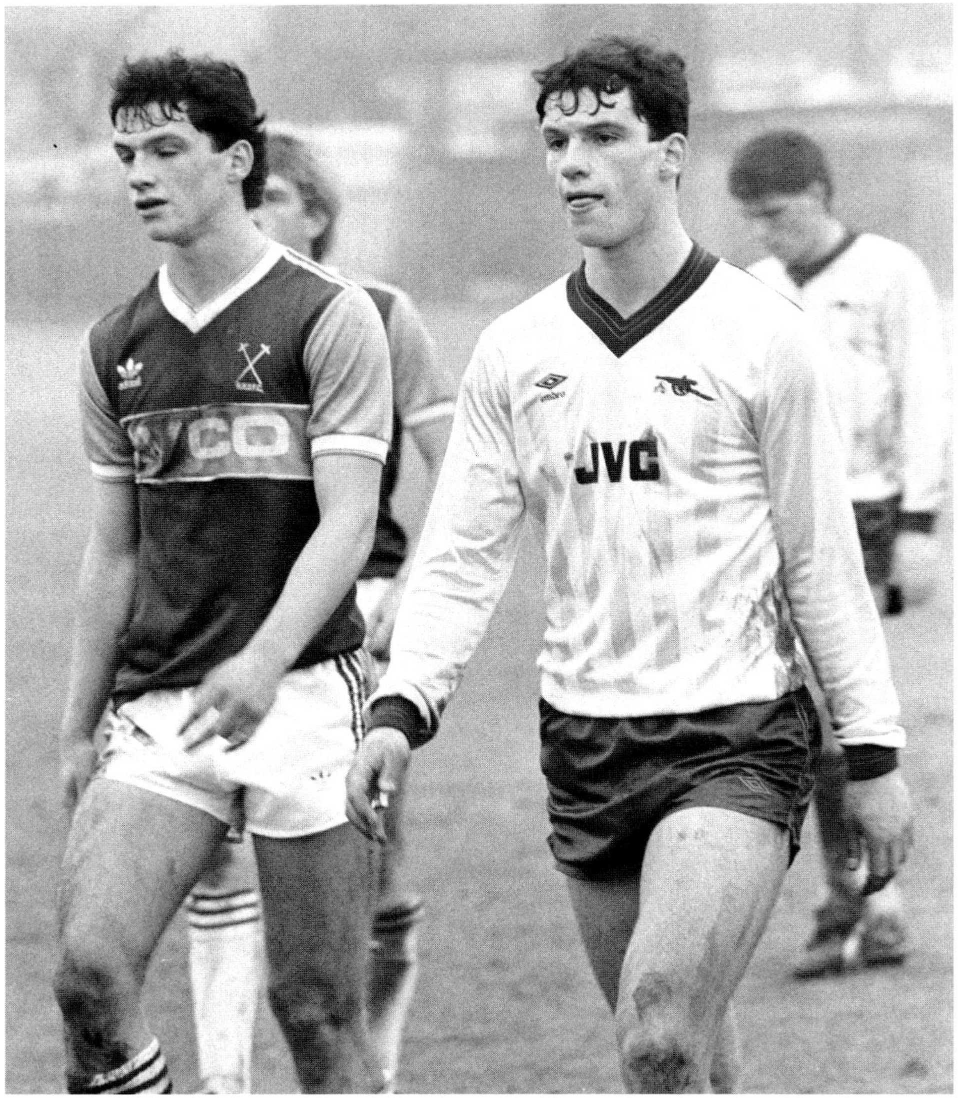

Double vision. No, you're not seeing things: Hammers' Eamonn Dolan came face to face with his twin brother Patrick of Arsenal in a youth match at Chadwell Heath.

Picture perfect. One of my favourite pictures is of Trevor Brooking scoring the match-winning goal in the 1980 FA Cup final against Arsenal. You're never 100% certain if you've got it 'in the can', but I was very pleased with this effort — as was our Trev.

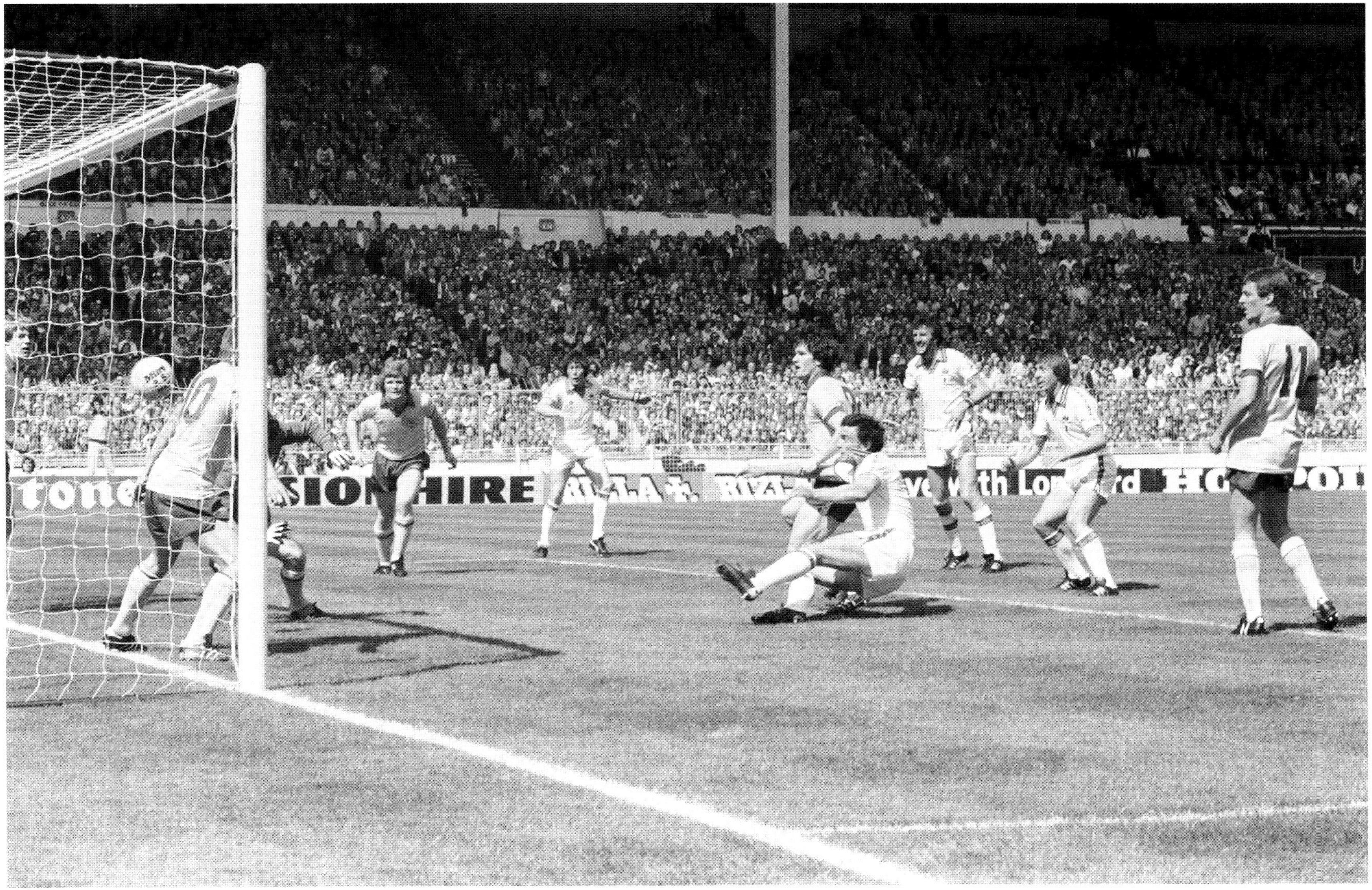

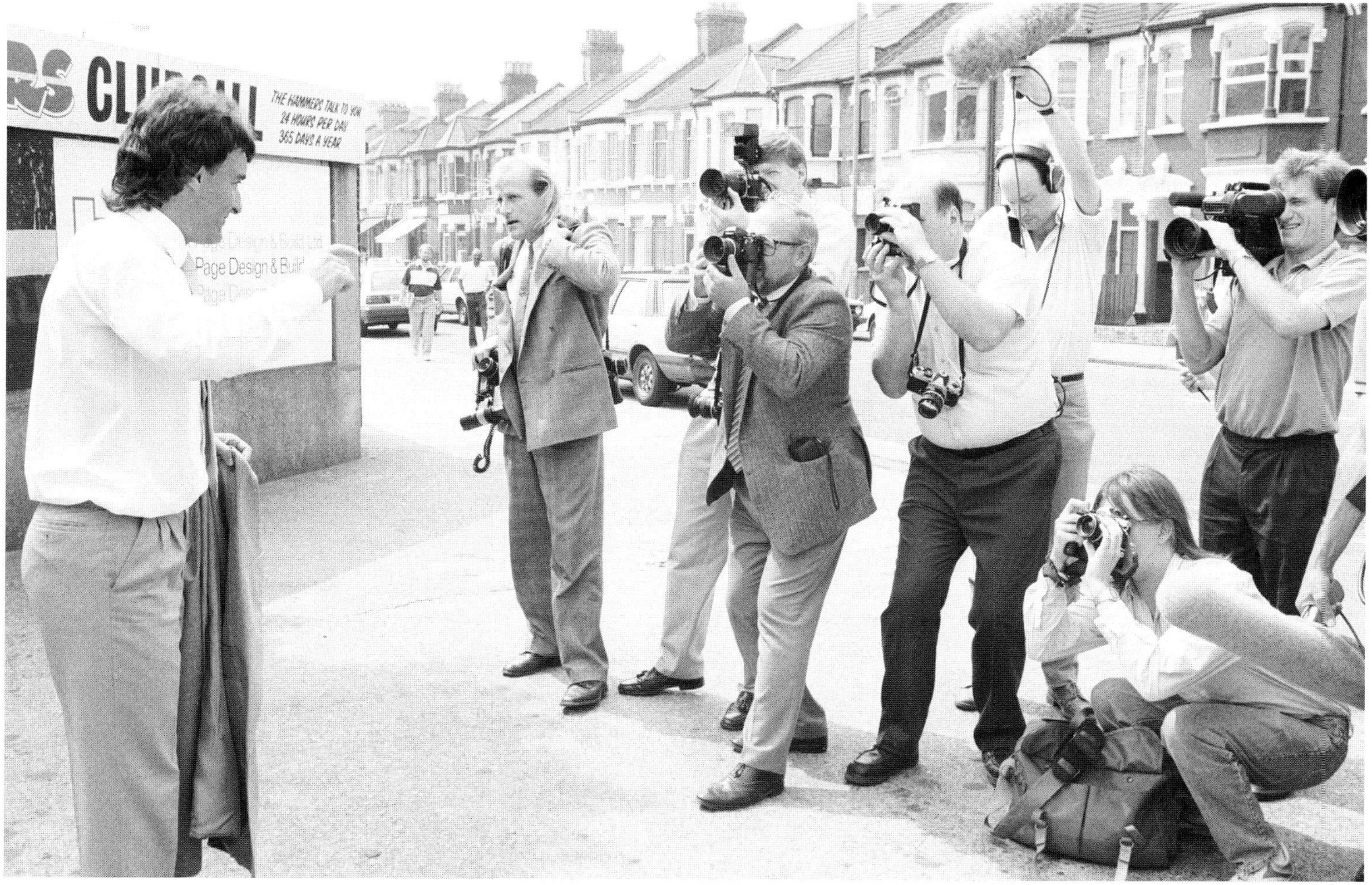

Face the press. Lou Macari poses for the photographers outside the gates at Upton Park on the morning of the press conference to announce his appointment as new Hammers' boss for the 1989–90 season.

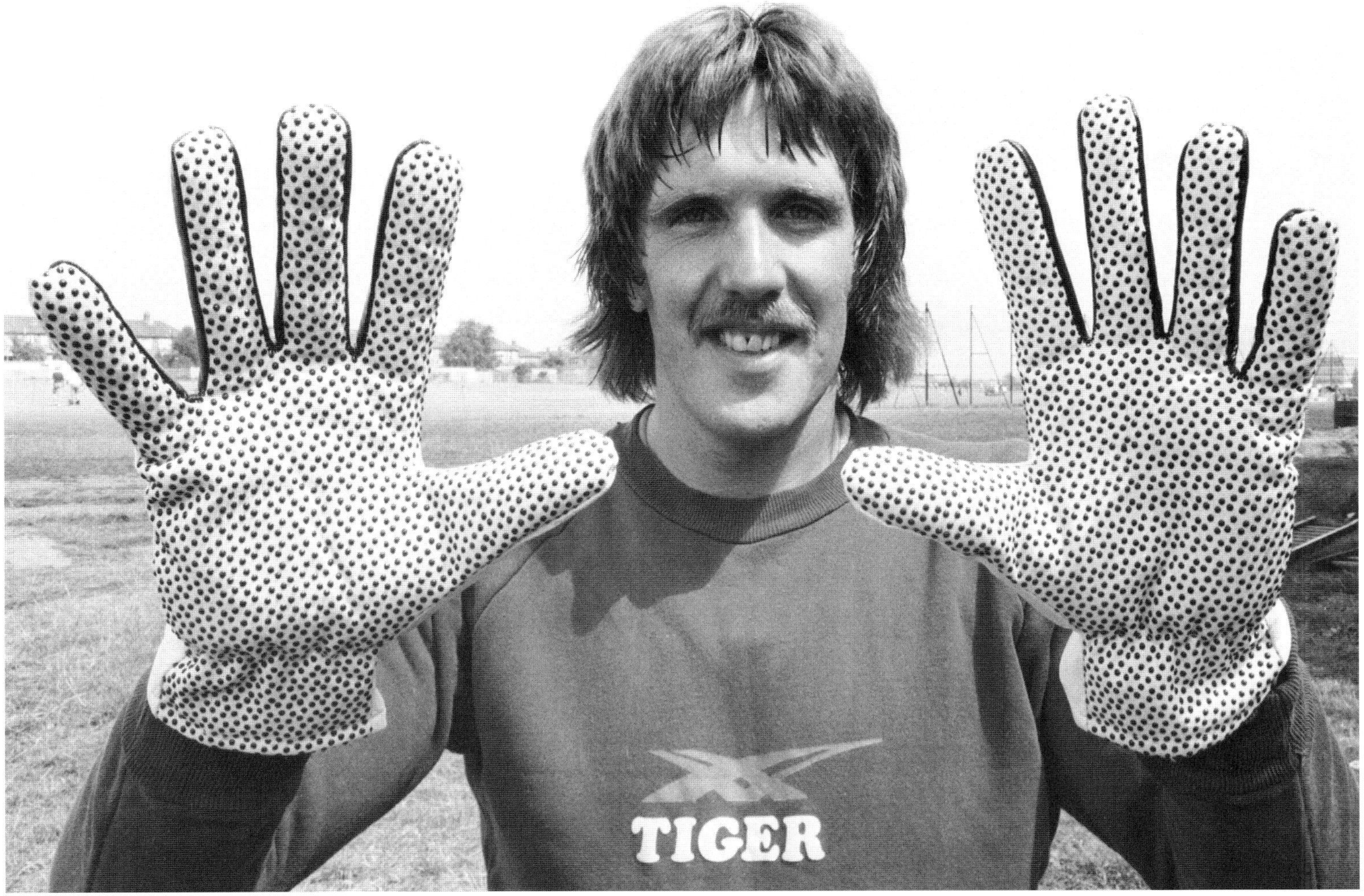

That's handy. 'Keeper Phil Parkes shows off his new gloves with a revolutionary non-slip dimple pattern which made him even harder to beat than ever.

Stumped. One of the highlights of the summer was the cricket match between Abridge and West Ham. John Lyall took a team down to his home village for a fund-raising match each year and his son, Murray, kept wicket for the local side. This picture shows Murray stumping George Parris, one of the better players on the Hammers' team.

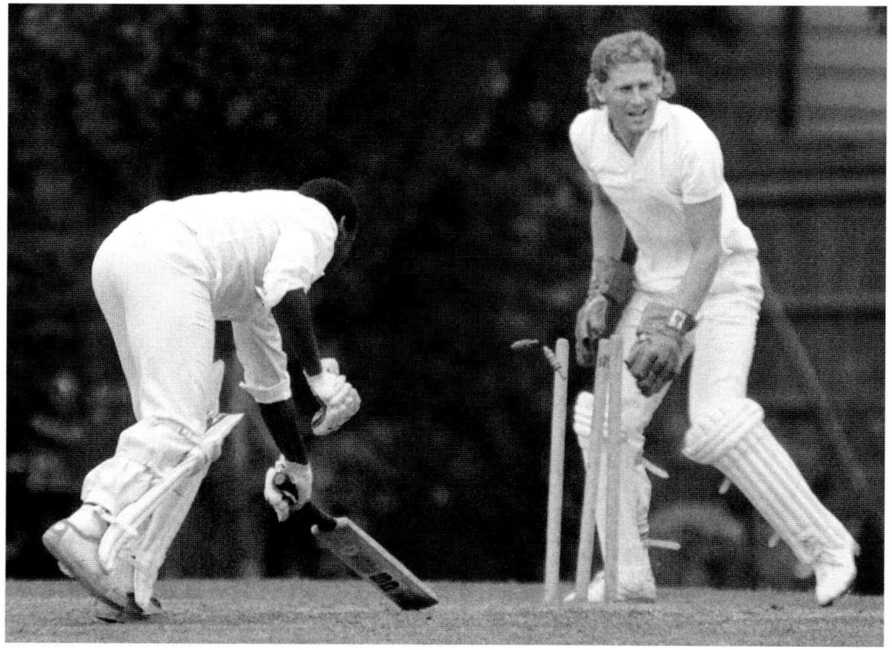

Cup of joy. Geoff Pike and Paul Allen lead the lap of honour around Wembley Stadium with the FA Cup after their famous victory over Arsenal.

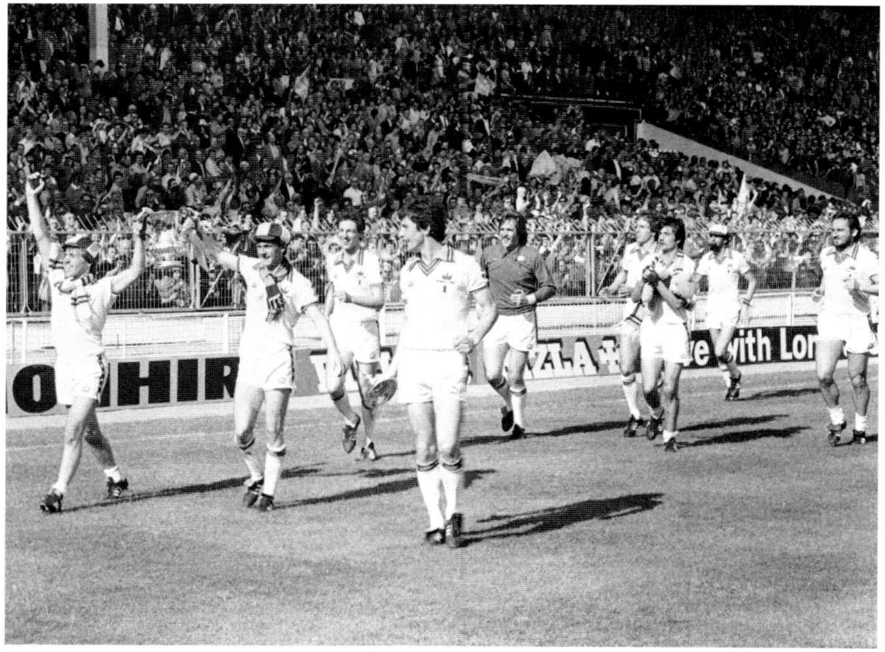

Get the message: a section of the fantastic support at Wembley for the 1980 FA Cup final including a banner aimed at me, I believe.

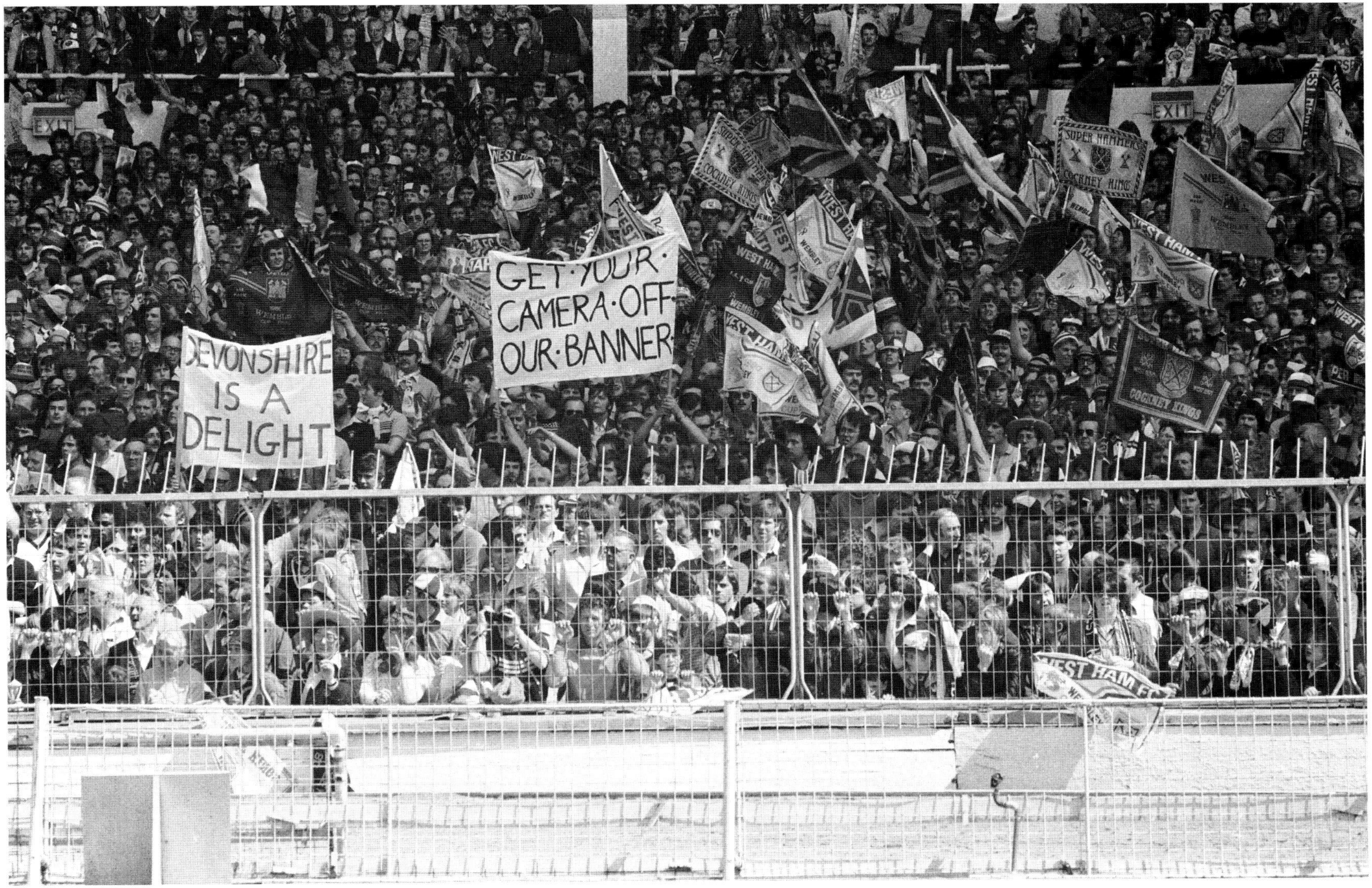
DEVONSHIRE IS A DELIGHT
GET·YOUR·CAMERA·OFF·OUR·BANNER
EXIT
EXIT
SUPER HAMMERS
COCKNEY KINGS
WEST HAM

Prodigal son. Hammers' favourite Pop Robson returns to Upton Park in April 1984 with Sunderland who gain their first away win in five months. Pop's old mate Trevor Brooking deflected the only goal of the game into the net.

Play it again. Trevor Brooking beats West Bromwich Albion's John Wile to score Hammers' second goal in their FA Cup third round replay at Upton Park in January 1980. Hammers won the match 2–1 to go through to the next round.

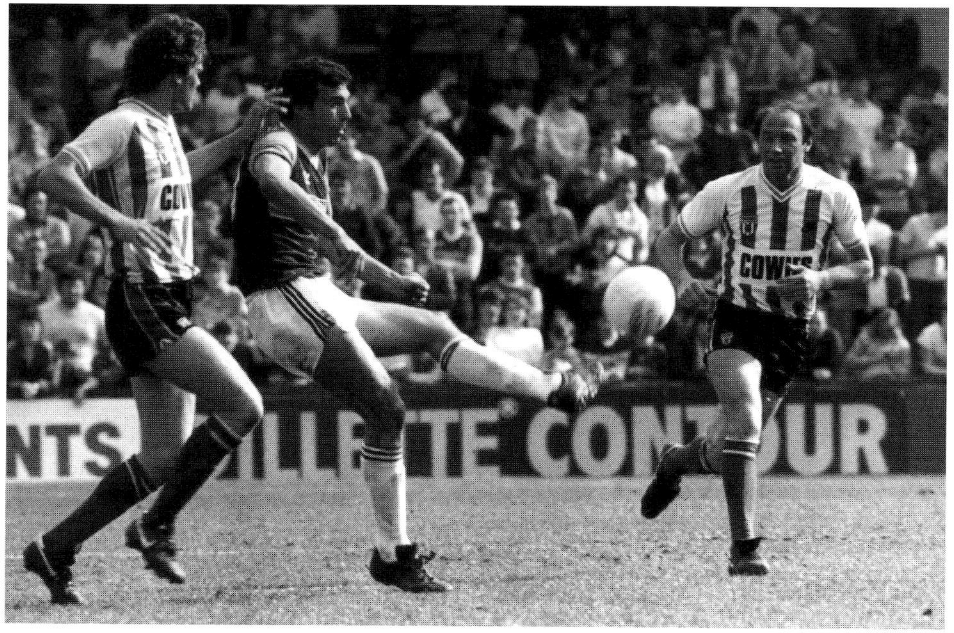

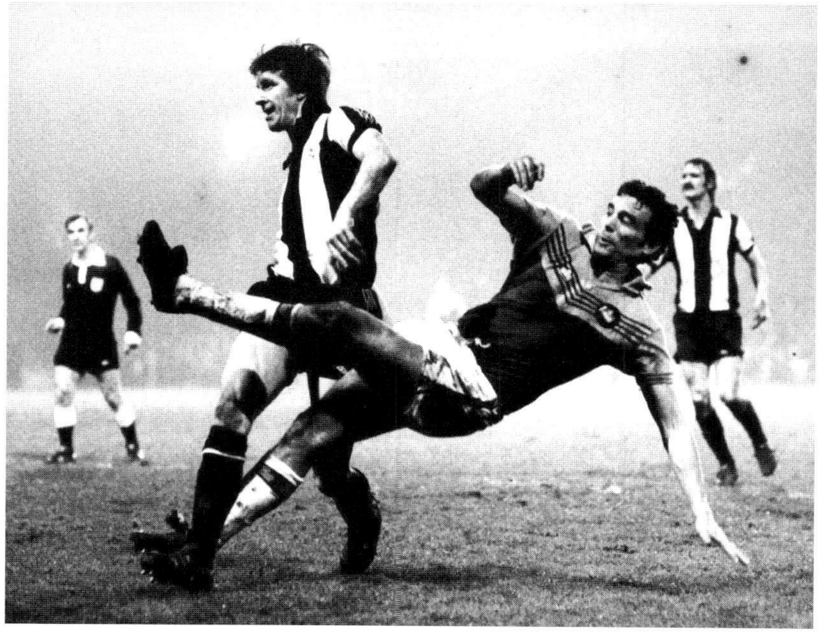

Up the pole. Mark Ward tries to escape from the rest of the players during pre-season training for the 1989–90 season.

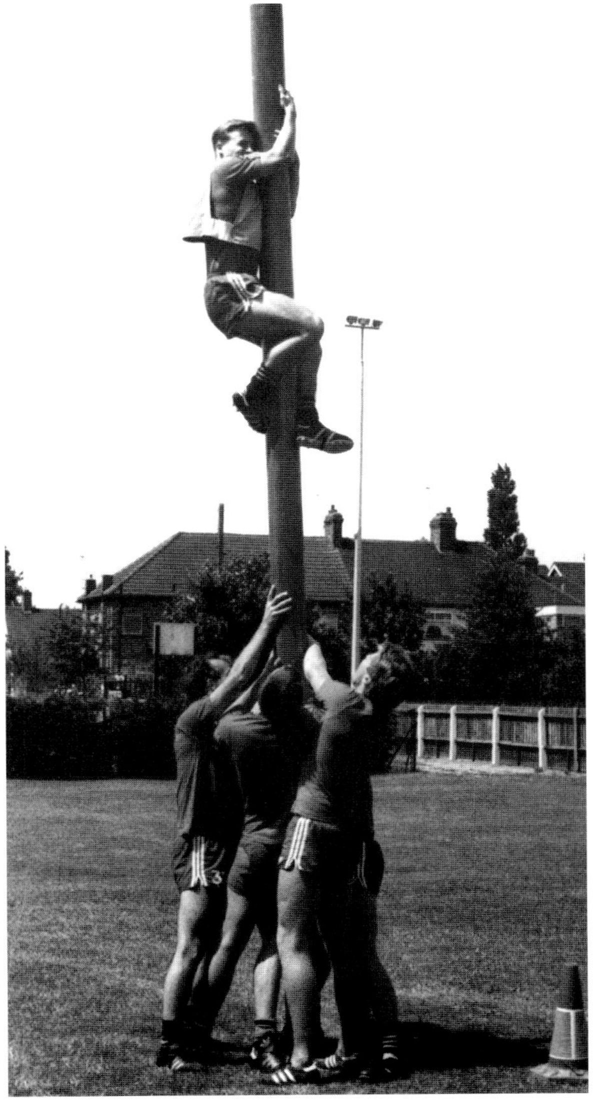

Me Tarzan. Paul Goddard is watched by Ernie Gregory as he attempts the new assault course at the Chadwell Heath training complex during a pre-season work-out.

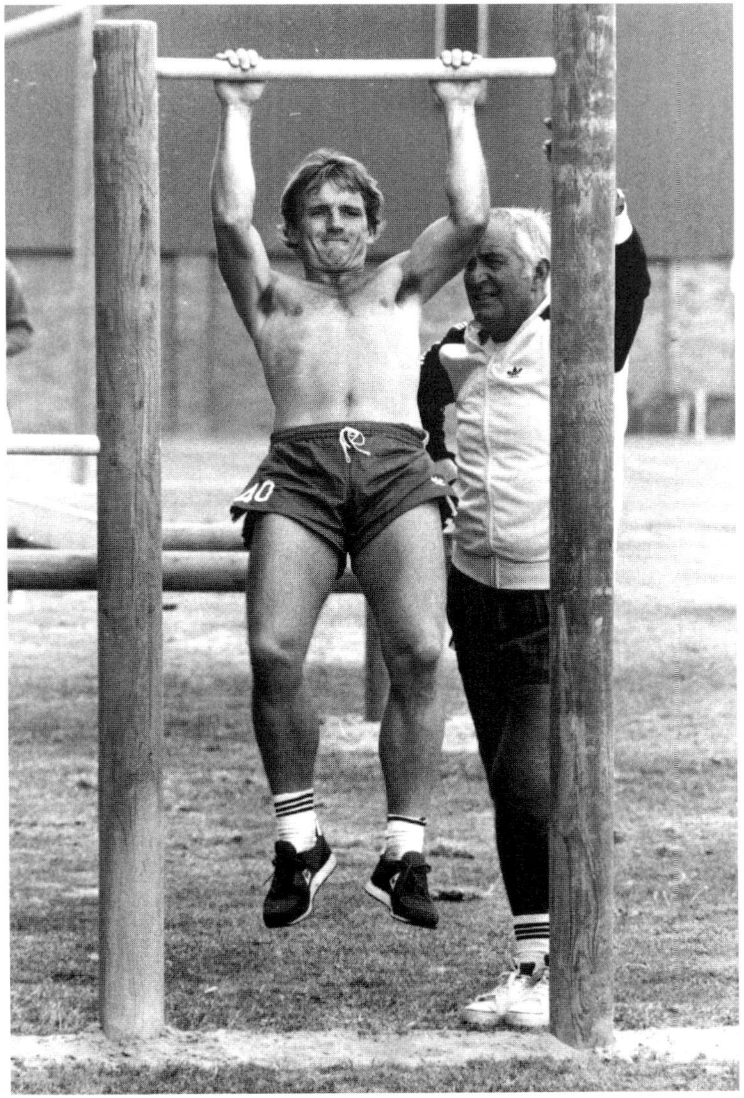

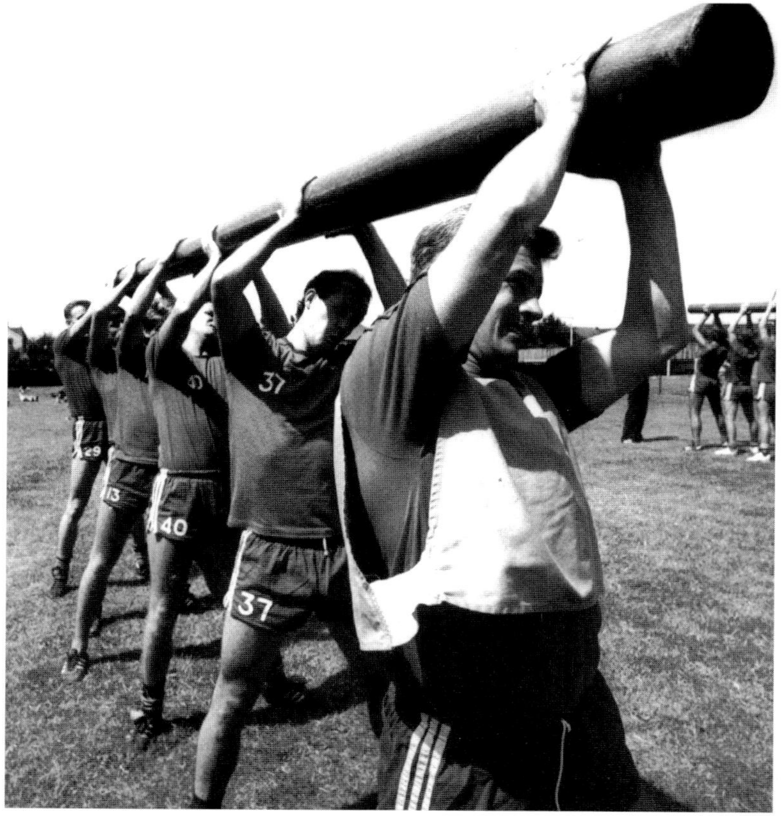

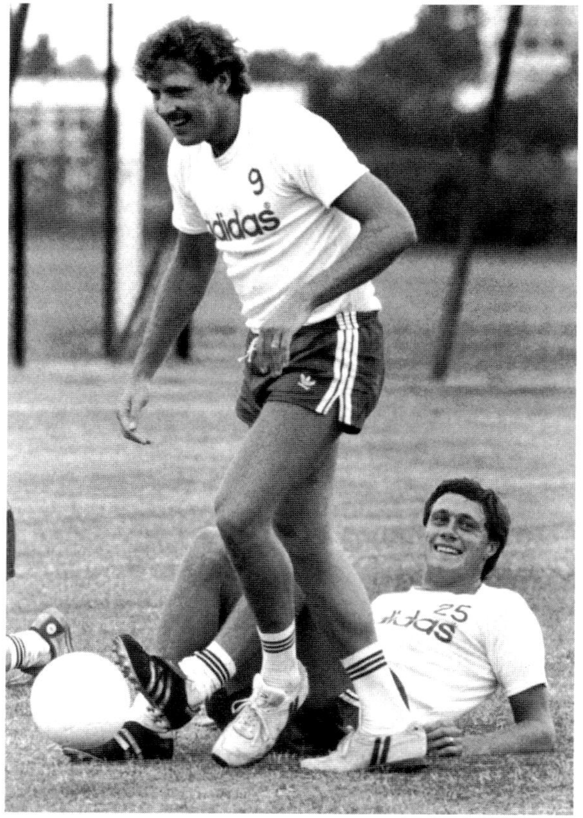

Take the strain. Mark Ward, Liam Brady, Tommy McQueen, Greg Campbell, Robert Reeves and Gary Strodder struggle during a pre-season log-rolling exercise.

No laughing matter. Dave Swindlehurst and a floored Steve Whitton find something funny during a training session at Chadwell Heath.

Smiler. Another of my favourite pictures is this one of Alan Devonshire, caught off guard during a training session clutching a football with the biggest of grins on his face.

Moving experience. Phil Parkes and fellow 'keeper John Vaughan find the new lightweight goalposts a doddle to shift.

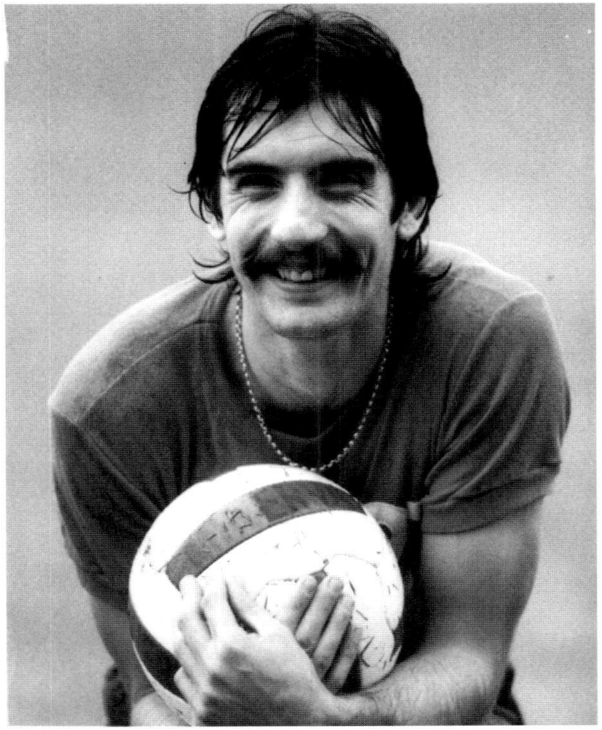

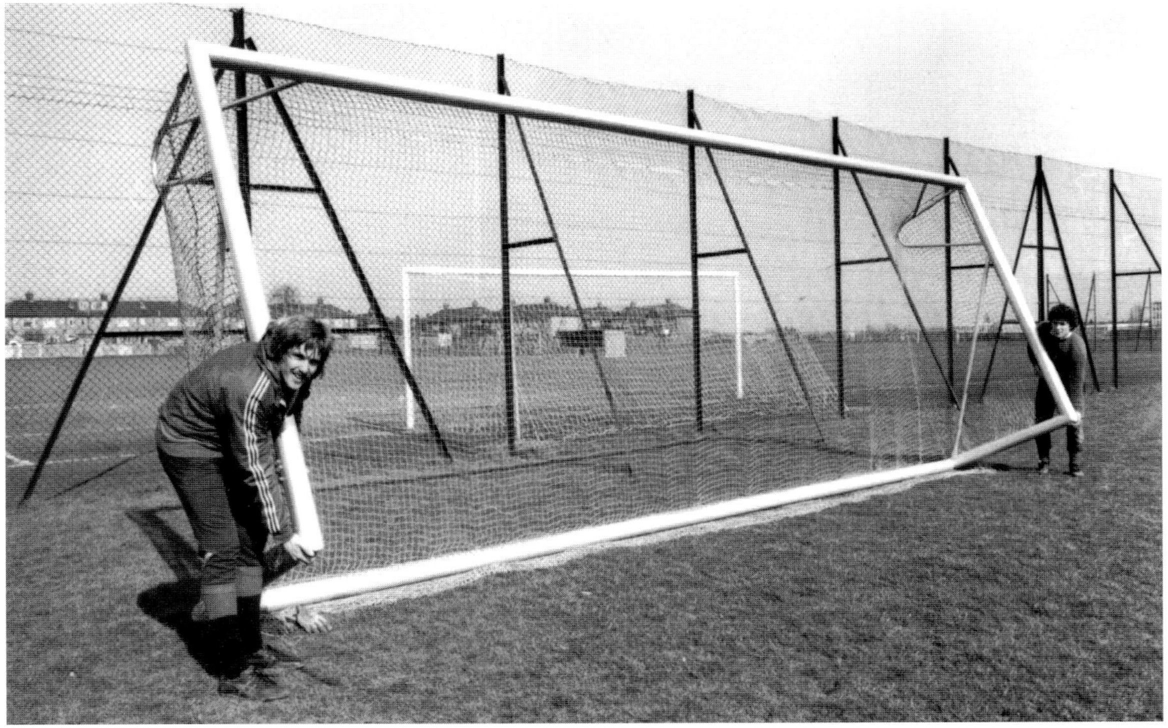

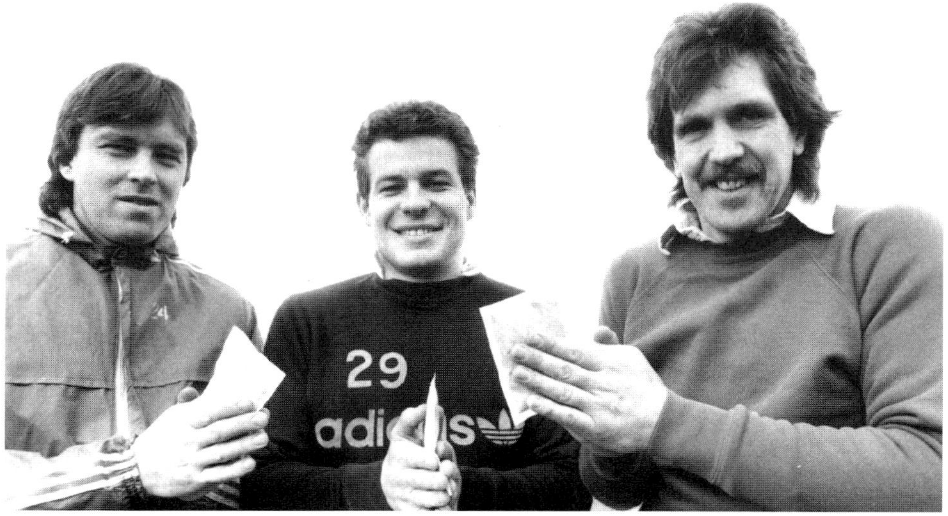

Winter warmers. Goalkeepers Tom McAlister, John Vaughan and Phil Parkes try out a new hand-warming idea. Thousands of these were handed out to the Upton Park crowd in a promotional offer.

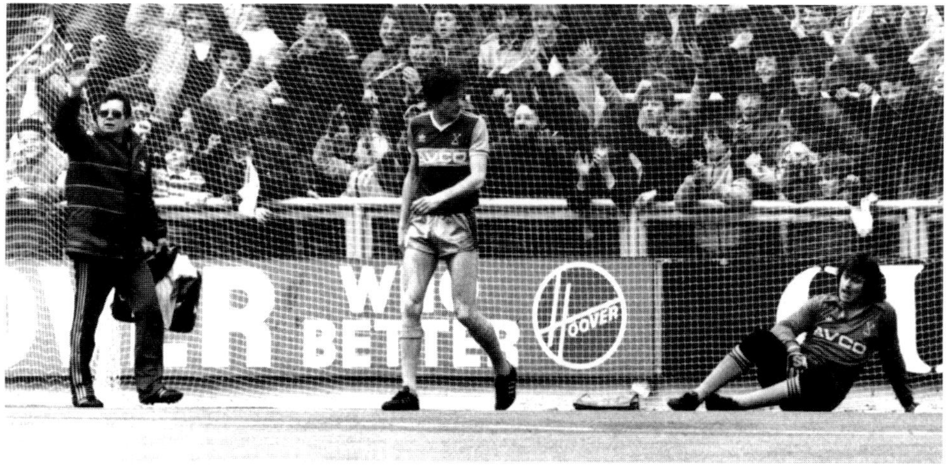

Down and out. Physio Rob Jenkins calls to the referee as 'keeper Tom McAlister is floored with broken ribs following a collision at Queens Park Rangers in April 1985. Ray Stewart took over in goal but Hammers lost 4–2. We dropped Tom and Rob off at the London Hospital en route back to Upton Park where he was patched up before being allowed home.

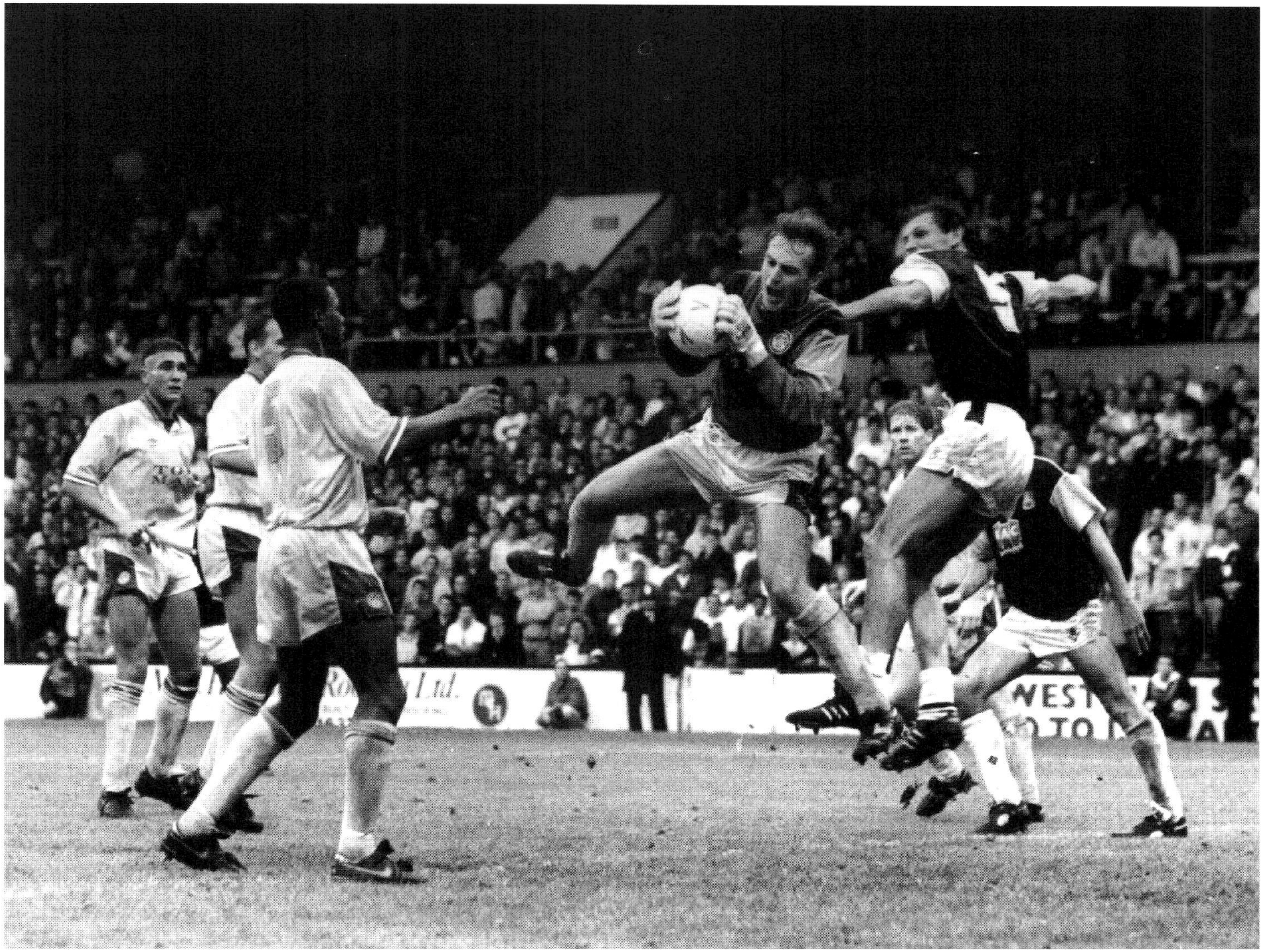

Happy Day. Alvin Martin puts ex-Hammer Mervyn Day under pressure with Leeds United leading 1–0 at Upton Park in October 1989. Alvin's efforts could not save the Hammers from losing the game by the single goal.

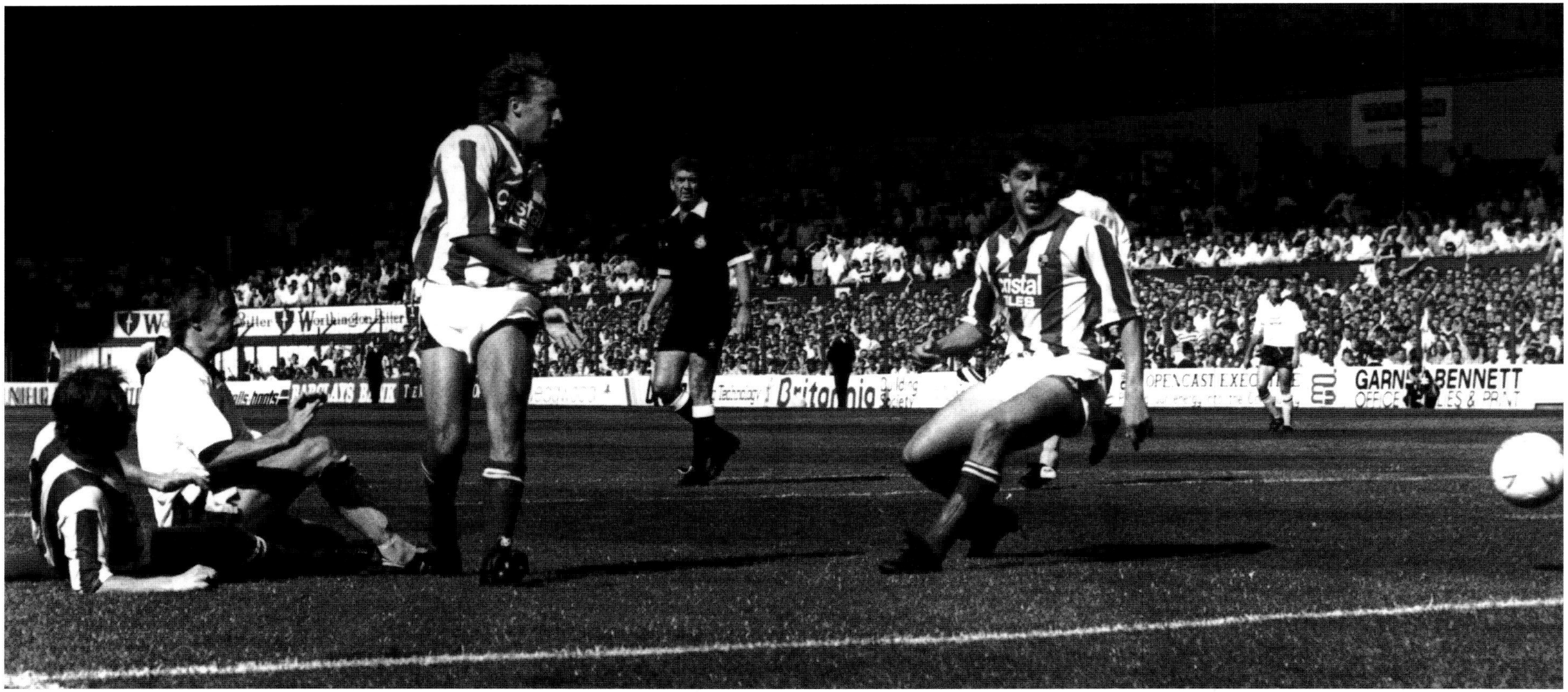

Bad break. The first day of the 1989–90 season, and Kevin Keen scores for West Ham to earn a 1–1 draw at Stoke City. The game was marred by a 55th-minute injury to Frank McAvennie who suffered a broken leg.

The right needle. Bobby Barnes doesn't know whether to laugh or cry as Doc Brill gives him his annual 'flu jab.

As I was saying. One-time Hammer Ken Brown turned out in goal for the Alvin Martin testimonial match but spent most of the match chatting to the fans on the terraces.

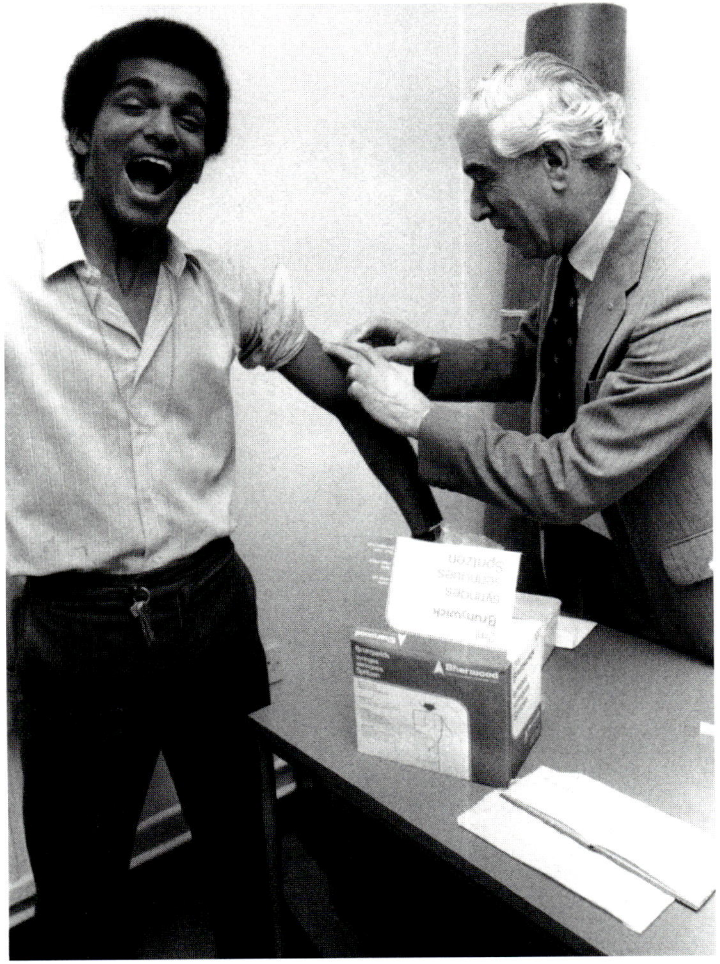

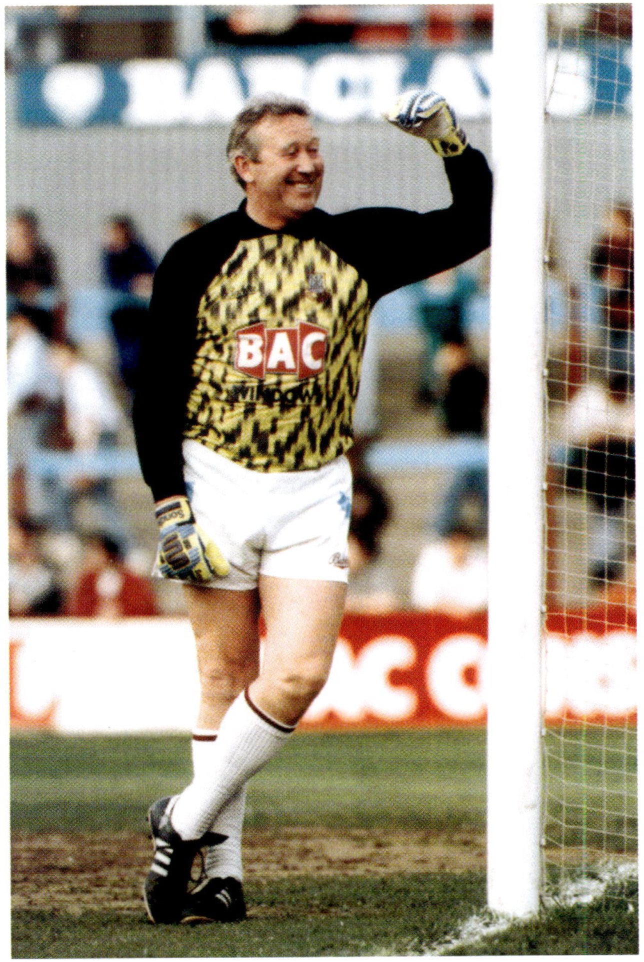

You beauty. Dave Swindlehurst wheels away after scoring, as Tony Cottee chases to add his congratulations. Swindles joined West Ham from Derby County in 1983 scoring 17 goals from his 71 league and cup outings.

Radio active. It's time for the draw for the quarter-final stage of the 1979–80 FA Cup and the West Ham players listen intently after training.

Mindless. West Ham were going out of the FA Cup in their fifth round tie at Birmingham City. The game was marred by pitch invasions by mindless idiots. I stood with Tony Cottee at the side of the pitch as I took this shot; he was not impressed!

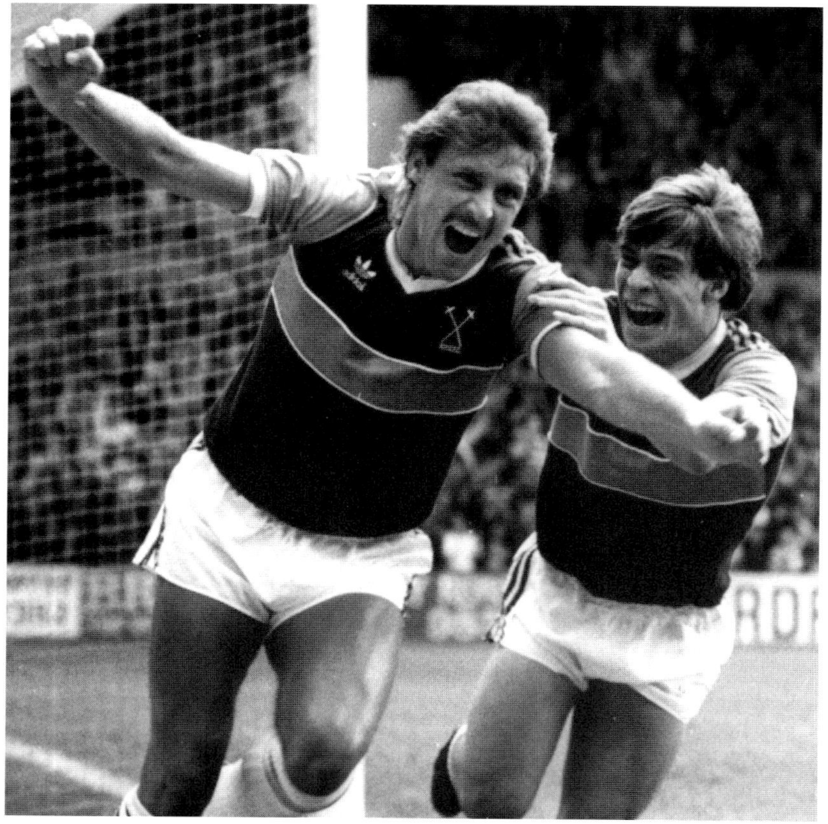

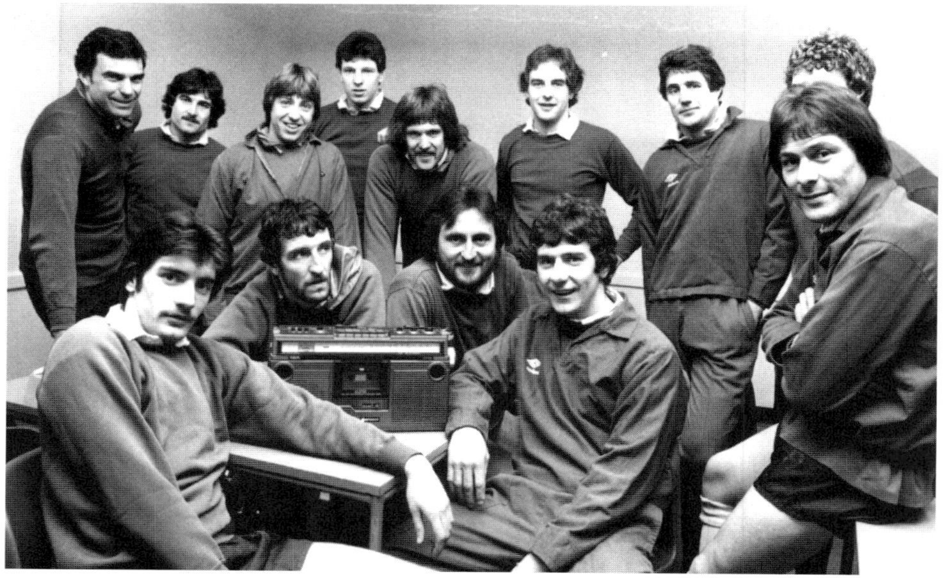

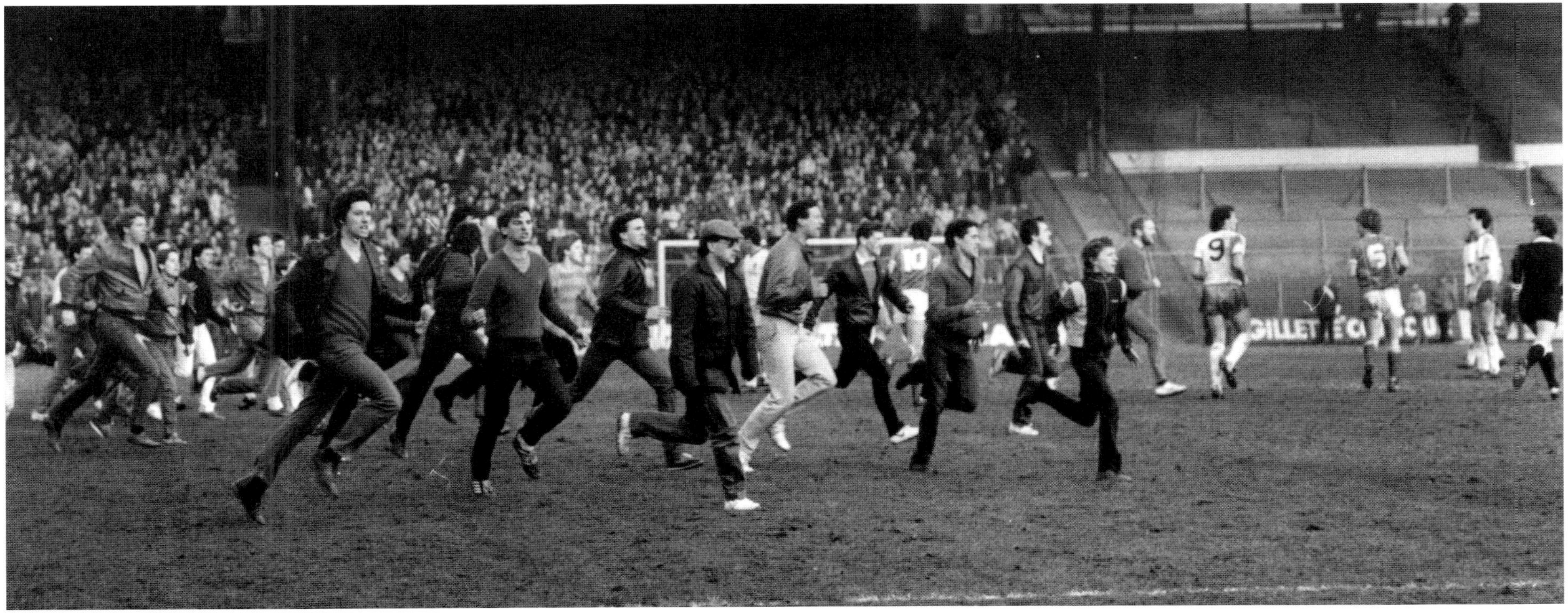

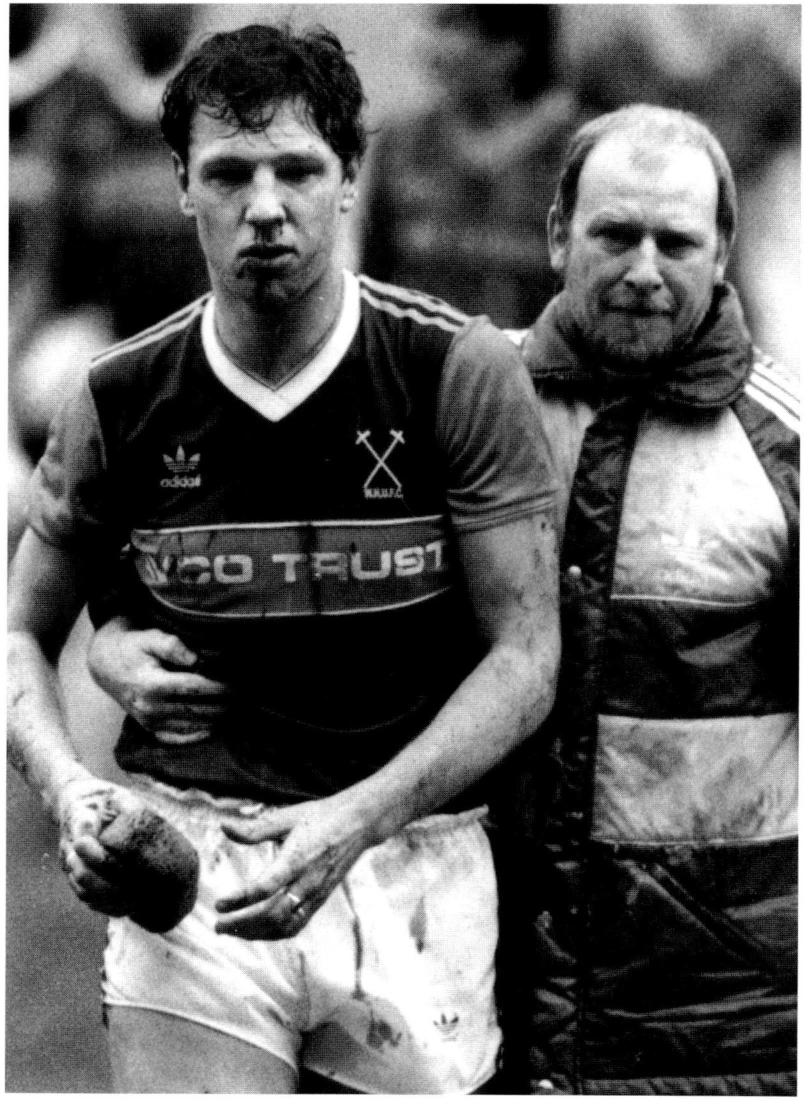

Plenty of claret. Physio Dave Gladstone escorts a blood-soaked Alvin Martin from the pitch to be patched up by the doctor. Typically for the tough Scouser he was soon back in the thick of the action.

. . . and stretch. A new innovation by manager John Lyall was the introduction of dance instructor Sarah Harwood to the training sessions. Gut feeling told me that their hearts were not really in it.

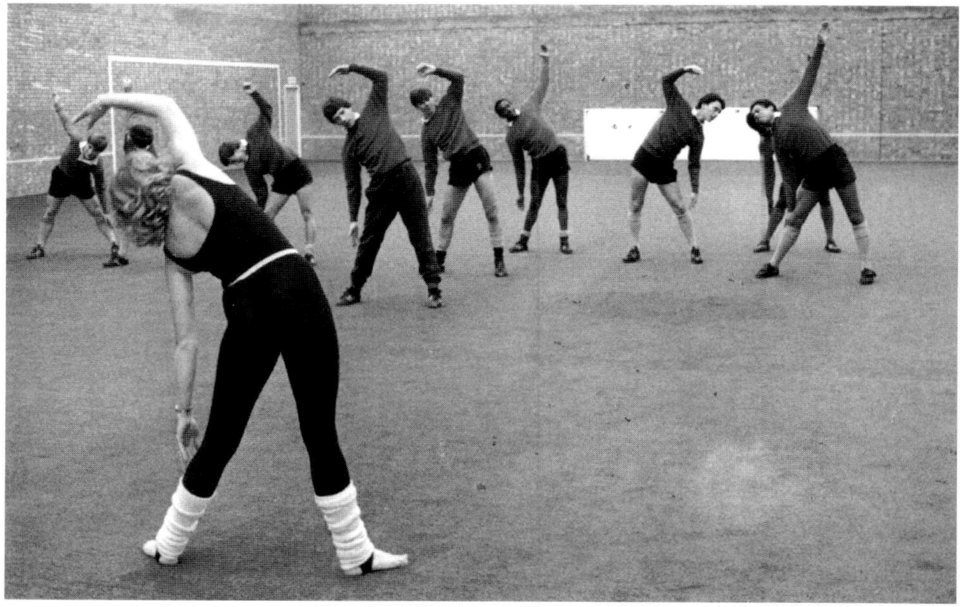

Steady boss. David Cross ushers John Lyall away from referee Clive Thomas on the Wembley pitch after the drawn 1981 League Cup final had ended in a storm of protests over Liverpool's goal, and an accusation of 'cheating'. Liverpool won the replay 2–1 at Villa Park.

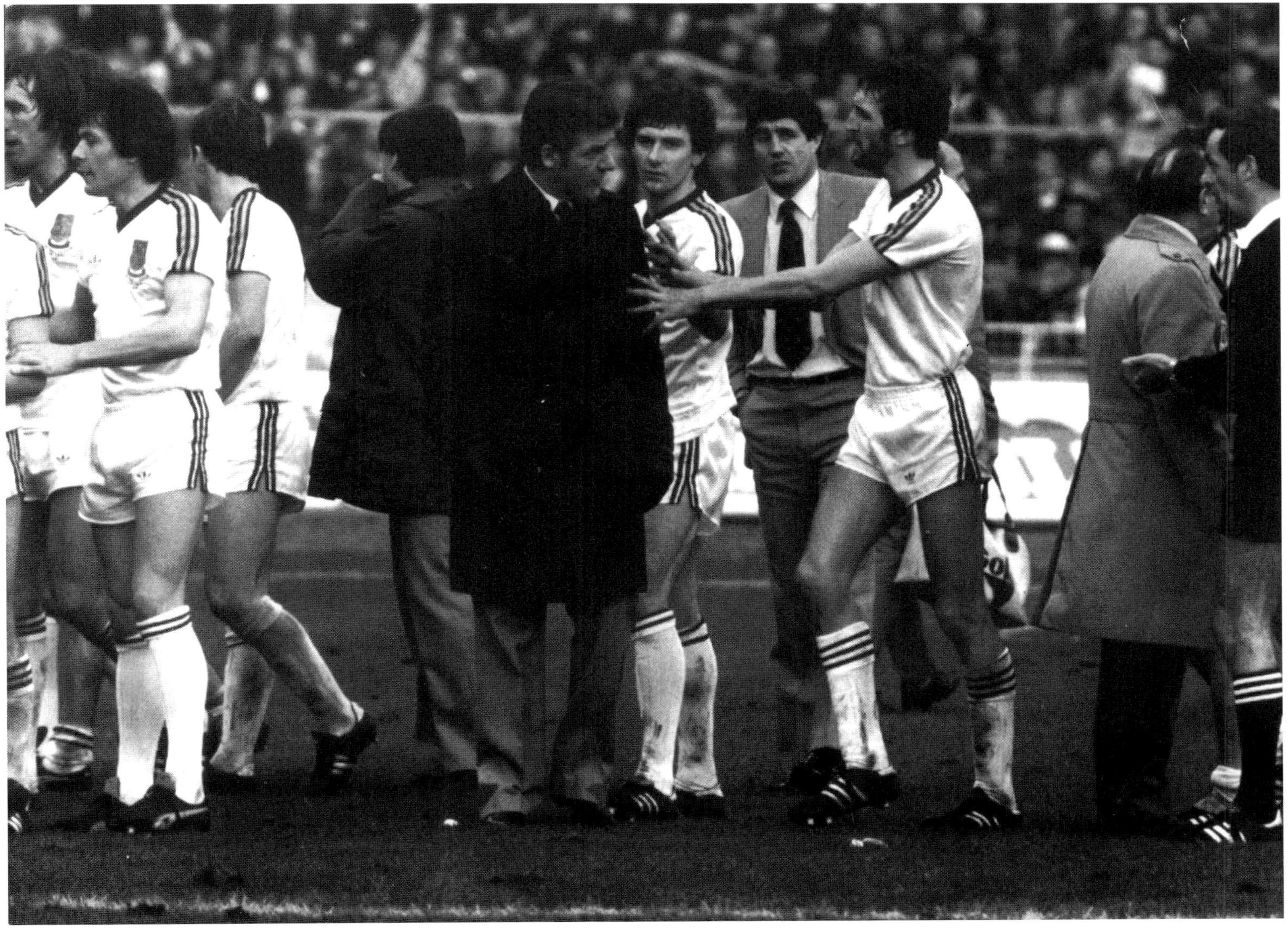

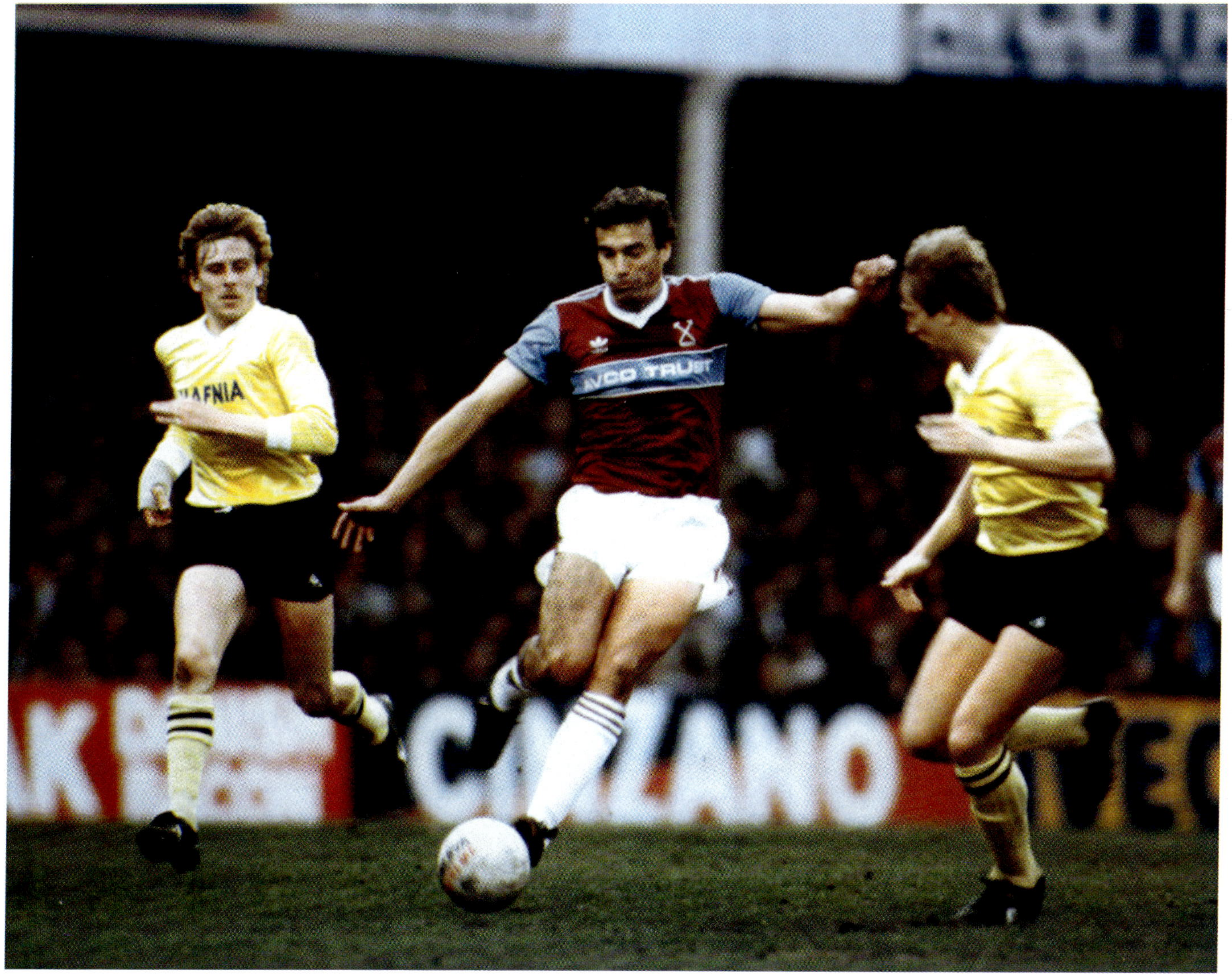

End of an era. Trevor Brooking in action on the Upton Park pitch for the last time on a May night in 1984. A 1–0 home defeat by Everton in the last match of the season couldn't stop the 25,425 faithful giving their hero a rousing send-off at the end of an illustrious career.

New Year's resolution for Paul Brush was to score more goals for the Hammers. Well, to be more precise, to score one goal for West Ham. He achieved his aim on 1st January 1985, with this looping header against QPR at Upton Park. What turned out to be Paul's only goal in the Claret and Blue couldn't stop Hammers from losing the match 3–1.

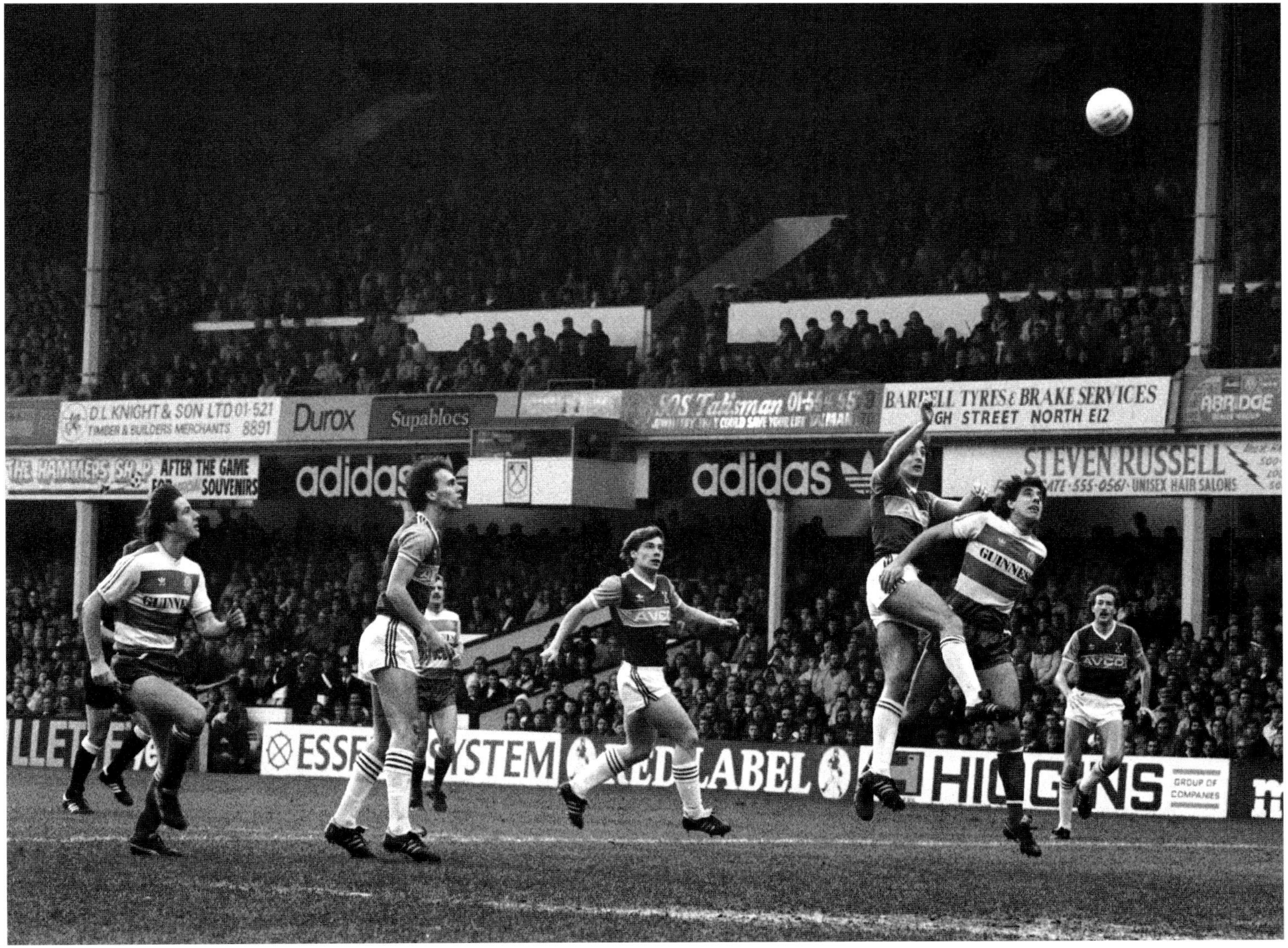

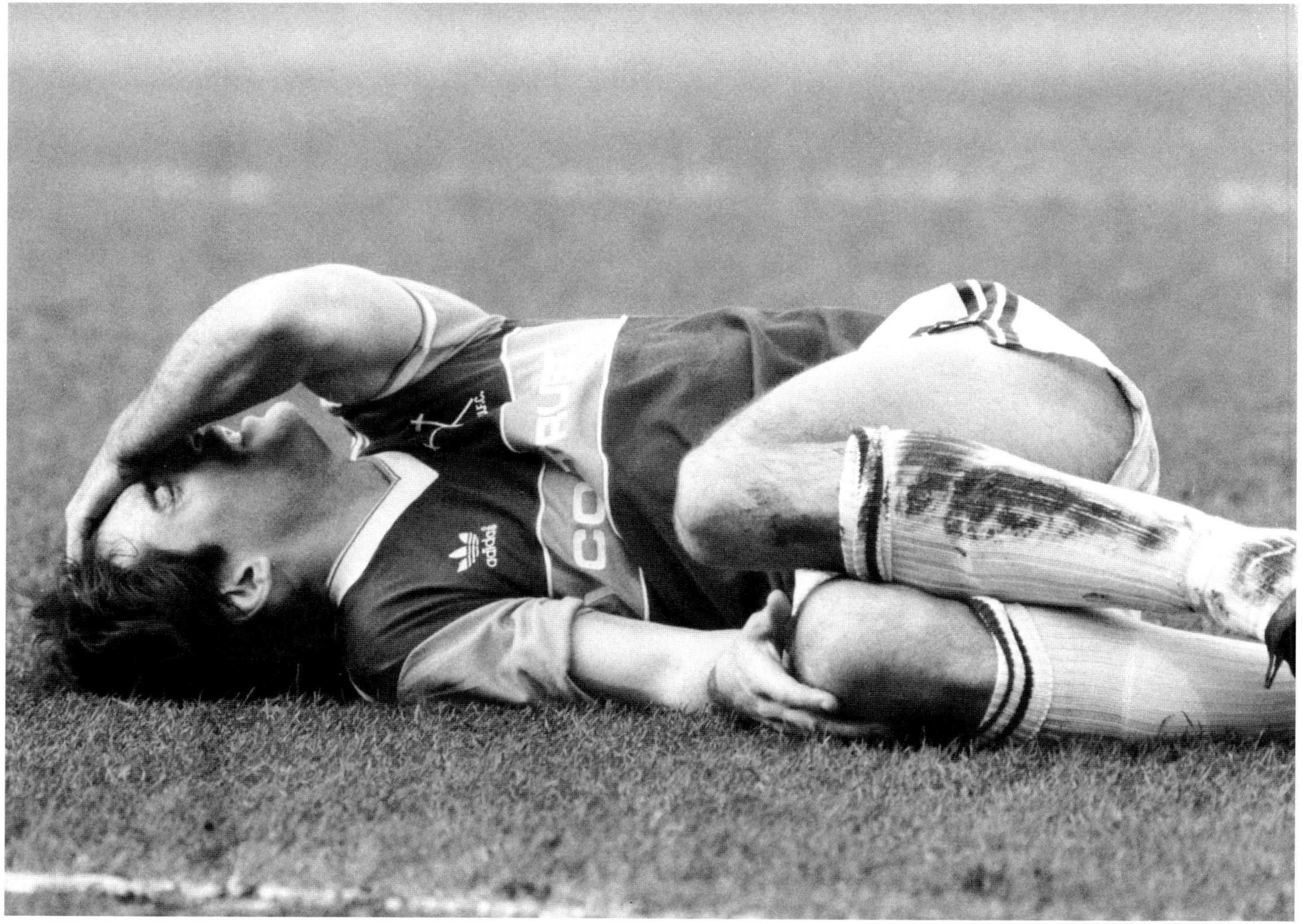

Dev-astating. A crunching tackle has left Hammers' midfield maestro Alan Devonshire writhing in agony after just fifteen minutes of the FA Cup third round tie against Wigan Athletic at Upton Park in January 1984. West Ham went on to win the match through a Ray Stewart spot-kick, but Dev's season was over after tearing his ankle ligaments.

Four he's a jolly good fellow. David Cross scores one of his four goals as he single-handedly demolishes Tottenham Hotspur 4–0 in Hammers' first away game of the 1981–82 season at White Hart Lane. Crossie went on to top-score that season with nineteen goals in all competitions.

United front. Alan Devonshire scores Hammers' second goal in a rare 3–2 victory over Manchester United at Old Trafford in the first away game of the 1986–87 season. Frank McAvennie had put the visitors ahead after just one minute and scored the winner in the 82nd minute, silencing most of the 43,306 crowd.

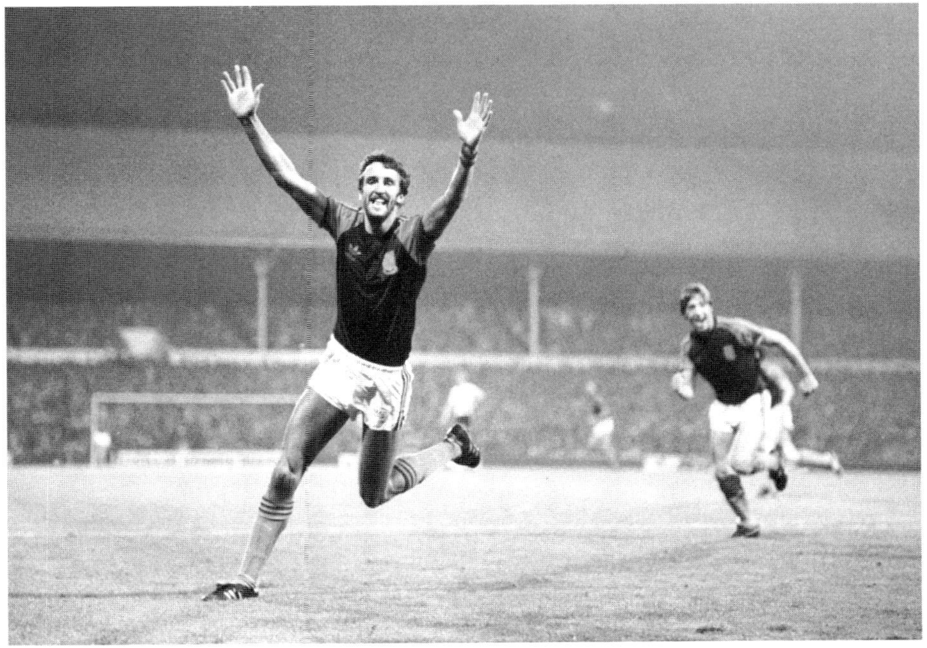

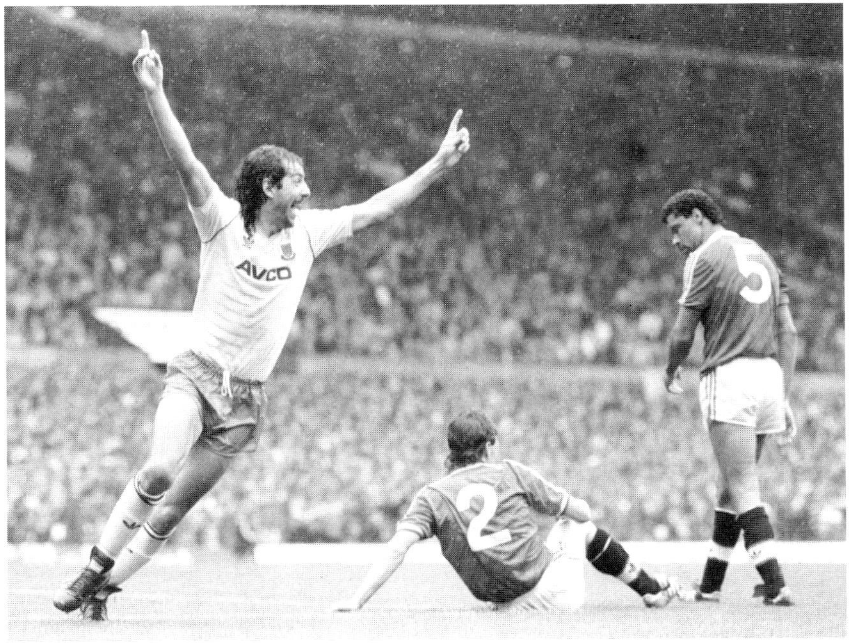

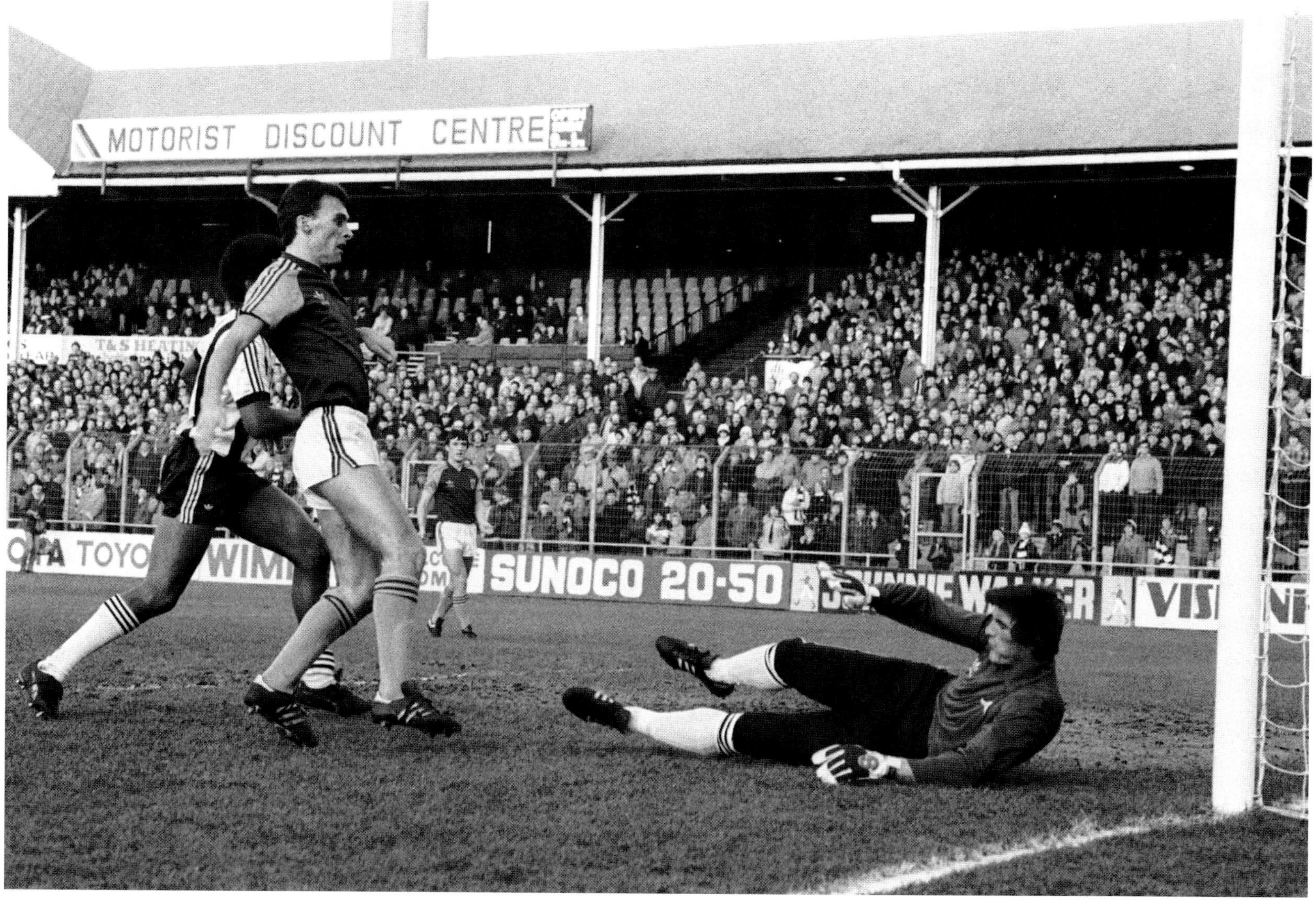
MOTORIST DISCOUNT CENTRE
SUNOCO 20-50

Debut delight. Eighteen-year-old Alan Dickens, making his West Ham debut at Notts County in December 1982, puts the visitors ahead after six minutes, latching on to the ball after Paul Allen's initial shot had been parried by 'keeper Avramovic.

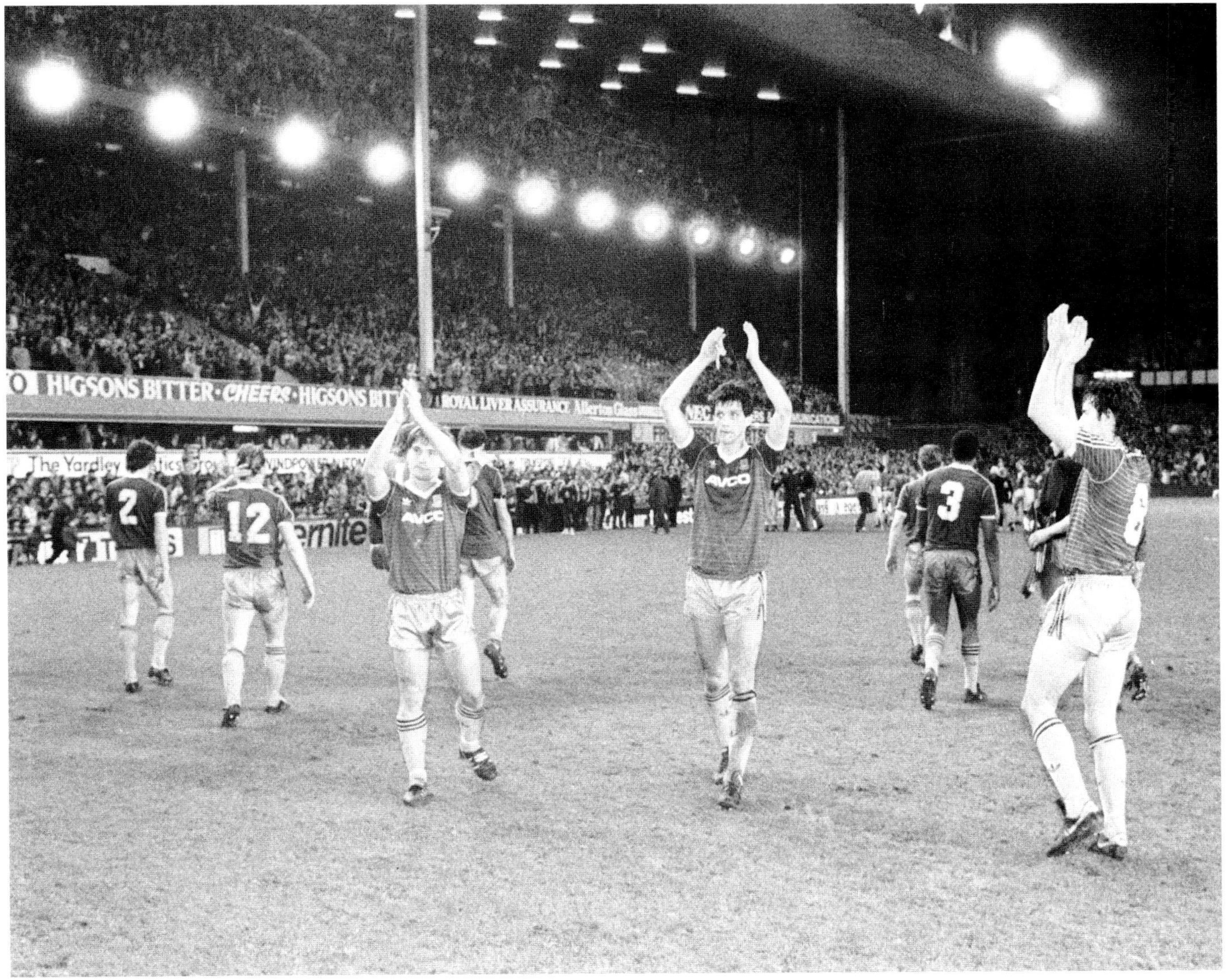

Compliments of the season. Hammers needed a draw in their last game of the 1985–86 season at Goodison Park to secure runners-up spot behind Liverpool. It proved a match too far for them as they went down 3–1 to an Everton side who pipped them into second place. At the end of the match, the West Ham players went to the 6,000 visiting fans to applaud them for their support during their most successful campaign.

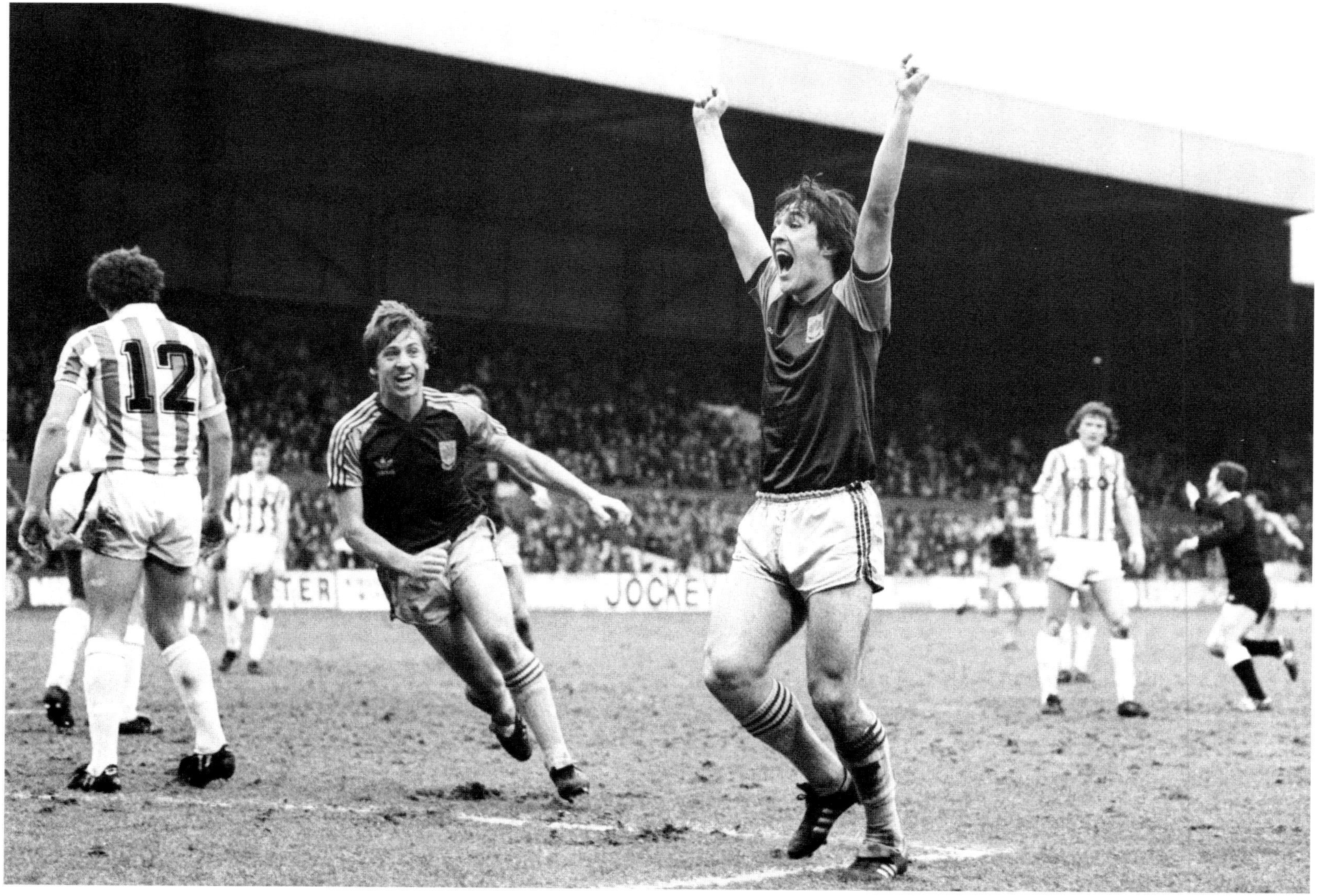
JOCKEY

François's first. Hammers trailed by a single Chapman goal at half time in a poor game at Stoke City in February 1982. François van der Elst pulled them level with his first strike for the club on 71 minutes, but his joy was short-lived when Maguire struck some eight minutes later to give City their first home win of the year.

Ince perfect. Paul Ince was drafted into the side for his debut in the home game against Southampton in the 1986–87 season and responded by scoring the opening goal with this diving header. Hammers won the game 3–1 with a goal from Alan Devonshire and a Tony Cottee penalty kick — which was won by Ince, who else?

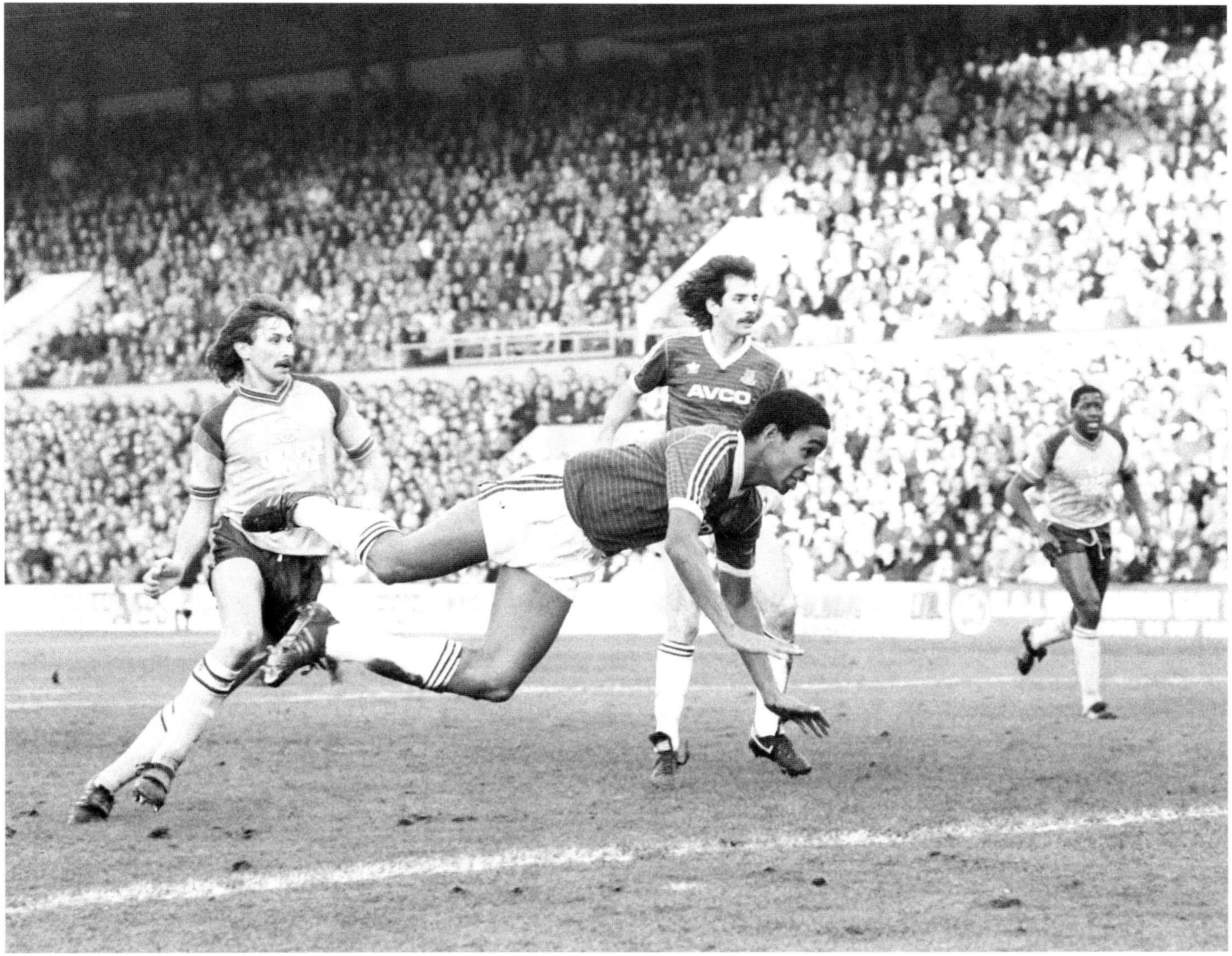

Come dancing. Scottish defender Ray Stewart was battling to regain fitness after a serious injury in the mid-'80s and was keen to try anything to help speed up his rehabilitation. I had already photographed him at the swimming pool, but I must admit that even I was surprised when he invited me along to a dance class full of women. Nice view though!

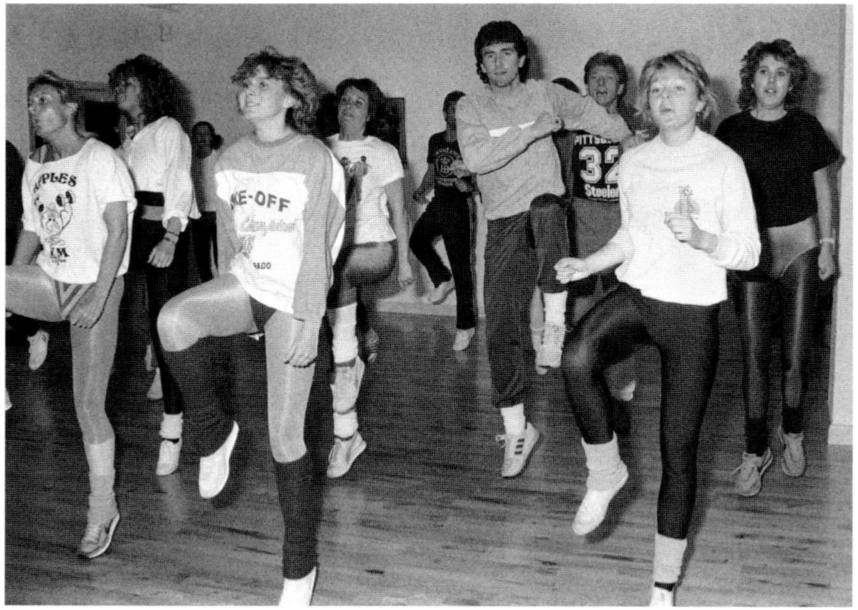

Keep-fit fan. Hammers' long-serving physio Rob Jenkins had a surprise in store when he retired after many years' service with the club. Ray Stewart had organised a collection among the players who bought Rob a rowing machine to enable him to keep fit in his retirement. In this picture Rob is joined by his son Billy who is holding a framed collection of photographs that I helped assemble from the archives.

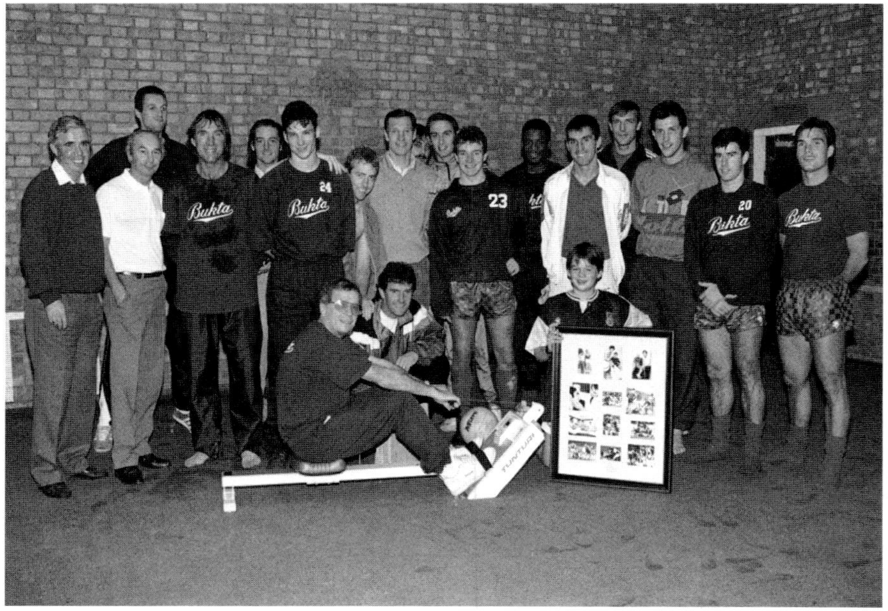

Superstar. I was particularly delighted when I got the call to photograph Liam Brady at his first day's training at Chadwell Heath. He is a player I have always admired and I decided to photograph him with my hero Billy Bonds. One of the highlights of my career was when, on a club trip to the Republic of Ireland, I took a stroll with Liam in Limerick and he was mobbed by the locals who treated him like a god.

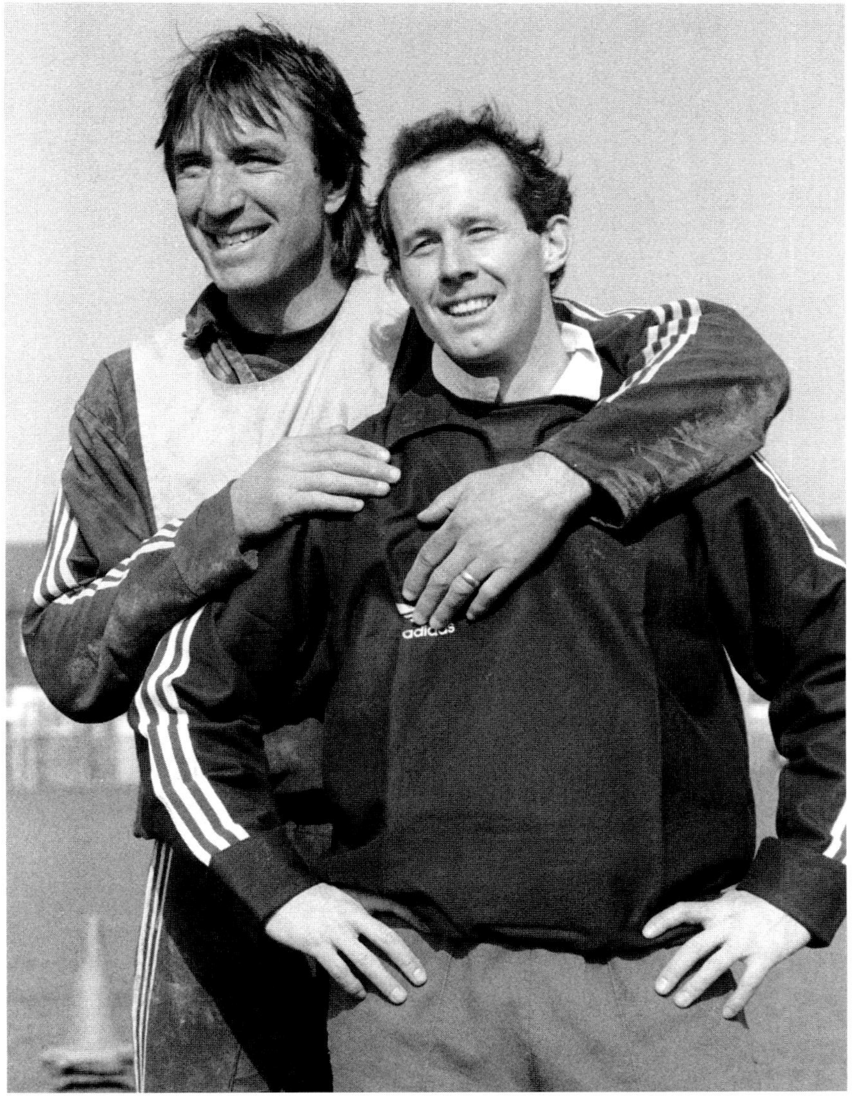

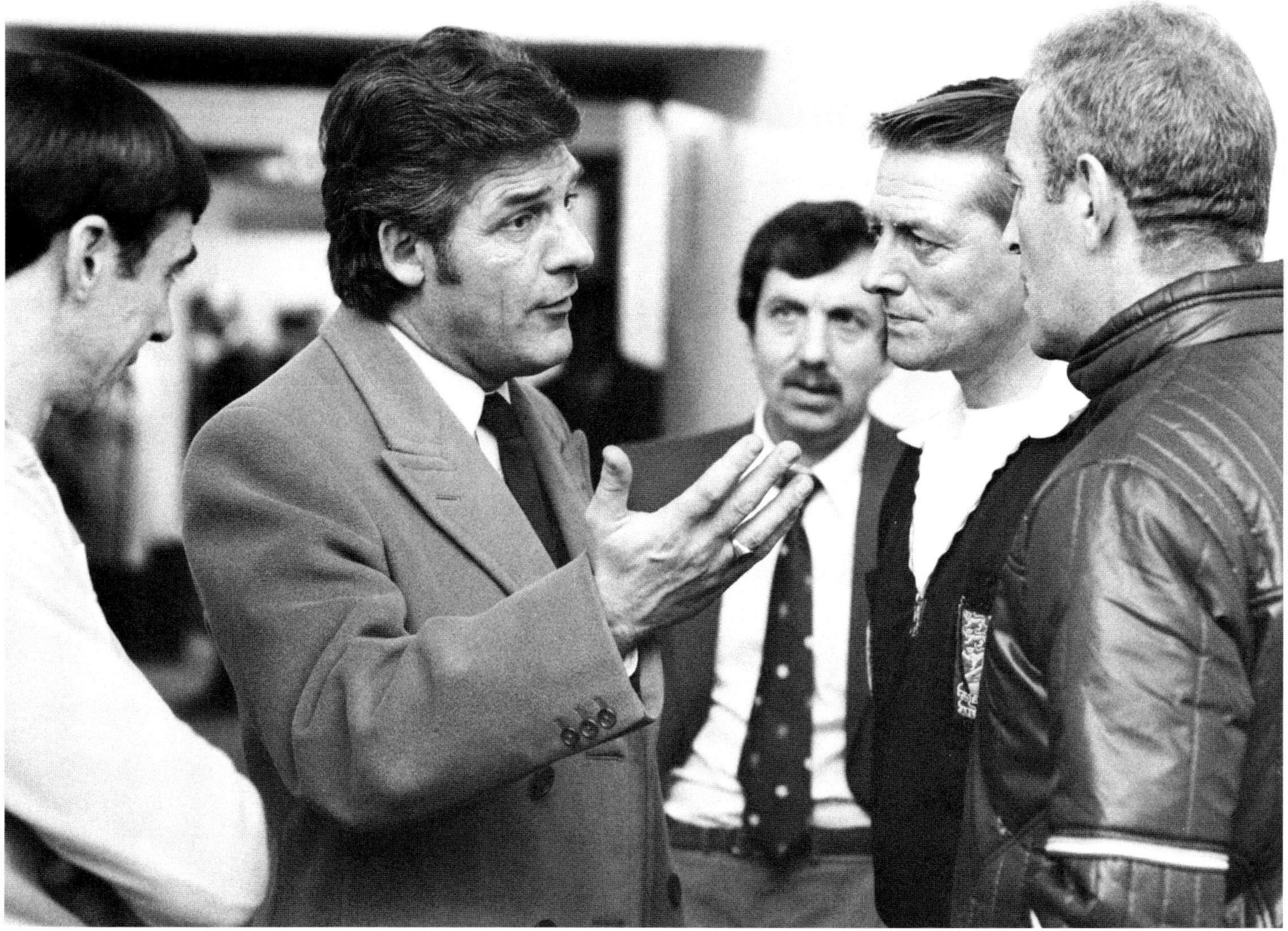

Let there be light. Hammers' manager John Lyall and his Coventry counterpart Dave Sexton discuss the problem with referee A. Glasson as a floodlight failure delays the match at Upton Park by some twenty minutes. Sexton must have wished that they hadn't found the fault as his side went on to lose the match 5–2 in November 1981.

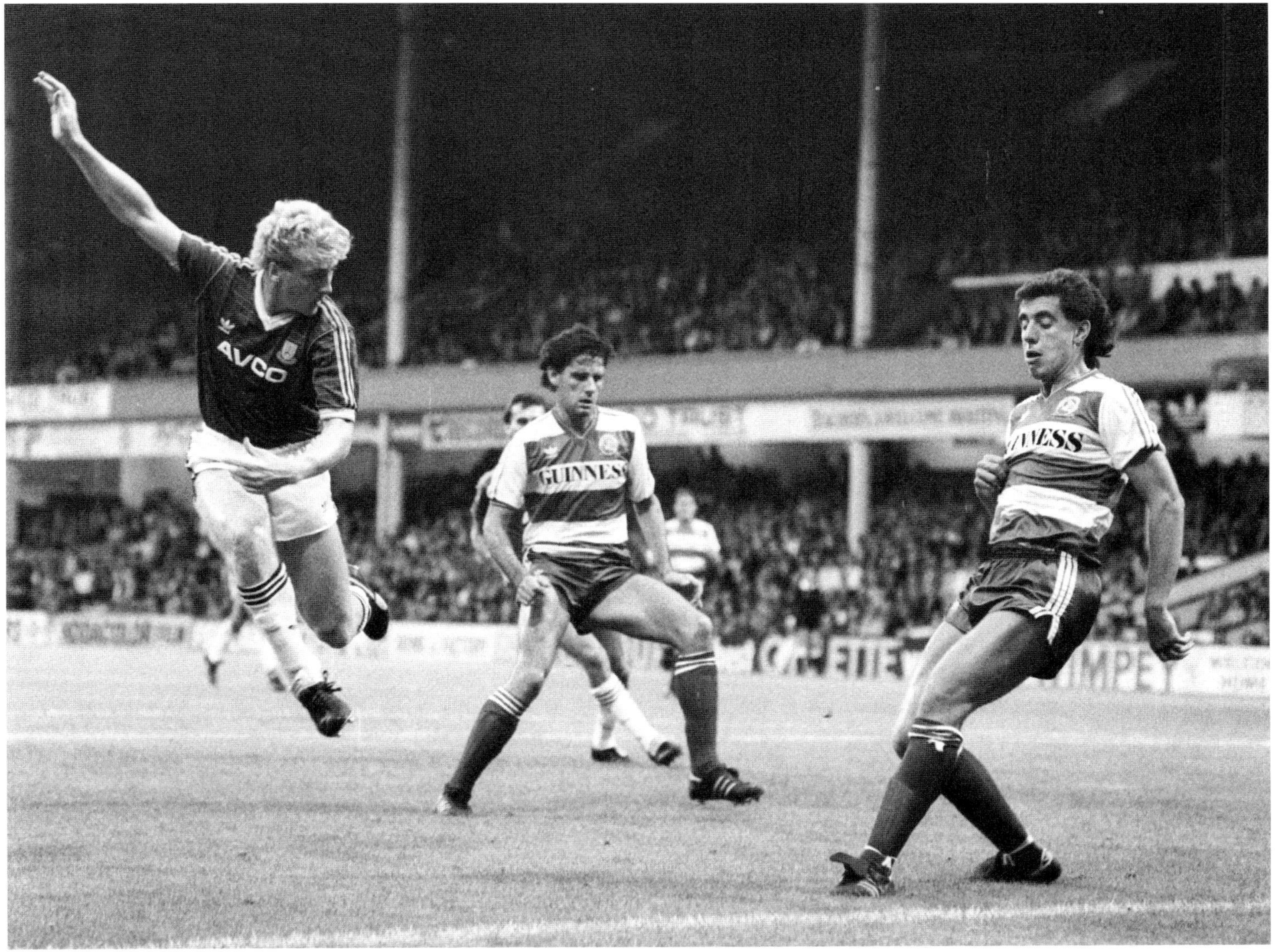

Frank who? This was one of a brace of goals that £340,000 signing Frank McAvennie scored on his home debut against QPR in August 1985, a 3–1 win for the Hammers. With a blackout of televised football that season, Frank remained somewhat of an unknown quantity, even though he scored 28 league and cup goals during the campaign.

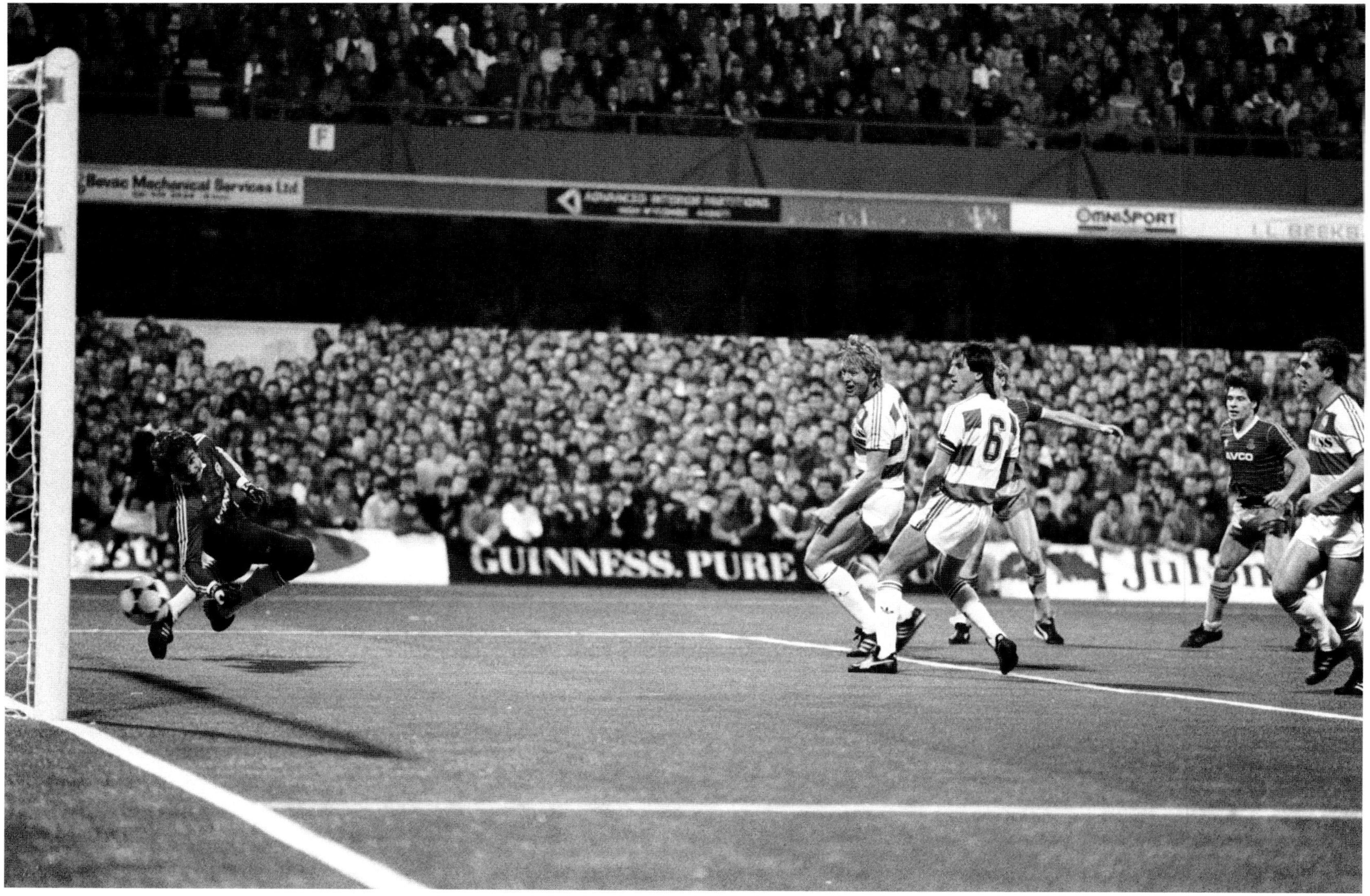
GUINNESS. PURE
OMNISPORT

Jet-lagged. Frank McAvennie flew back from Australia the day before West Ham were due to play at Loftus Road in the 1985–86 season, but nobody seriously expected him to play. Not only did he complete the match but he scored this 73rd-minute winner to give Hammers a rare win on a plastic pitch.

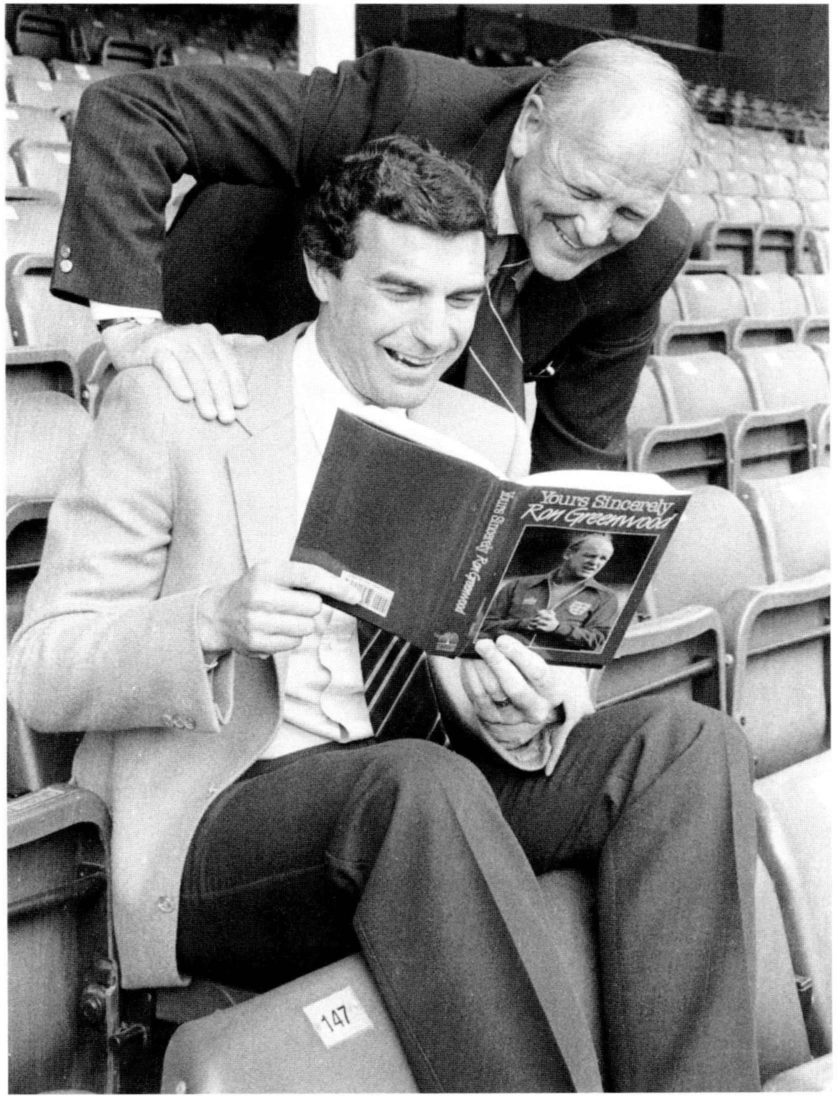

Let's have a look. Trevor Brooking tries to get a peek over Ron Greenwood's shoulder at the Upton Park launch of the former West Ham and England manager's autobiography. I don't expect that Ron had a bad word to say about one of West Ham's favourite sons.

Happy New Year . . . and a happy new career. Tony Cottee scores on his West Ham debut on 1st January 1983, beating Ray Clemence in the Spurs goal after Joe Gallagher's header had rebounded off of the crossbar. The seventeen-year-old, born in West Ham, went on to become one of the club's most prolific goalscorers in his two spells at Upton Park and we became great friends over the years we worked together — and still are to this day.

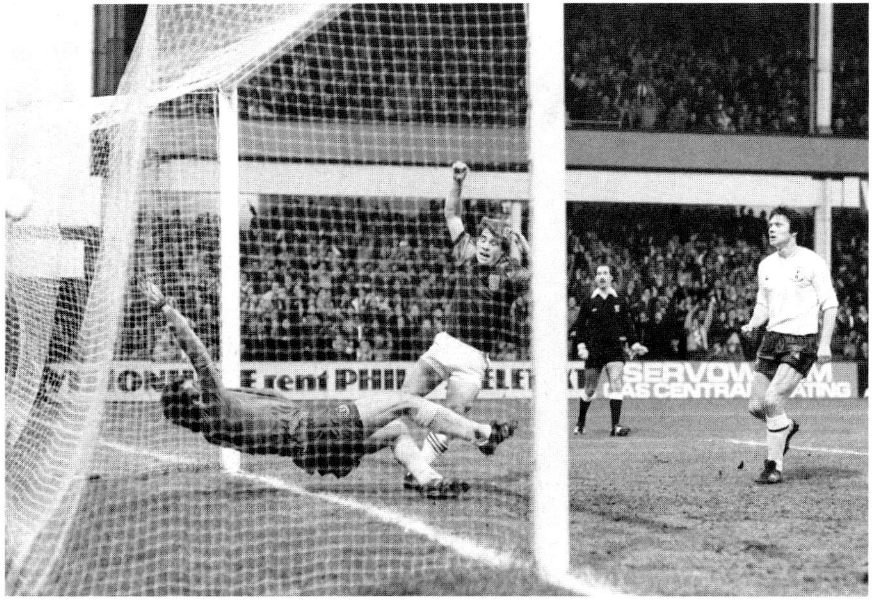

Lifesaver. This goal by Tony Cottee, against Ipswich Town at Portman Road, gave West Ham the win they needed for Division One survival in the 1984–85 season. Although they had appeared to be safe, other results during this last month of the season would have meant the drop but for this 1–0 victory.

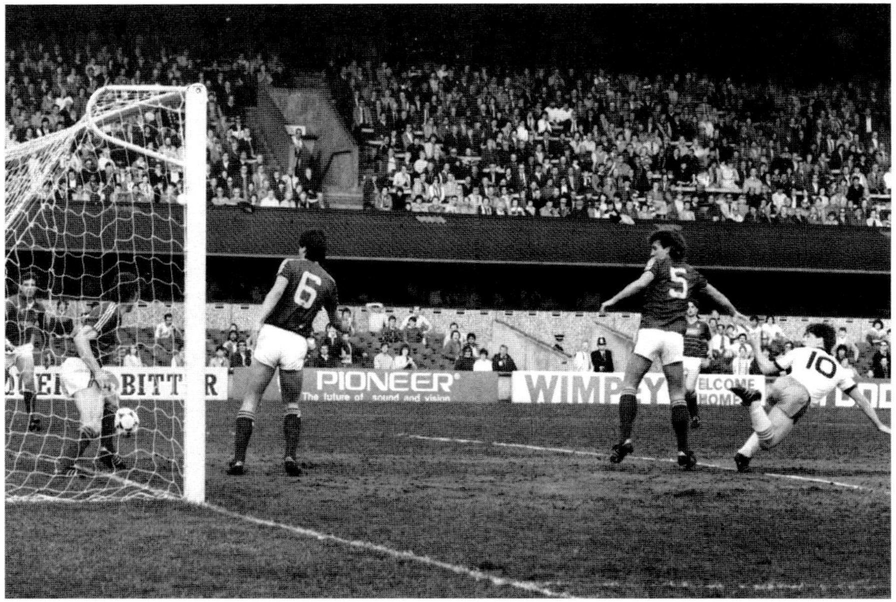

Dead and Bury-ied. West Ham stormed to a 10–0 victory in this Milk Cup second round, second leg tie against Bury at Upton Park. This was one of four goals that Tony Cottee scored that night in October 1983. Strangely enough, John Lyall signed the Bury central defender Paul Hilton not long afterwards! I once asked Hilts what his manager had said at half-time as Bury trailed 5–0 in this game. 'If you lot don't pull your socks up we're going to get beat ten tonight!' was the reply.

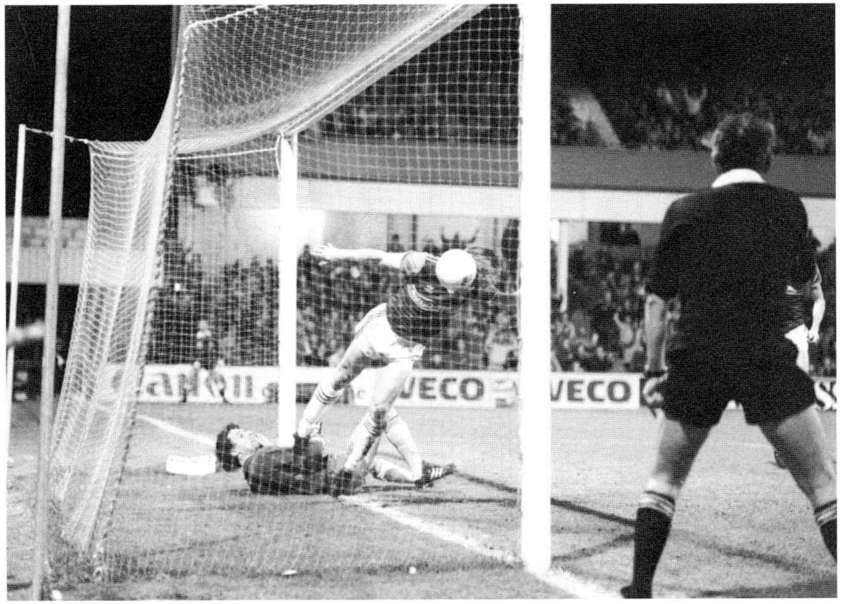

Stretch fabric. Manchester United's Mike Duxbury gets a firm grip on David Kelly's shirt as the West Ham striker tries to break through at Old Trafford in September 1988. Kelly didn't get through, and neither did any of his team-mates as Hammers went down 2–0.

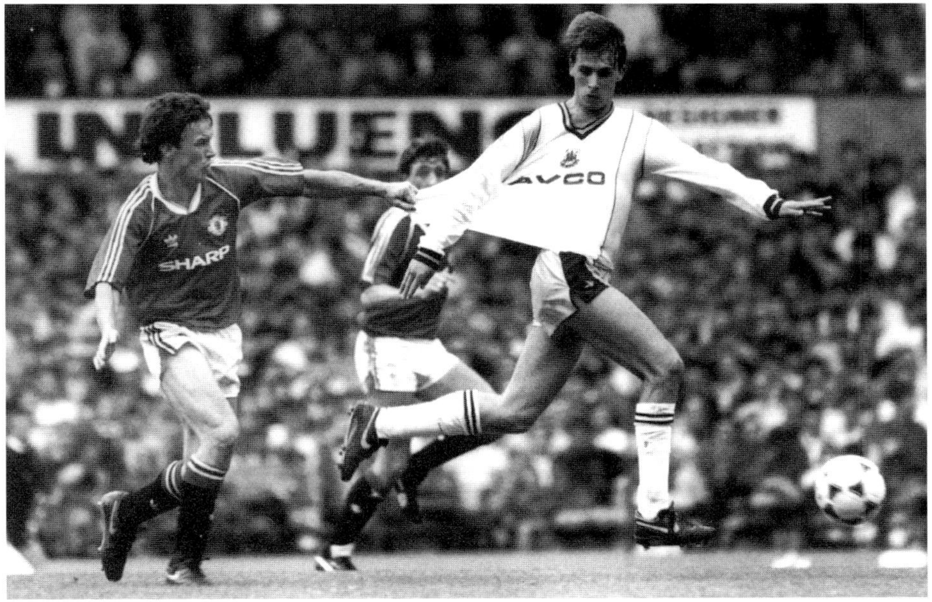

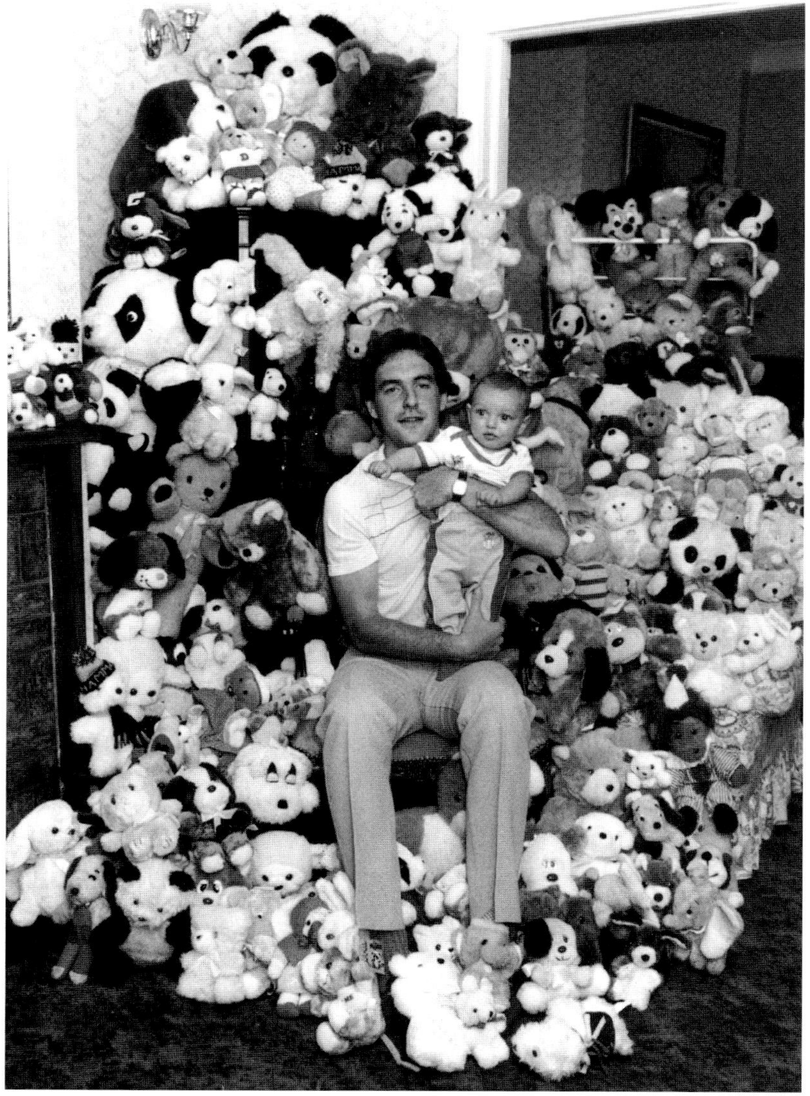

Tragedy. Football paled into insignificance in August 1985 when Paul Brush's wife, Marilyn, died following a courageous battle against leukaemia. She had been diagnosed during a routine pregnancy test when she was carrying their first child, Peter. Paul, one of my best mates at the club, is pictured with a seven-month-old Peter amid a mountain of cuddly toys donated by friends and supporters in memory of Marilyn, who had always loved such toys. Paul requested these instead of flowers at the funeral and they were later distributed among several children's hospitals.

The 1990s

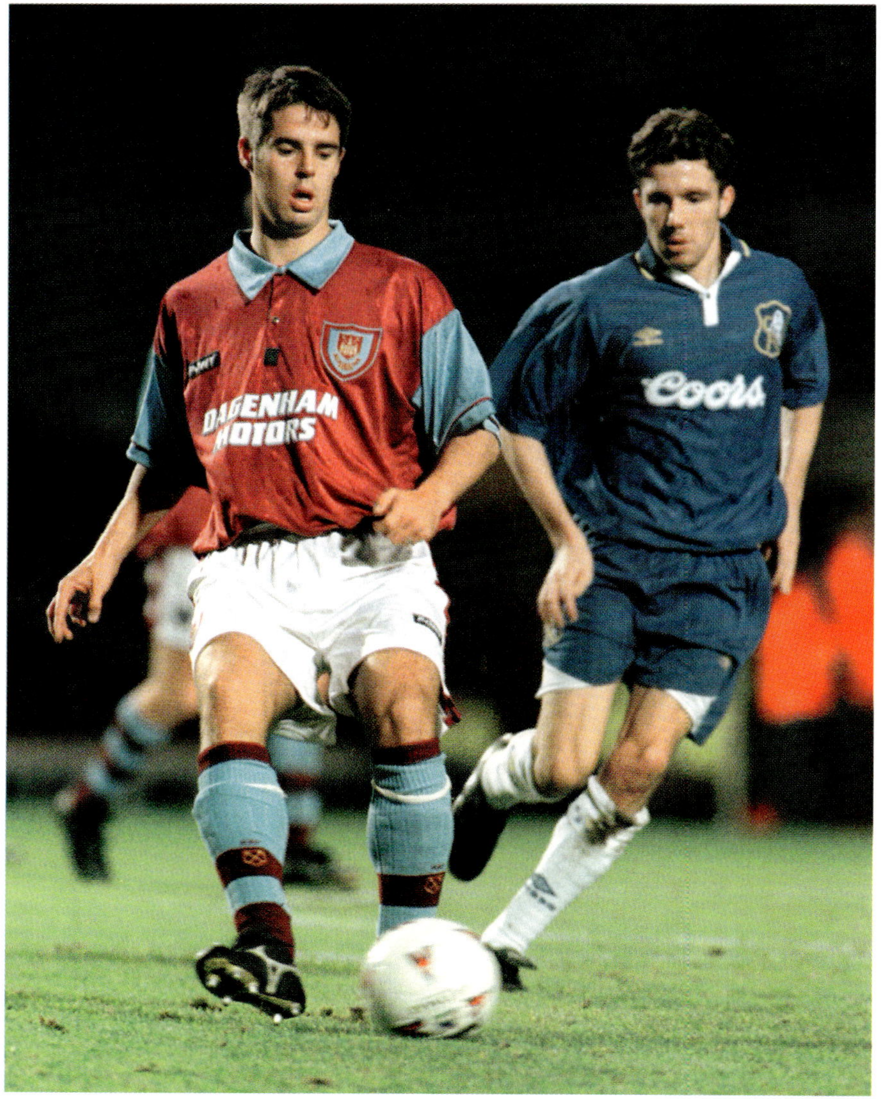

Dream on you Hammers' fans. Jamie Redknapp dons the Claret and Blue for a guest appearance in Alvin Martin's Testimonial match. Wouldn't you just love to see him in Hammers' kit every week?

Well done mate. Manager Billy Bonds and his assistant Harry Redknapp relax with a beer in the Upton Park medical room after winning promotion, beating Cambridge United 2–0 in the final game of the 1992–93 season.

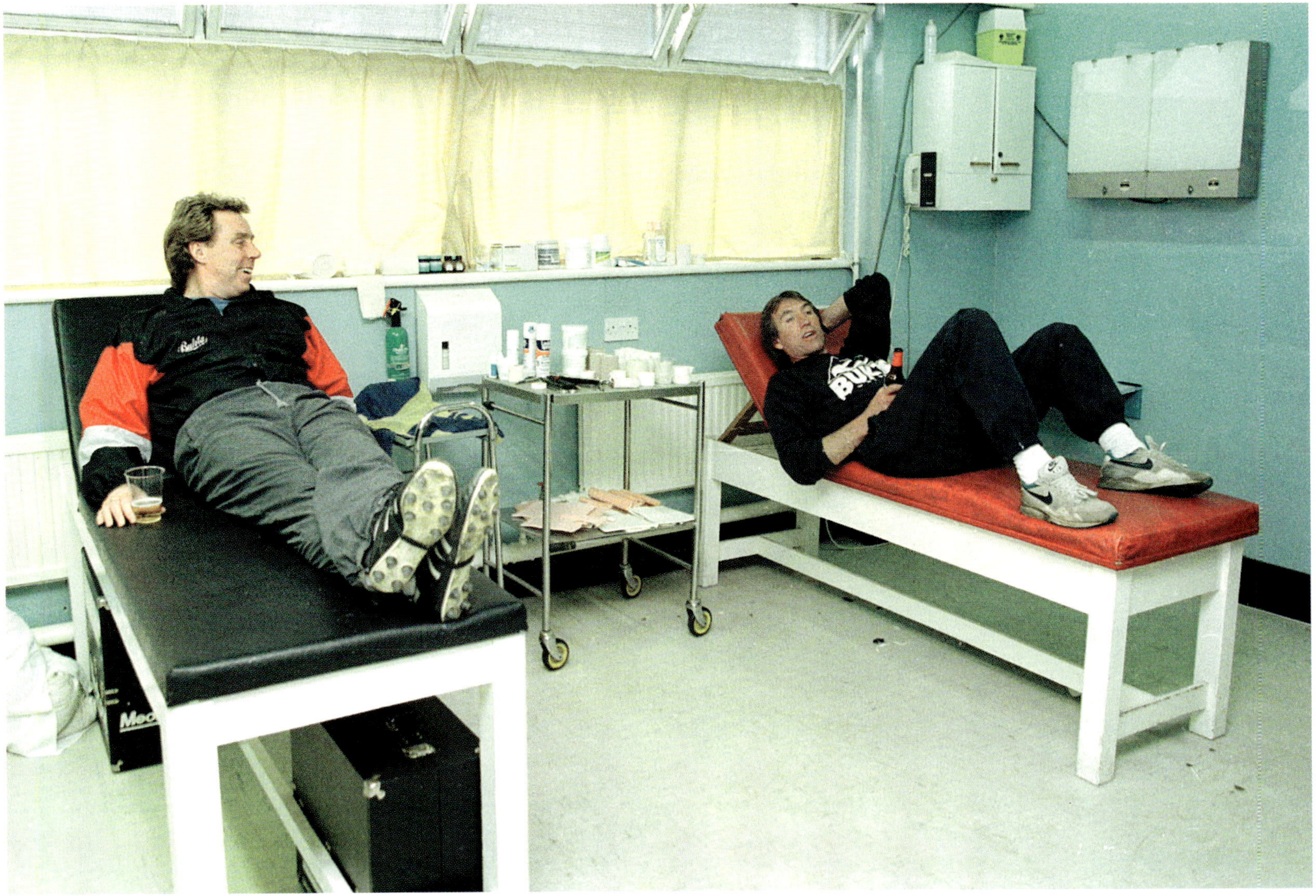

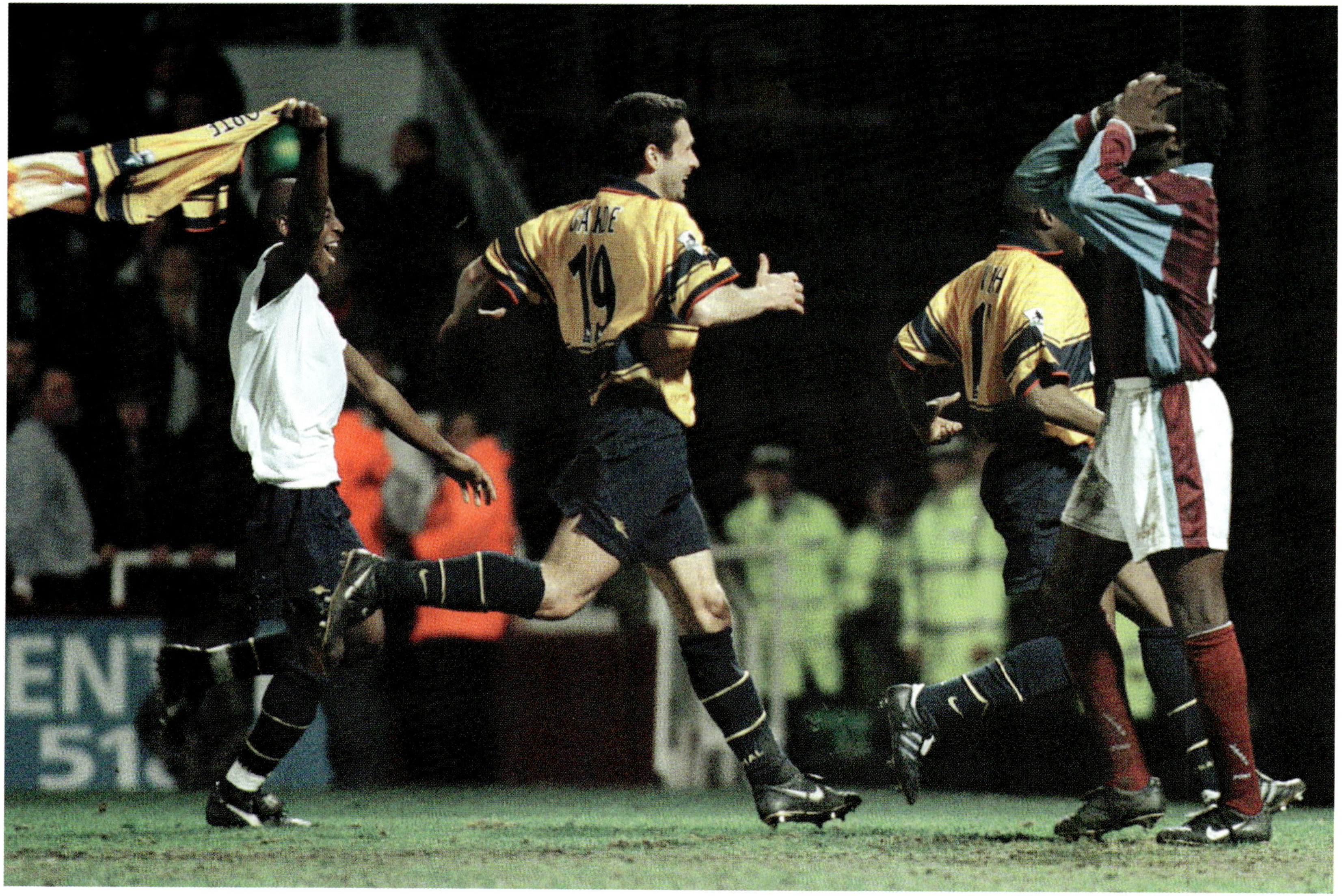

Aboohoo. Samassi Abou holds his head in anguish after missing his spot-kick in the FA Cup quarter-final penalty shoot-out against Arsenal as the victorious Gunners celebrate in the background.

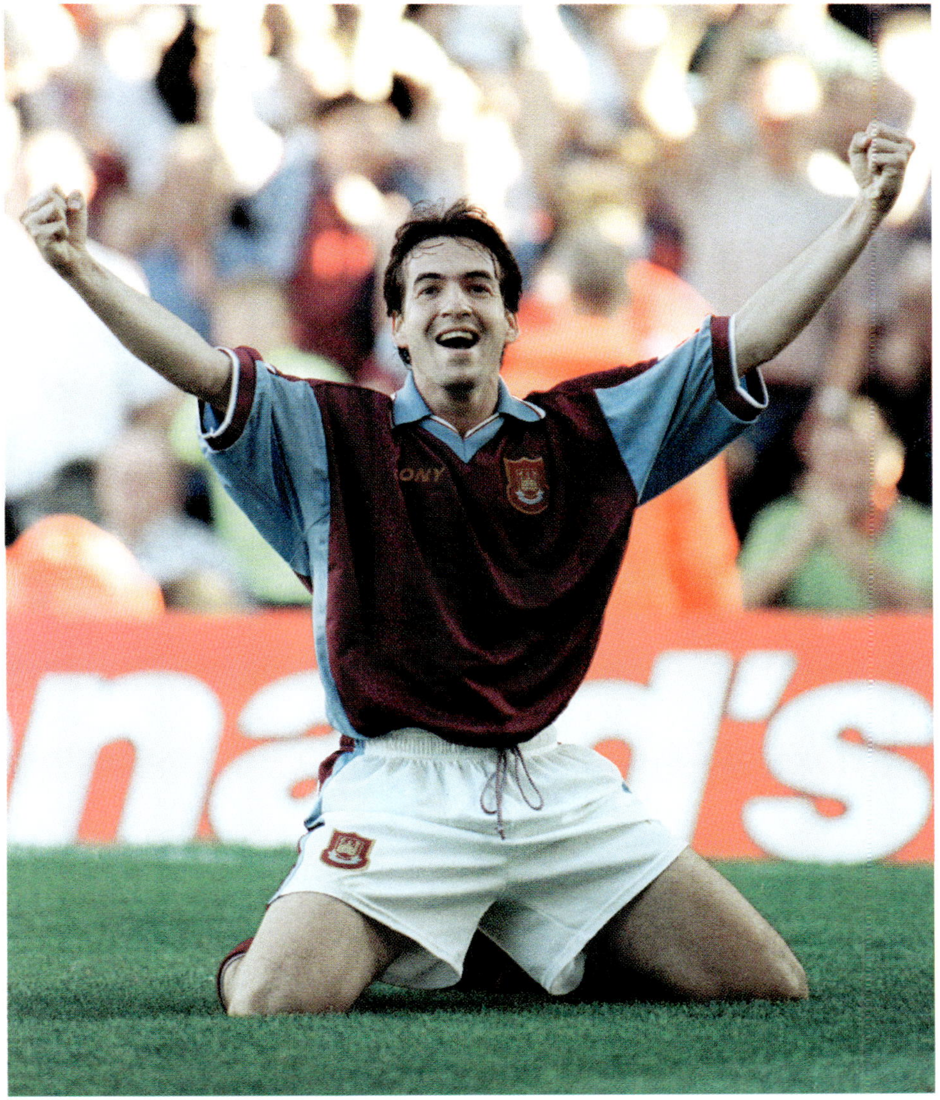

Brilliant Berky. Eyal Berkovic celebrates in his usual enthusiastic style after scoring at Upton Park.

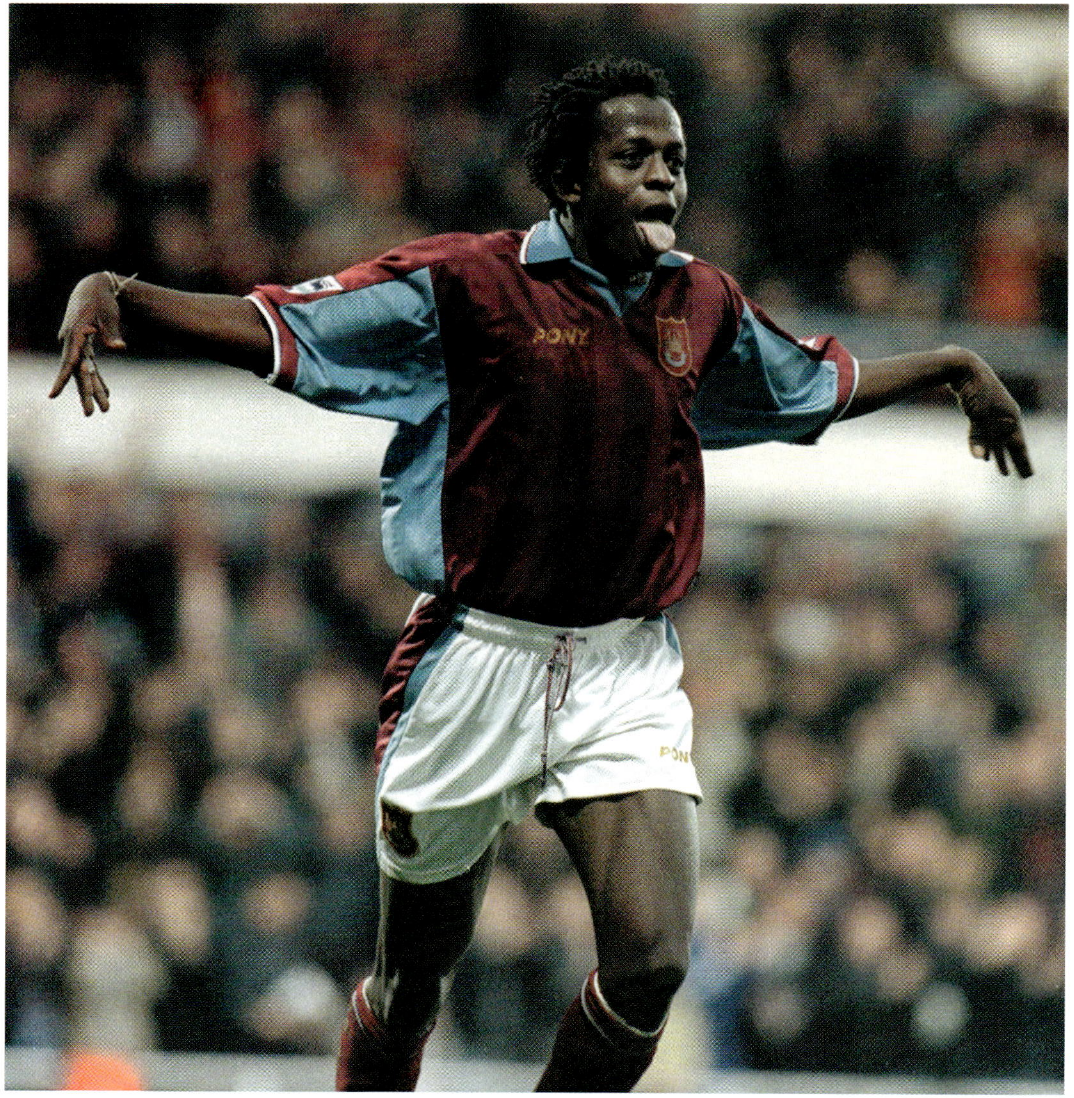

He flies like a bird. Samassi Abou takes flight to celebrate his goal against Barnsley at Upton Park.

Memories. I was lucky enough to visit ex-Hammer Danny McGowan with Terry Connolly, an old friend who tracks down players from the old days. Dublin-born Danny played for the club between 1948 and 1954 making 83 appearances and it was a privilege to meet and talk to him. Sadly Danny passed away some months after our meeting.

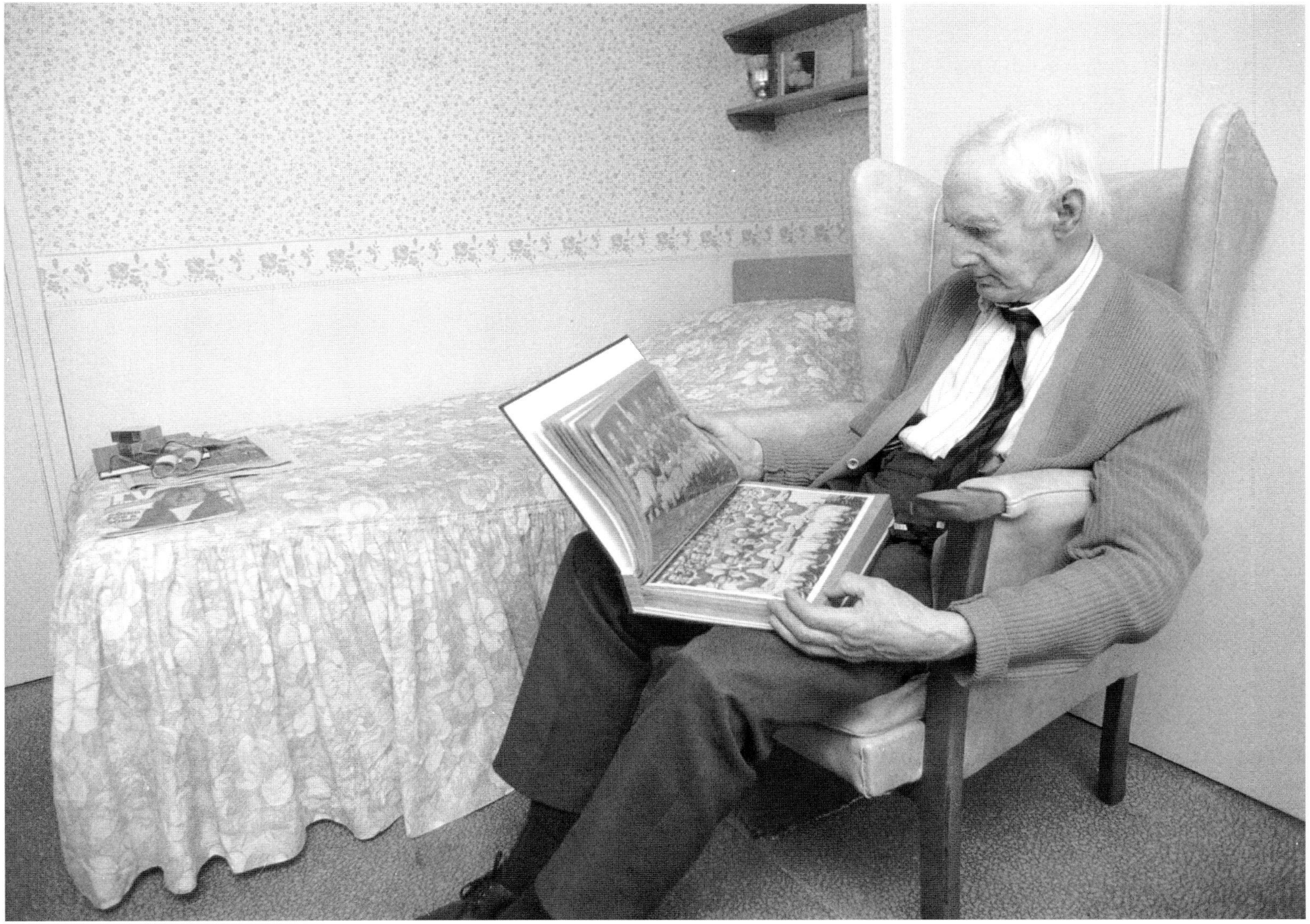

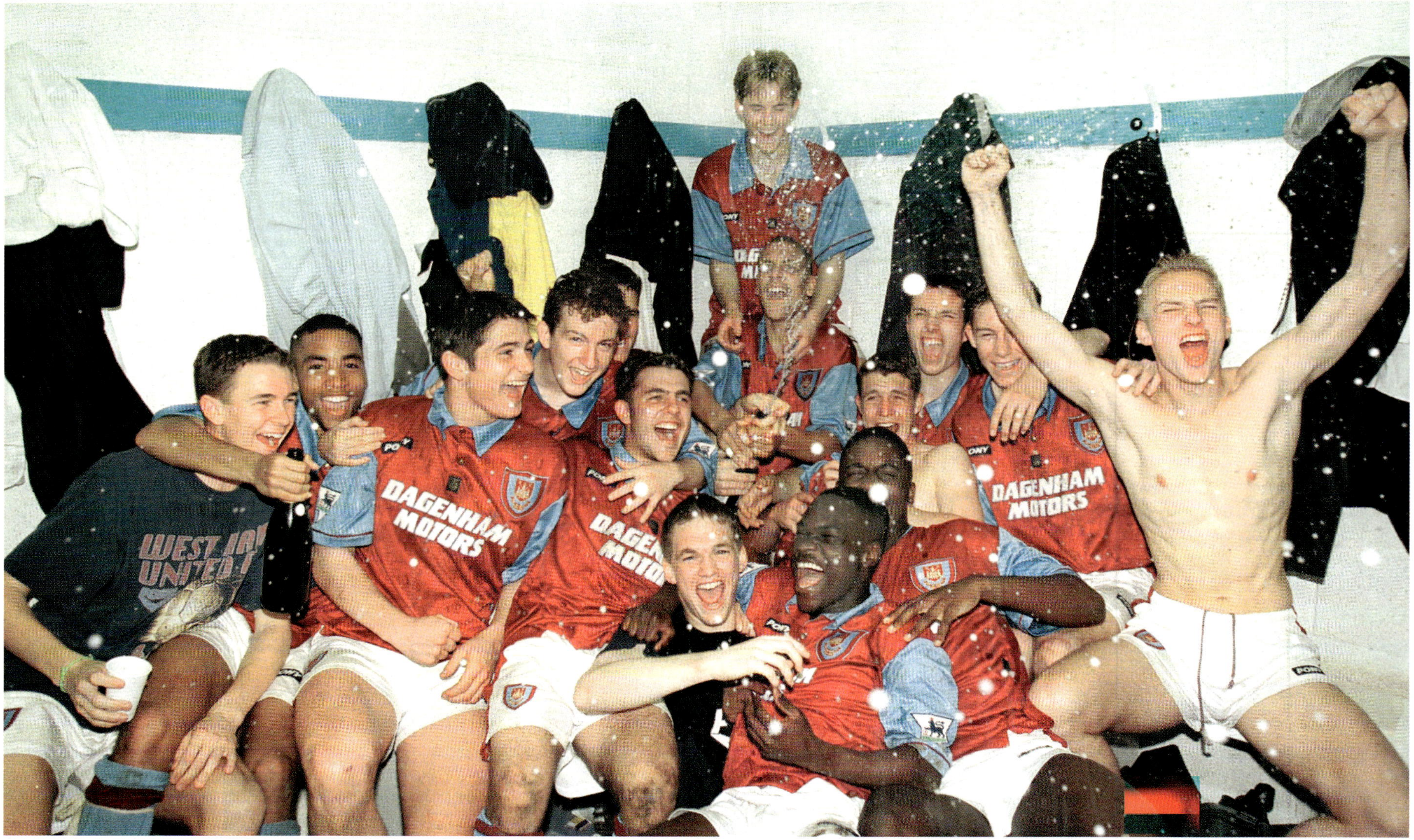
DAGENHAM
MOTORS
DAGENHAM
MOTORS

Just champion. The champagne flows as the West Ham youngsters celebrate their South East Counties League title in the Chadwell Heath dressing room at the end of the 1996–97 campaign.

Sharp-shooter. I had just treated myself to a new lens (a 400mm f2.8 Canon autofocus) and was keen to try it out, even though the 1997–98 season was coming to an end. Our last away match was at Selhurst Park, so I shot the match on the new optic. This picture of Andy Impey holding off the challenge of Crystal Palace's Dean Gordon was one of the pick of the images from the match — sharp enough to cut yourself on!

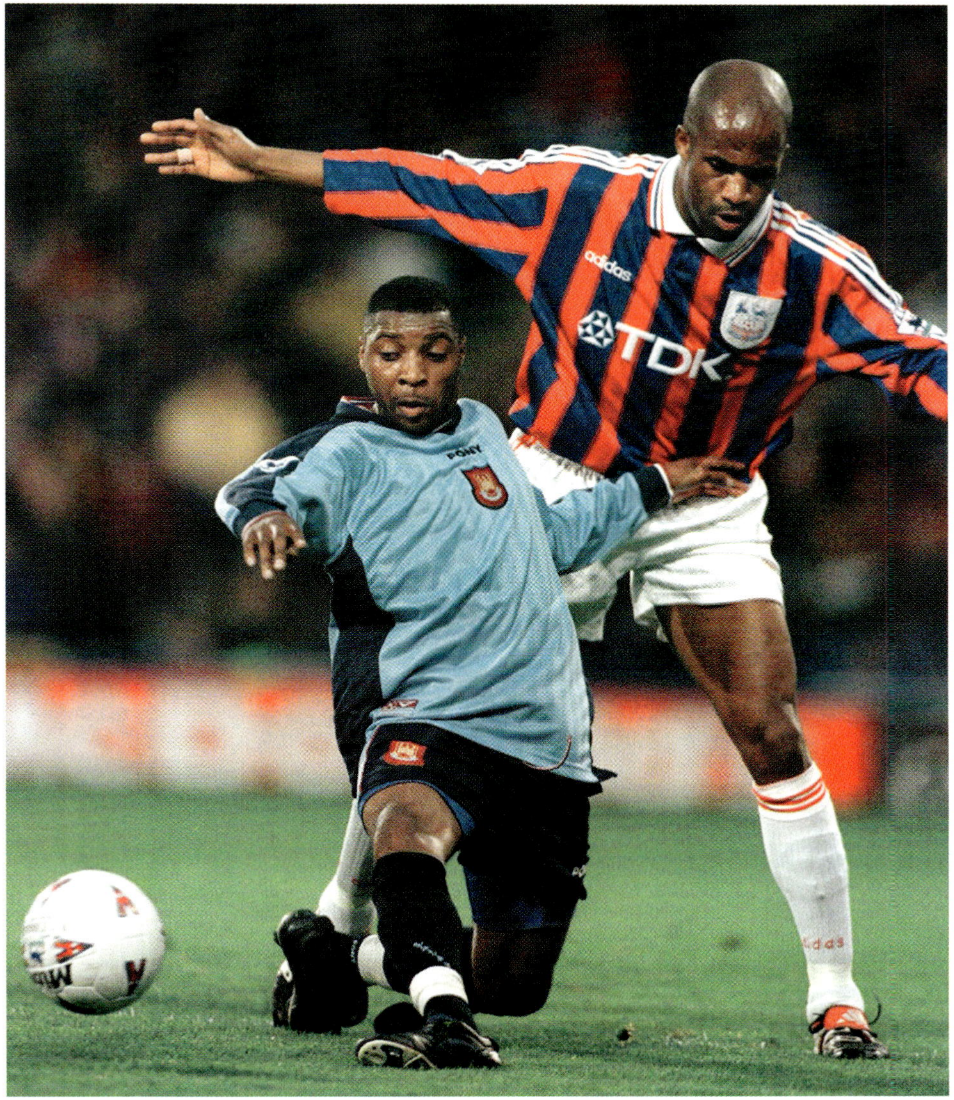

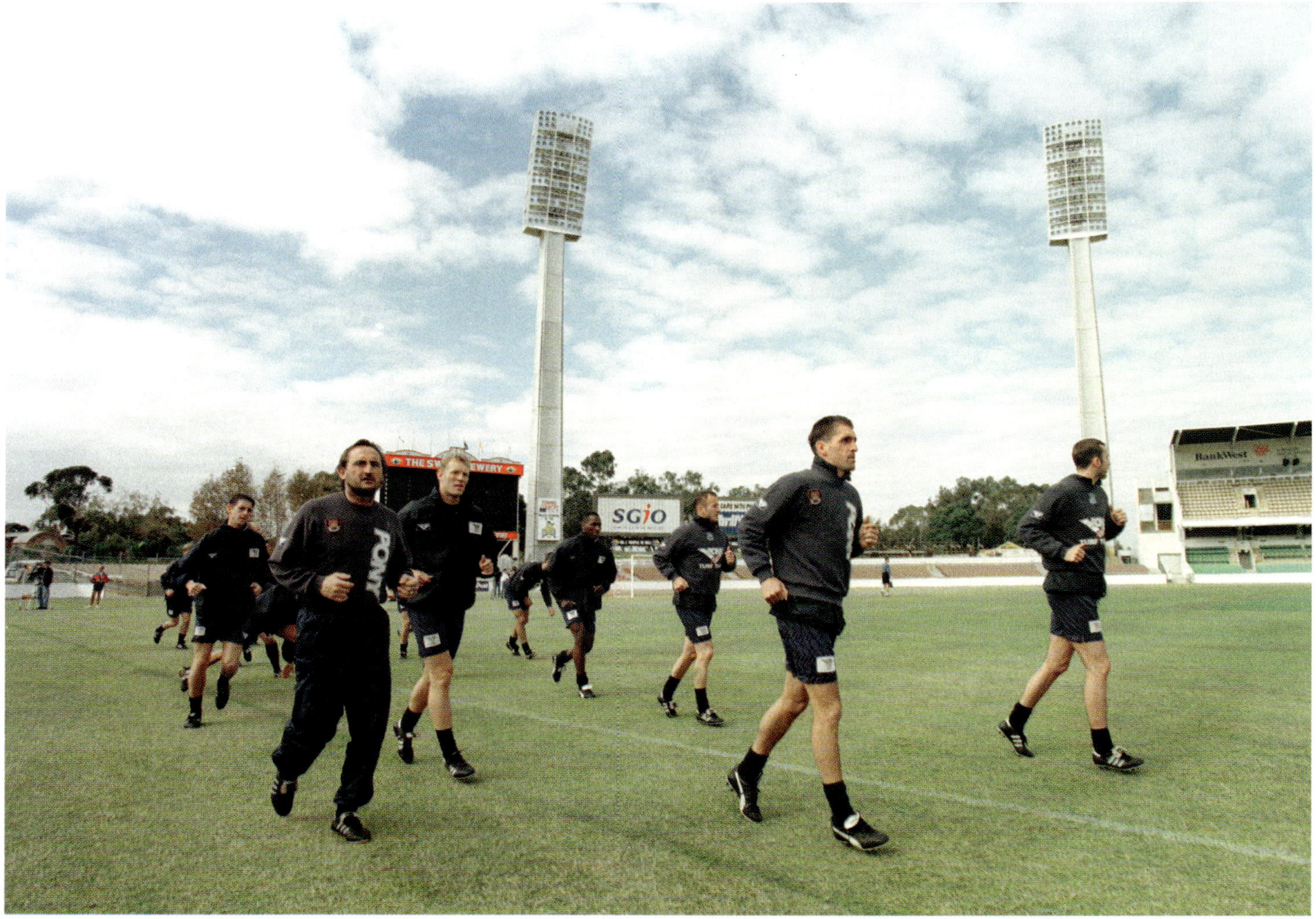

Down under. Frank Lampard leads a training session at the WACA in Perth during Hammers' Centenary Tour of Australia in 1995. The club invited me along on this trip of a lifetime which took in four cities — Perth, Sydney, Melbourne and Brisbane — and ended with a six-day holiday on Surfers' Paradise.

High jinks. Steve Jones scores an acrobatic goal in a pre-season friendly against Portsmouth at Fratton Park.

Collectors' item: Joey Beauchamp sporting a West Ham shirt. This rare picture was taken, ironically, in a pre-season friendly at Oxford United, the club he was signed from in June 1994. The player failed to settle at his new club and moved on to Swindon Town on the eve of the season without kicking a ball in anger.

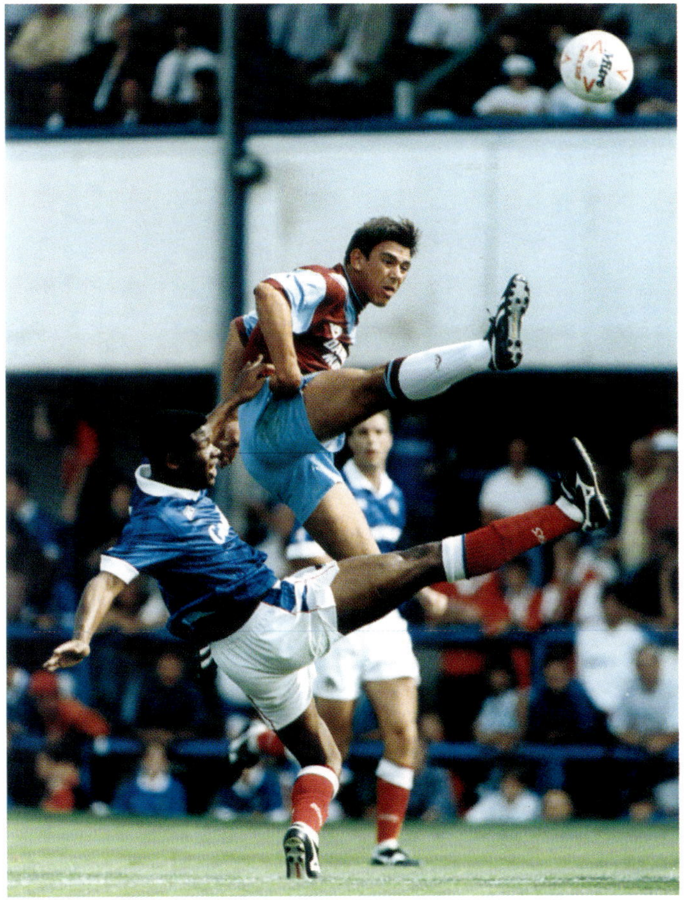

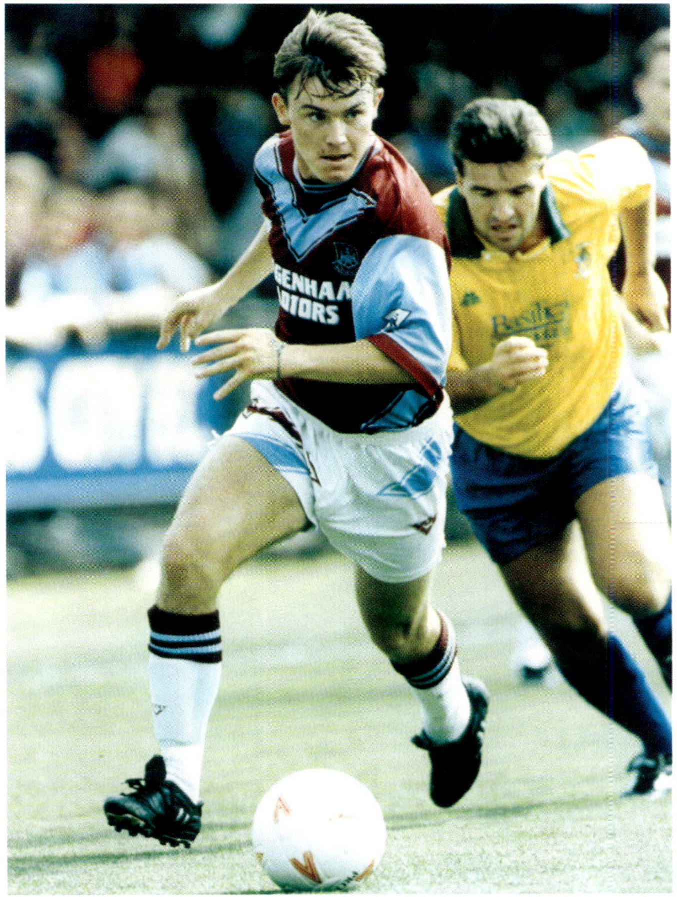

Gotcha! Alvin Martin gets a tight hold on Tony Cottee as the Hammers' marksman returns for his second spell at the club in September 1994.

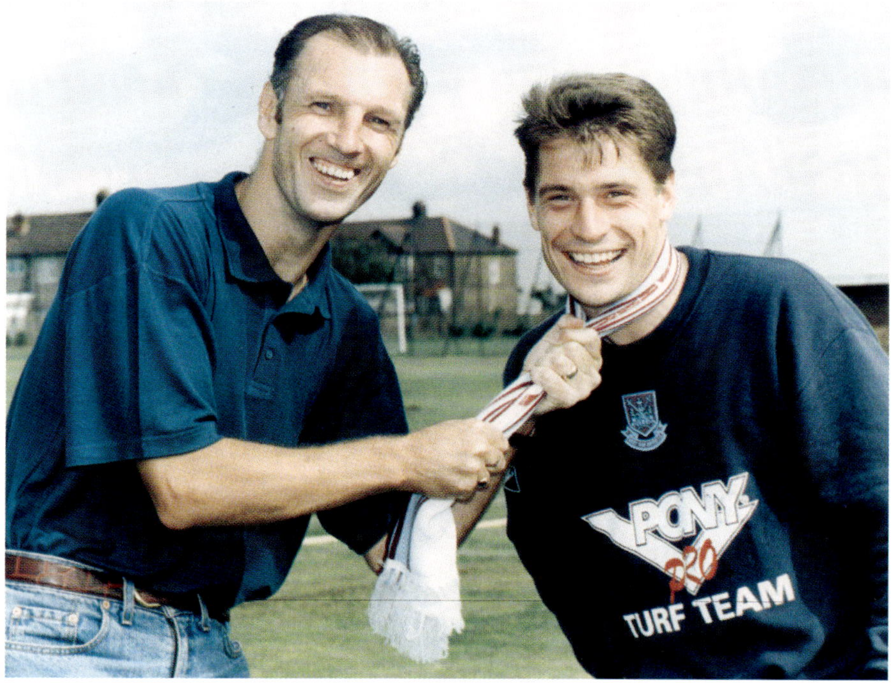

Future star. A very young-looking Rio Ferdinand signs schoolboy forms for West Ham on the Upton Park pitch watched by his mum, brother Anton and Frank Lampard.

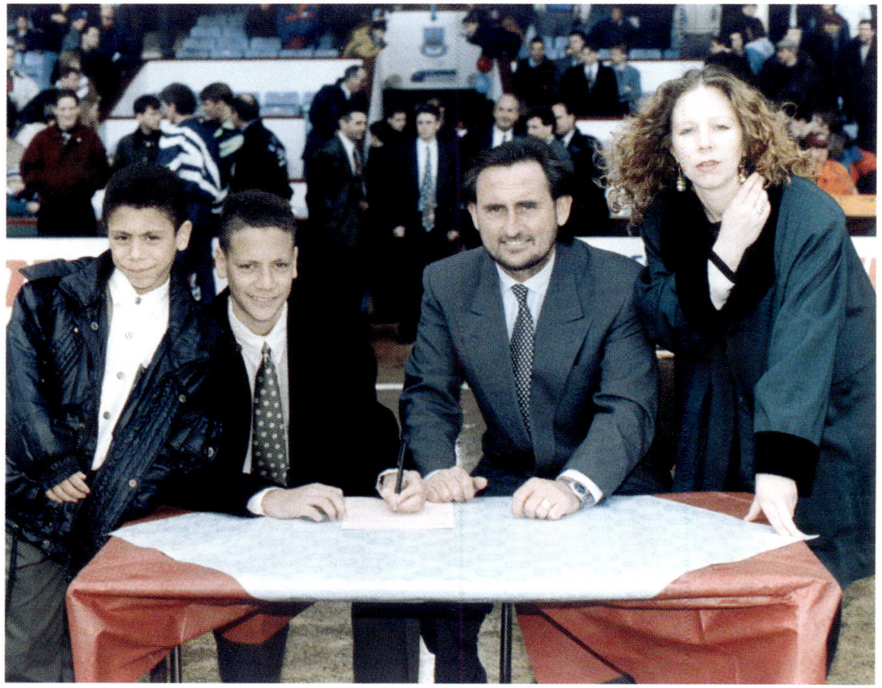

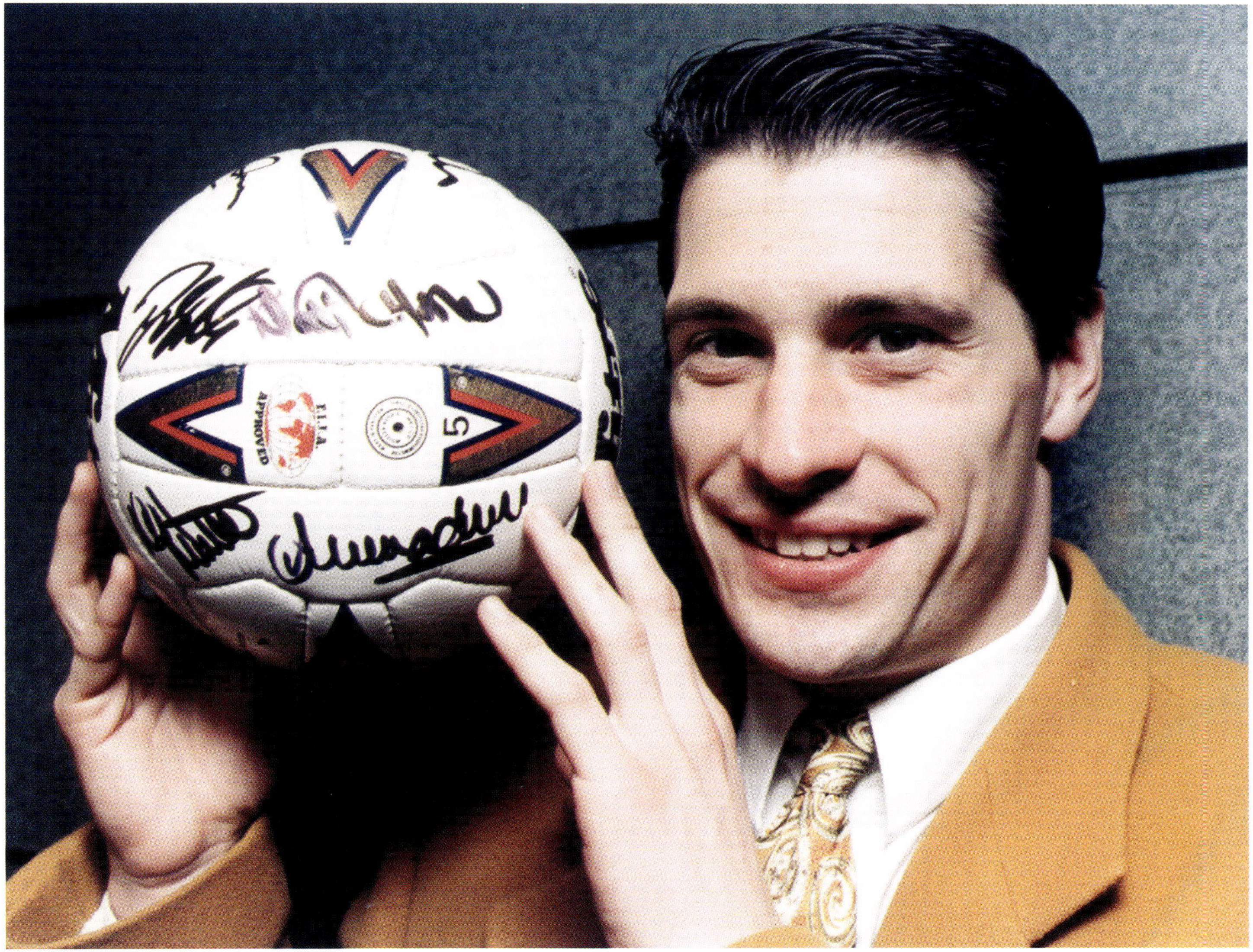

Having a ball. Tony Cottee proudly shows off the match ball, signed by his team-mates, presented to him after his hat-trick in the 3–0 win over Manchester City in December 1994.

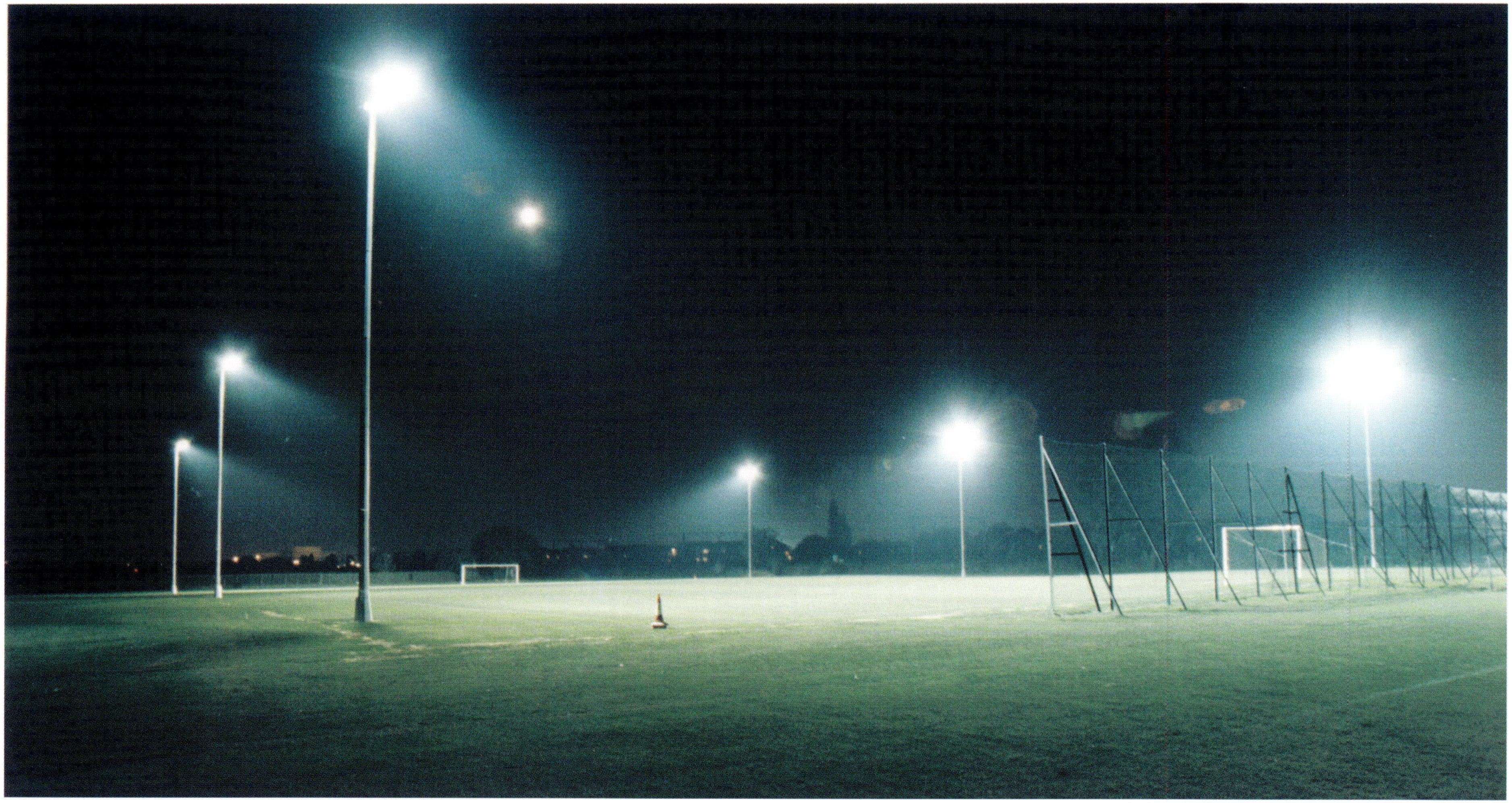

Switched on. A moody shot of the training ground at Chadwell Heath and the new floodlighting installation.

Perfect Pottsy. A classic stock action shot of West Ham's Mr Reliable, Steve Potts. Pottsy never lets us down and is one of the few local lads in the side these days.

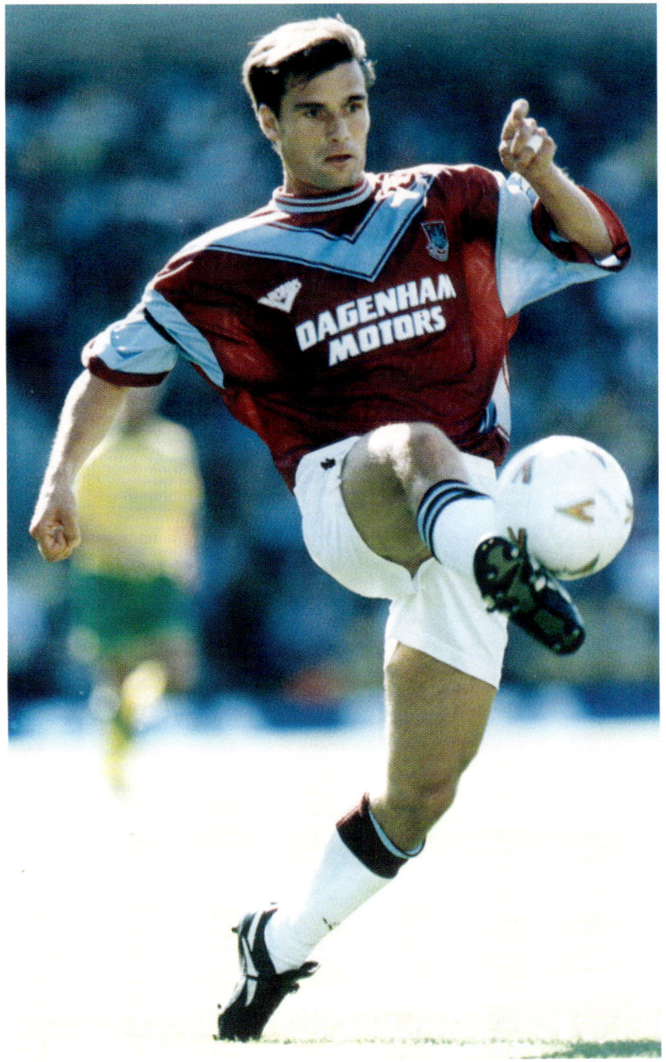

Hair we go. Ian Bishop in full flight with his long locks flowing in the breeze. Bish tended to change his hairstyles as often as his socks!

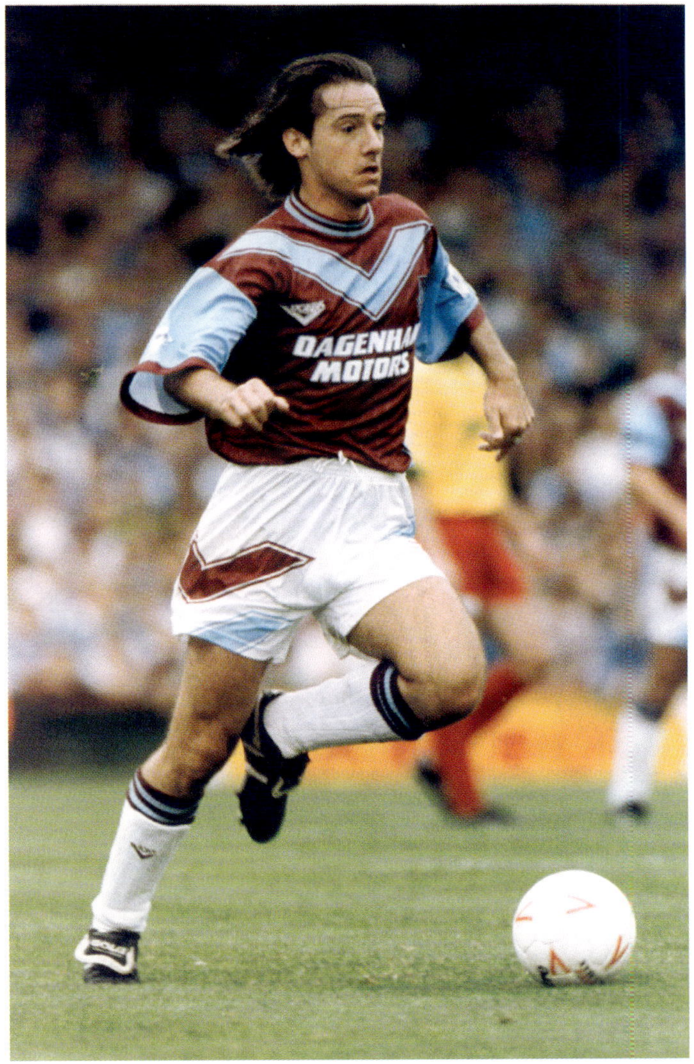

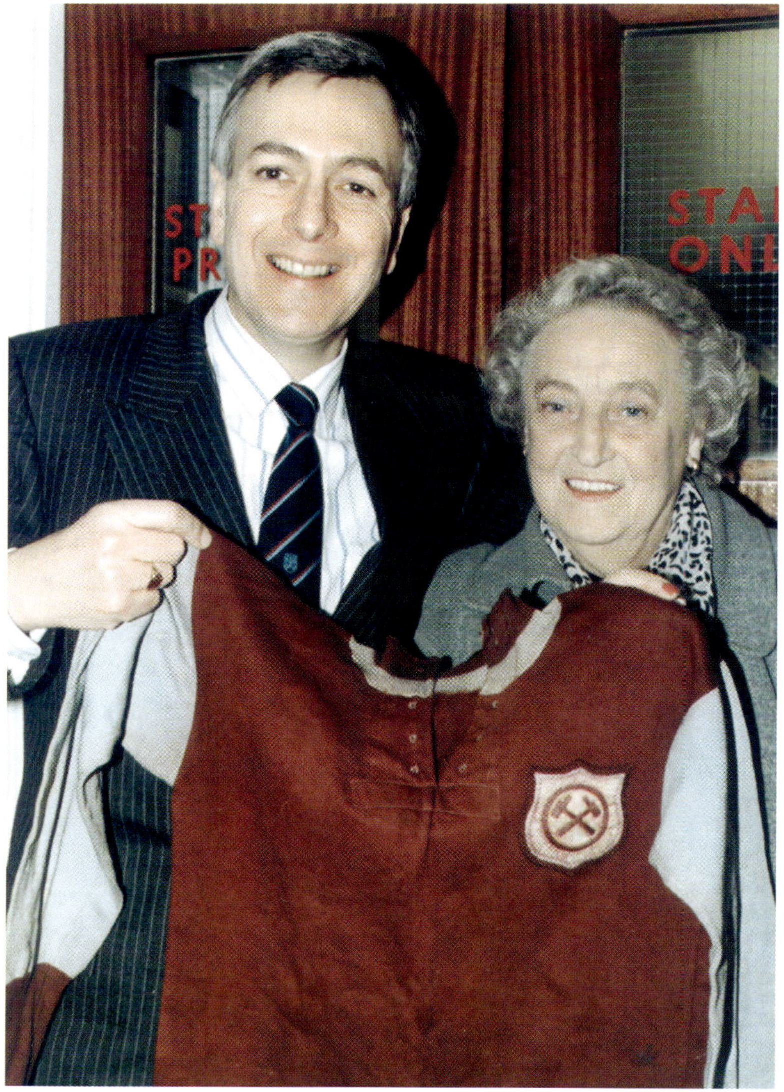

Piece of history. Miss Dorothy Young presents West Ham United chairman Terence Brown with the shirt worn by her father, Jack Young, in the 1923 FA Cup final.

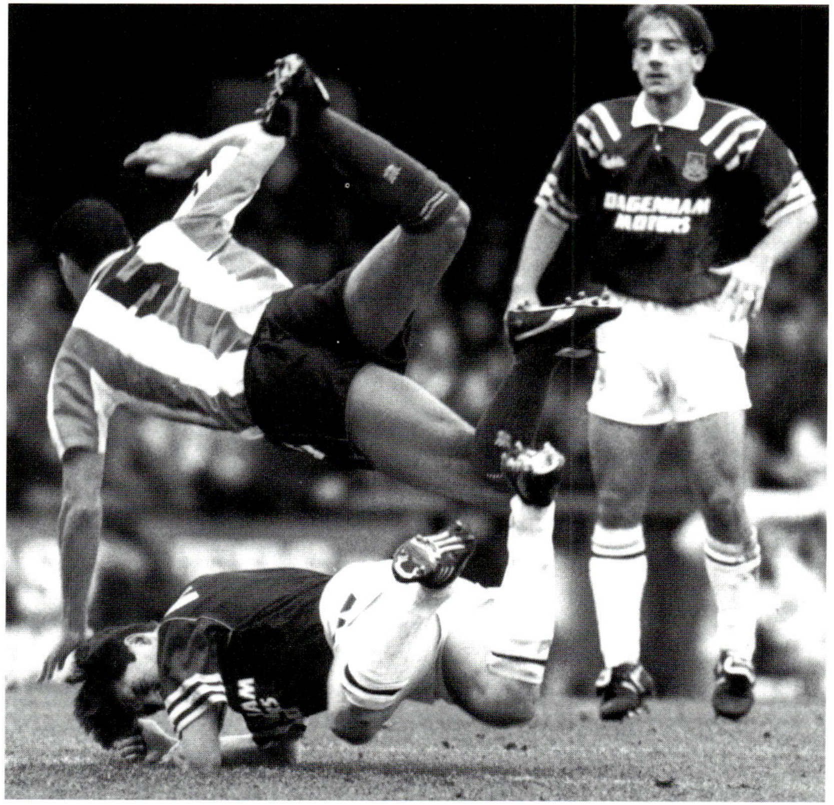

Over my shoulder. Brentford's Shane Westley goes flying as he and Trevor Morley clash at Griffin Park in a dour 0–0 draw five days before Christmas 1992.

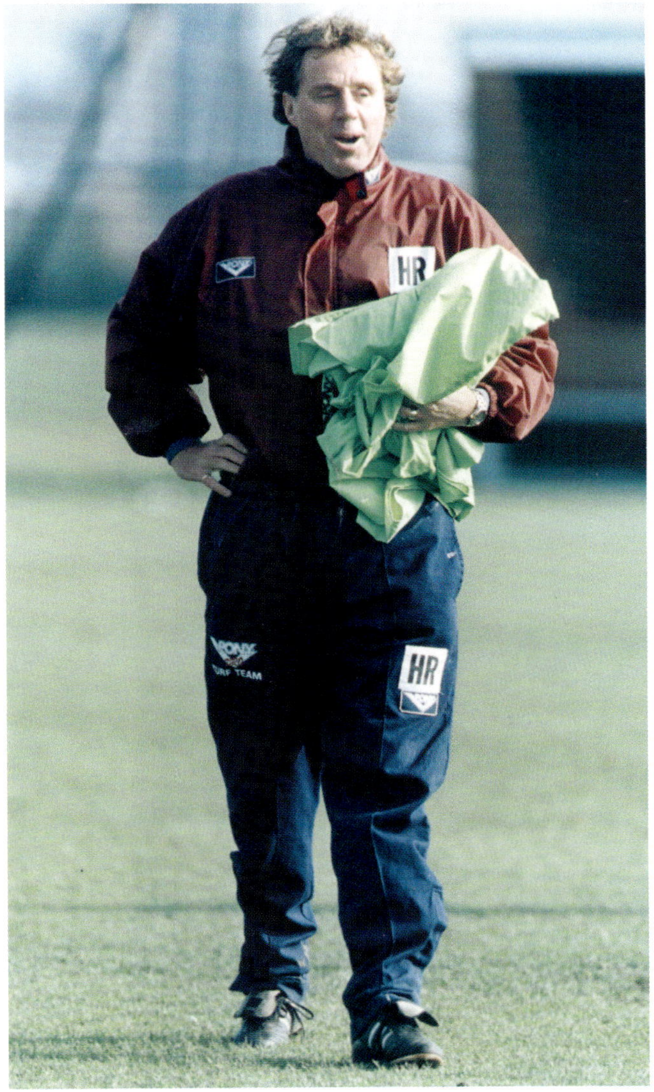

Joker. Harry Redknapp finds something to smile about as he collects the bibs after a training session at Chadwell Heath.

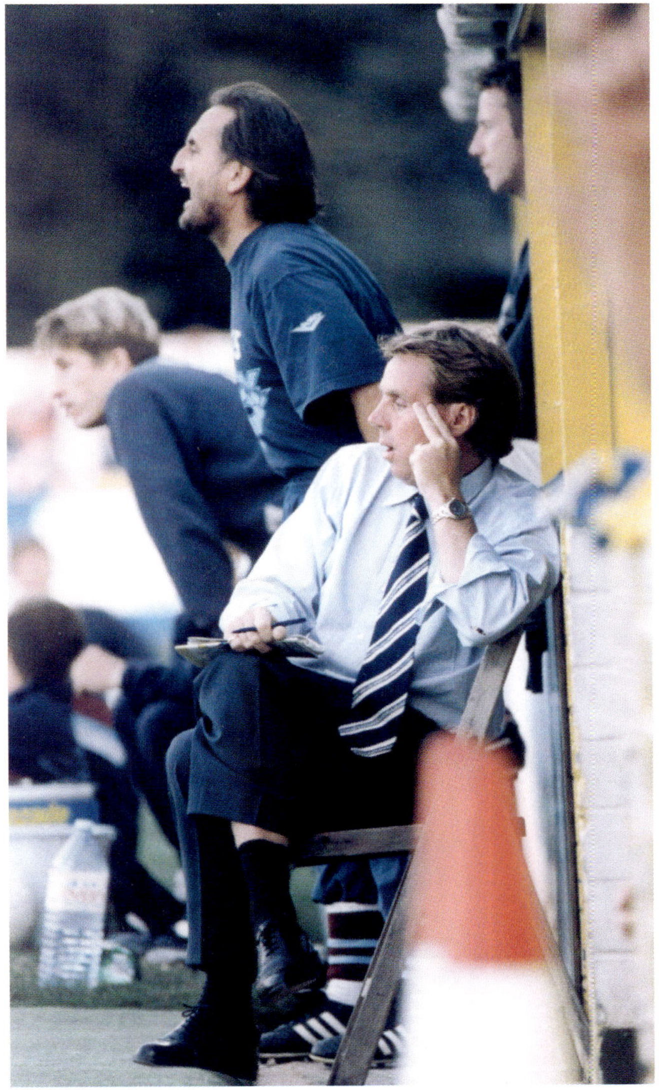

Taking note. Clipboard in hand, Harry Redknapp watches intently from the dugout during a pre-season match at Sutton.

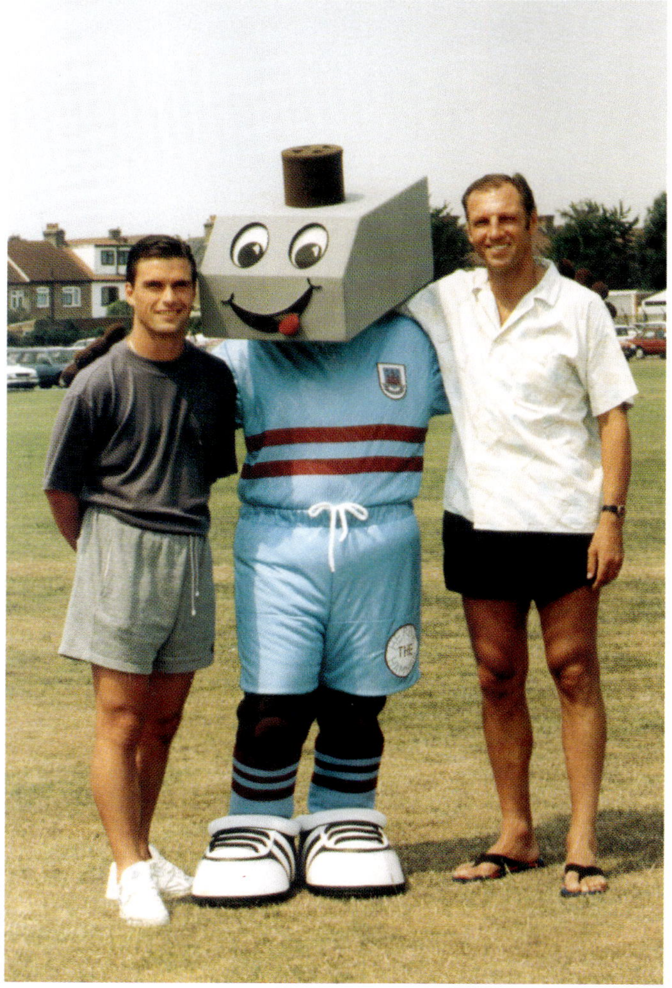

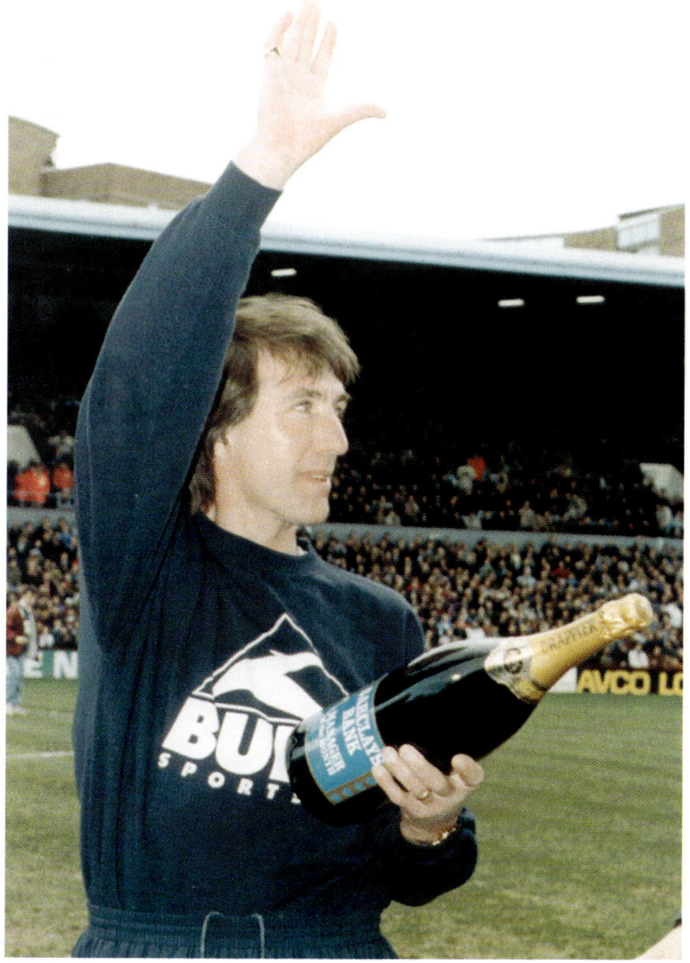

'Ello Herbie. Steve Potts and Alvin Martin get to know Hammers' new mascot Herbie the Hammer at the training ground. Nice boots, Herbie!

Main man. Billy Bonds acknowledges the cheers of the crowd as he collects a Barclays Manager of the Month award during his brief reign.

Pot of gold. The grey skies above the East Stand show off this rainbow over Priory Court to its full effect.

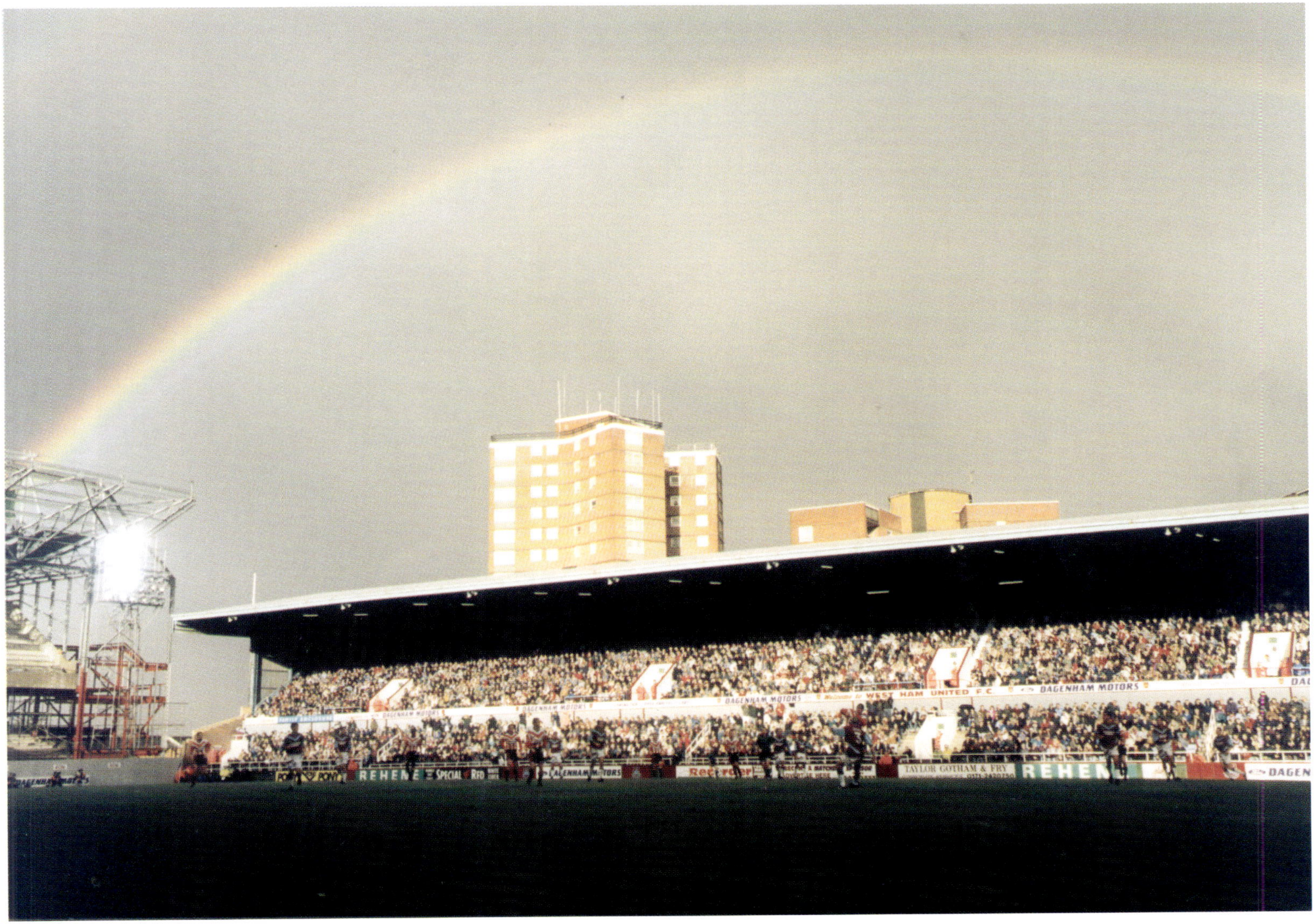
DAGENHAM MOTORS

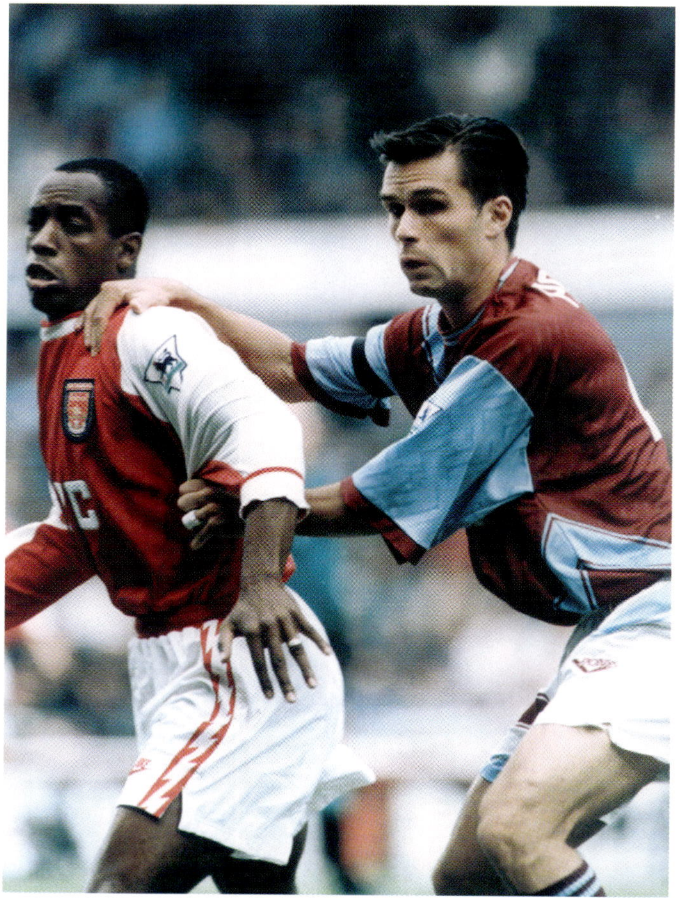

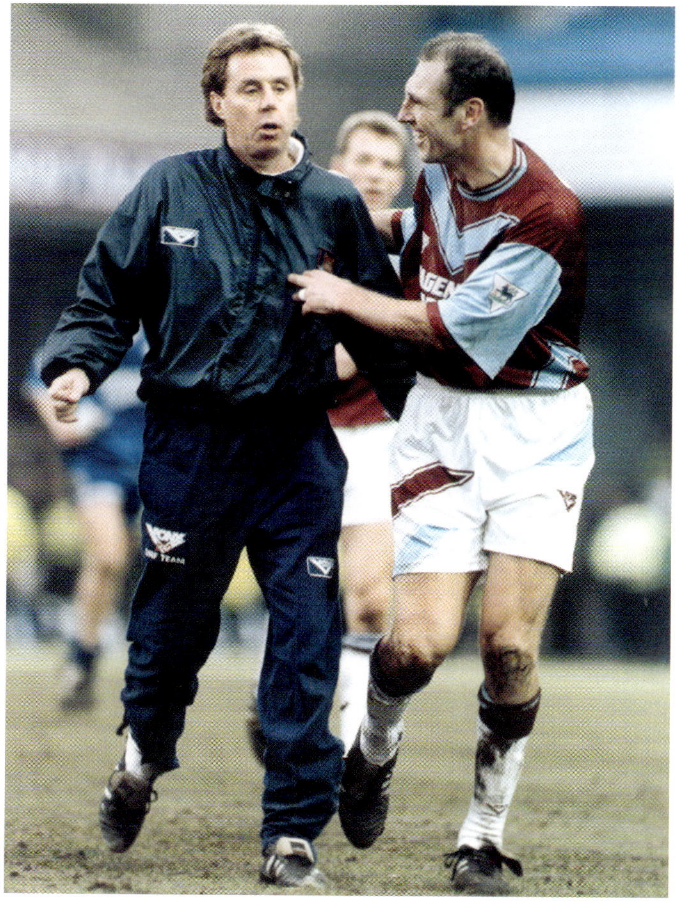

Get a grip, son. Steve Potts finds Arsenal's Ian Wright a real handful.

Cheer up boss. Hammers have just won a vital late season game at bottom club Leicester in April 1995 and look to have saved themselves from relegation. A smiling Alvin Martin tries to get manager Harry Redknapp to lighten up a bit.

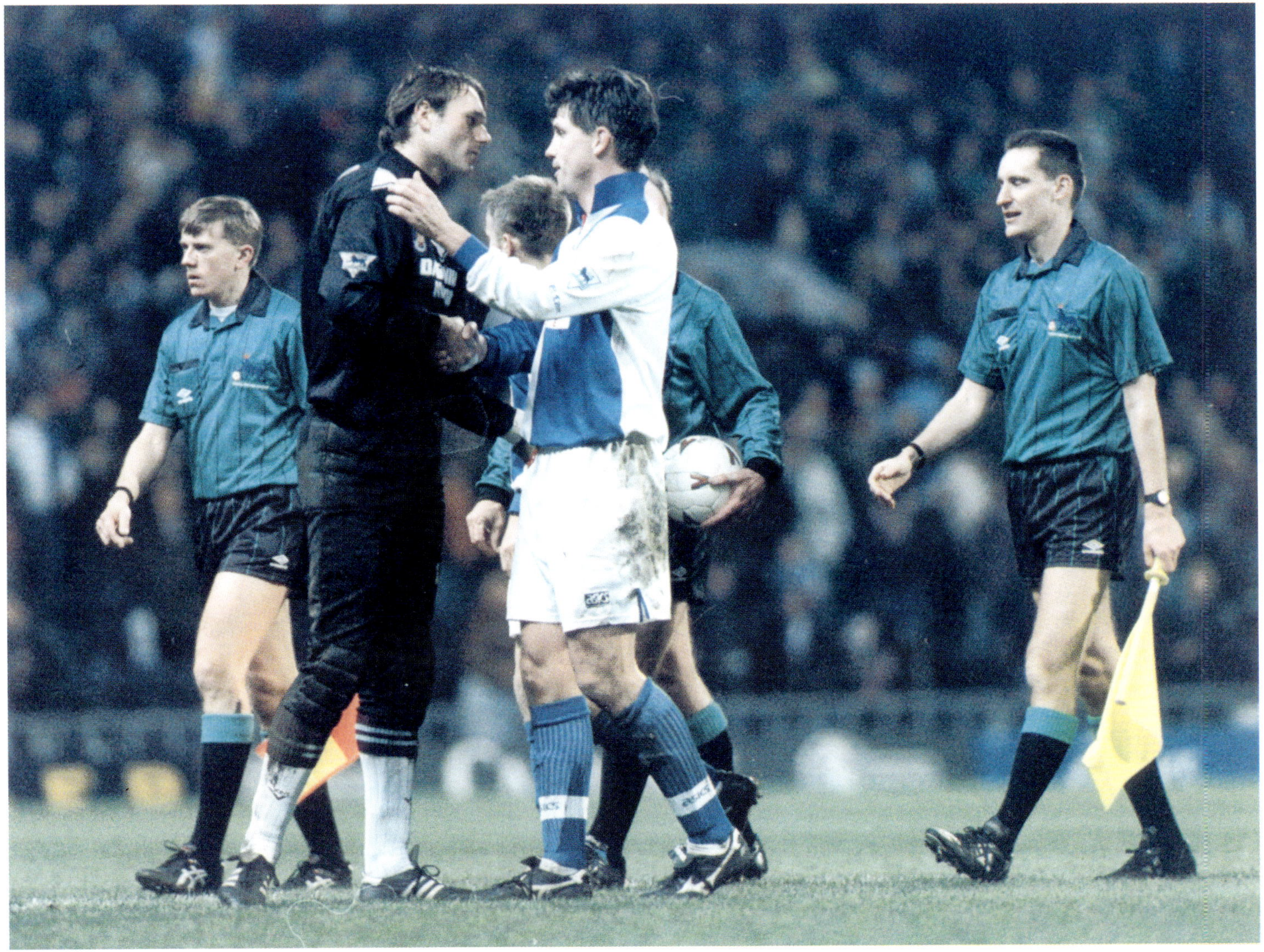

Bad luck mate. Ex-Hammer Tony Gale commiserates with Ludek Miklosko after West Ham had surrendered a 2–1 lead at Blackburn in January 1994. Alan Shearer did the damage with a hat-trick, including two penalties, as the home side won 4–2.

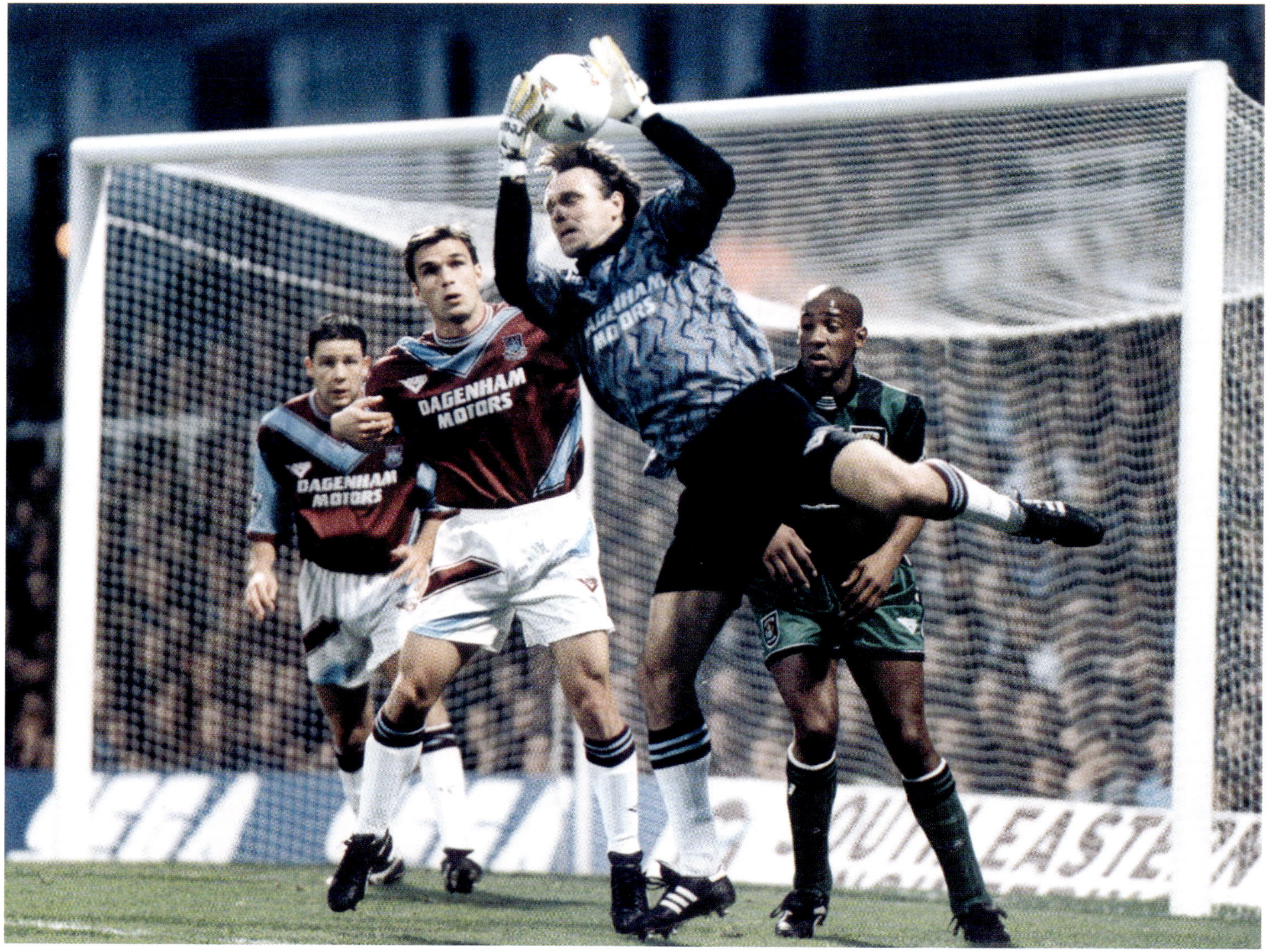

'Keeper's ball. Ludek Miklosko gets a safe pair of hands to the ball as Steve Potts and Dion Dublin look on during a home match against Coventry.

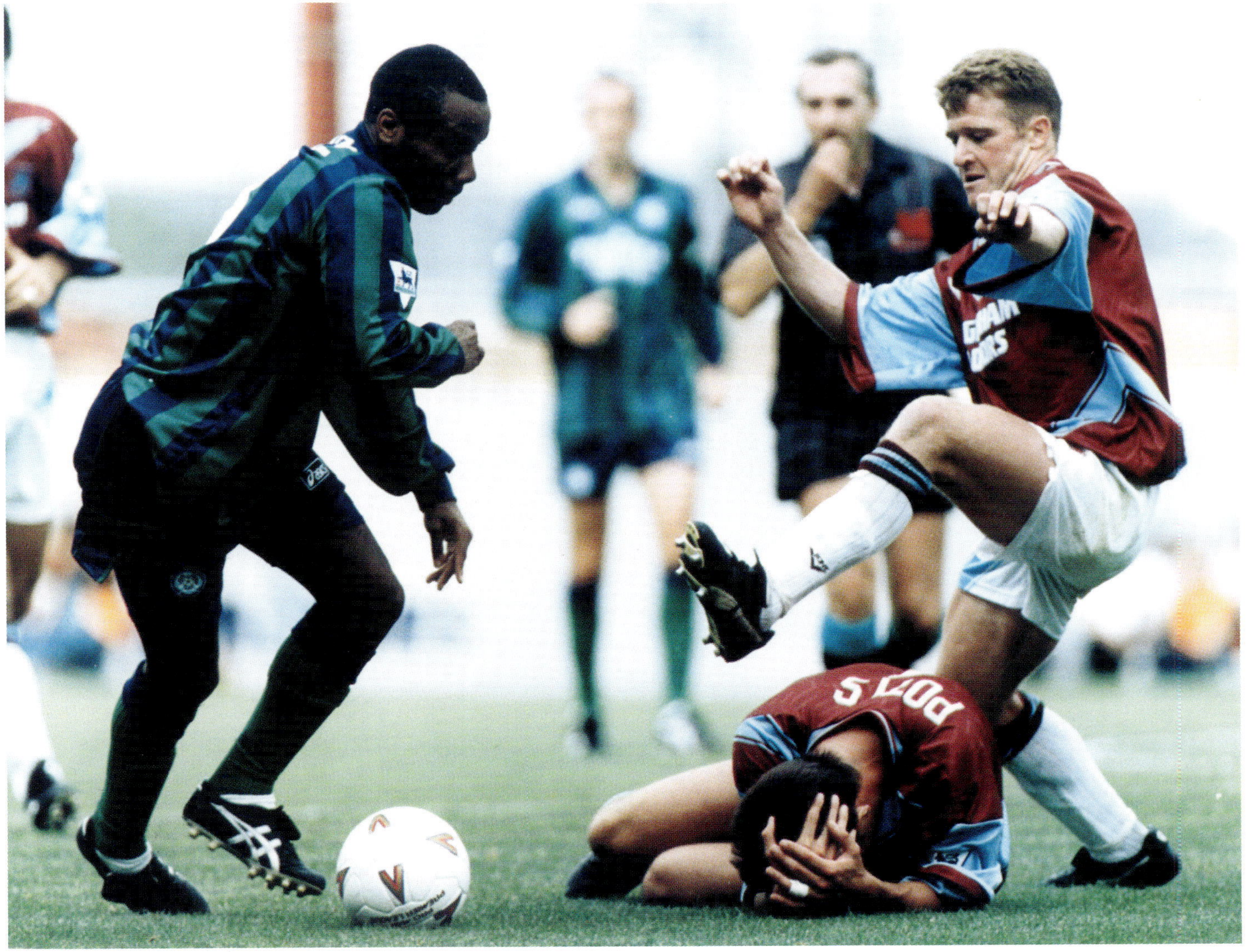

On me 'ead, son. Steve Potts takes evasive action as team-mate Peter Butler comes too close for comfort with his studs.

In the driving seat. Julian Dicks takes the wheel at the launch of the Dagenham Motors sponsorship. Team-mates Alvin Martin, Clive Allen, Tony Gale, Steve Potts and Stuart Slater grab a ride.

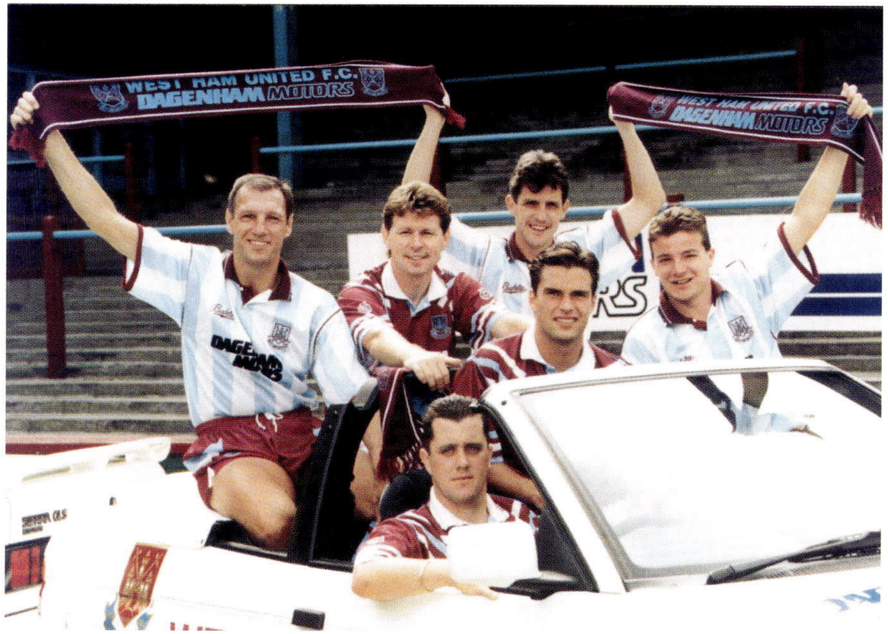

Hamming it up. Geoff Hurst and Martin Peters join Dagenham Motors chairman David Philip in the sponsors' lounge. Geoff jokingly reminds everybody about that famous 4–2 victory at Wembley in 1966.

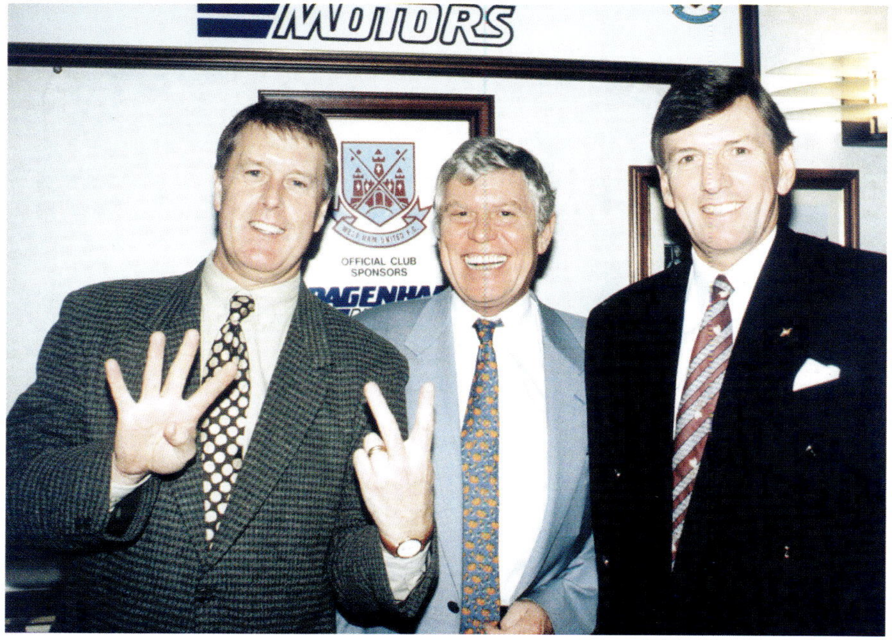

Swift return. John Lyall, sacked by West Ham, makes a quick return to Upton Park as manager of Ipswich Town in September 1990. John, pictured in the dugout making a point to his assistant Mick McGiven, saw his new side lose 3–1.

Crack. Colin Foster suffers a broken nose in this collision with Wimbledon's John Fashanu at Selhurst Park in August 1991. Hammers lost the match 2–0.

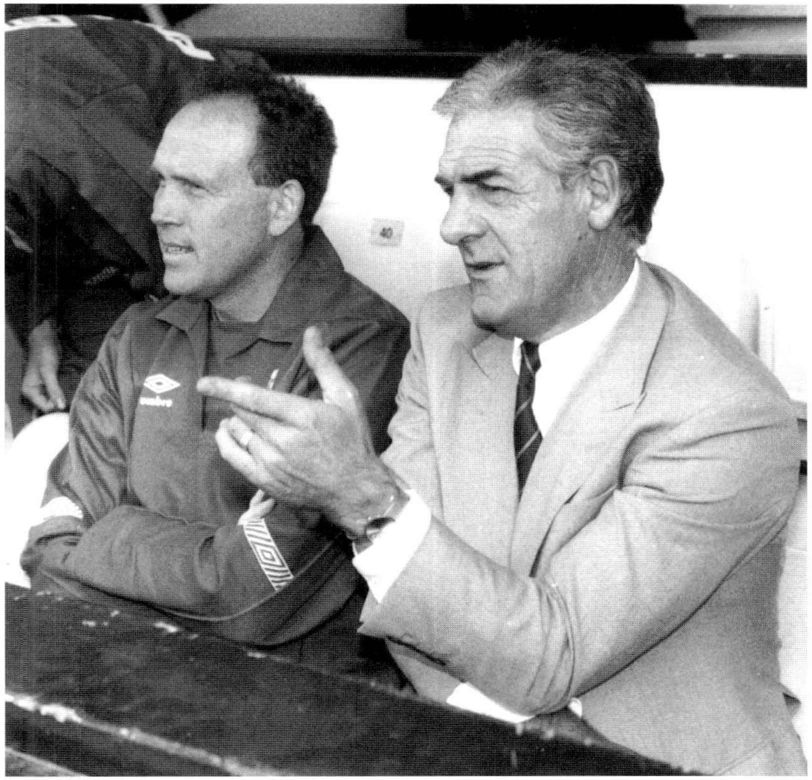

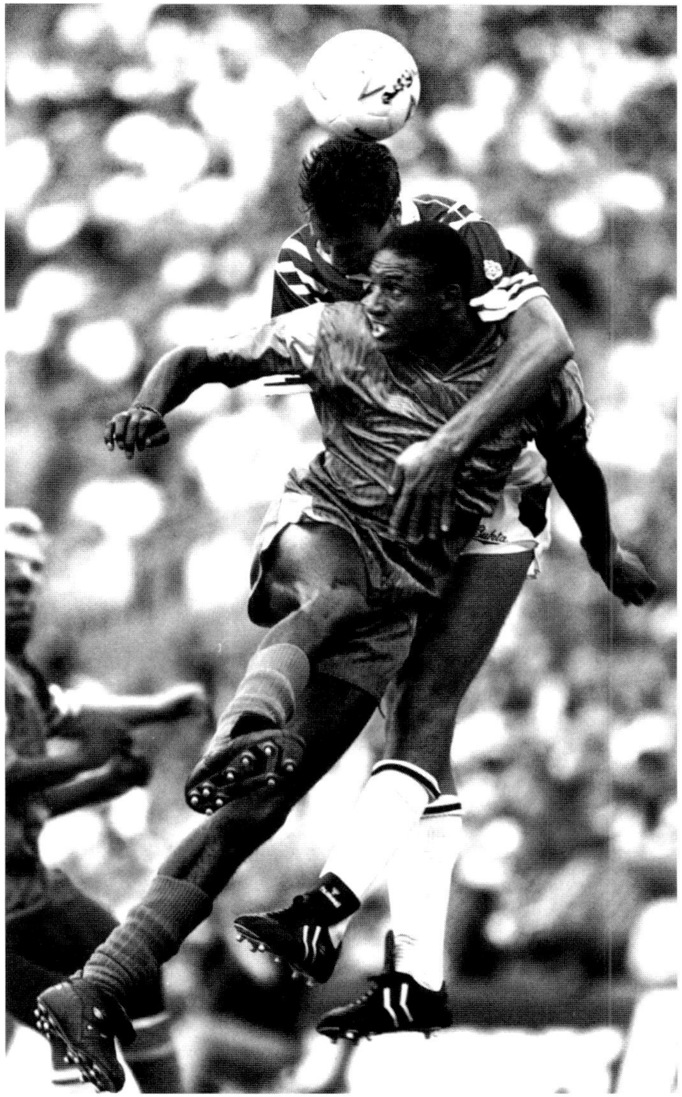

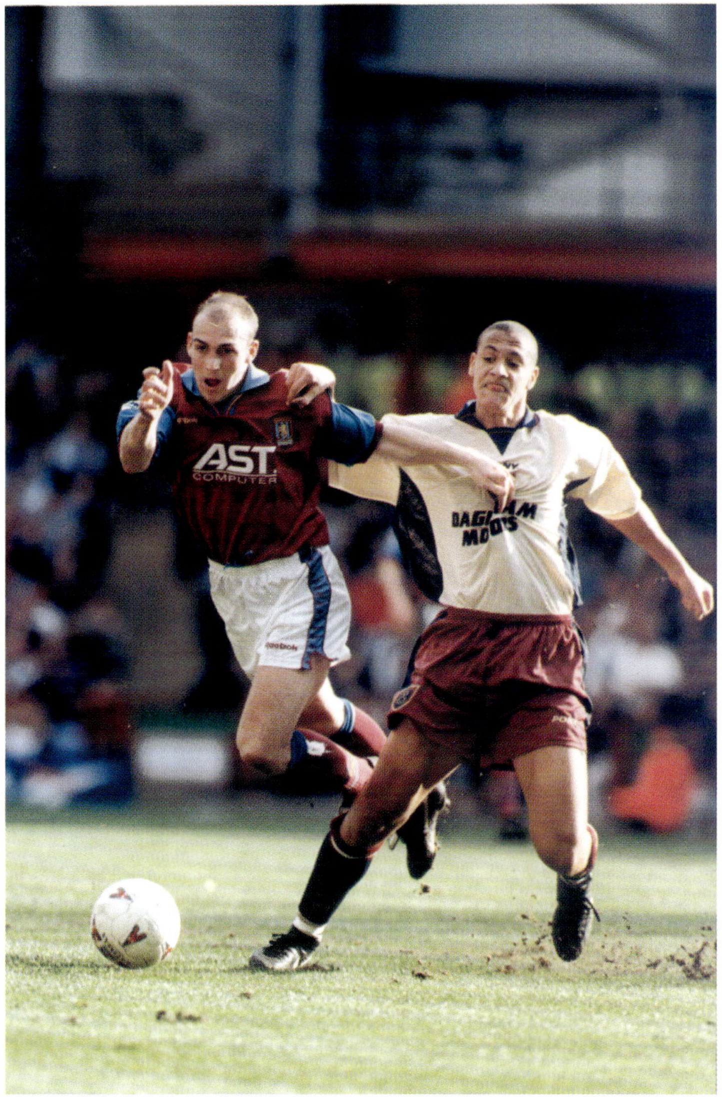

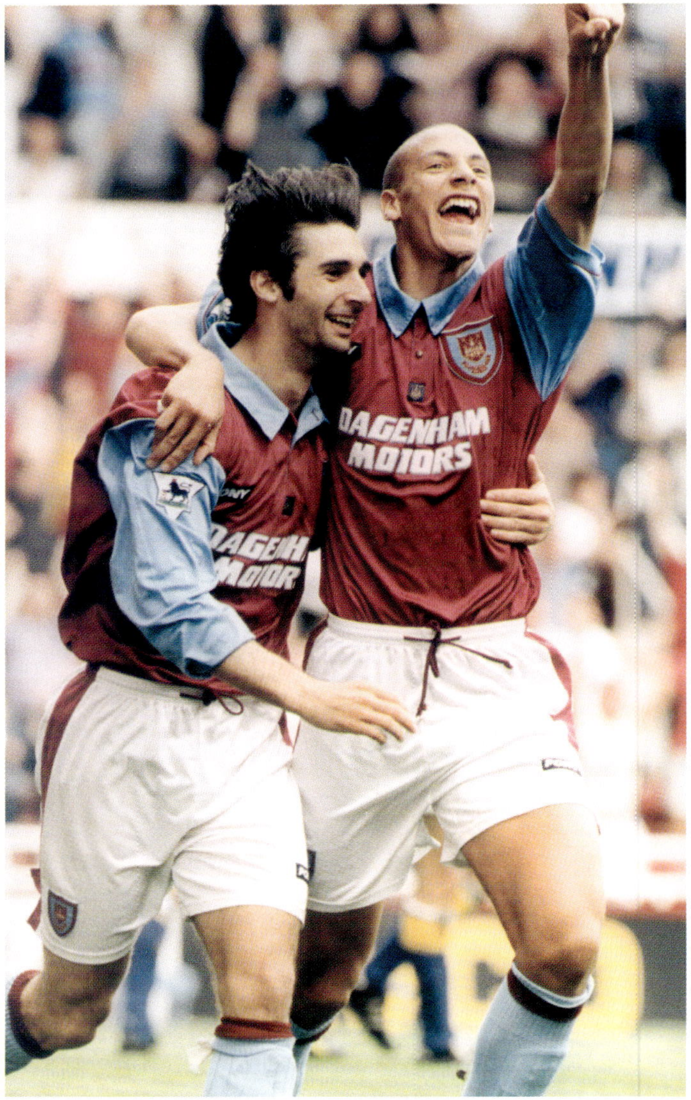

Ecru is the colour. Rio Ferdinand and Mark Draper of Aston Villa tussle in a late-season goalless draw at Villa Park in 1997. Note the ecru-coloured kit which made a rare appearance that day.

Happy Hammers. Rio Ferdinand celebrates with goalscorer Paul Kitson at Upton Park in a 5–1 win over Sheffield Wednesday in May 1997.

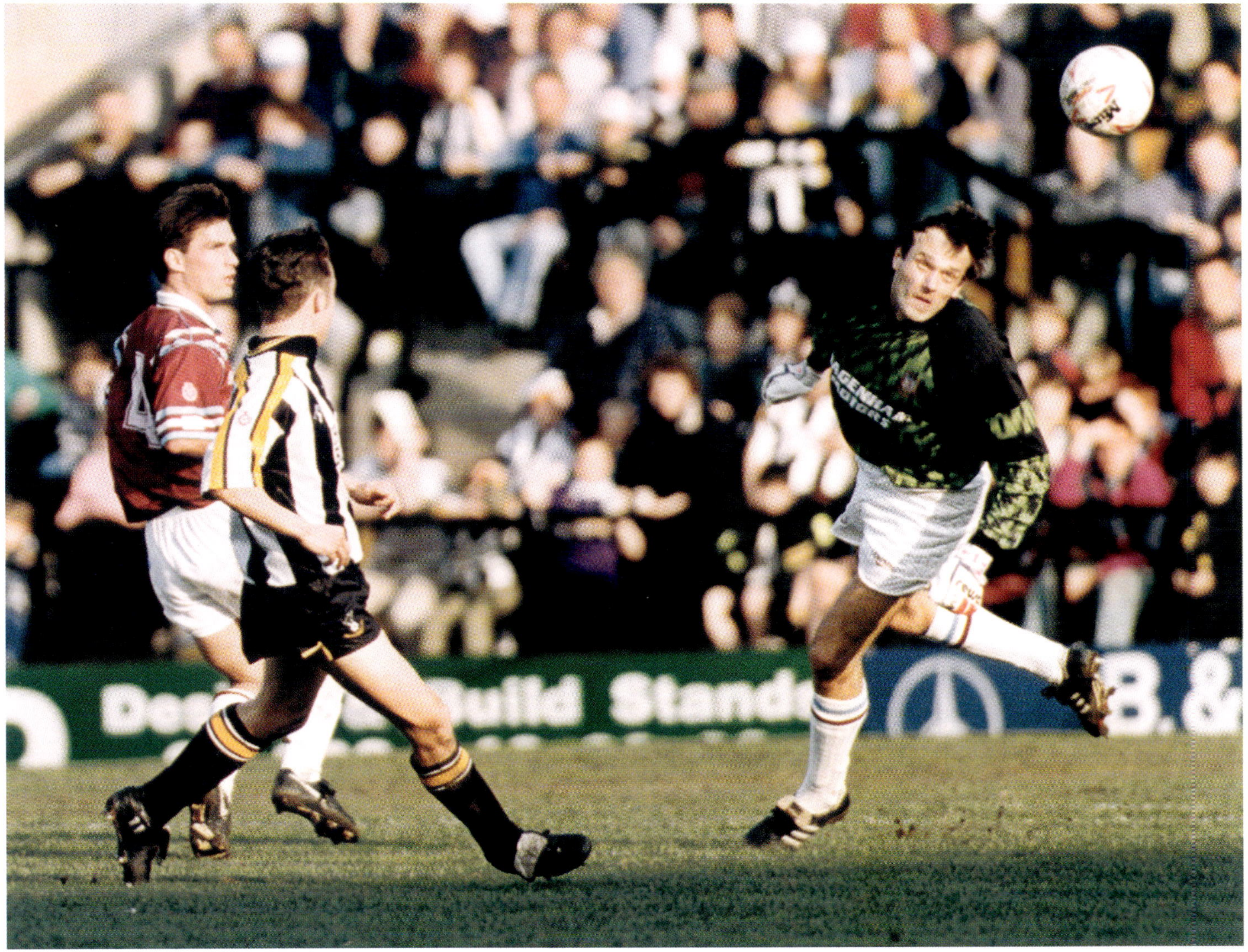

Look mum, no hands. Goalkeeper Ludek Miklosko turns defender as he comes out of his area to head the ball clear, with Steve Potts and a Notts County forward closing in.

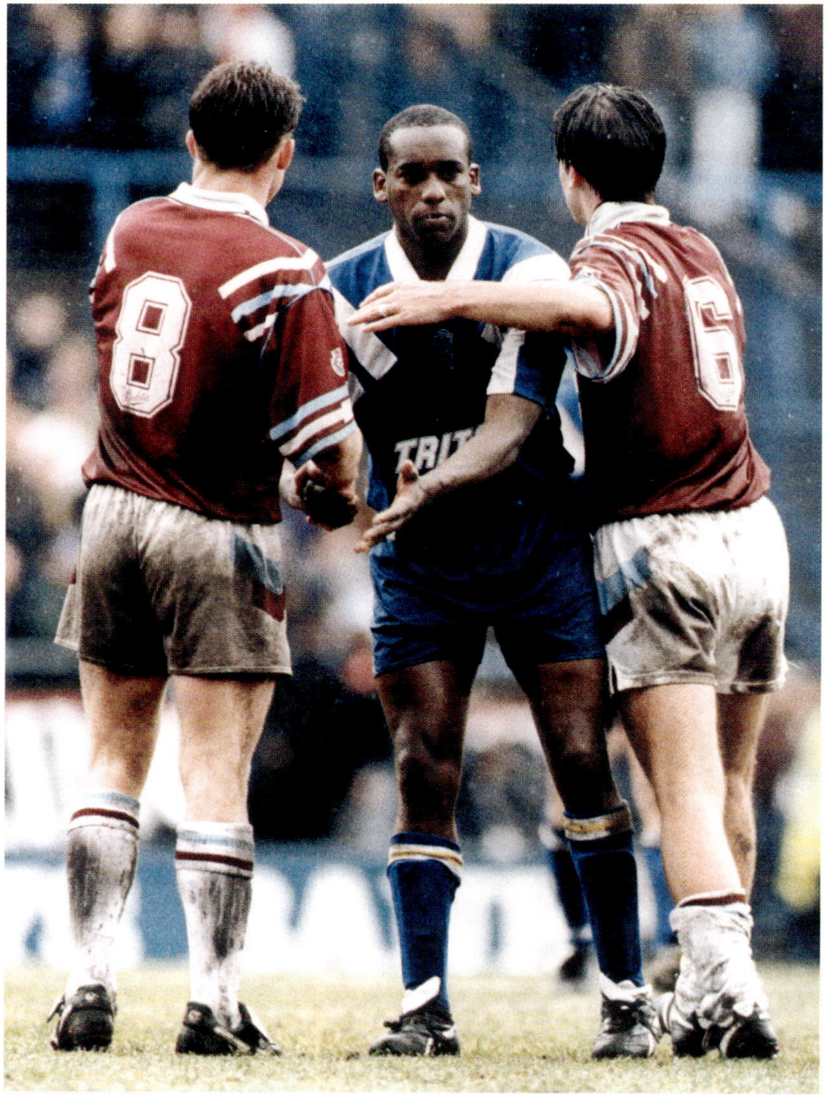

Late-late show. Ex-Hammer George Parris shows his disappointment as Peter Butler and Ian Bishop console him at the end of a rain-soaked match at Birmingham City in April 1993. West Ham snatched a 2–1 victory with two late goals to keep their push for promotion on course when all had seemed lost.

Fancy that. Party time for the players as they don fancy dress for their Christmas bash.

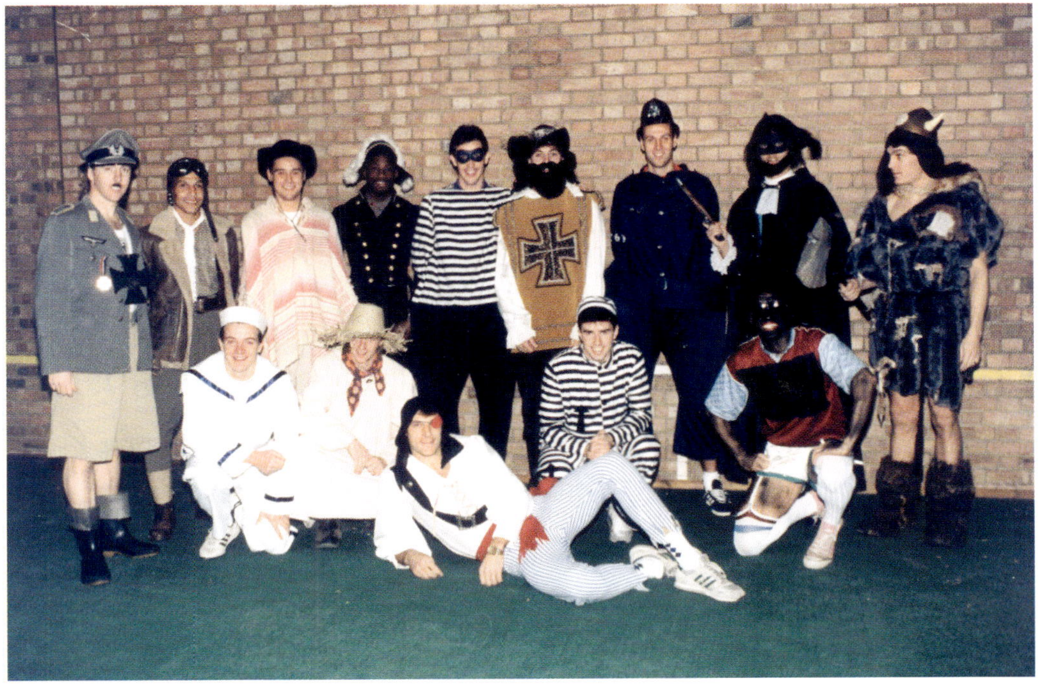

Like your style. Good mates George Parris and Steve Potts dress up as a pirate and a Teddy Boy respectively and set off for the players' Christmas party.

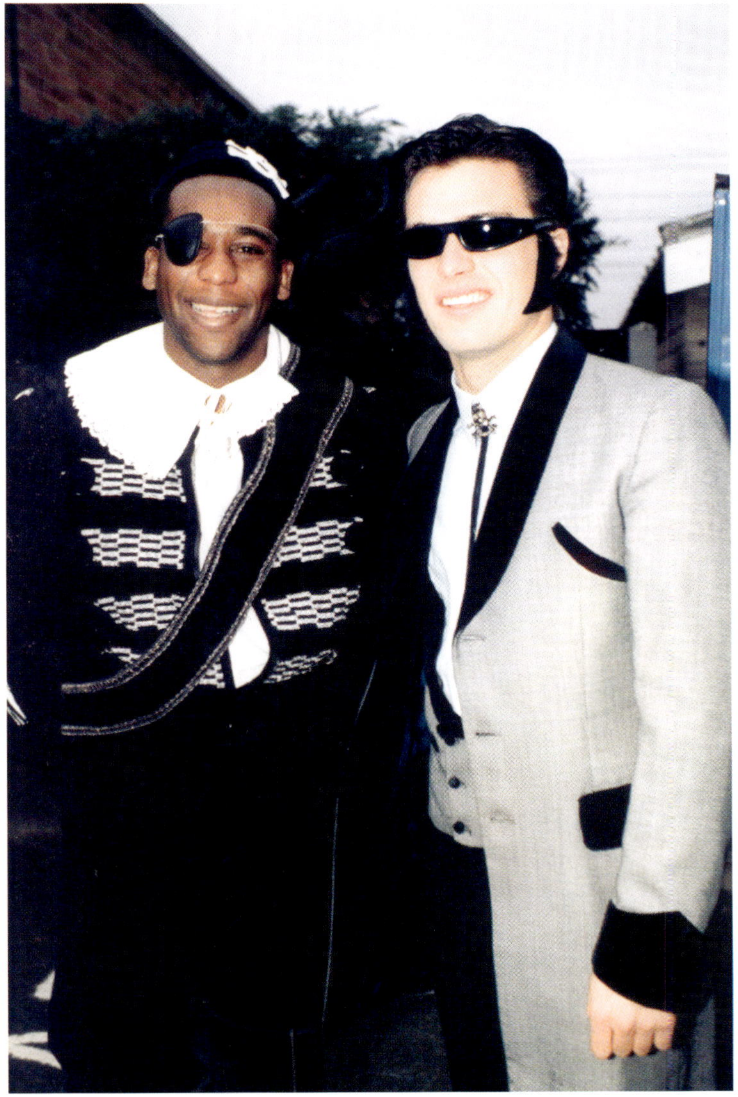

Funny, that. Alvin Martin and Pat Holland can obviously see the lighter side of Billy Bonds's autobiography at the Upton Park book launch.

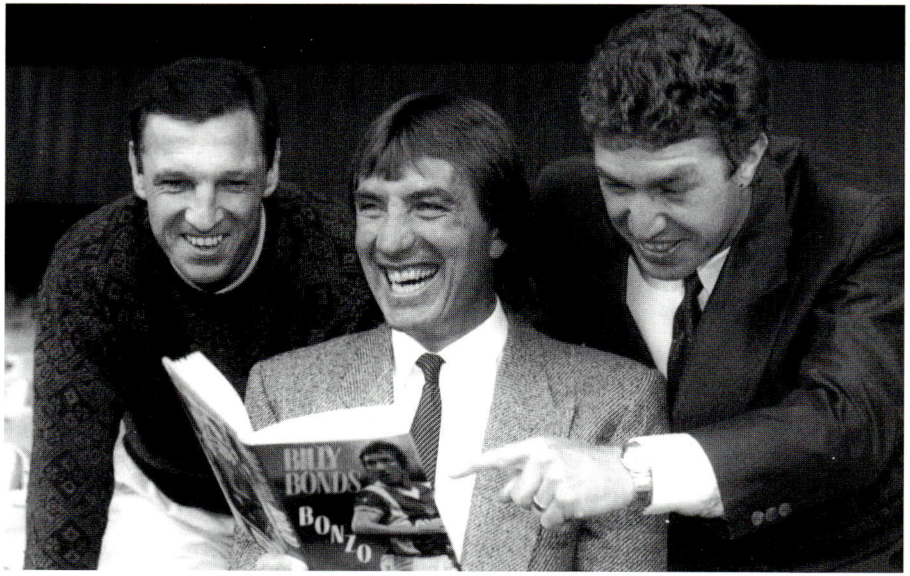

Listen. Manager Harry Redknapp makes his point from the dugout.

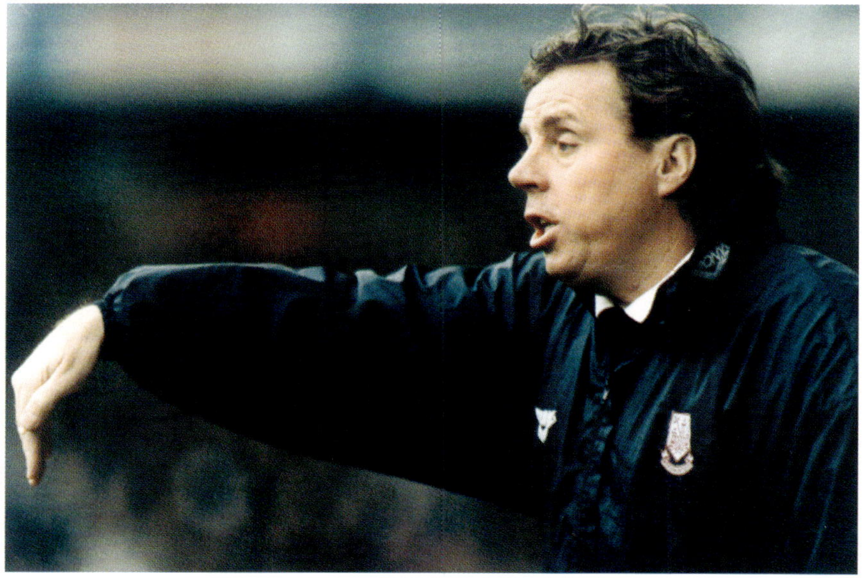

Green stuff. There's grass under there somewhere: the Upton park pitch disappears under a sea of bodies following Hammers' promotion-winning 2–0 victory over Cambridge United in May 1993.

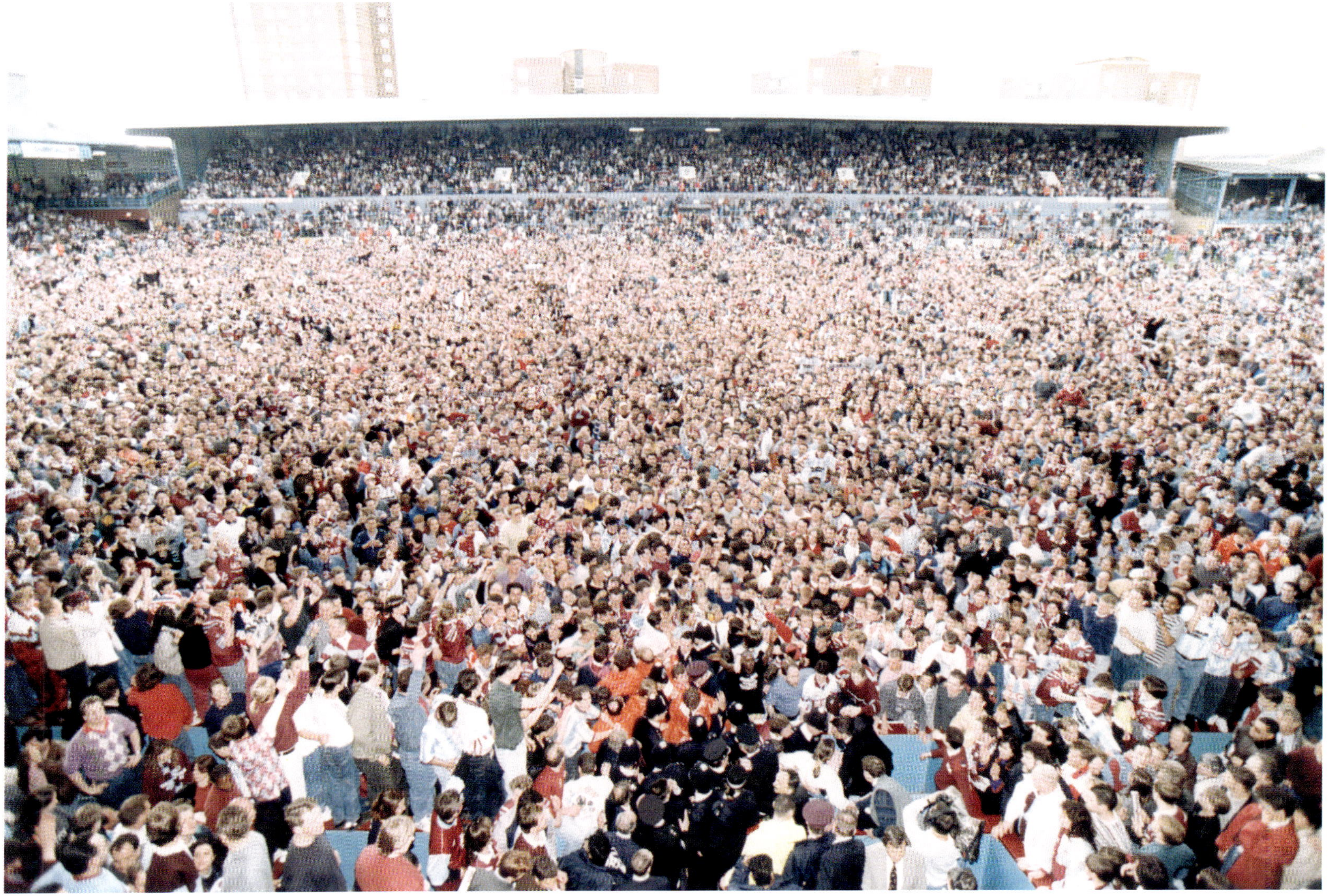

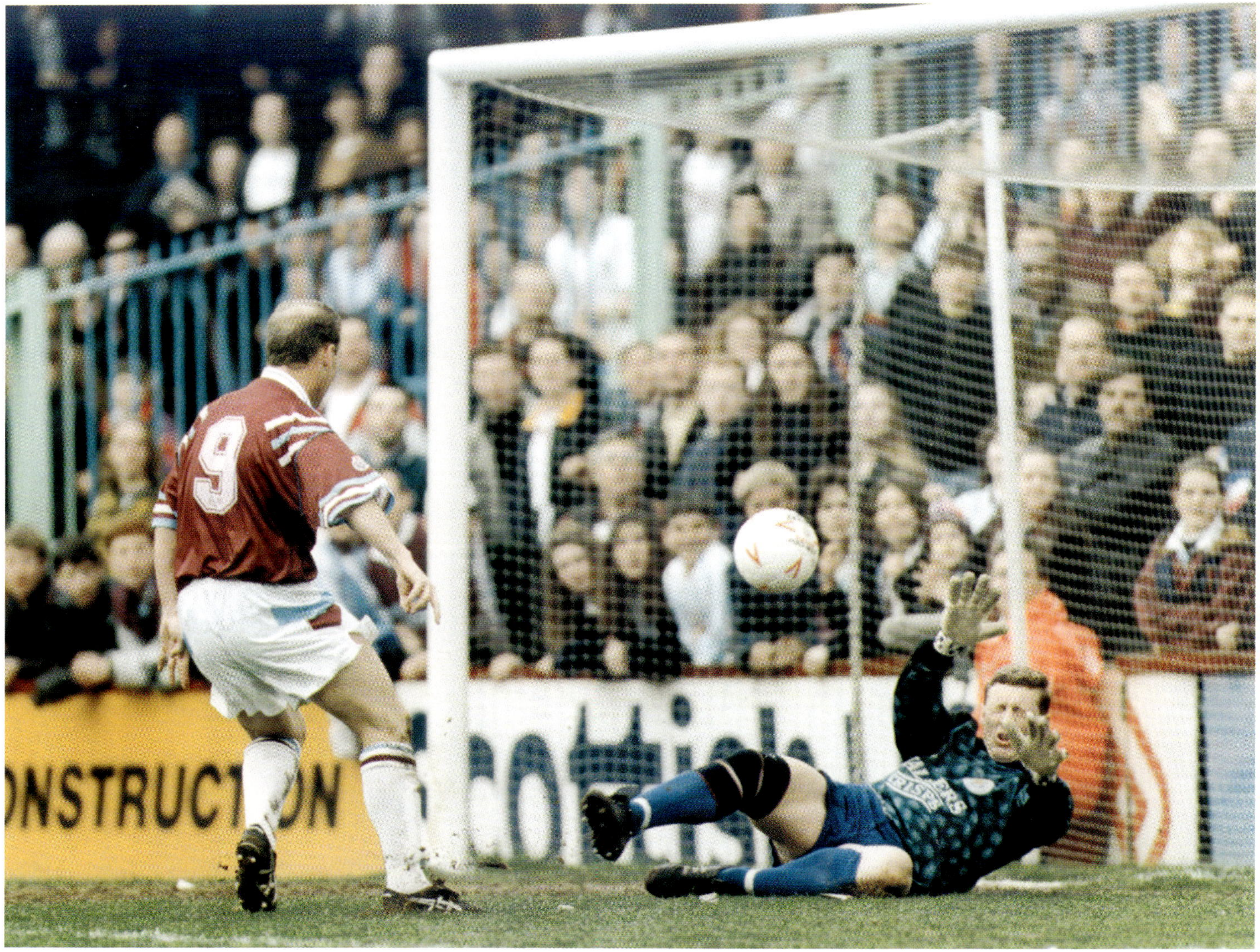

Sunday service. On-loan David Speedie scores in the 3–0 win over Leicester City as Hammers go for promotion in April 1993. David scored twice in this televised Sunday game but still failed to win over the Hammers' fans.

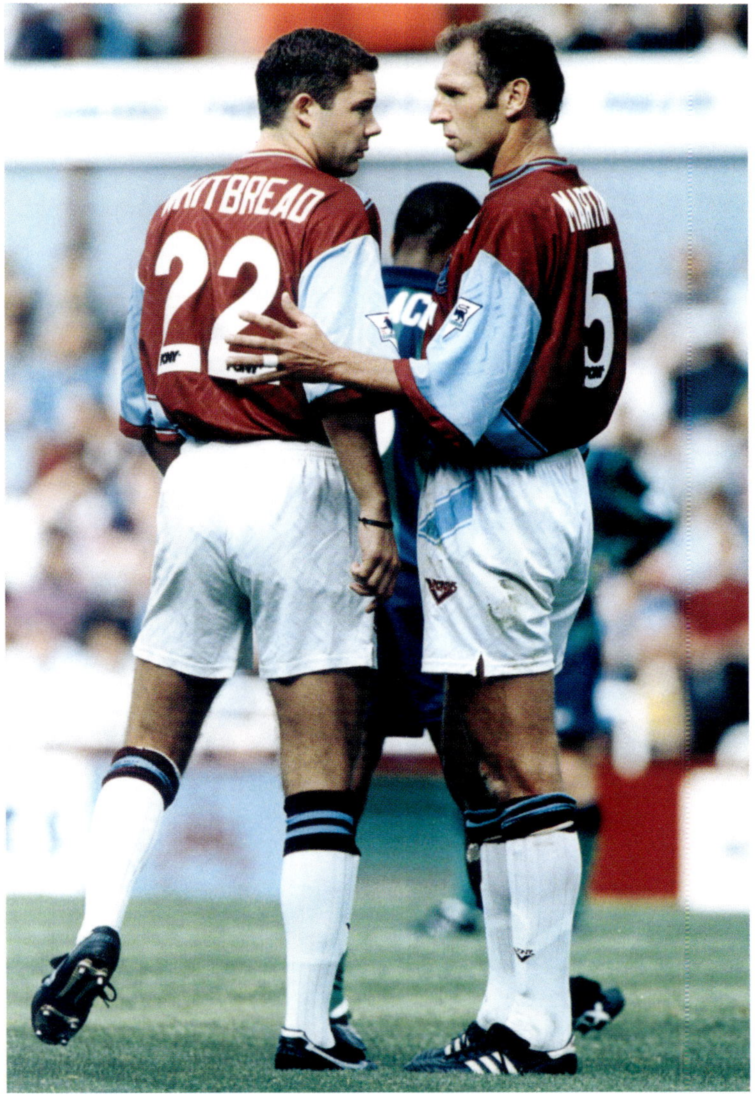

Words of wisdom. You're about to make your debut for your new club as a 70th-minute substitute against Leeds United: could Adrian Whitbread have anyone better to offer advice than Alvin Martin in this 1994 goalless draw at Upton Park?

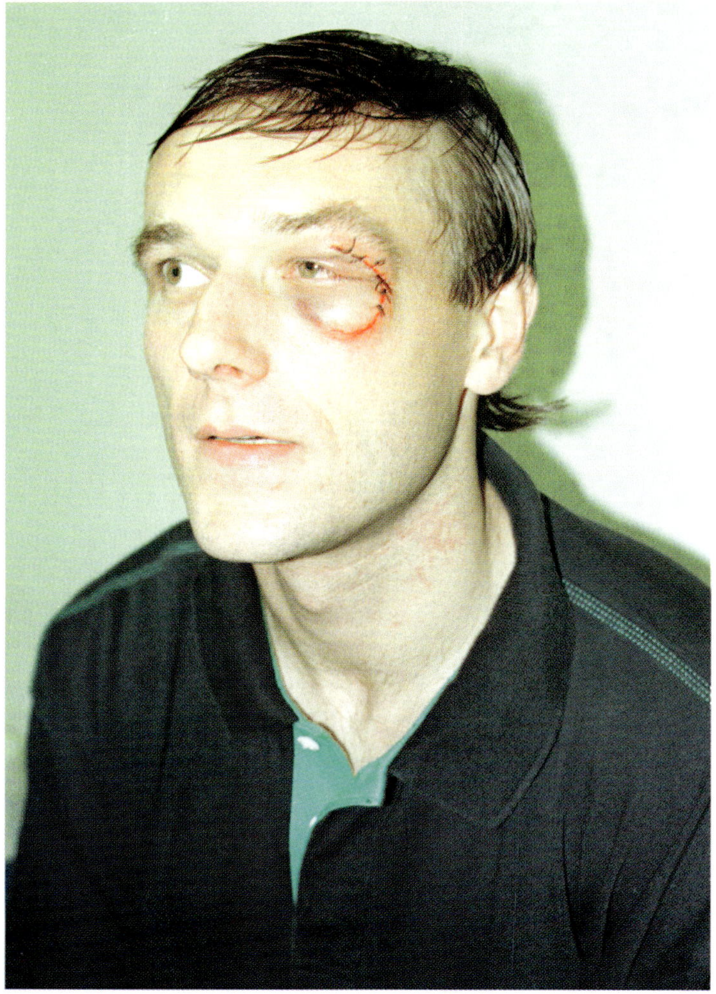

One in the eye. Ludek Miklosko was battered black and blue at Elland Road in 1994 and Hammers trailed 2–0 at half-time. The Czech 'keeper had a dreadful eye wound stitched during the interval and played the second half in which Jeroen Boere scored a brace to level the scores. After the match Harry Redknapp asked me to get a shot of Ludo's injury which, after much persuasion, he allowed me to do.

Ooh, that hurts. Alvin Martin winces as physio John Green takes a look at his sore ankle in the treatment room.

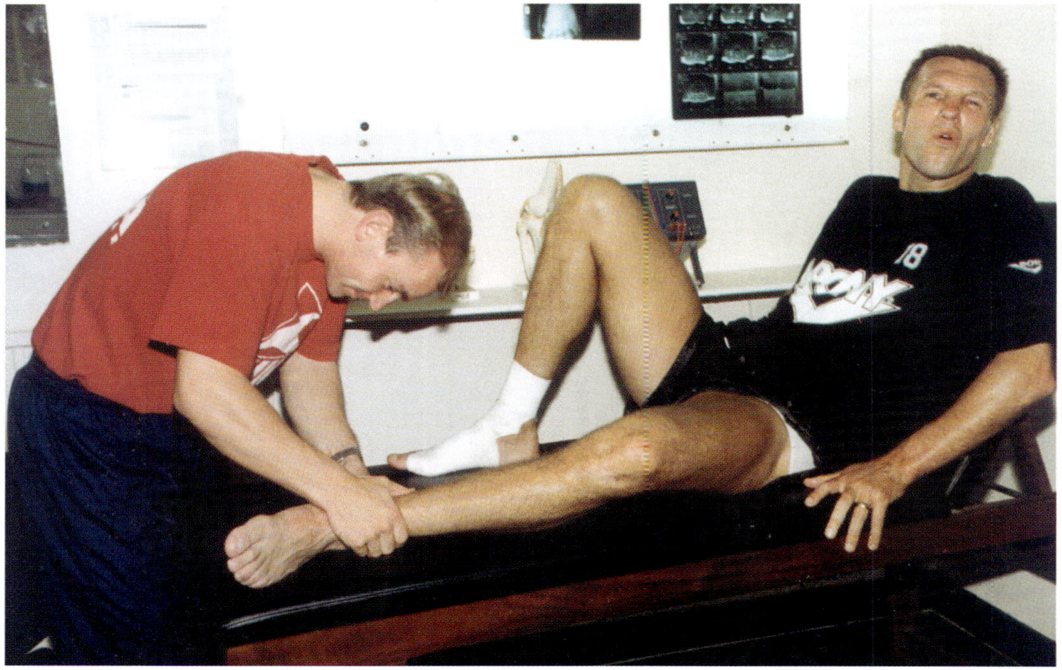

Boxing clever. World Heavyweight Boxing Champion Lennox Lewis puts Trevor Morley, Steve Jones, Tony Gale and Matty Holmes through their paces on a visit to the Chadwell Heath training ground.

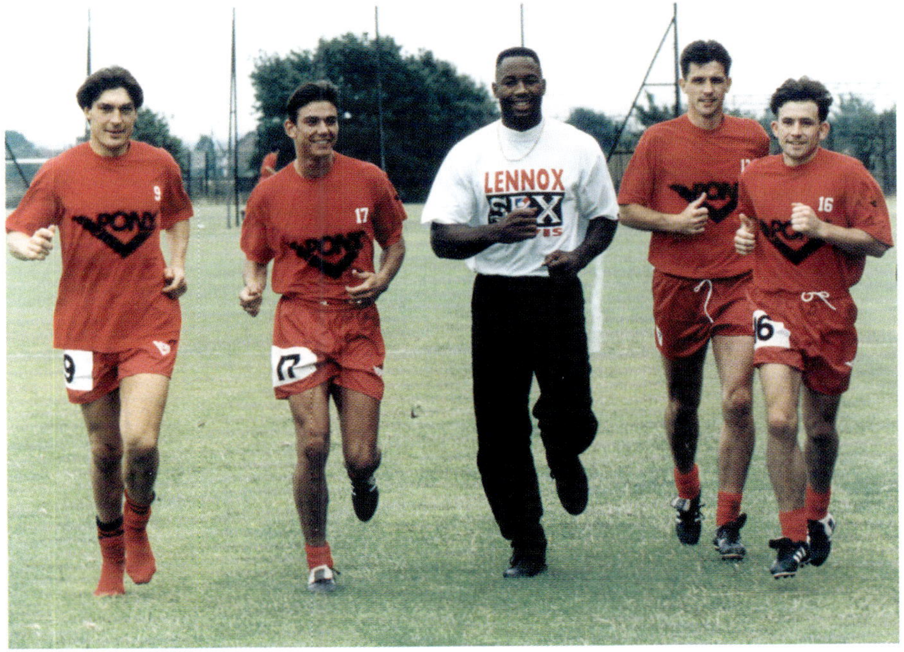

Feet of strength. Herbie the Hammer and Ronald McDonald insisted on having a kick-about when I had finished a photo shoot at the training ground. Sensibly, the players let them get on with it. Have you seen the size of those boots?!

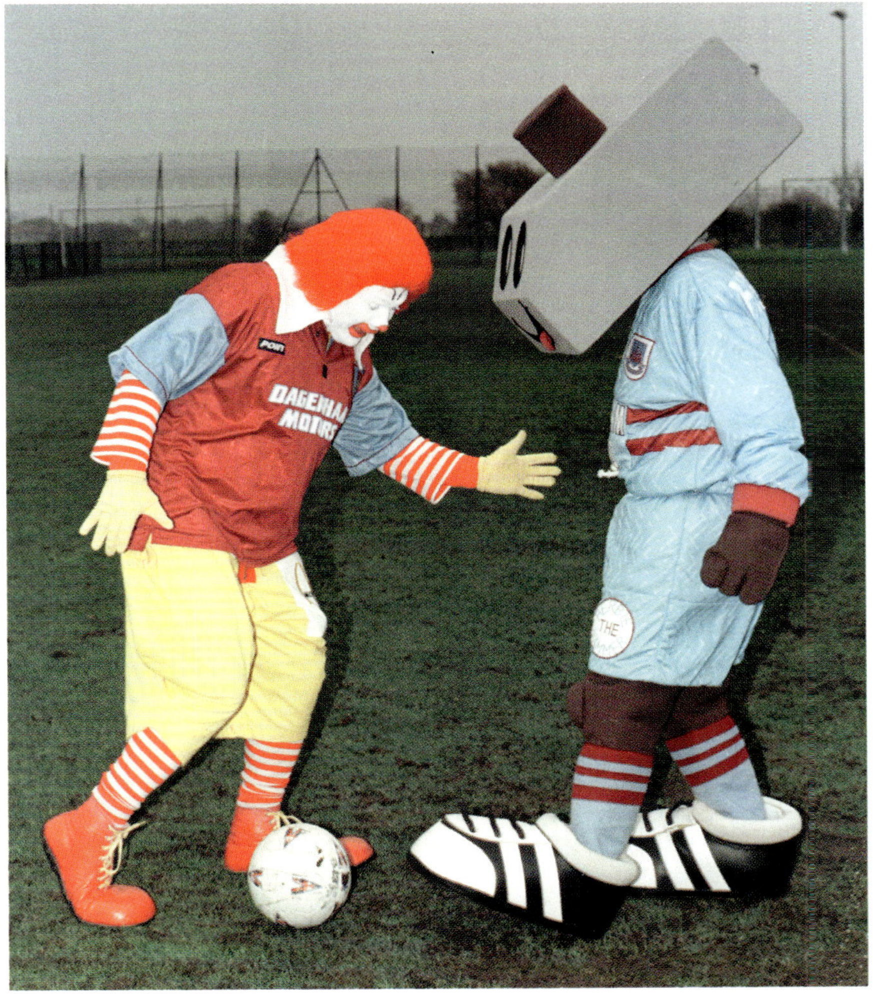

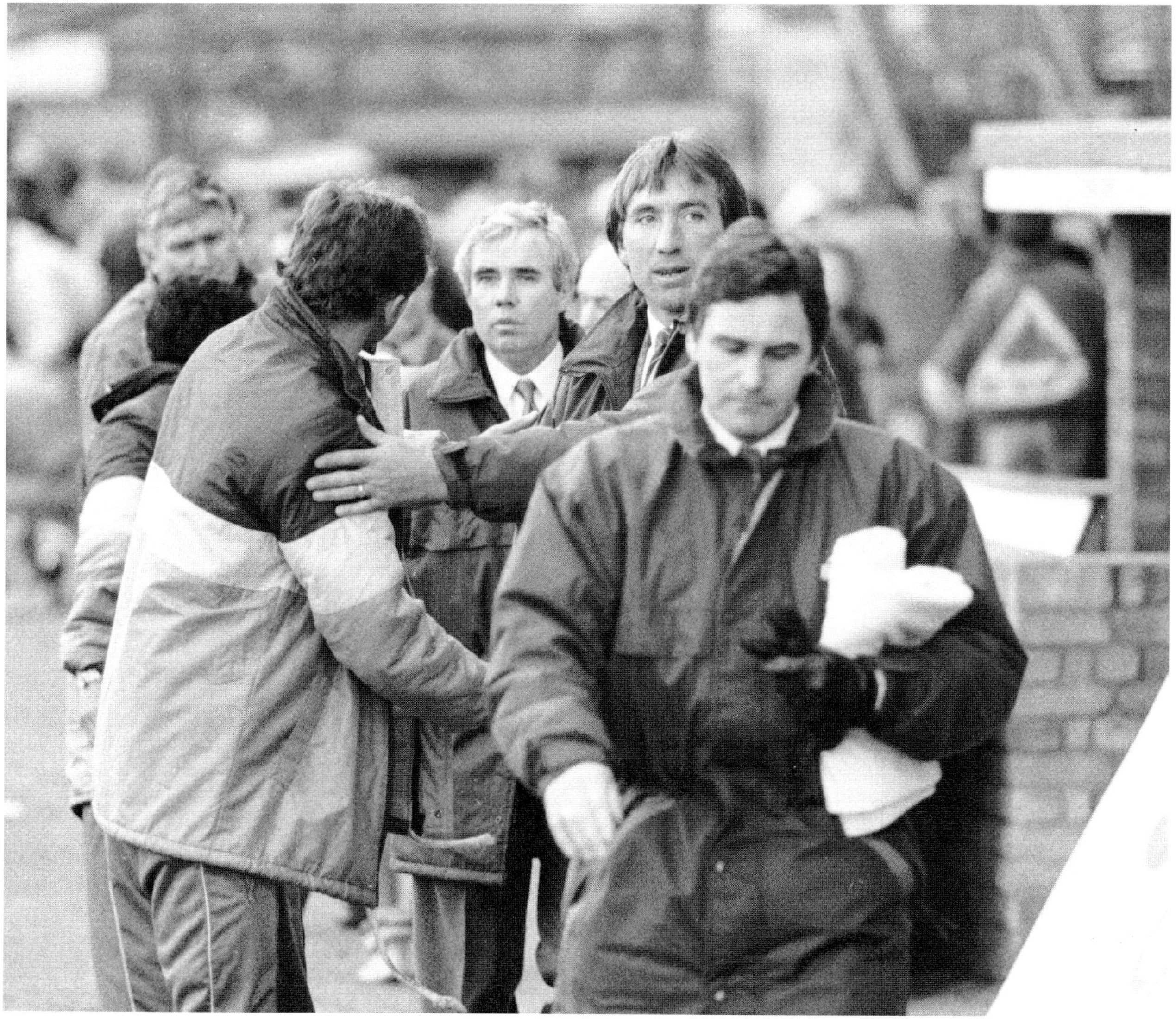

I'm in charge. Billy Bonds leaves the Swindon pitch after Hammers' 2–2 draw in February 1990. Bonzo had been called in to take charge a couple of hours before kick-off when it became clear that Lou Macari was not going to turn up to face his old club. Lou, facing an FA charge concerning his time at Swindon, resigned shortly afterwards and Bonds was installed as the new manager in time for the following match.

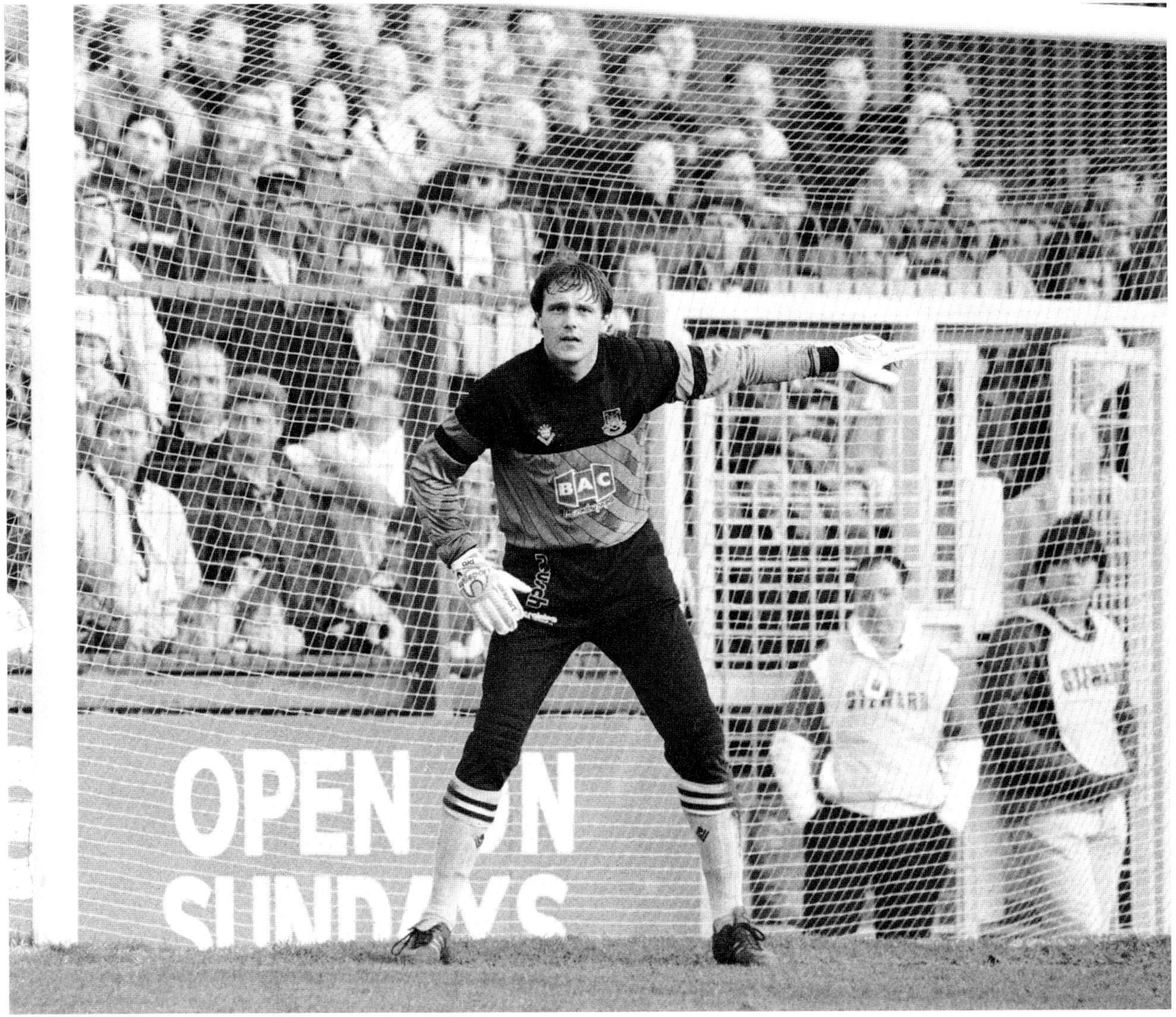

Where's the boss? Ludek Miklosko makes his debut for the Hammers in the now infamous Sunday match at Swindon Town when Lou Macari went AWOL *shortly before resigning as manager. Lou had signed Ludo from Banik Ostrava for £300,000 a few days earlier and the giant Czech 'keeper had a competent start, although he was beaten twice in a 2–2 draw.*

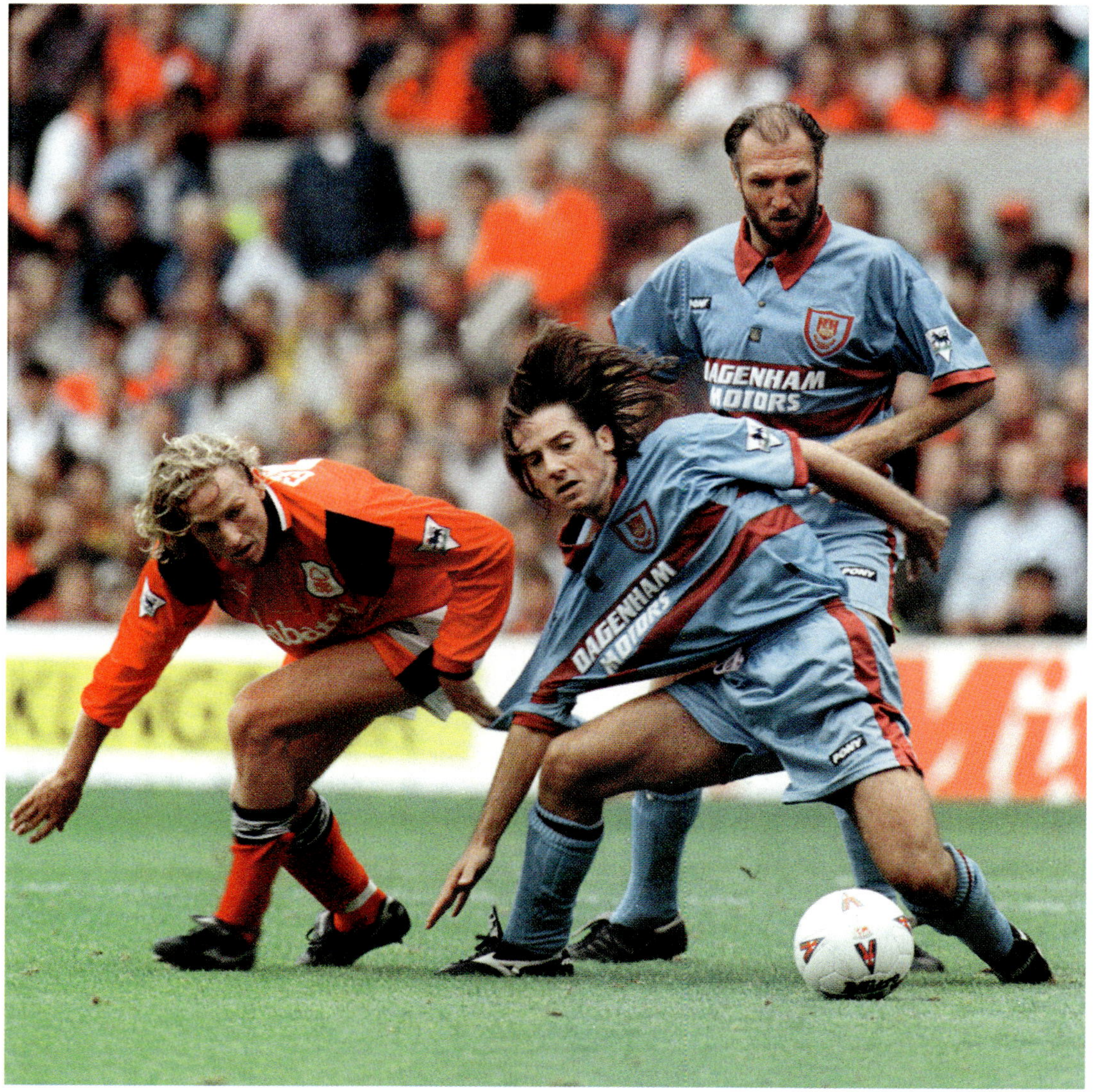

I've pulled. Ian Bishop got a tug from Scott Gemmill when West Ham visited Nottingham Forest in their second away fixture of the 1995–96 season. Martin Allen put Hammers into a 14th-minute lead but Don Hutchison gave away a penalty which Stuart Pearce converted to share the points.

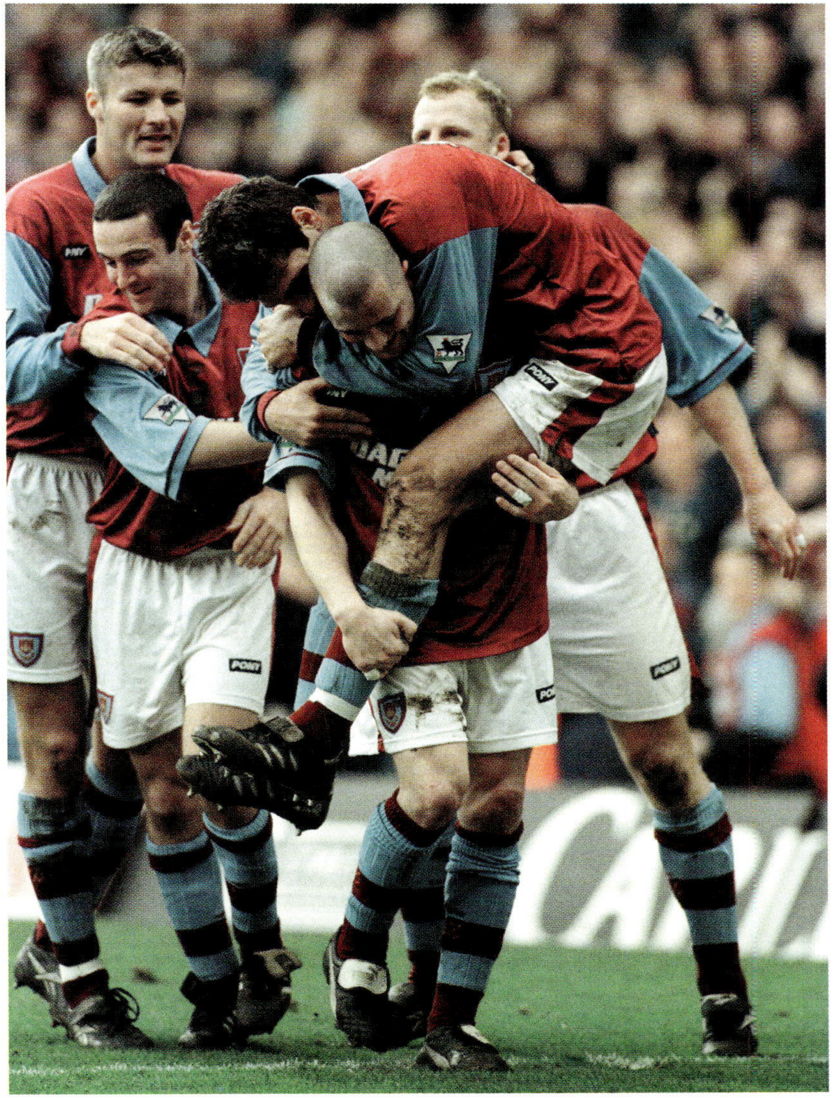

Bad day at the office. Julian Dicks celebrates his 83rd-minute goal as Hammers crush Manchester City 4–2 at Upton Park in March 1996. It was a bad day for City as Miklosko saved Keith Curle's spot-kick and Steve Lomas, destined to join and captain the Hammers, was sent off for two bookable offences. City were relegated at the end of the season!

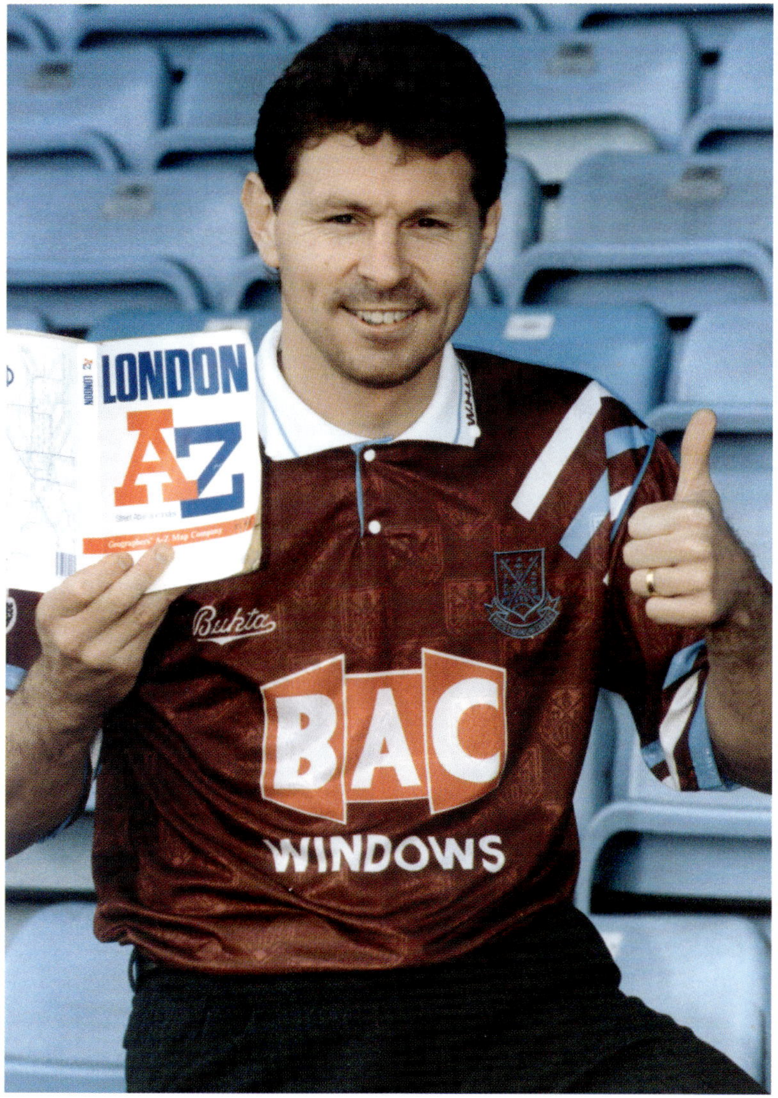

Capital. When Clive Allen signed for West Ham from Chelsea in March 1992 they became his sixth London club. My old A–Z finally came in useful.

What do you think of it so far? Harry Redknapp's face shows exactly what. This picture, taken in Germany when we played a pre-season game against TSV Munich in 1995, is not one of H's favourites — obviously. I hope he will forgive me for using it just one more time.

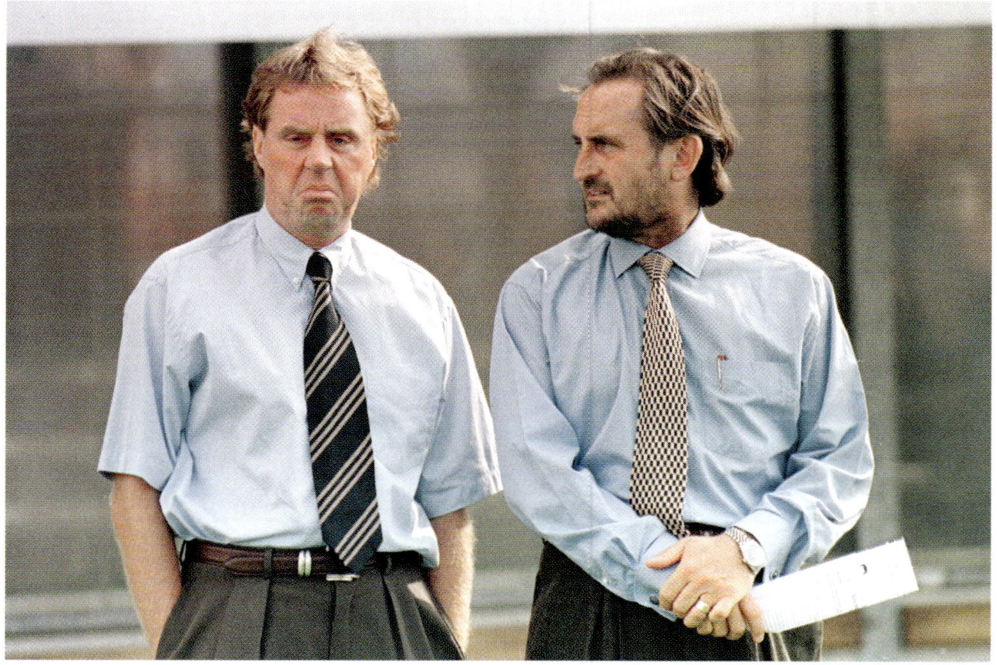

No prisoners. Julian Dicks gets in a typical challenge on Manchester City's German striker Uwe Rosler in the 4–2 win at Upton Park in March 1996.

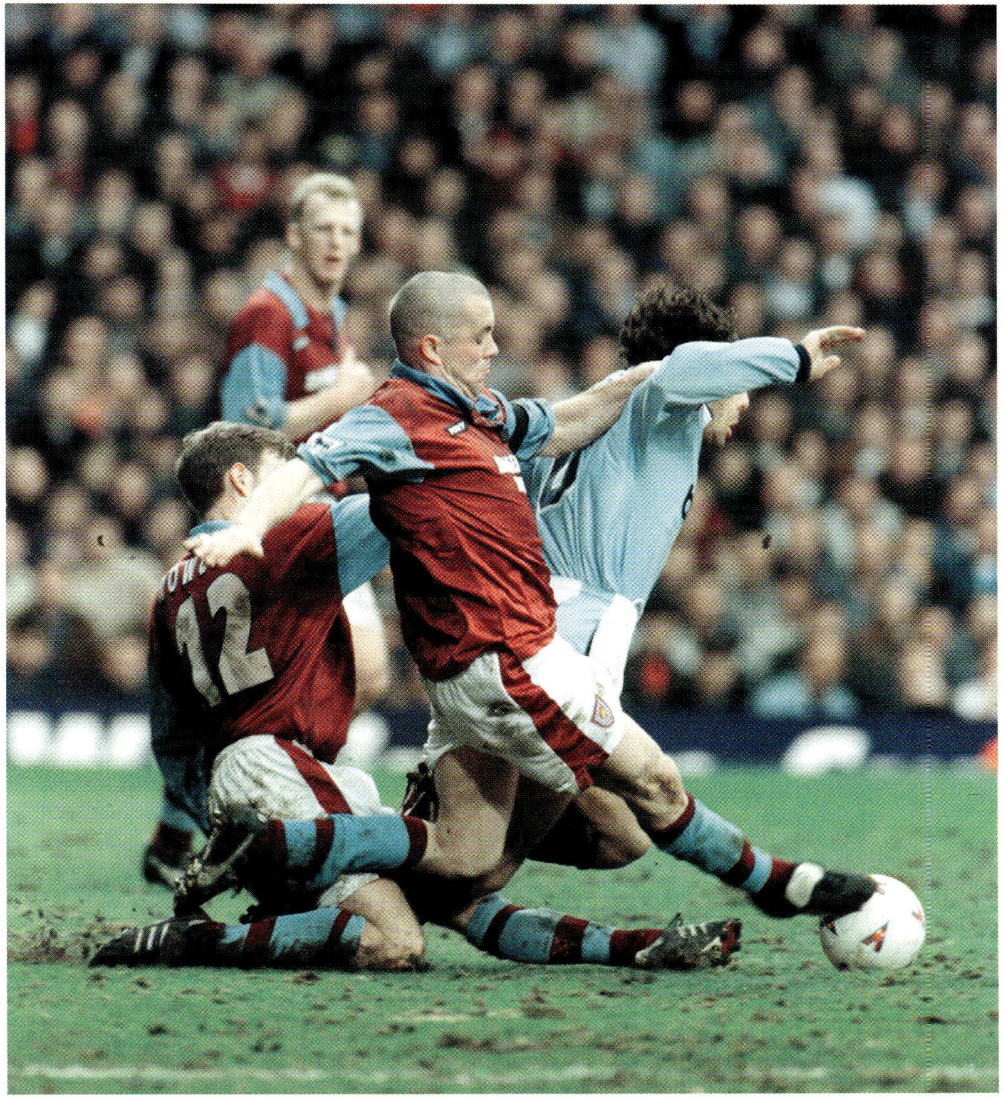

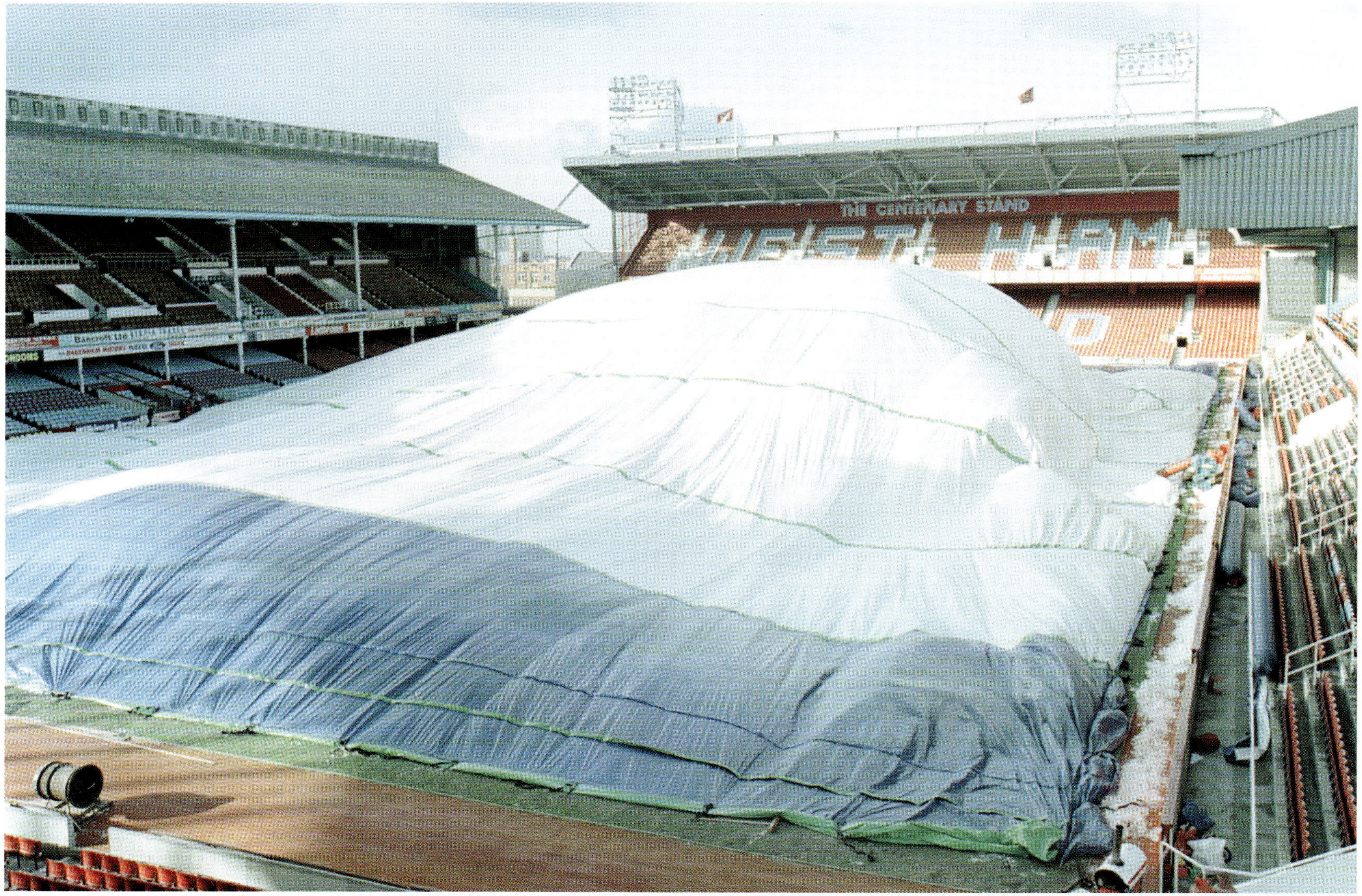
THE CENTENARY STAND
WEST HAM
Bancroft Ltd
DAGENHAM MOTORS IVECO

The balloon goes up. A pretty spectacular shot of the giant hot air balloon which covered the entire Upton Park pitch to keep the frost at bay. This has now been made redundant by the revolutionary new under-soil heating and drainage system installed during the close season of 1998.

When Harry met Dani. I'm always telling Harry Redknapp not to be photographed next to those good-looking young footballers. Never was this advice more apt than with Portuguese heart-throb Dani. You'll never learn, H!

Oh bother! Les Sealey kicks out at the post in frustration as West Ham go down 3–0 at Newcastle in a Monday-night Sky TV match in March 1996. Les finally got his chance to keep goal for his beloved Hammers when Ludek Miklosko cried off through injury. It was not Les's first appearance in the first team, however, as he was called upon as an outfield sub at Highbury earlier in the same season!

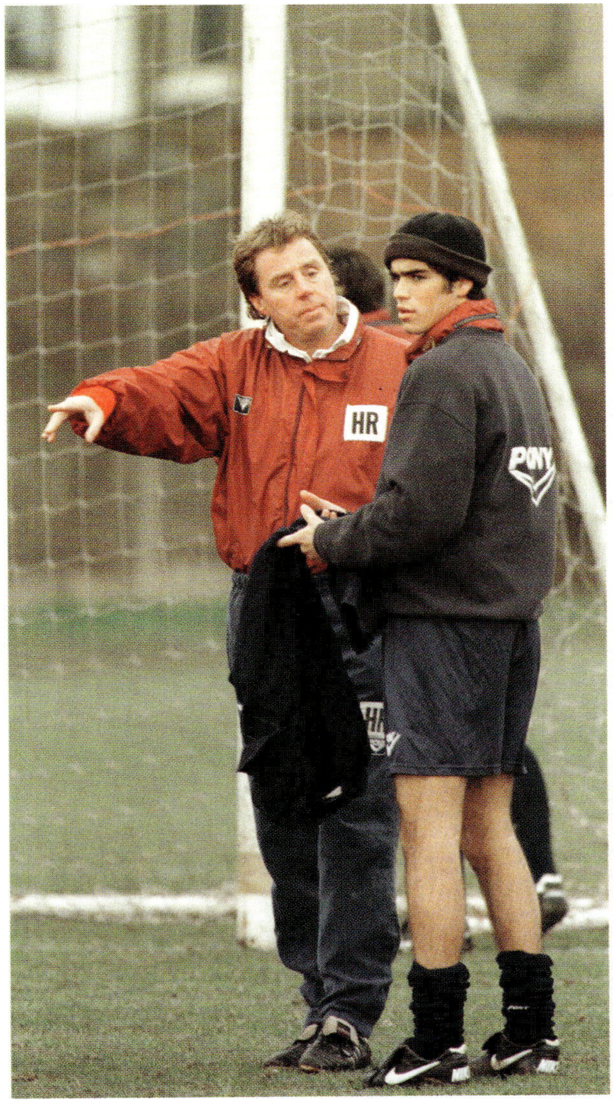

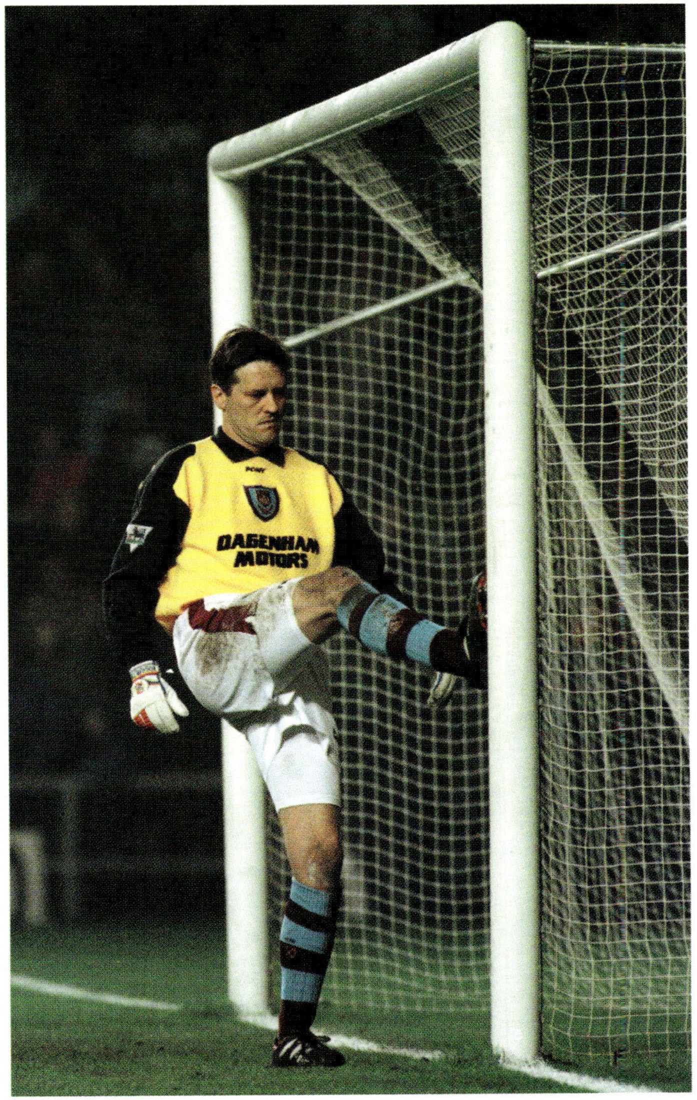

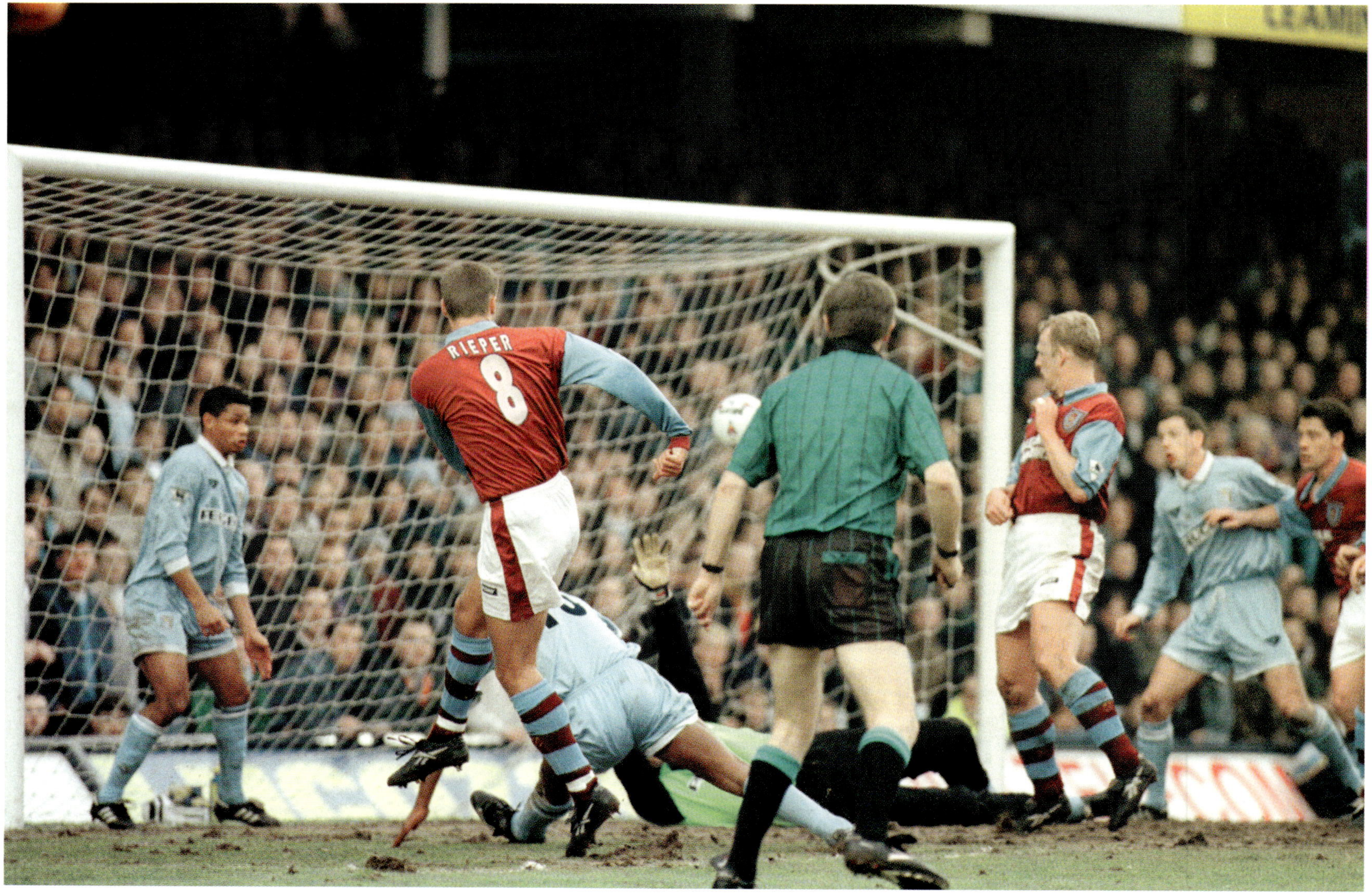
RIEPER
8

If it's Coventry, then it must be a Marc Rieper goal. Well, that might be a bit of an exaggeration, but Hammers' Great Dane did seem to have a penchant for scoring against the Sky Blues. This goal at Highfield Road in a March 1996 draw followed his goal earlier in the season when Hammers beat Coventry 3–2 at Upton Park. The following season Rieps again scored in both matches with Coventry, including an own goal in the away game!

Whoa there. Aussie Robbie Slater hangs on to Sasa Curcic's shirt in an effort to stop the Bolton midfielder's progress. Although Wanderers had made a late run to avoid relegation, this 1–0 defeat at Upton Park virtually condemned them to the drop.

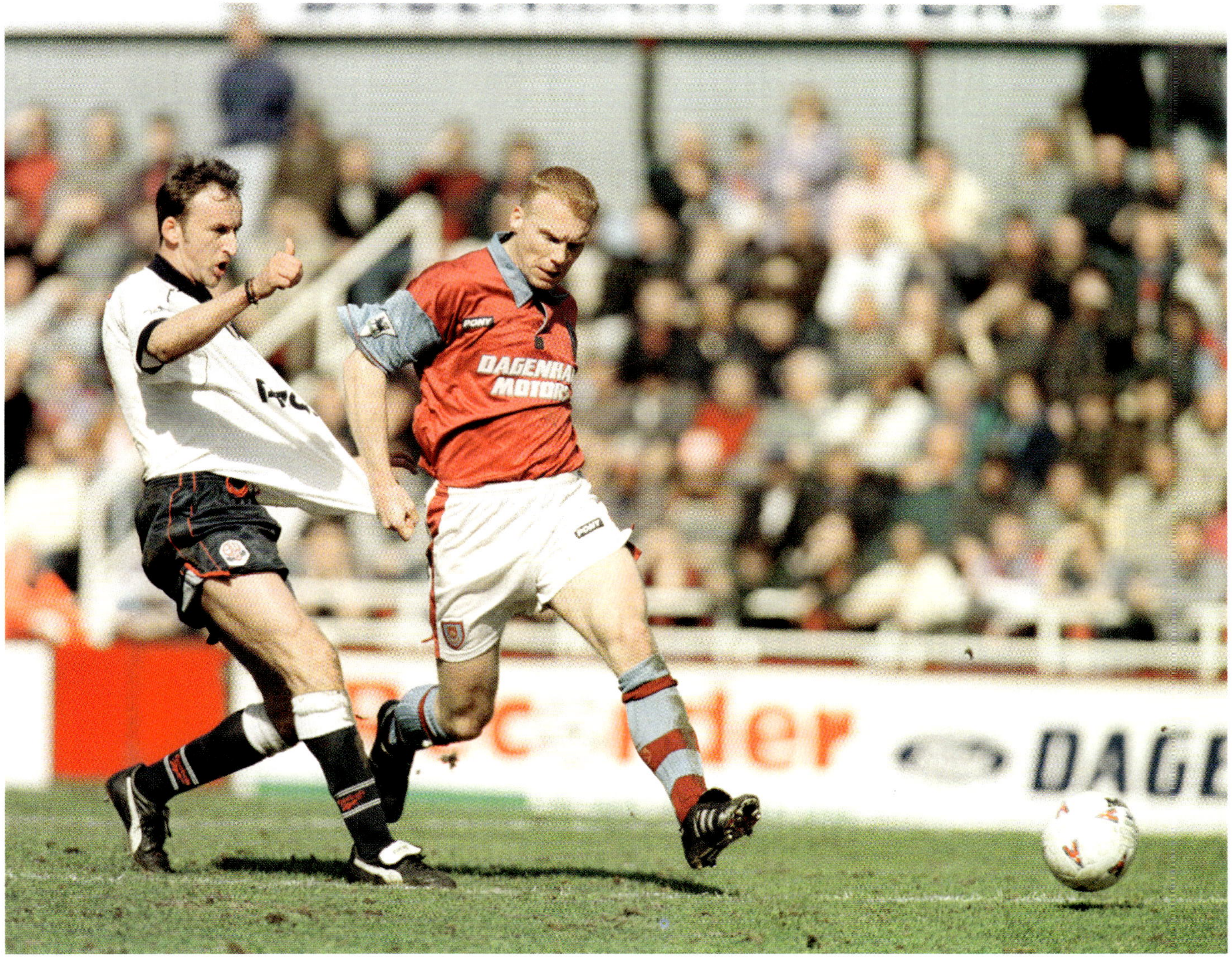

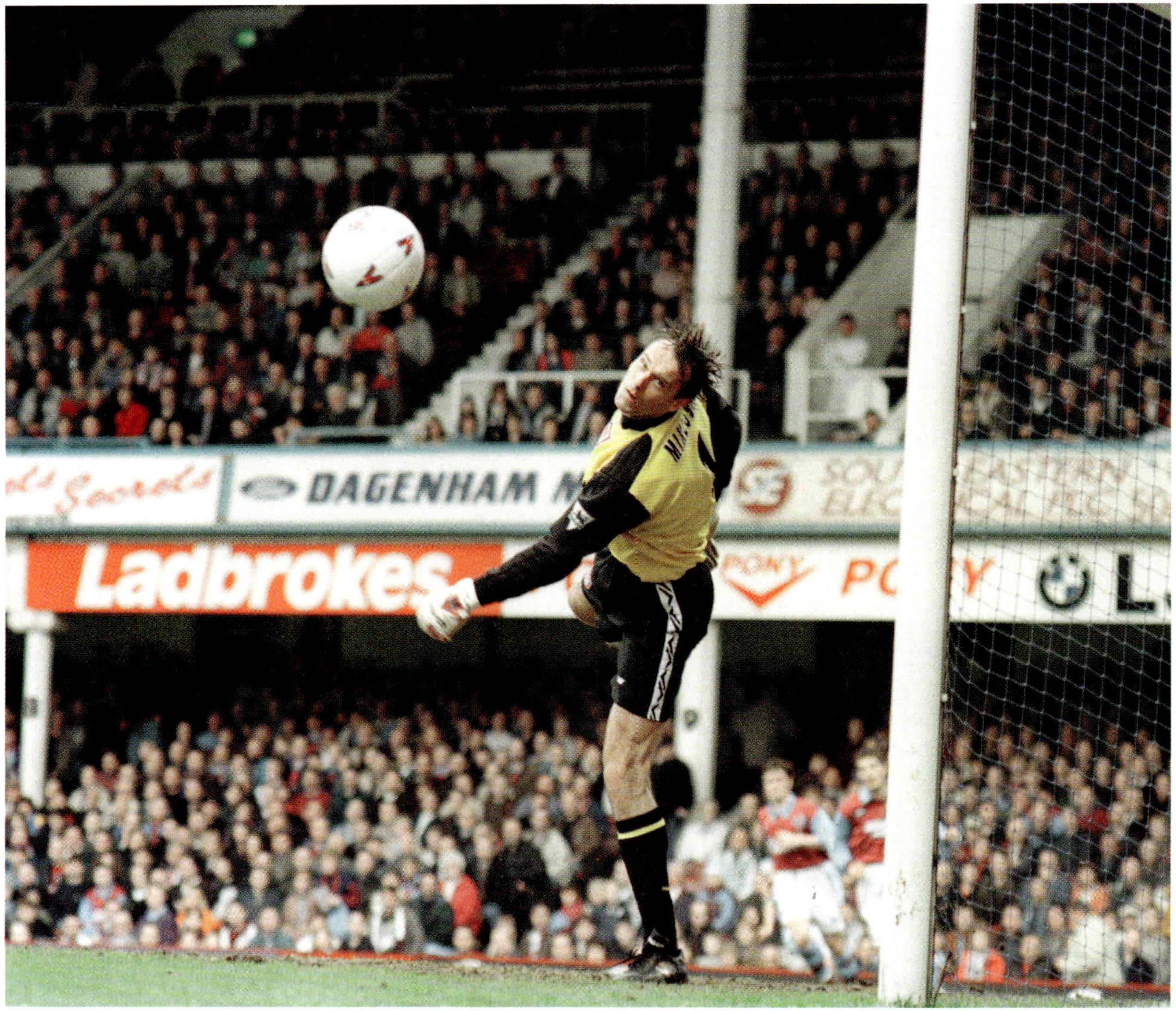

Numero uno. Ludek Miklosko palms the ball away to safety in front of the Centenary Stand at Upton Park.

One for the boys. It's not all sweaty footballers with hairy legs in this job, you know. On rare occasions I had the pleasure of photo shoots with dancer Donna Derby who modelled clothing for the Hammers' Shop as a favour to her Aunt Beattie who worked there. Donna is now married to comedian Bradley Walsh — an Arsenal fan!

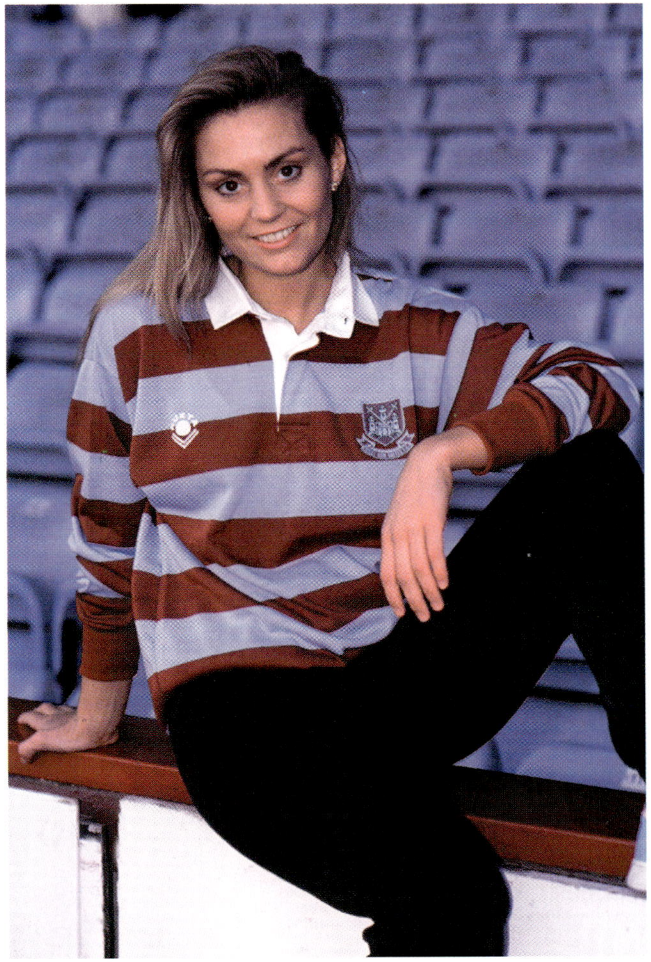

One for the girls. When Dani joined West Ham on loan in 1996, one national newspaper splashed the back page headline 'Lock up your daughters' in reference to his smouldering good looks and playboy image. Can't for the life of me see why!

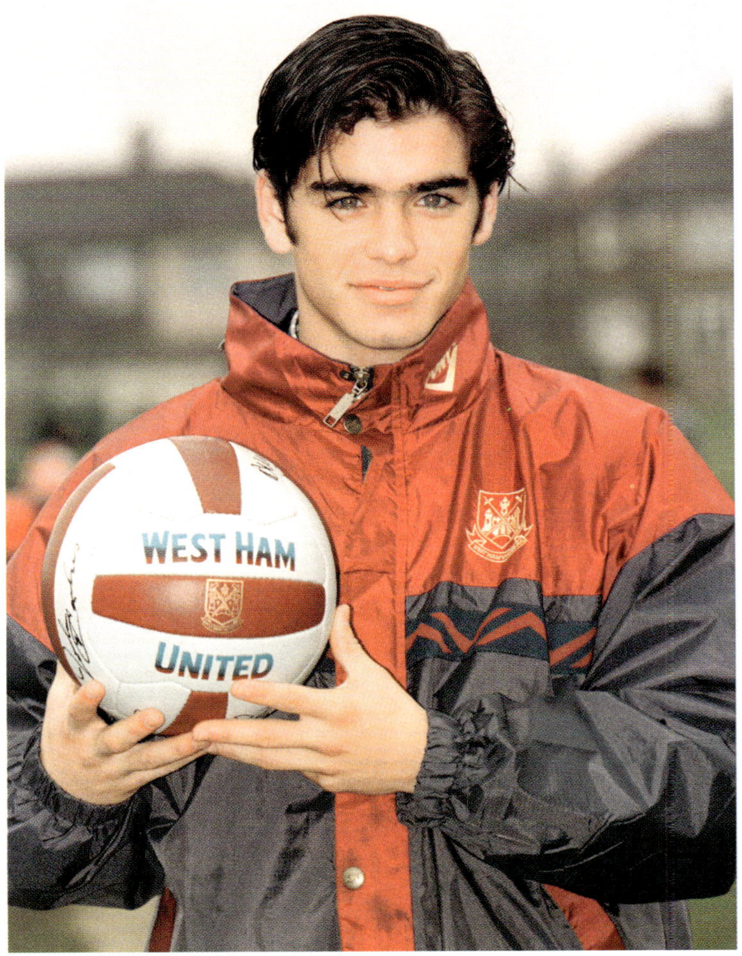

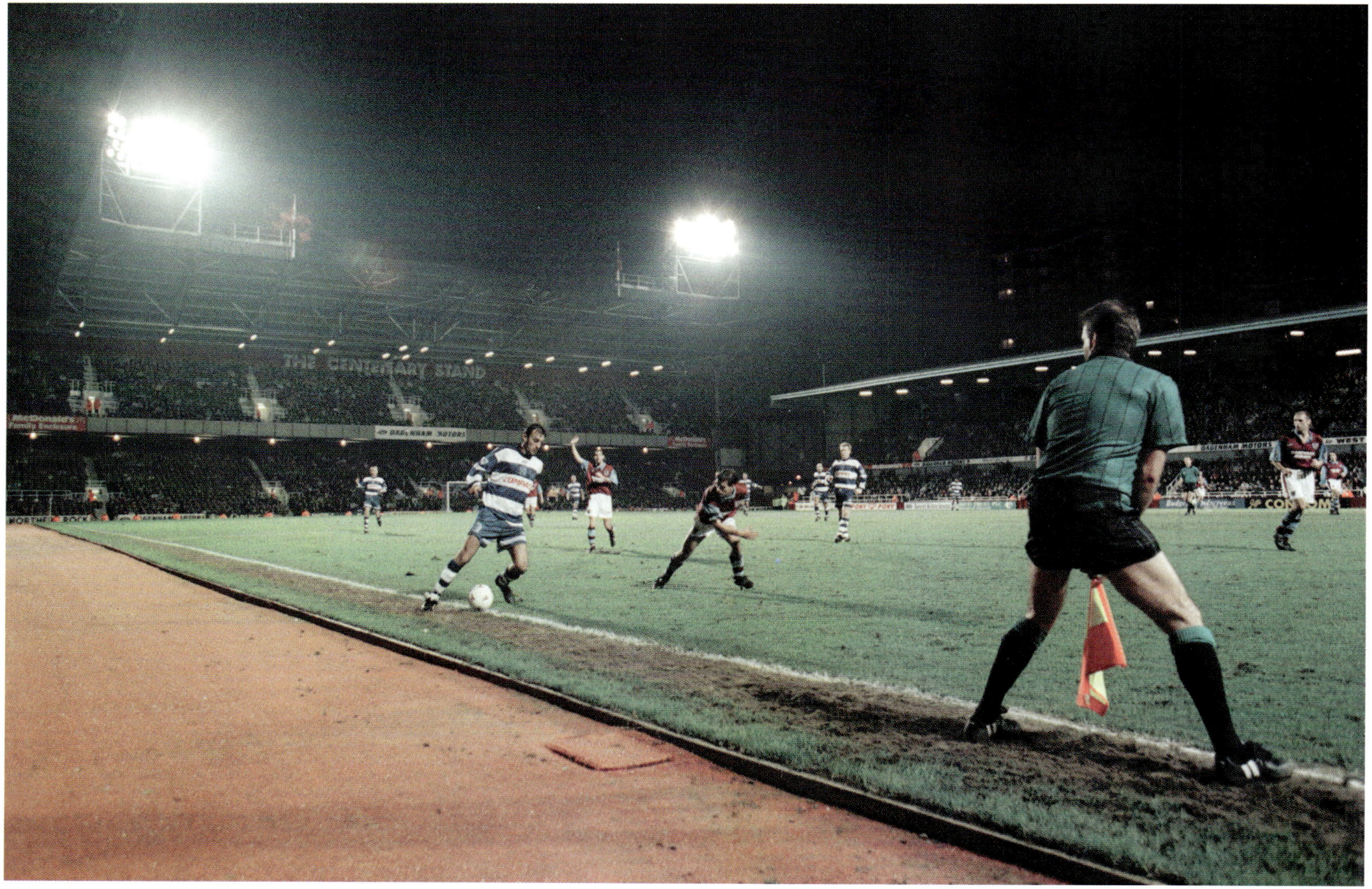
THE CENTENARY STAND

Light work. I was asked to take a picture to illustrate the new floodlighting installation at Upton Park. I think that this wide-angle shot captures the mood of a night match in West Ham's compact stadium which many people think can be worth a goal start to the home side.

Celebrate. This has got to be one of my favourite goal celebration shots. Iain Dowie had just scored in the home match against Blackburn Rovers in 1995. It was his first goal since he rejoined the Hammers but, sadly, was not a match-winner as that man Alan Shearer scored an 89th-minute equaliser. Nevertheless, I think that the delight of scoring is evident in Dowie's expression; likewise with Tony Cottee in the background.

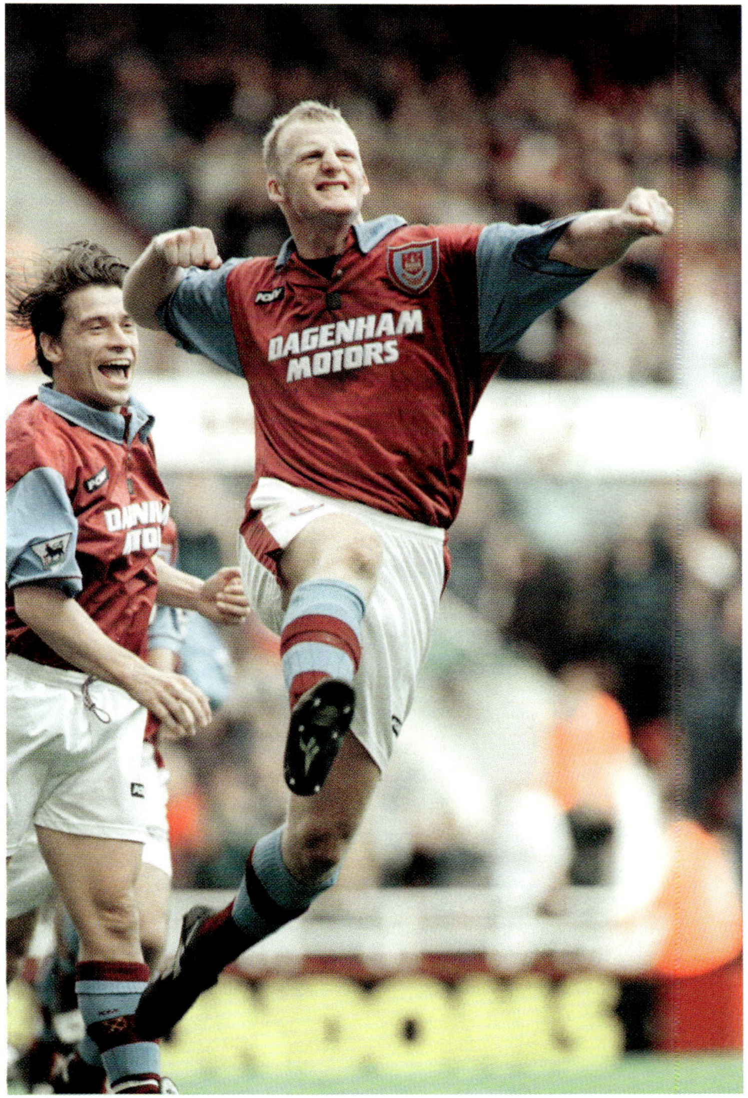

Where are they now? Julian Dicks sends Sheffield Wednesday's Danny Wilson sprawling during a match at Hillsborough in 1992. After taking Barnsley to the Premiership as their manager in 1997–98, although just for the one season, Danny was appointed boss of Sheffield Wednesday in July 1998 in succession to Ron Atkinson.

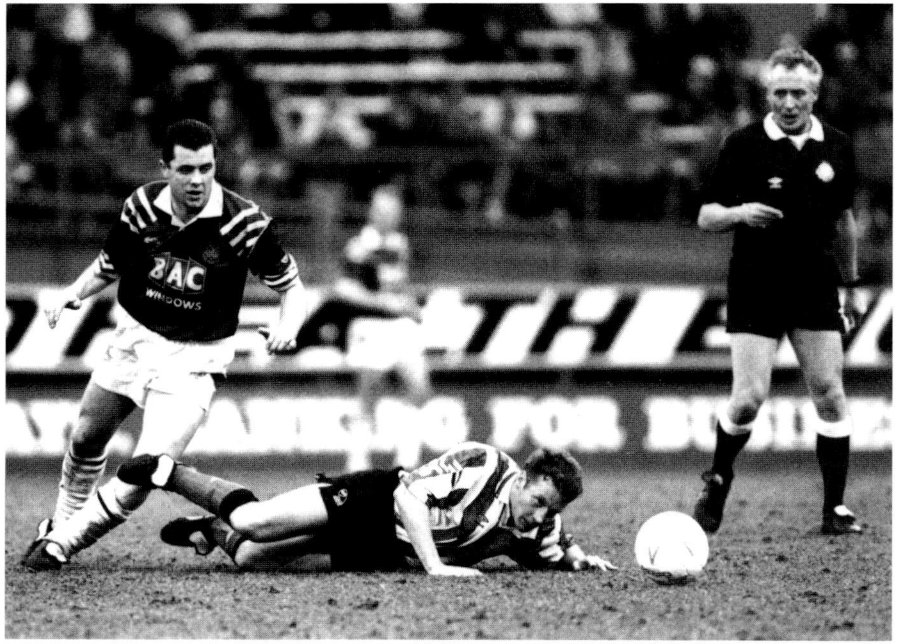

Heartache. There was grave concern for Hammers' Ilford-born George Parris who, after coming on as substitute against Arsenal in March 1992, collapsed on the Upton Park pitch. Club doctor Ges Steinbergs was urgently called for and, after some delay, George was revived and helped from the pitch. There were later rumours of a mystery heart problem and George's appearances were limited until he moved to Birmingham City in March 1993 in an effort to find first-team football.

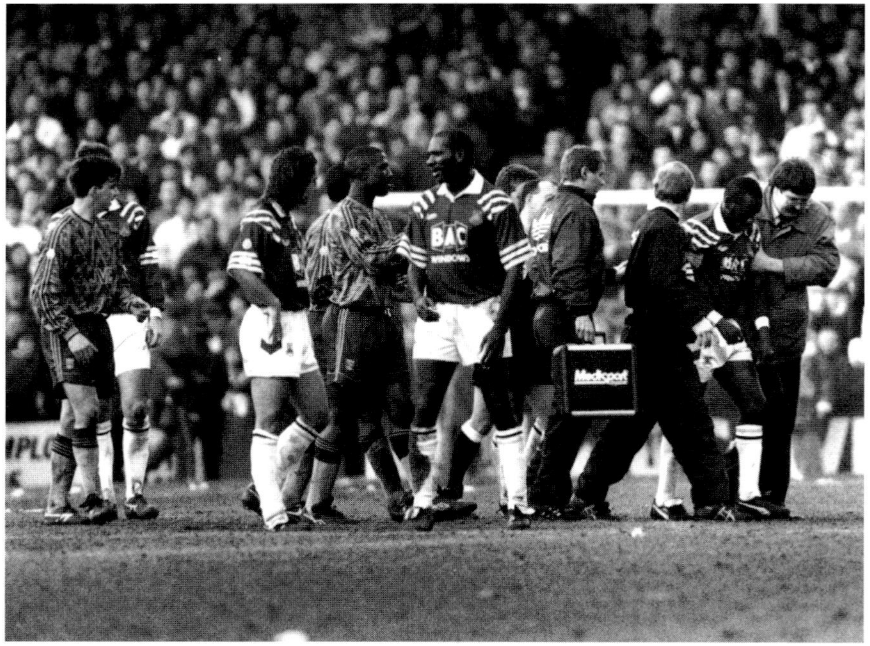

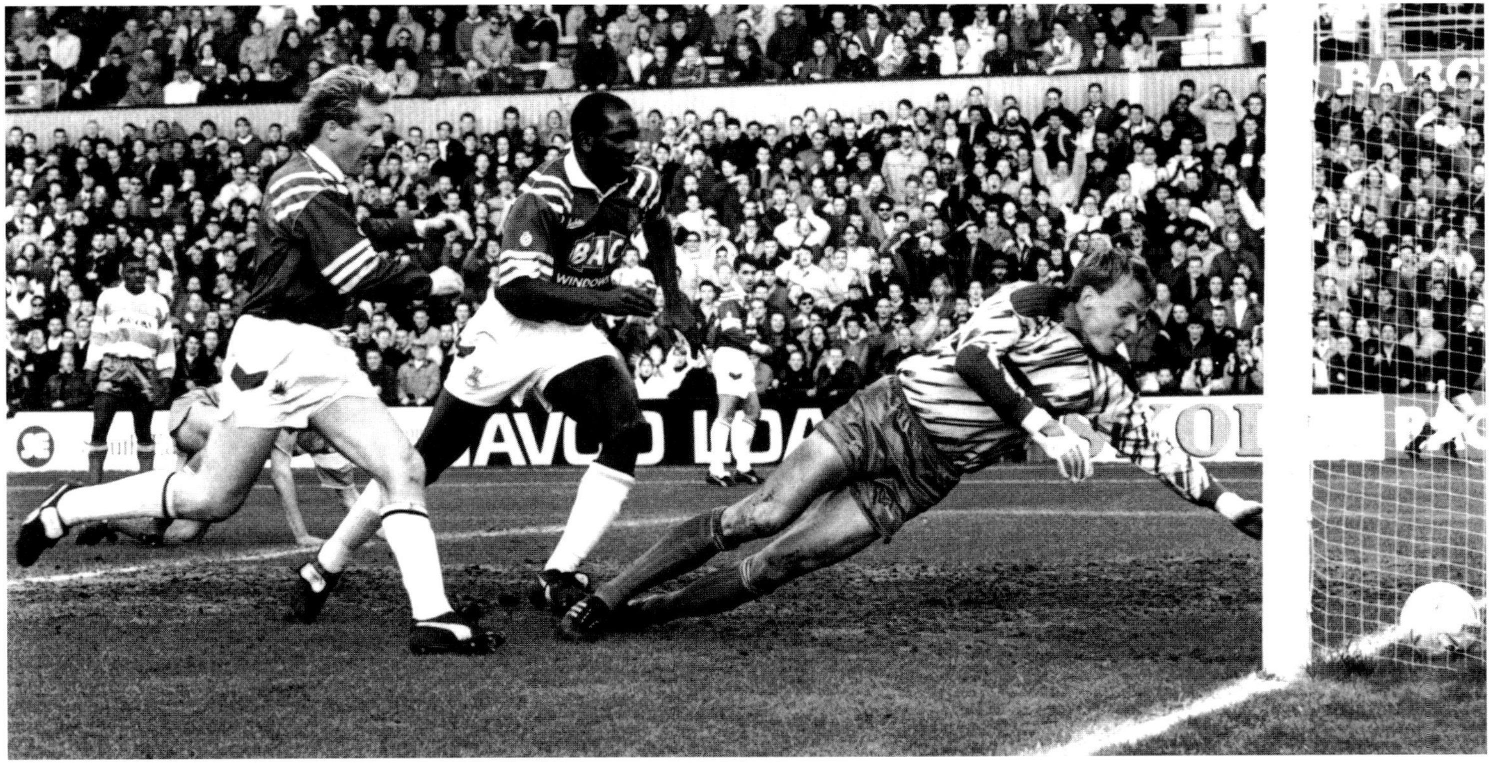

Lost points. Mike Small strikes in the 28th minute of the home match against QPR in the 1991–92 season to give Hammers the lead. The game ended in a 2–2 draw with Bradley Allen netting twice against his cousin Martin's side. More vital lost points in the season in which West Ham finished rock bottom of the league.

Sinking feeling. This match was the one that consigned West Ham to the second division, or Barclays League Division One as it became on the formation of the Premiership. Ex-Hammer Stewart Robson challenges Mitchell Thomas as Coventry beat West Ham by the only goal at Highfield Road in April 1992.

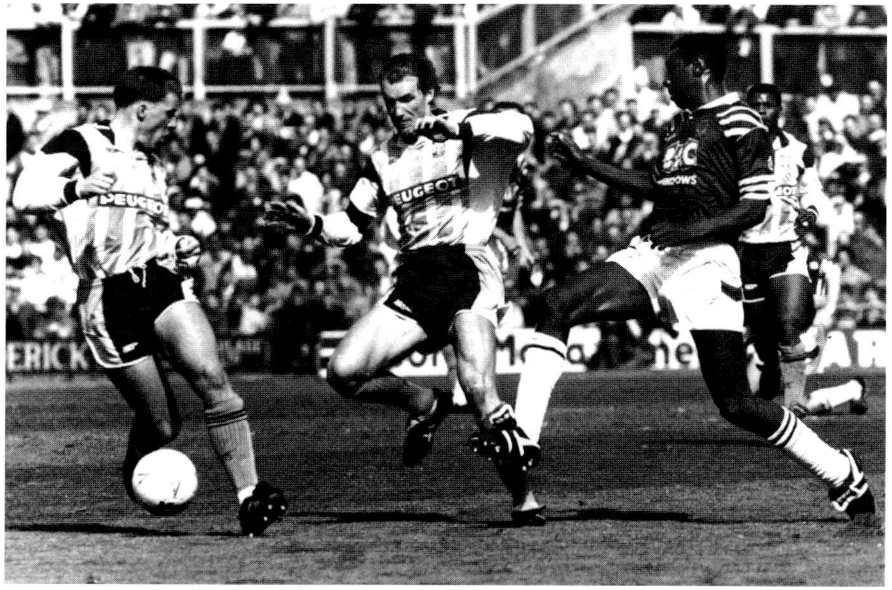

Stars on Sunday. The ITV boys were quick to welcome West Ham into the Barclays League and made their first match of the 1992–93 season, at Barnsley, their live Sunday game. Clive Allen scored this, the first of his fifteen goals for the coming season, to give Hammers a 1–0 victory and set them on their way for promotion to the Premiership some nine months later.

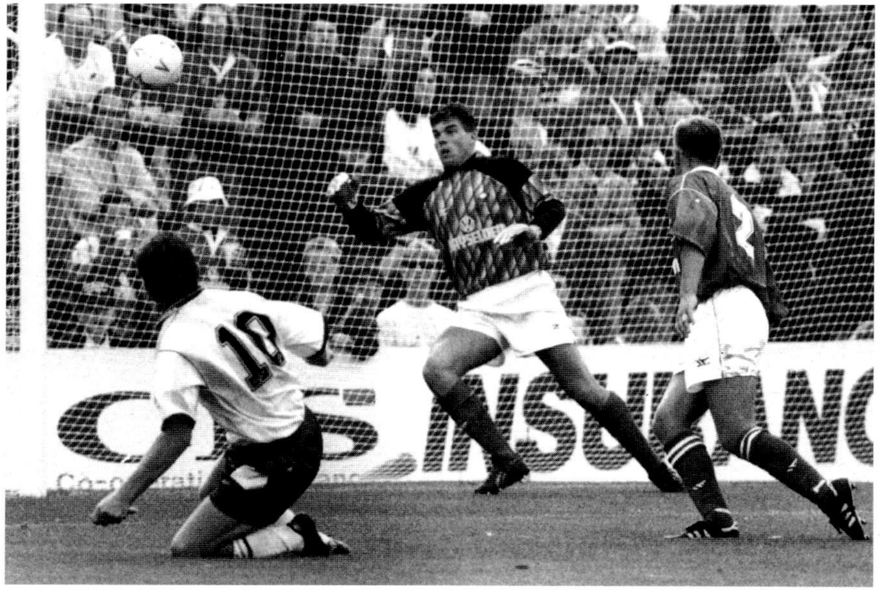

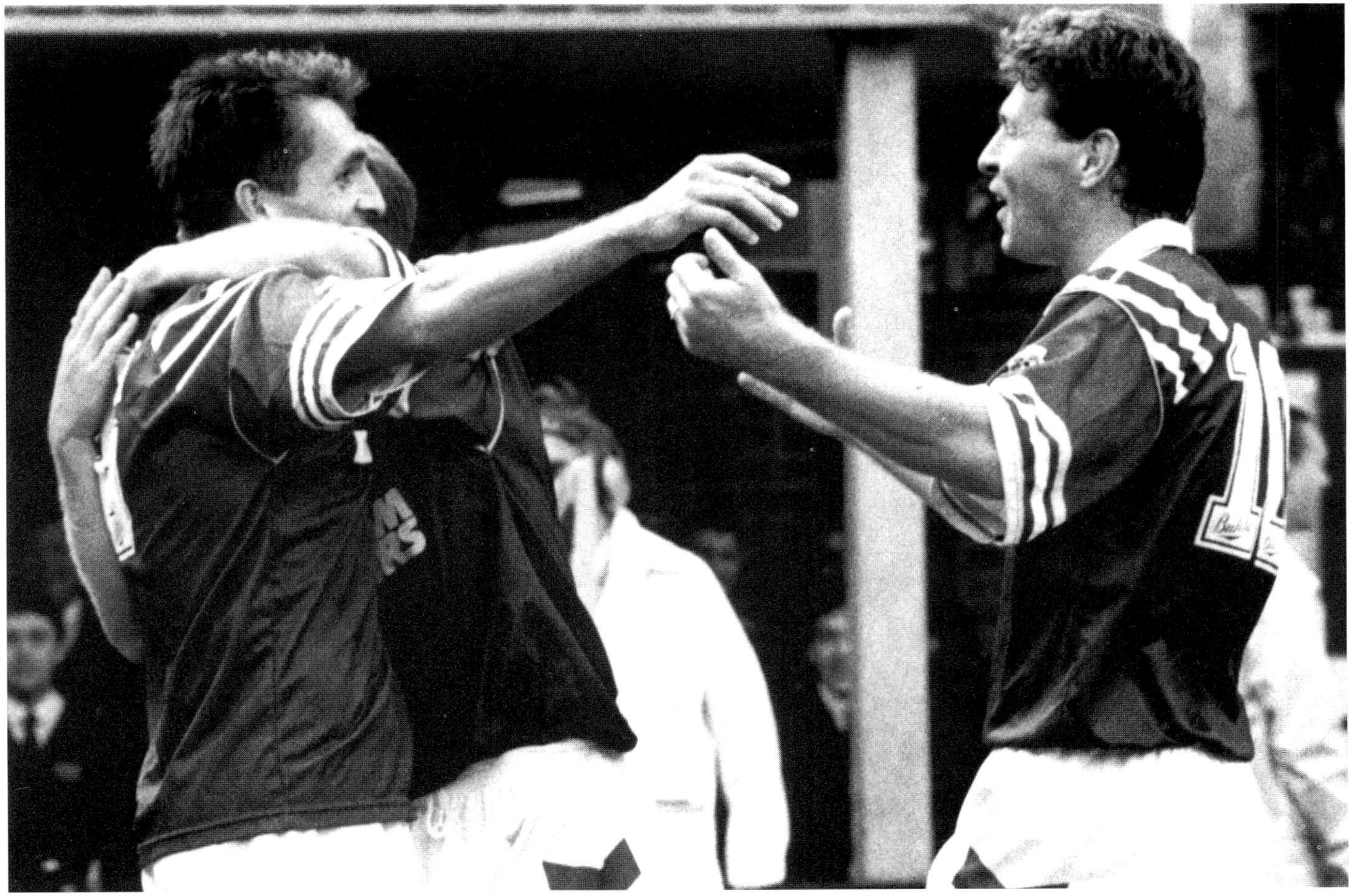

Kissing cousins? Not quite, but Clive and Martin Allen are certainly good friends as they celebrate their goals that beat Watford 2–1 at Upton Park early in the 1992–93 season.

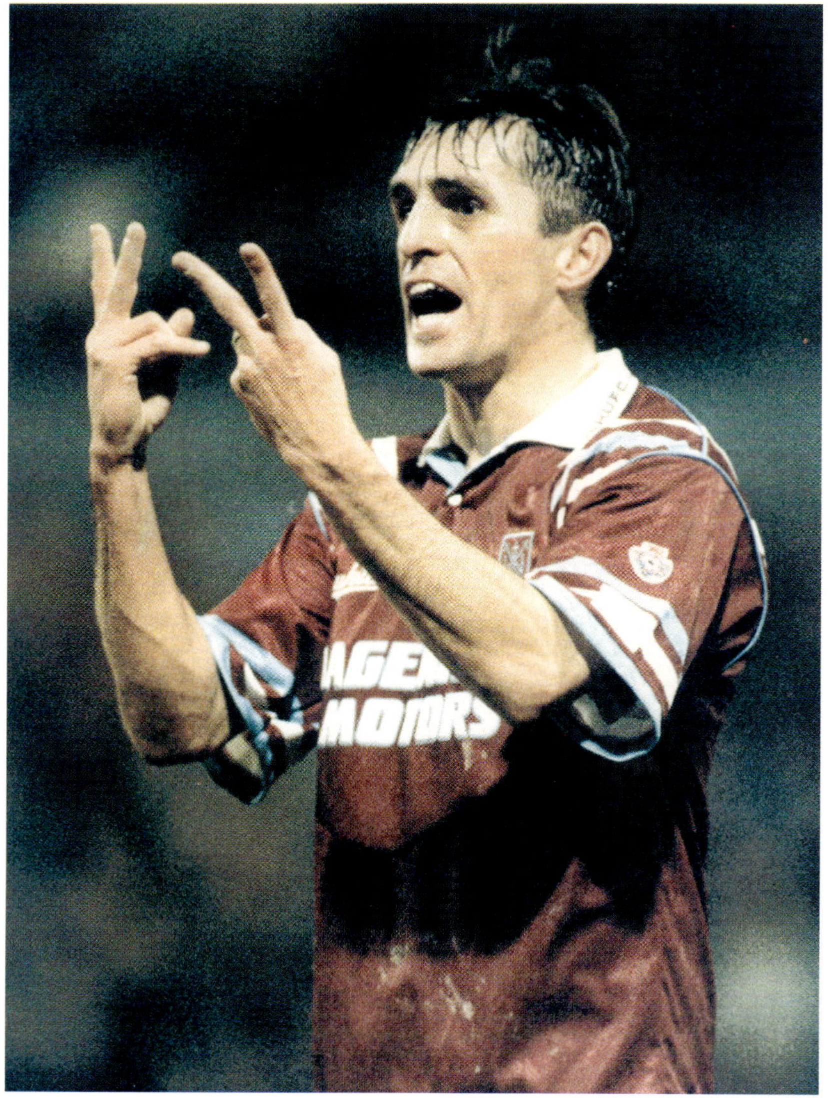

Harvey Smith? No, it's just 'Mad Dog' Martin Allen trying to make his point to his team-mates during the heat of the action.

Seeing red. Julian Dicks makes the long, lonely walk back to the Molineux dressing room after being shown the red card for a second bookable offence as Hammers drew 0–0 against Wolves in 1992. Dicksie had a running battle with Steve Bull throughout the match and the final fracas left referee Allison little choice.

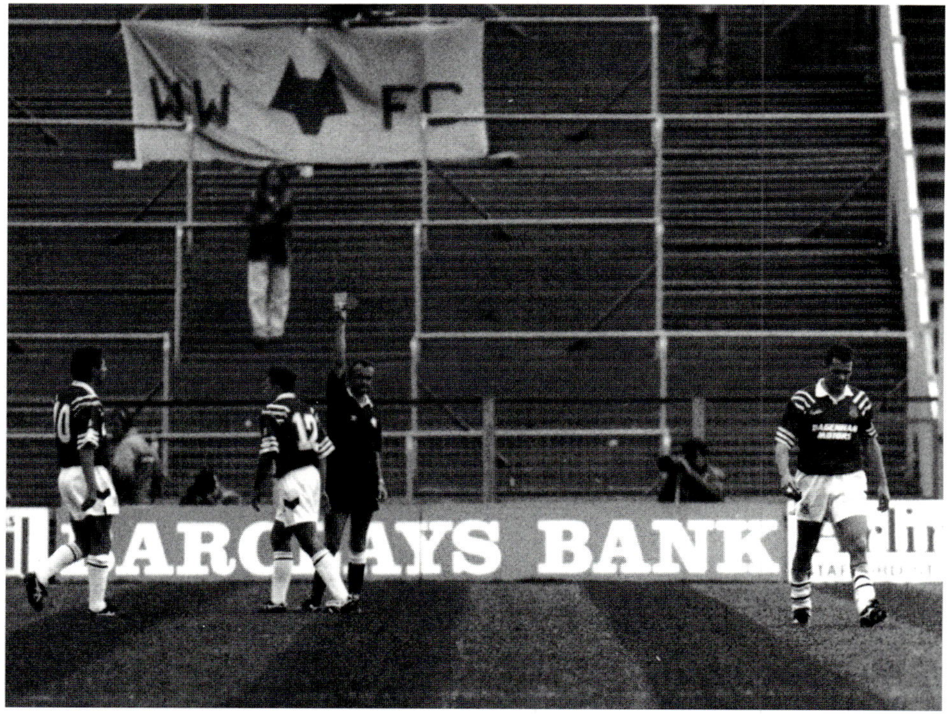

Dale's debut. Dale Gordon, a £750,000 summer signing from Norwich, makes his debut in the first game of the 1993–94 season as Hammers entertain Wimbledon at Upton Park. Dale clashes with Dons' Robbie Earle as the home side go down 2–0 on a hot, sunny afternoon.

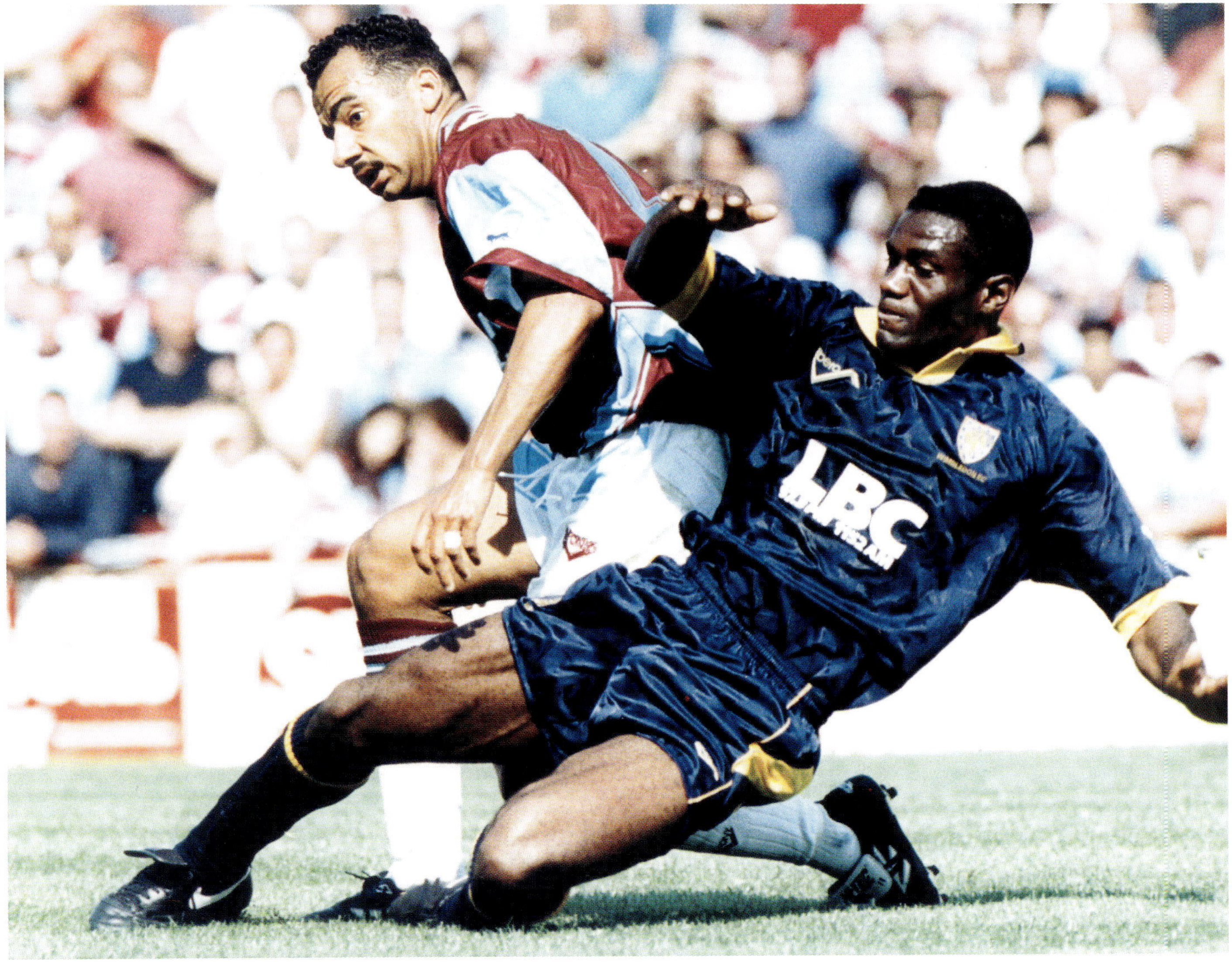

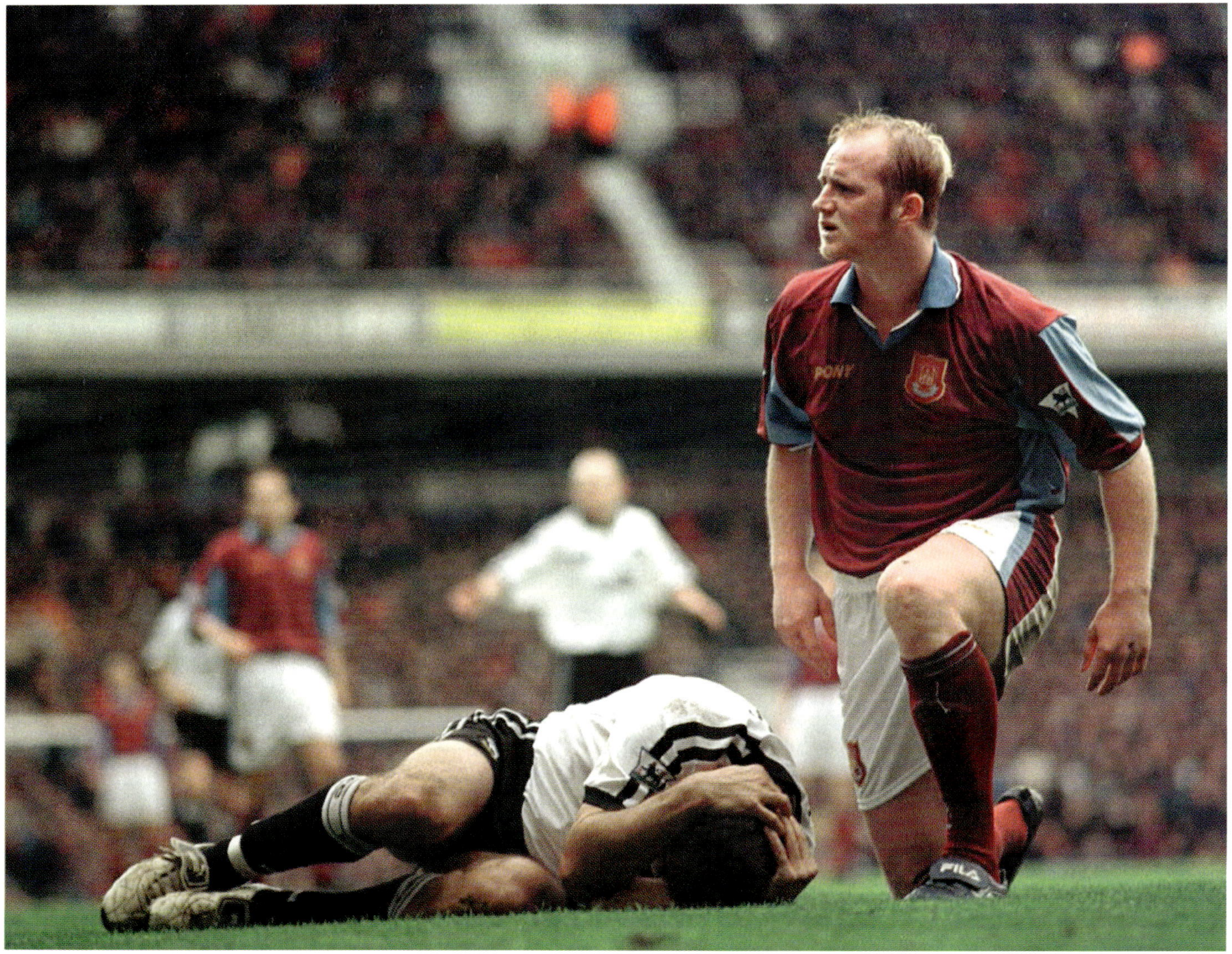

Oh no, John. Derby County's Igor Stimac clutches his head in agony following a clash with Hammers' fiery Welsh striker John Hartson during their league clash at Upton Park in 1998. Big John was shown the red card for hitting out in retaliation and missed the last four games of the season.

Play it again. Canadian 'keeper Craig Forrest cannot conceal his delight after saving a penalty in the FA Cup fifth round replay shoot-out at Ewood Park in 1998. After 90 minutes of normal time and 30 minutes' extra time, the teams were still deadlocked. Hammers held their nerve in the penalty shoot-out to win through to a London derby against Arsenal — where they lost the replay in another penalty shoot-out.

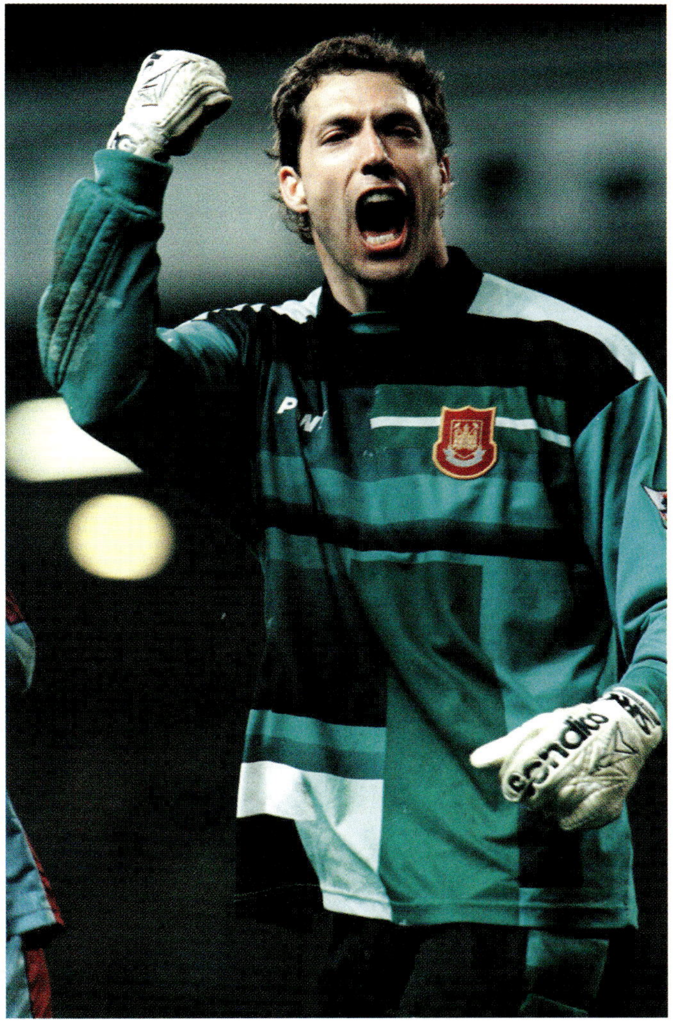

Well done, son. Martin Allen and Tim Breacker congratulate team-mate Peter Butler on his first-ever goal for West Ham in a 2–1 win over Peterborough at Upton Park in February 1993. Buts scored one more goal that season in a 4–0 home win over Brentford.

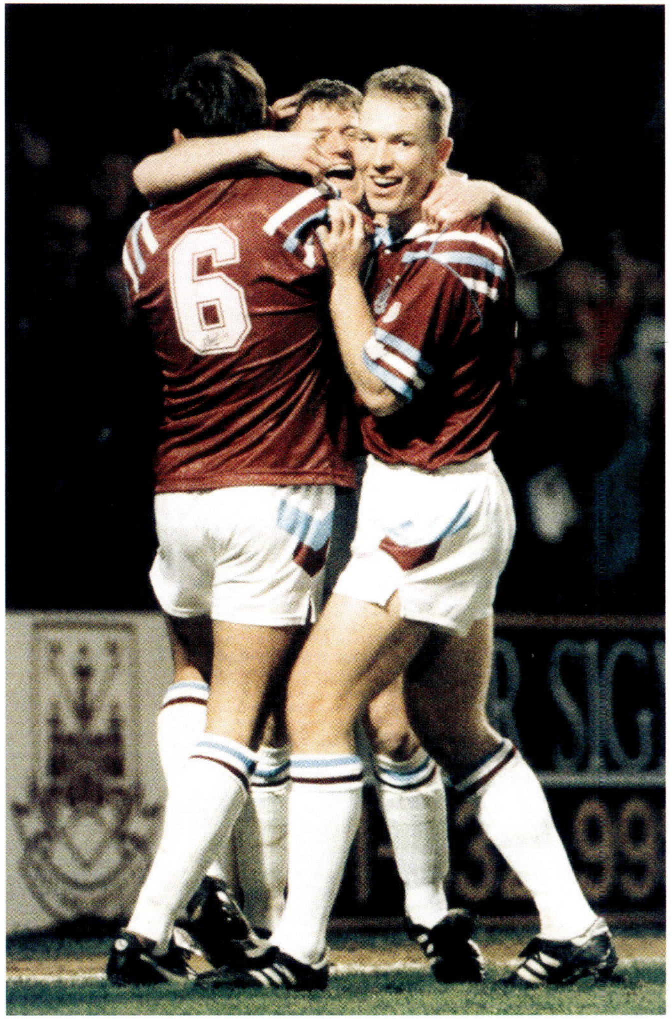

Spot of bother. Paul Kitson scores the second of his two goals in the 2–2 home draw with Everton in April 1997. With West Ham leading 2–0, they were awarded a penalty and Kits was urged by the crowd to take the spot-kick for his hat-trick; he missed — and Everton struck back to snatch a draw. Manager Harry Redknapp was not amused.

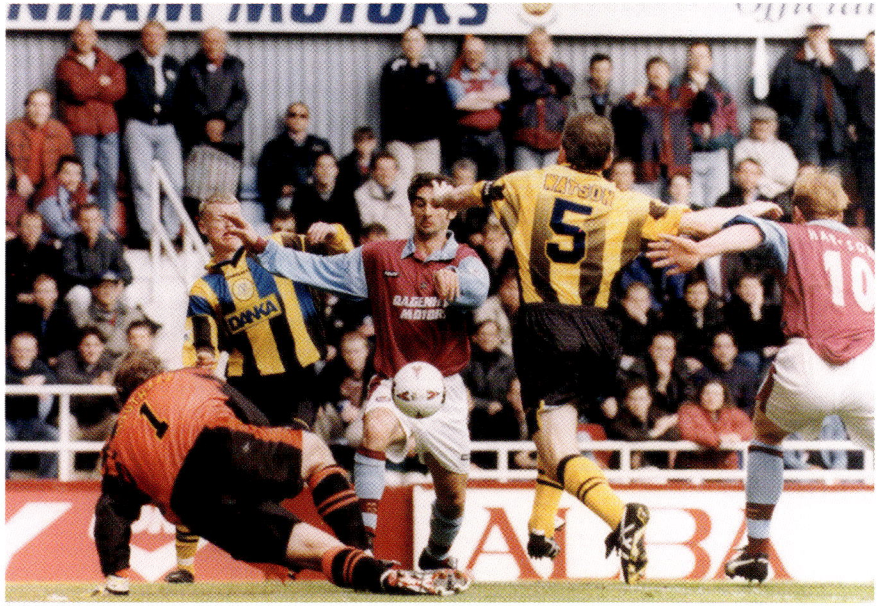

Keen as mustard. Kevin Keen hits the winner for West Ham against Watford at Vicarage Road in February 1993. It was to be Kevin's penultimate season for the Hammers as he moved to Wolves for £300,000 in October 1994 having made 263 appearances in the Claret and Blue.

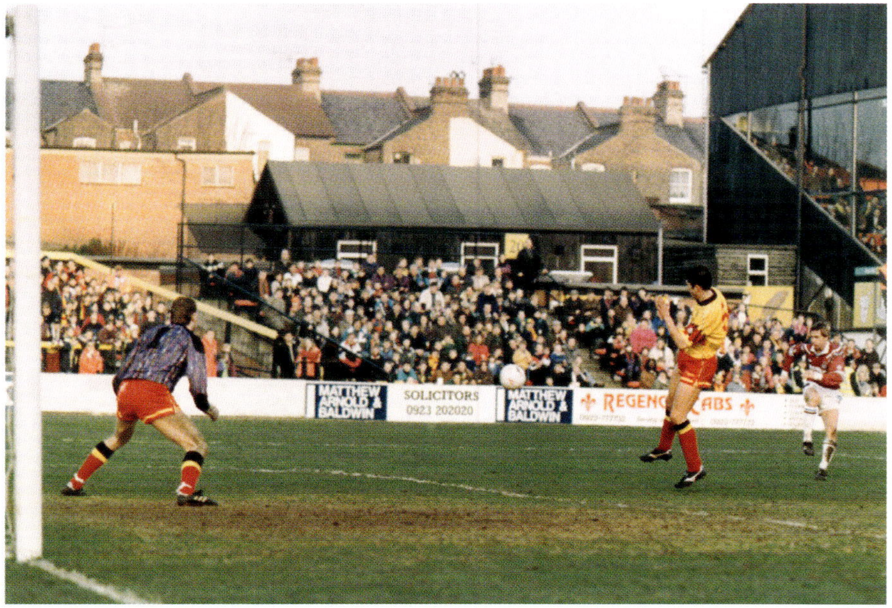

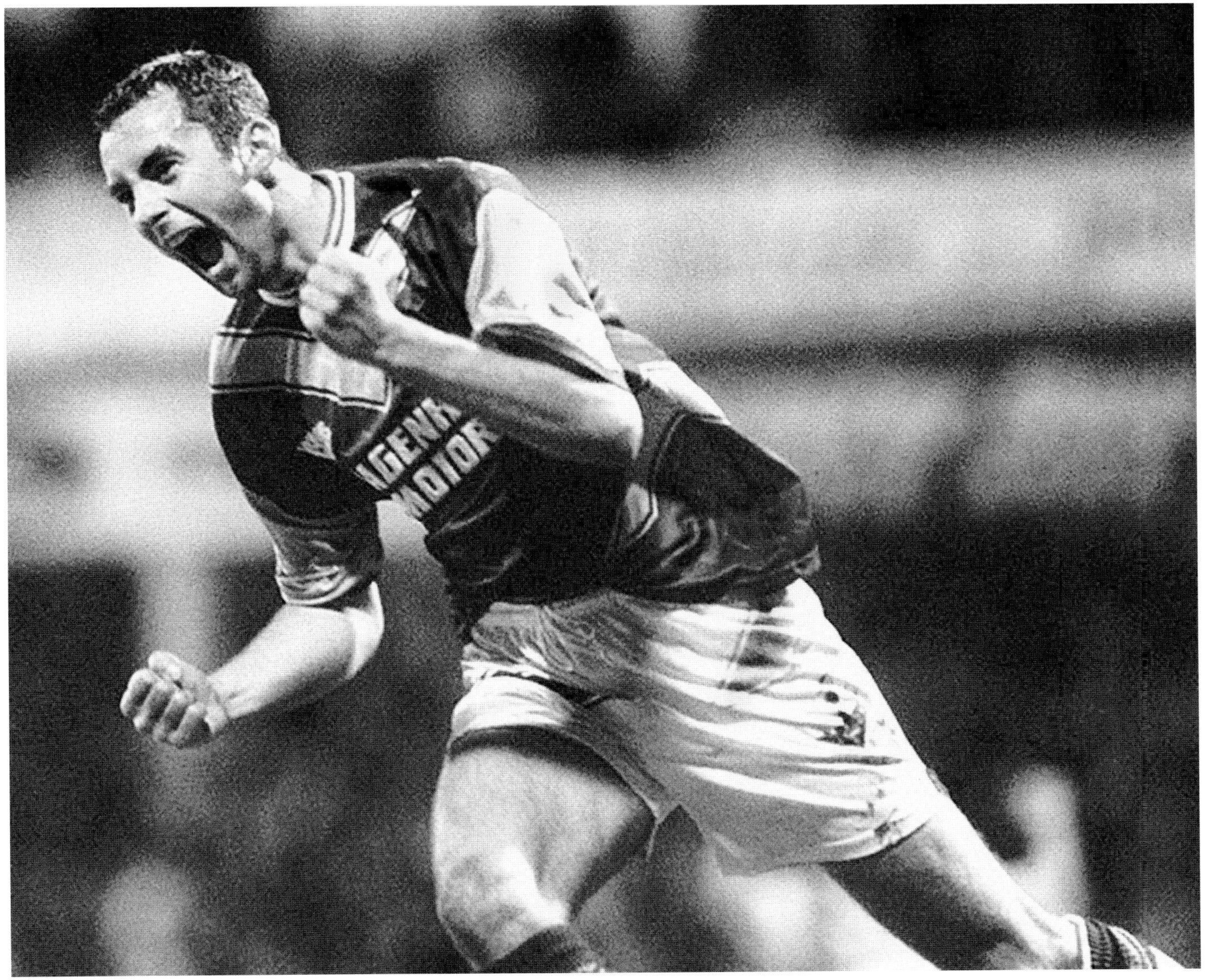

Don's delight. There's no hiding his pleasure as Don Hutchison celebrates a brace of goals against his old club, Liverpool, during the penultimate home match of the 1994–95 season. West Ham won the match 3–0 and, with one more home game to come against Manchester United, ensured Premiership football for another season. An added bonus for Hammers' fans was a draw with United to rob them of the title in favour of Blackburn Rovers.

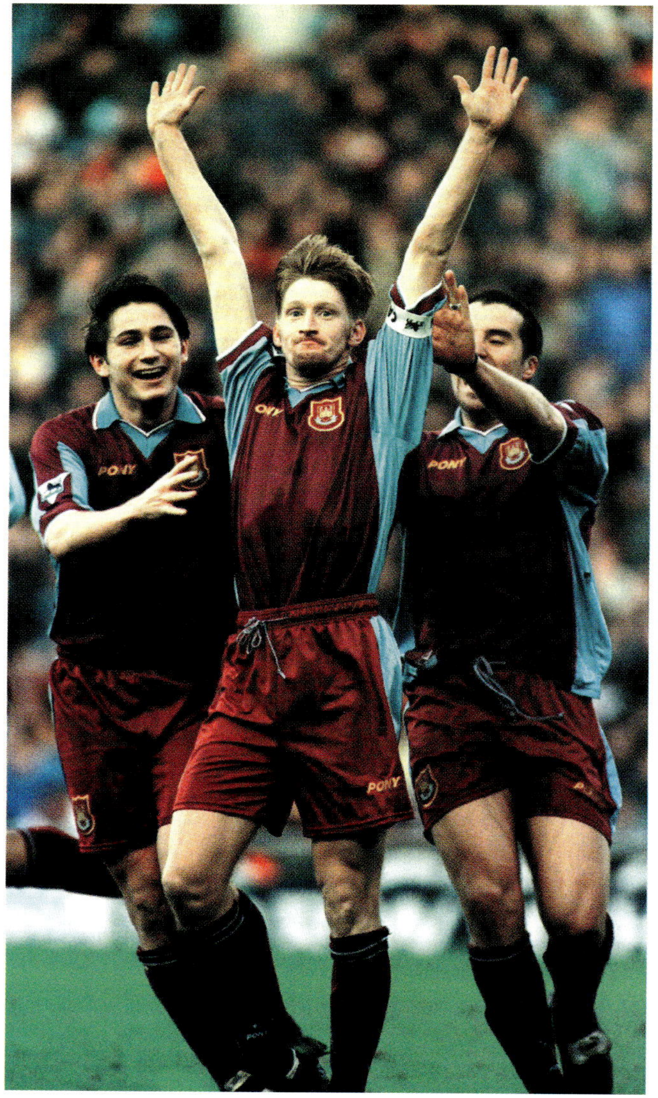

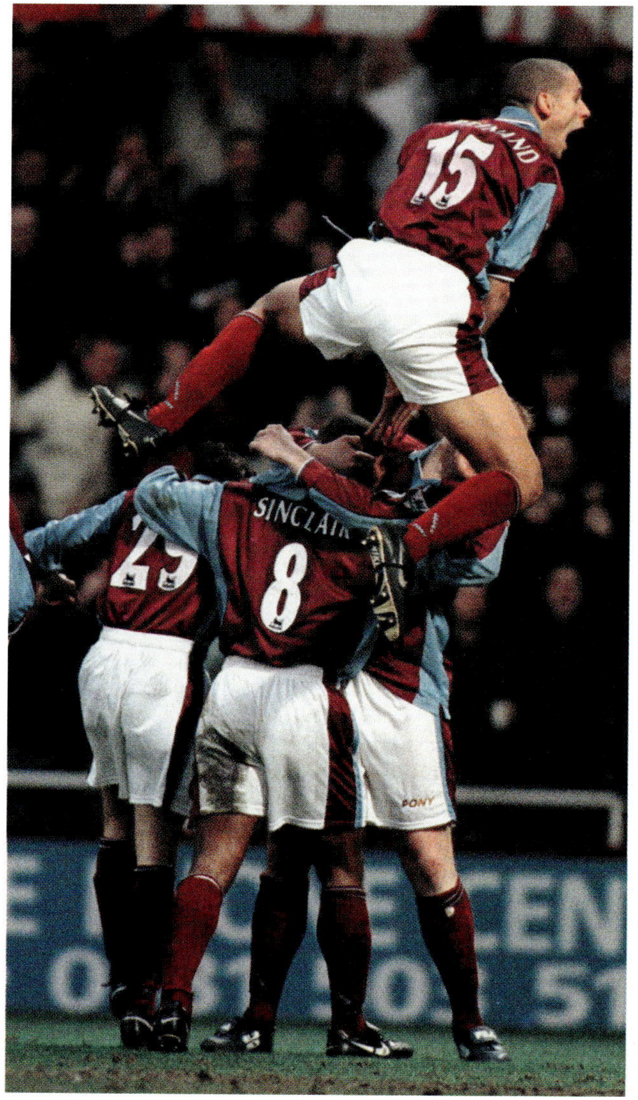

Captain's innings. Steve Lomas holds his arms aloft in both celebration and relief after scoring the winning goal in the 1998 FA Cup tie against his old club, Manchester City, at Maine Road. City had earlier missed a penalty and the chance to go 2–1 ahead. Frank Lampard and Ian Pearce look equally pleased with their skipper's effort.

Over the top. Rio Ferdinand joins in the celebrations following Trevor Sinclair's second goal in the home league match against Everton in January 1998. As usual with the shy and retiring Rio, he is very restrained in his celebrations.

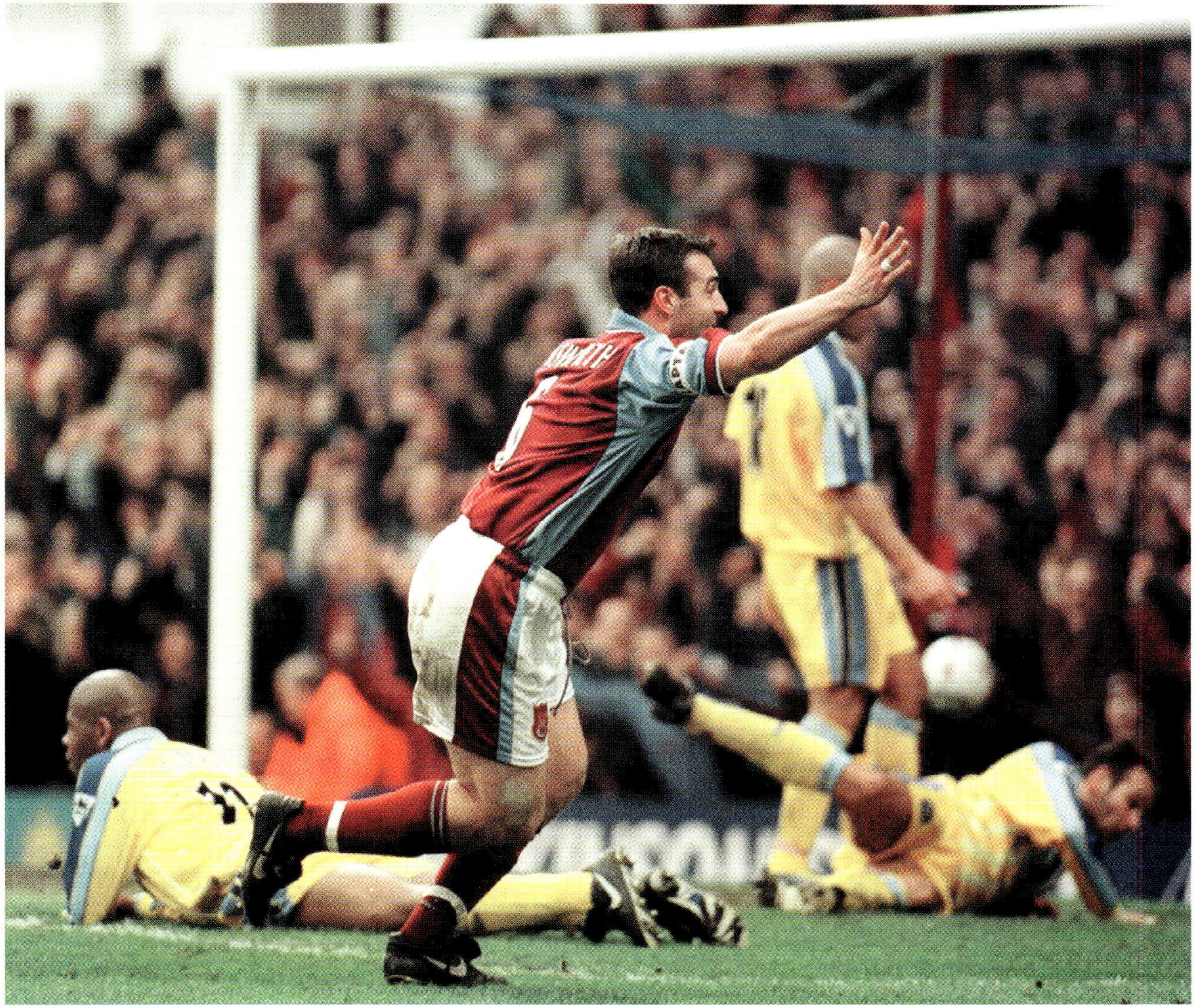

David's delight. Defender David Unsworth wheels away in delight after scoring the winning goal against Chelsea at Upton Park in March 1998. Trevor Sinclair had equalised after Charvet had given Chelsea the lead, but Unsie popped up to secure the three points.

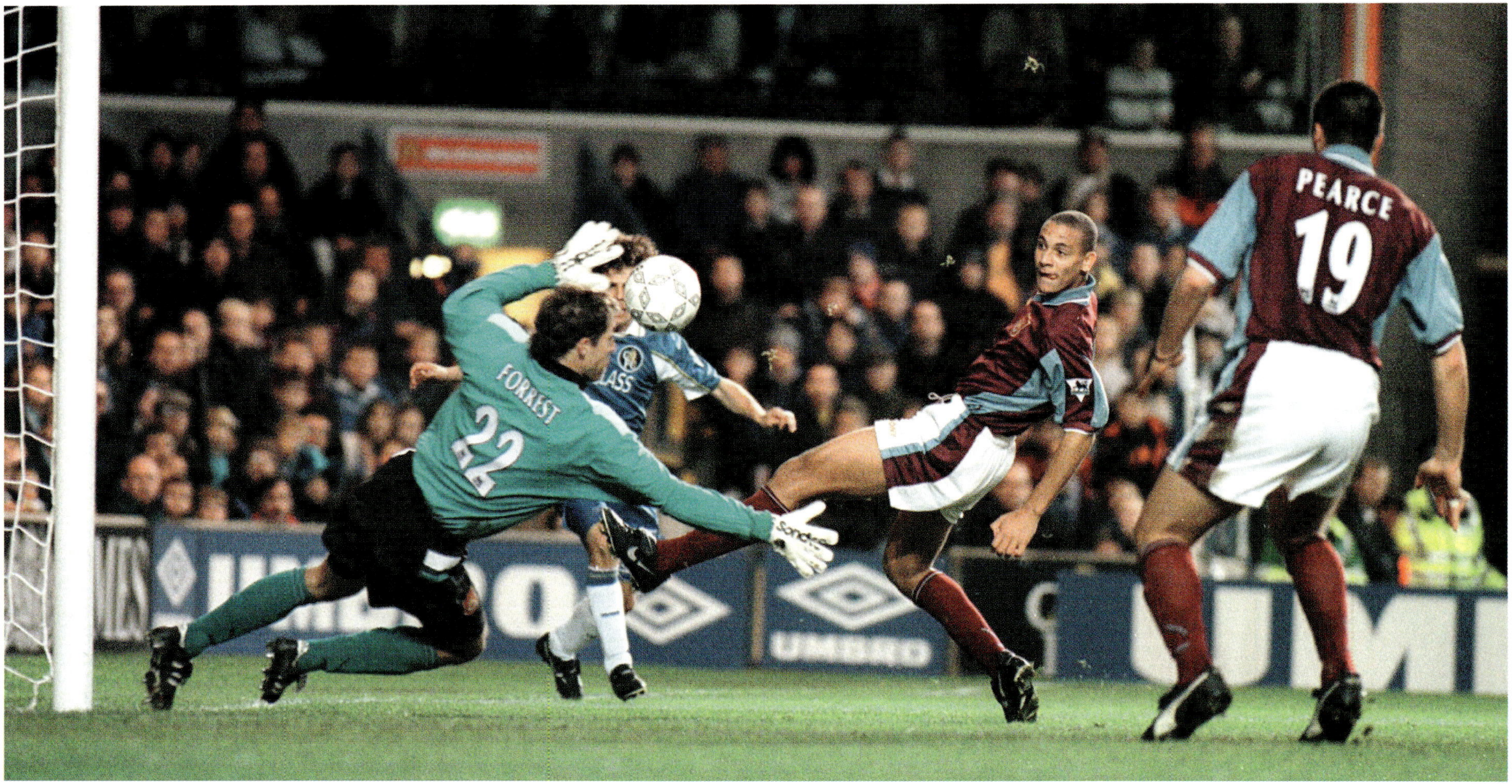
PEARCE
19
FORREST
22
UMBRO
UMBRO

What a picture! Now this is a great goal picture by anyone's standards. All the action is encompassed in one shot. Only trouble is: the scorer is Rio Ferdinand and the 'keeper is team-mate Craig Forrest! It's own-goal time at Stamford Bridge as Hammers go down 2–1 during the 1997–98 season.

No Futre in it. Another one of Harry Redknapp's 'foreign army' for the 1996–97 season was former Portuguese superstar Paulo Futre. Paulo was signed on the proviso that, if his long-standing injury proved too much to overcome, both parties would tear up the contract by mutual consent. In the event he made four starts for the Hammers before succumbing to the old injury and returning to Portugal.

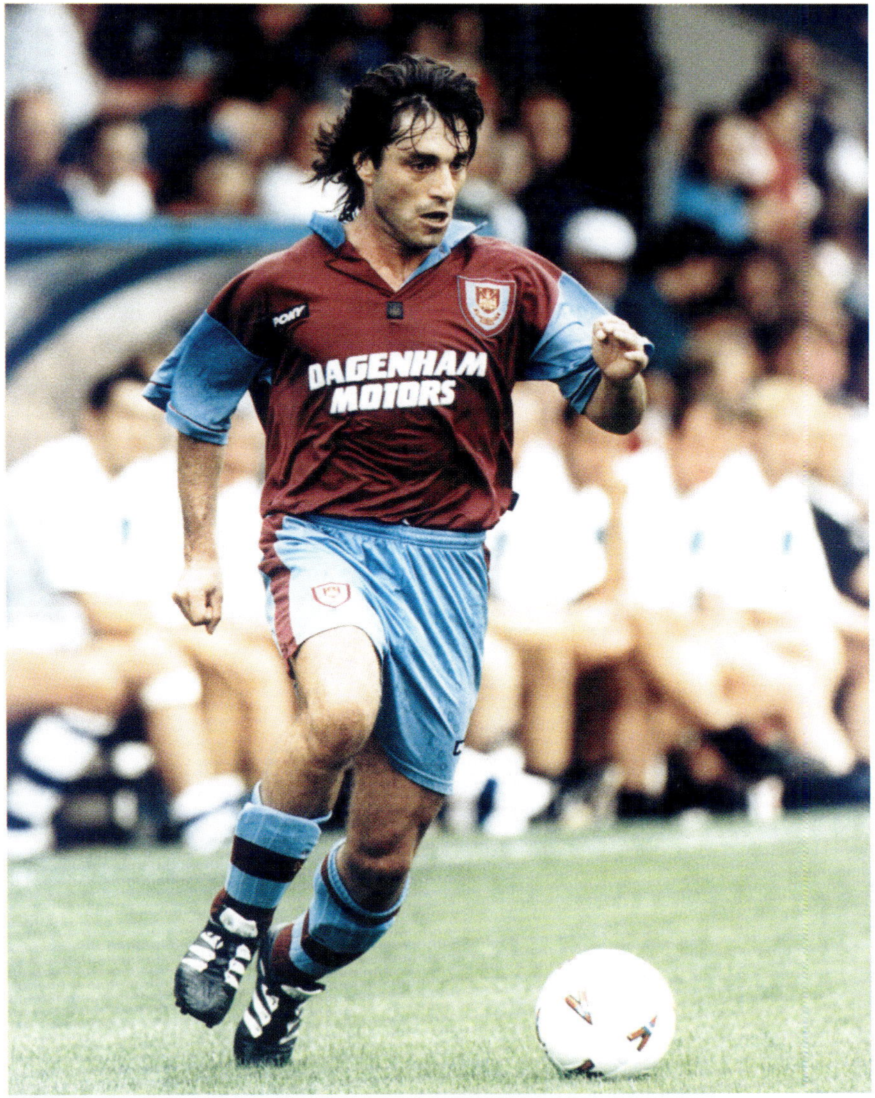

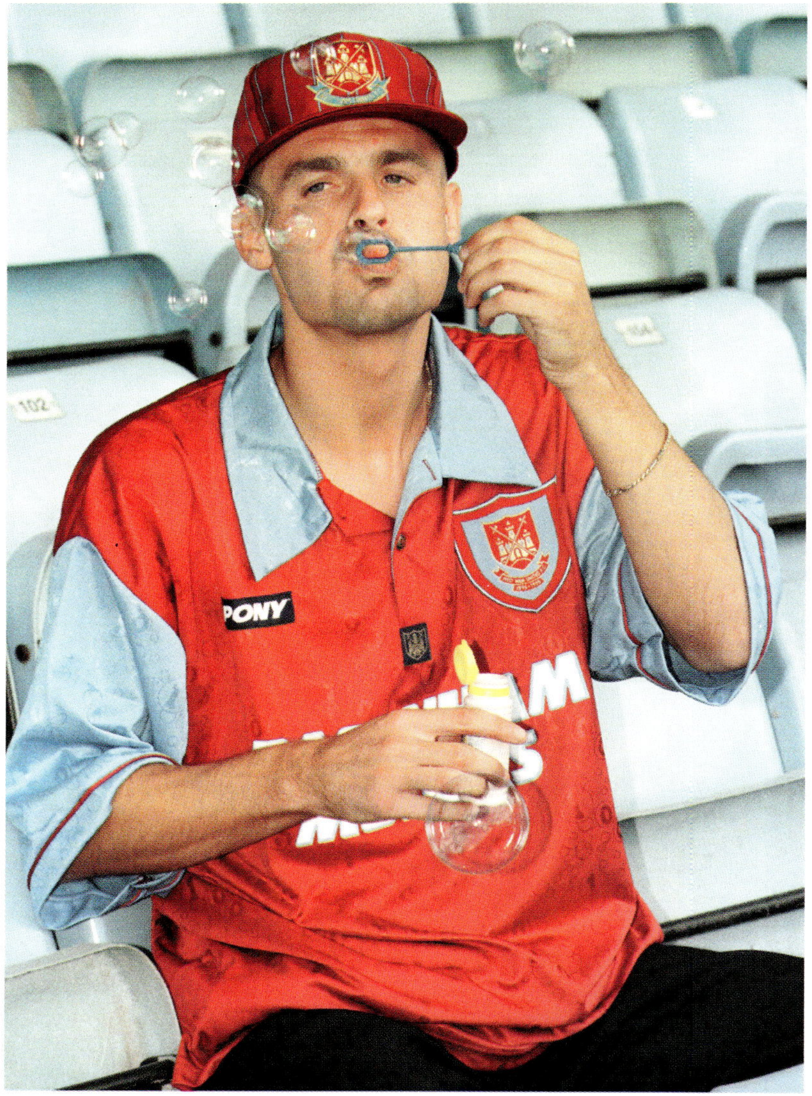

I'm forever blowing bubbles. Marco Boogers joined West Ham from Sparta Rotterdam in the summer of 1995 and was happily blowing bubbles at the photo call to announce his signing. Things turned sour for the Dutchman when, in the second match of the season, he was shown the red card for a lunging tackle on Gary Neville at Old Trafford. Marco made just four appearances as substitute that season and was never seen again!

Say cheese. Spectators at a Hammers' warm-up game before the 1996–97 season were recently signed Romanian international Florin Raducioiu and fellow-countryman Ilie Dumitrescu who had joined the club the previous season. Whatever the whys and wherefores of their short careers at the club, I personally got on quite well with the pair of them during their stay.

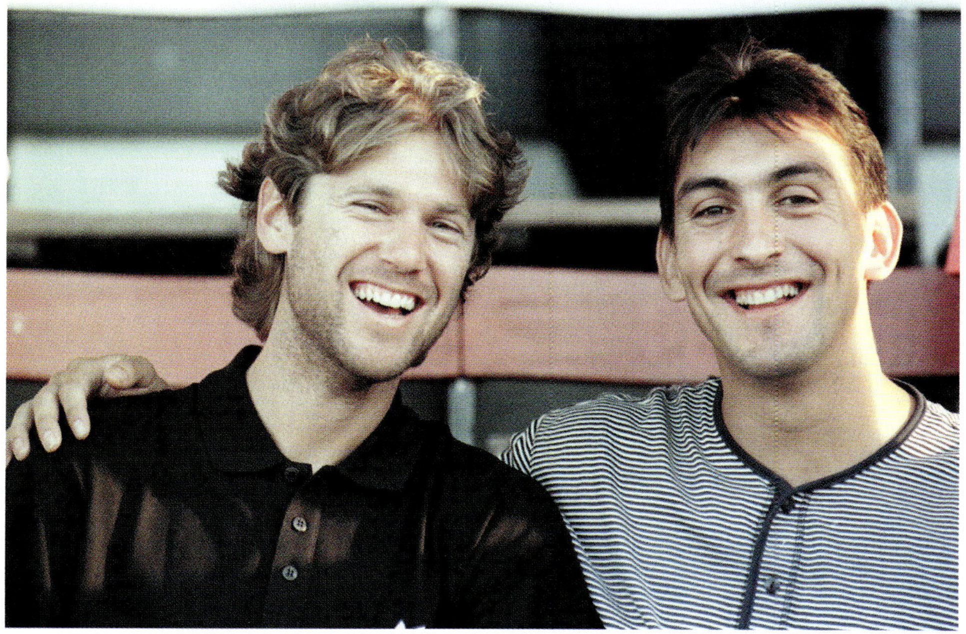

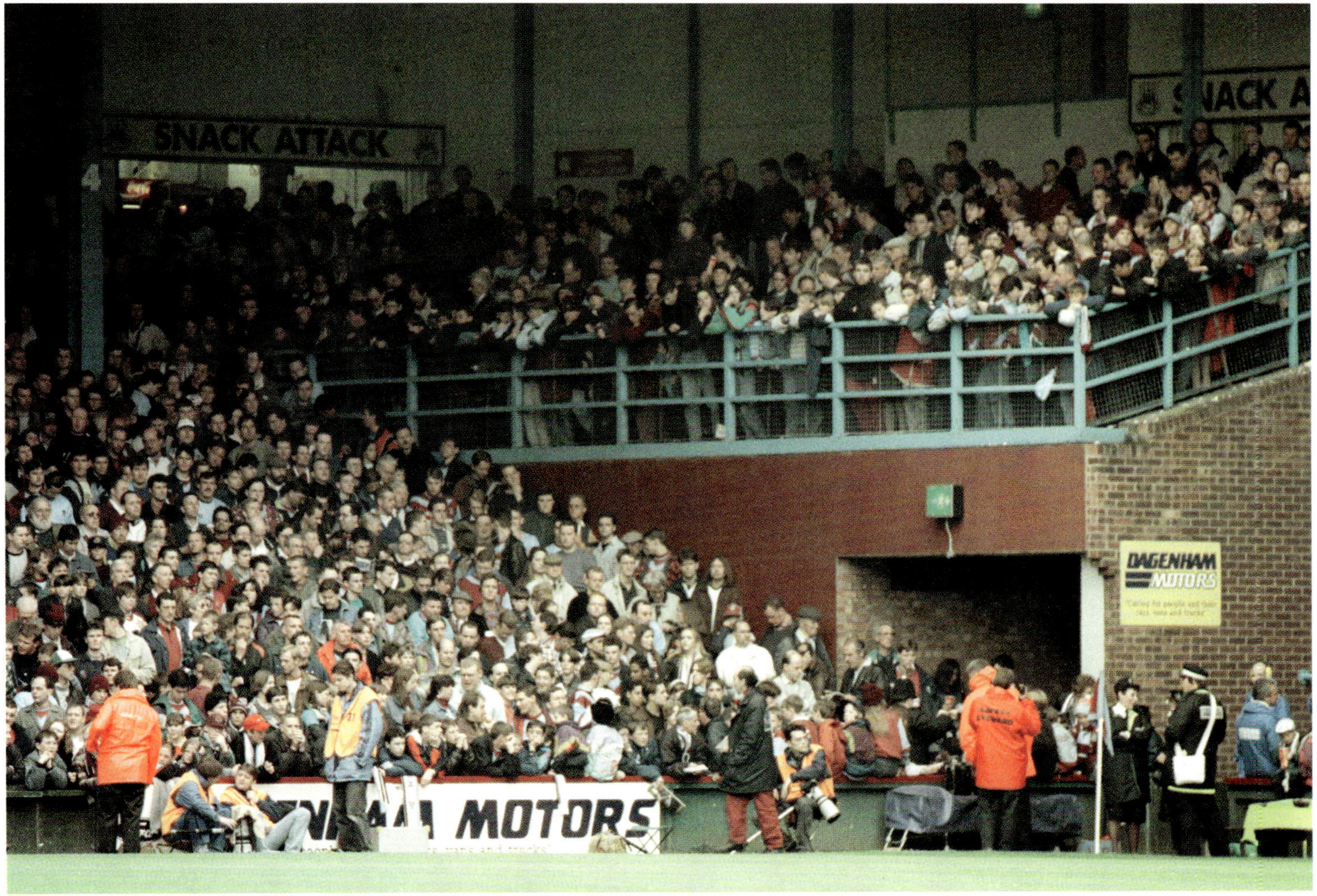

Fans' last stand. The North Bank terracing was in use for the last time for the final home game of the 1993–94 season when West Ham drew 3–3 with Southampton. A crowd of 26,952 watched the game that day. I stood on that terrace in my younger days, so it was sad to see it go in some ways, but you can't stand in the way of progress.

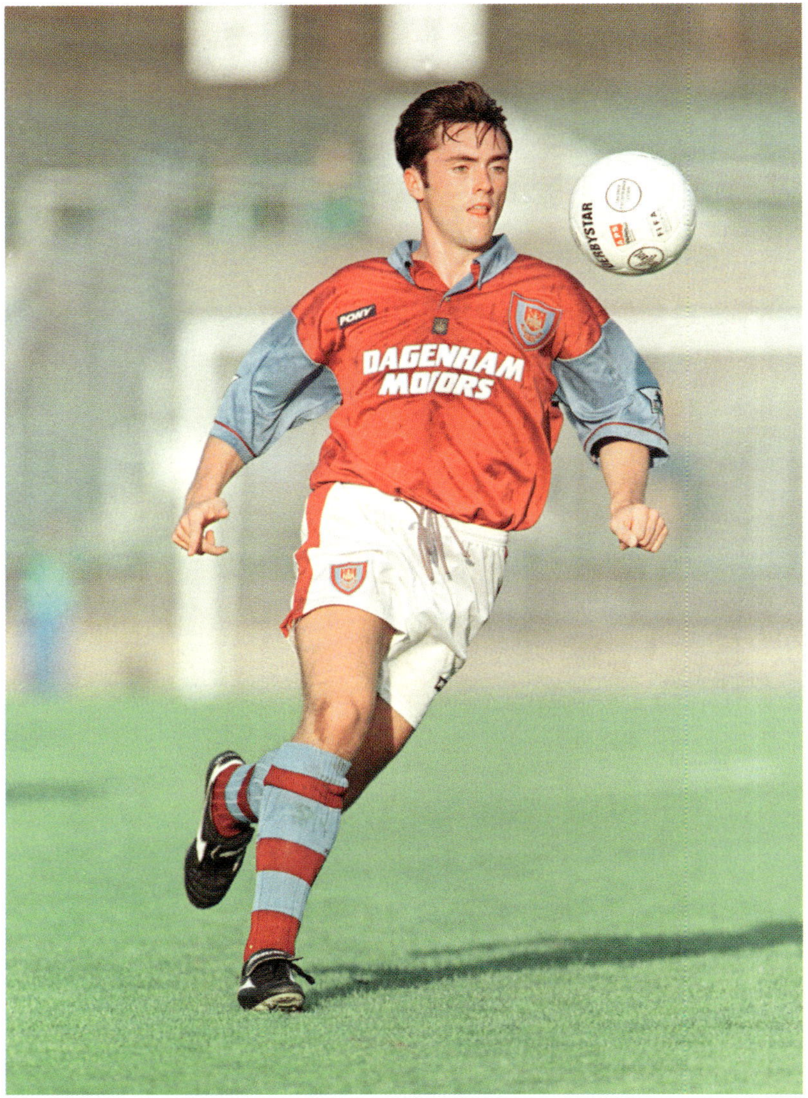
PONY
DAGENHAM MOTORS

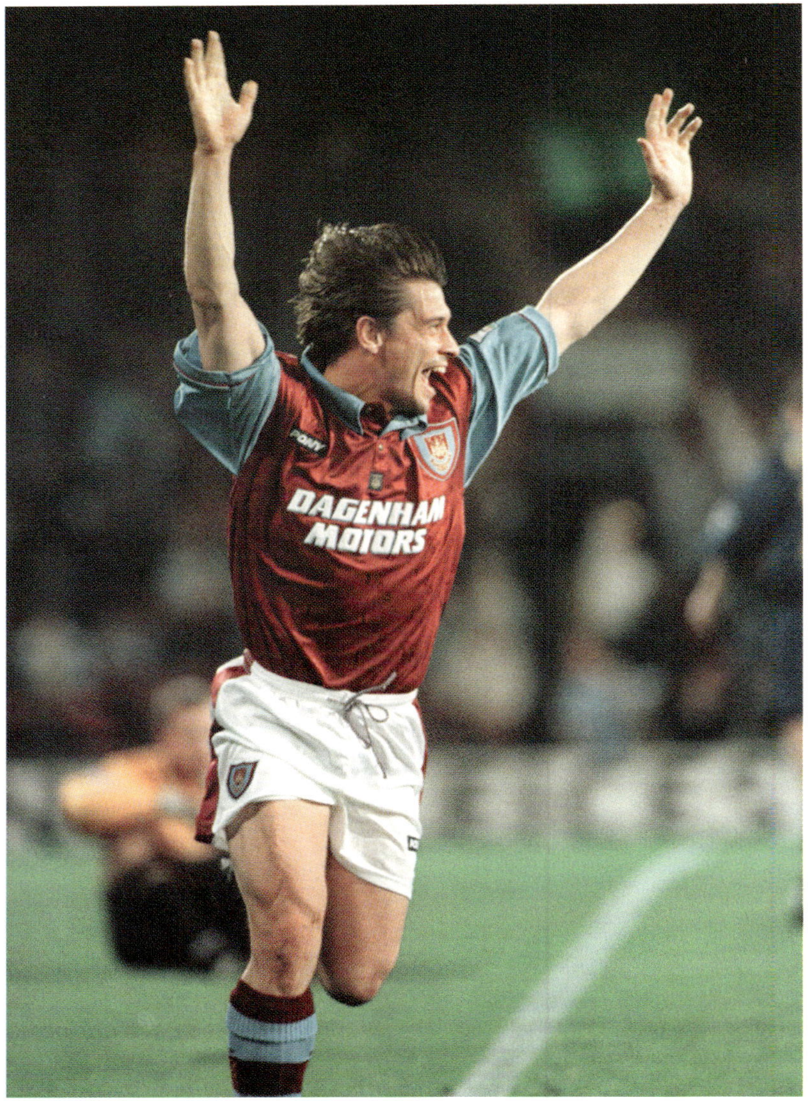
PONY
DAGENHAM MOTORS

Stock market. Pre-season matches give me a chance to concentrate on shooting stock shots of individual players. This strong shot of Danny Williamson was taken in Germany in 1995 when we played TSV Munich 1860 in a match to celebrate the 30th anniversary of the two sides meeting in the 1965 European Cup Winners' Cup Final at Wembley, which Hammers won 2–0.

Happy chappie. Tony Cottee's 18th-minute winner at Wimbledon in October 1995 was his first league goal for six months. No wonder he looks so delighted with himself.

Stars of the future. West Ham's exciting young defender Rio Ferdinand gets the better of Coventry's Darren Huckerby on this occasion. Both players are tipped for great things in the future.

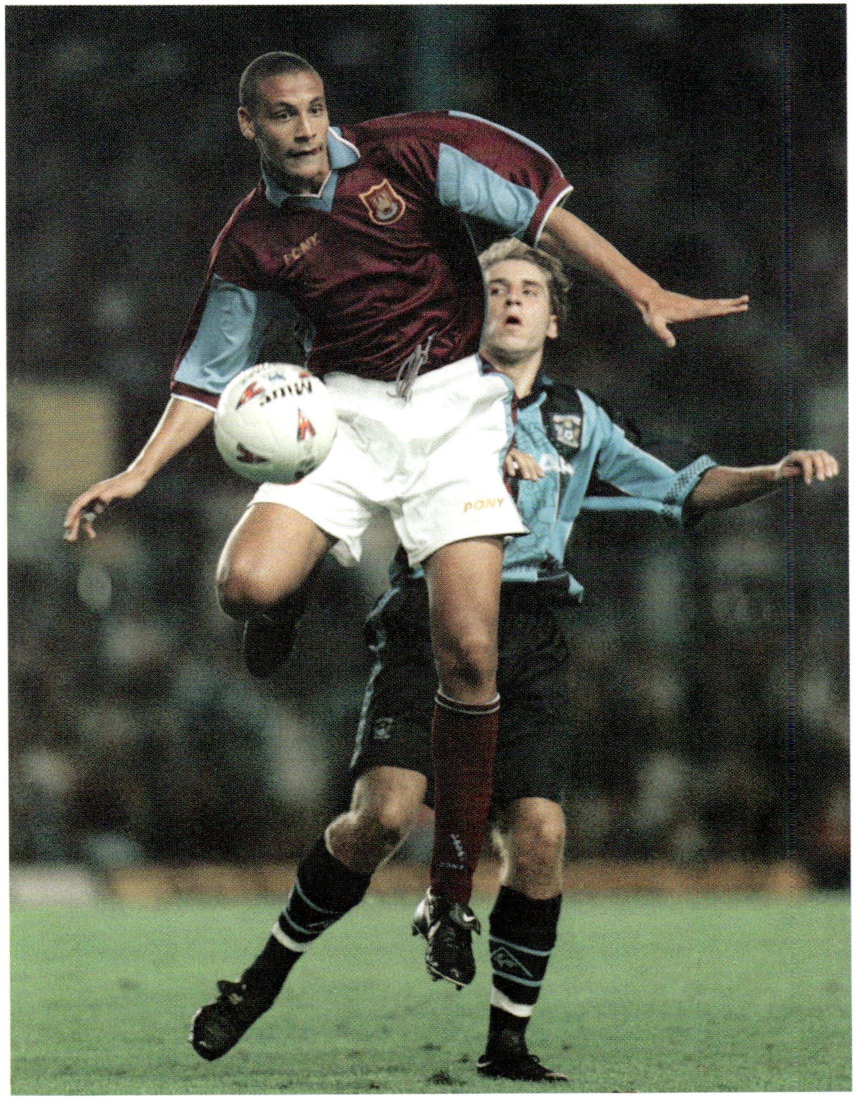

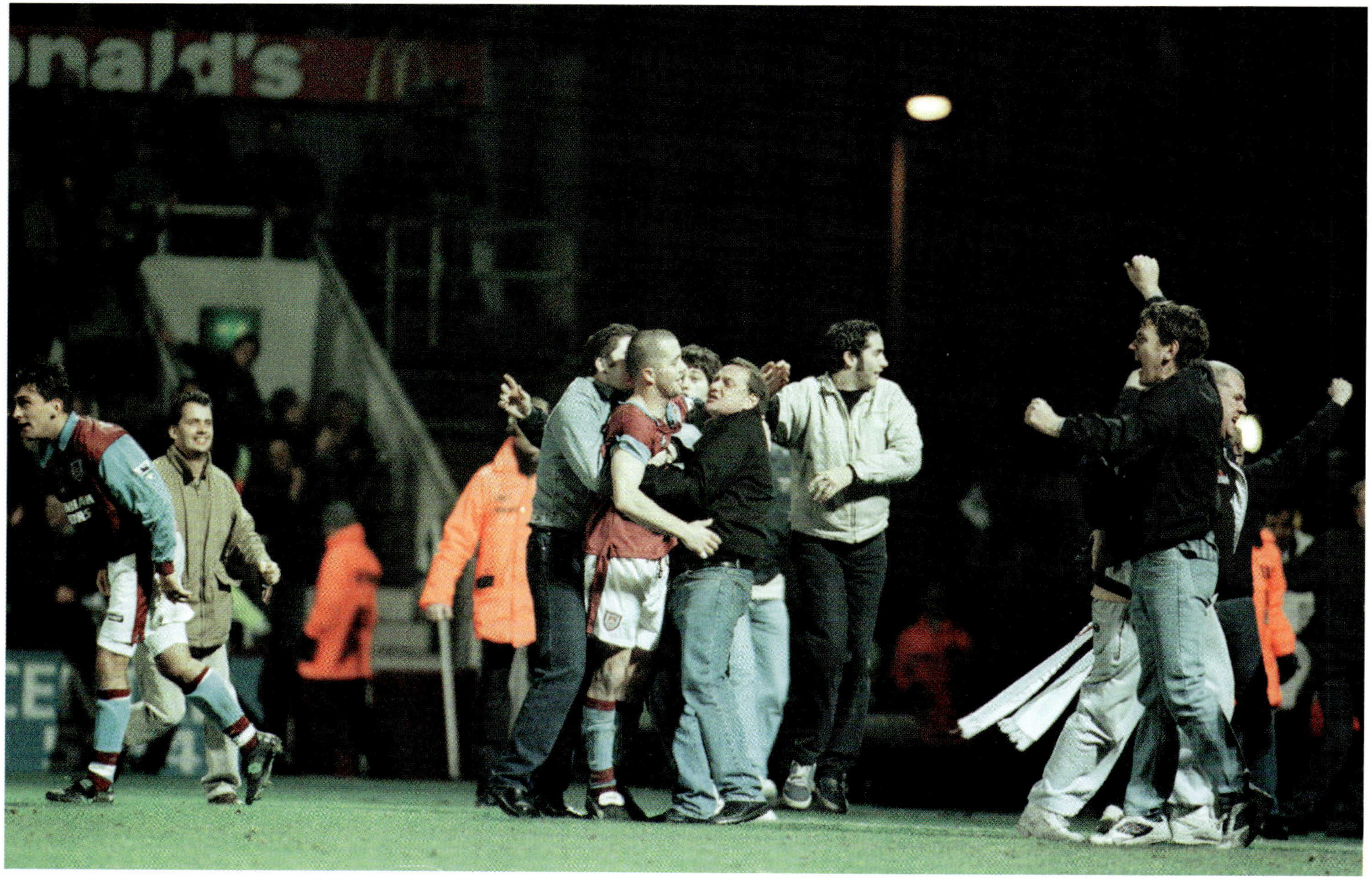

Spot-on Dicksie. Julian Dicks is mobbed by joyous fans after his spot-kick had put West Ham level against Manchester United at Upton Park in December 1996. Hammers had trailed 2–0 until late in the game when Florin Raducioiu pulled a goal back on 78 minutes before Dicks's equaliser two minutes later.

Cheers and tears. Rio Ferdinand and Frank Lampard celebrate their call-ups into the full England squad and the Under-21 squad respectively. Just days after I took this picture of the pair celebrating at Chadwell Heath, Rio was charged with a drink-driving offence and was withdrawn from the squad by England coach Glenn Hoddle. Happily, as we now all know, young Rio was finally given his chance and was a member of the England squad for the World Cup Finals in France '98.

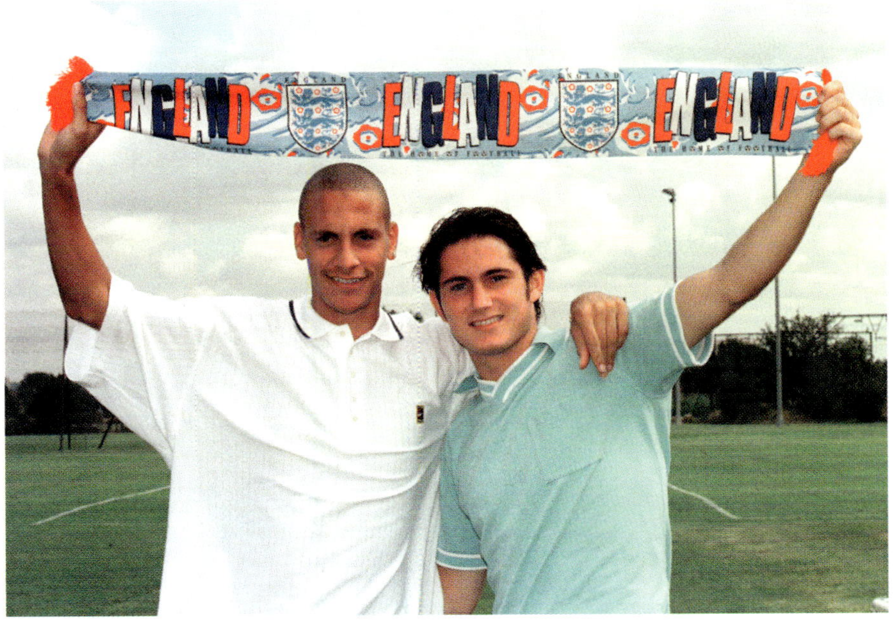

Goal-hanging. John Hartson joined West Ham from near neighbours Arsenal in February 1997 in what many 'experts' claimed to be an overpriced deal. John's five goals from eleven starts during the remainder of the season were crucial to Hammers' survival and made it look like money well spent.

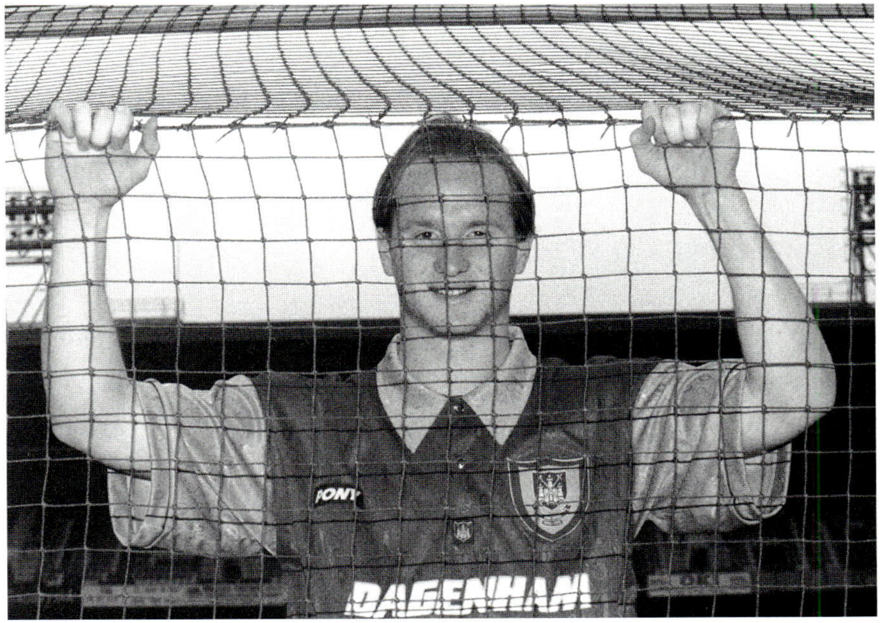

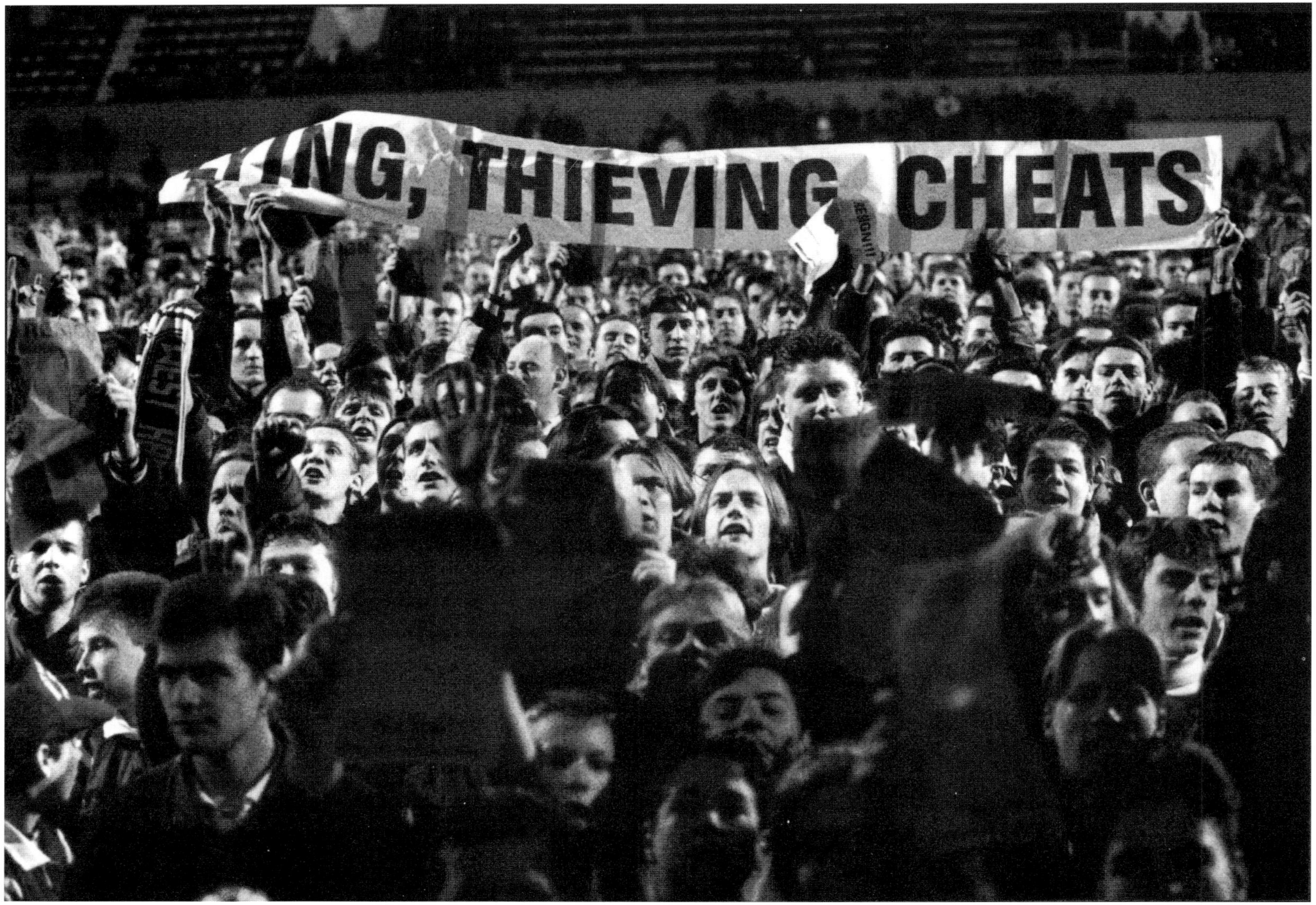
THIEVING CHEATS

Banner man. The West Ham fans make their feelings towards the Board of Directors known with a post-match pitch demonstration against the infamous Hammers' Bond scheme.

Ali oops. Everybody was impressed with Tunisian goalkeeper Ali Boumnijel whom Harry Redknapp included in the squad for the pre-1997–98 season tour of Scotland. Ironically, Craig Forrest, the Canadian 'keeper signed from Ipswich weeks earlier, made his debut on the tour and it was clear that there was no place for Ali. Nothing more was heard from him until the 1998 World Cup squads were announced and he was named in the Tunisian line-up.

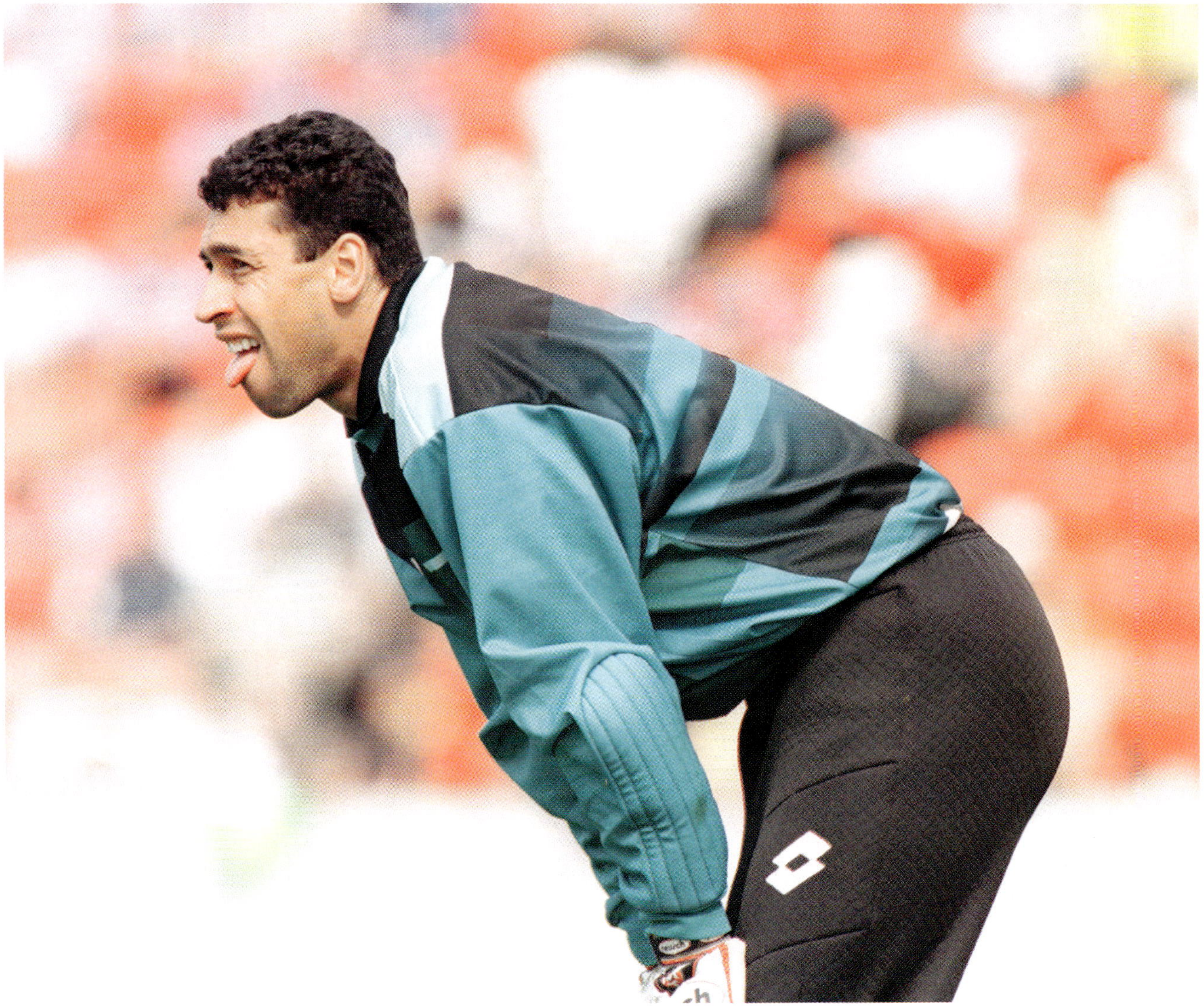

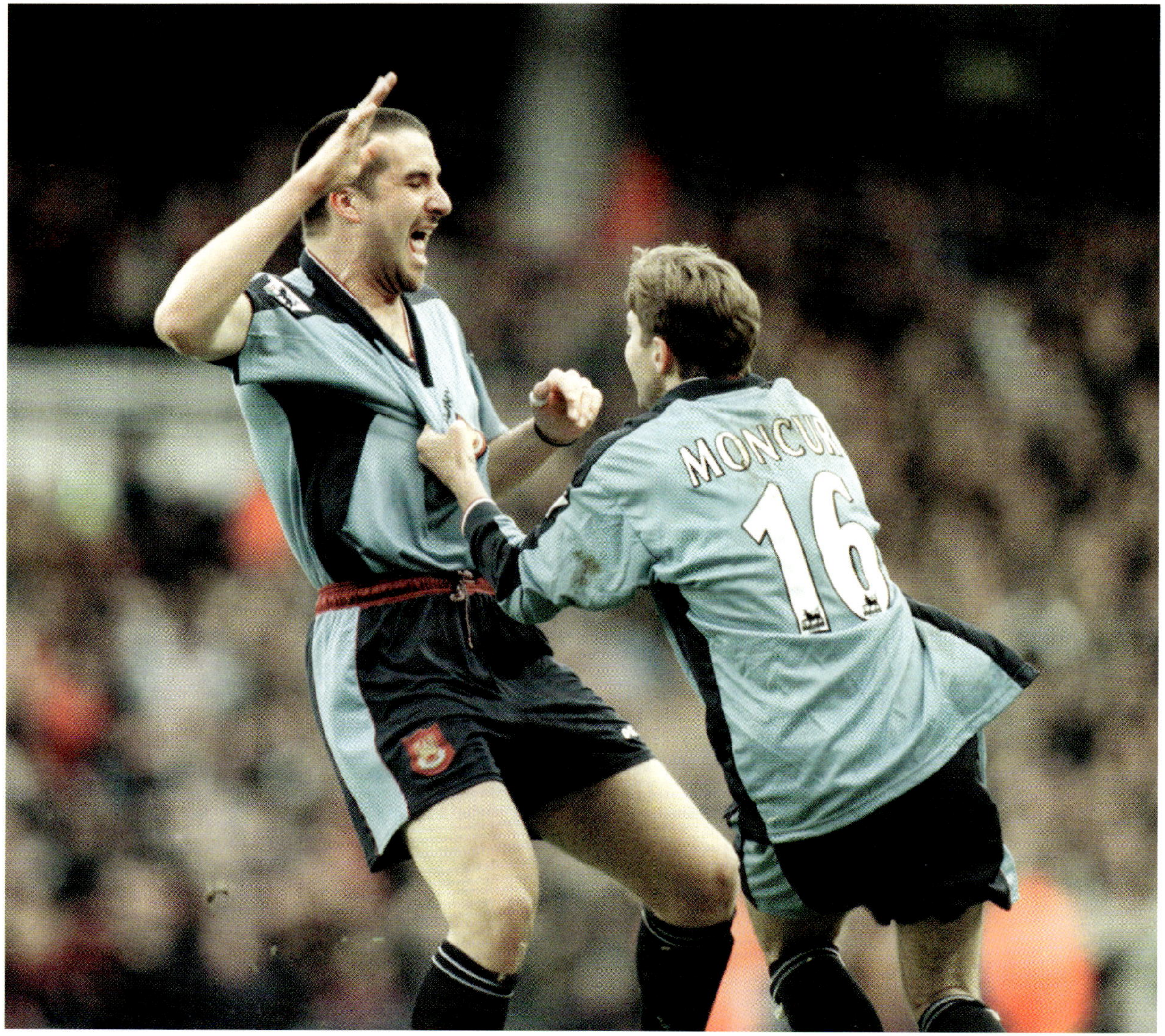

Hero and villain. John Moncur congratulates a delighted Ian Pearce after the latter's goal had put West Ham ahead in the FA Cup sixth round tie at Highbury in March 1998. Sadly for Pearce, he conceded a disputed penalty later in the match which Dennis Bergkamp converted to force a replay — which Hammers lost in a penalty shoot-out.

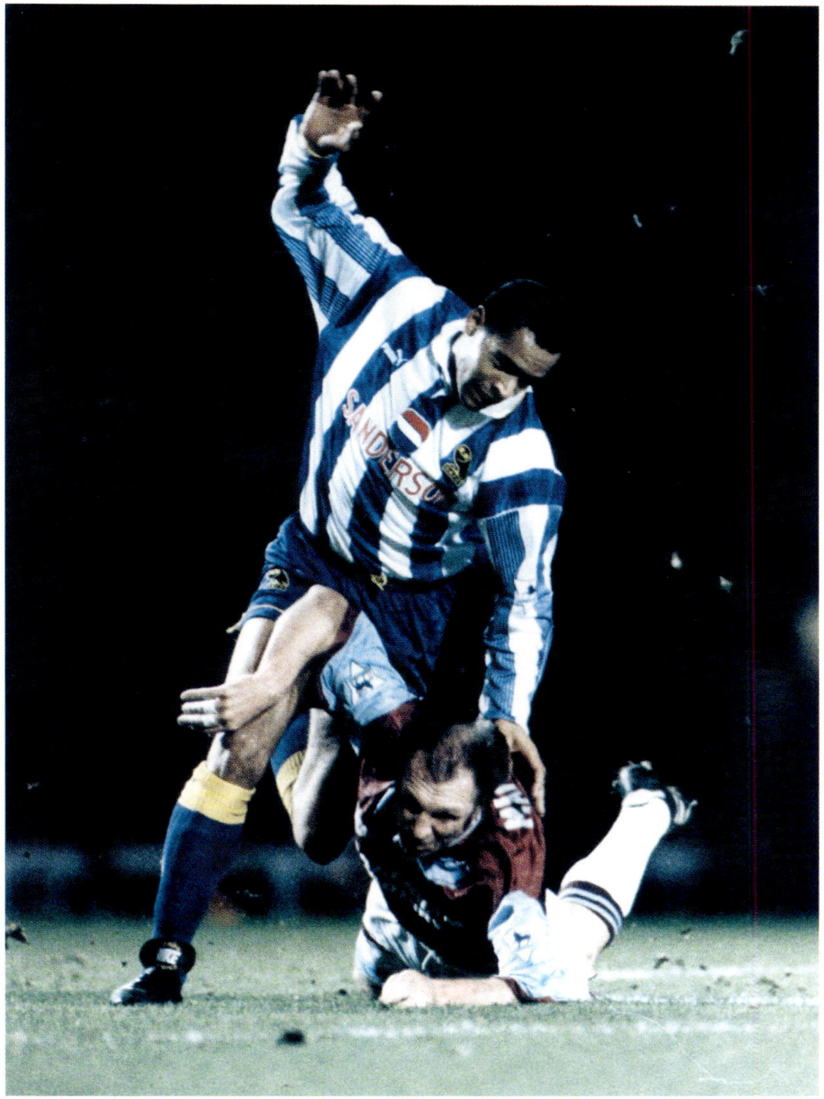

Off you go. Alvin Martin stumbles into Sheffield Wednesday's Mark Bright on the halfway line and is shown the red card by referee Paul Danson, despite the West Ham man's protestations. A second sending-off, for Tim Breacker, sees Hammers lose the 1995 match 2–0. Referee Danson later made an about turn after studying a video of the incident, reducing Martin's red card to yellow.

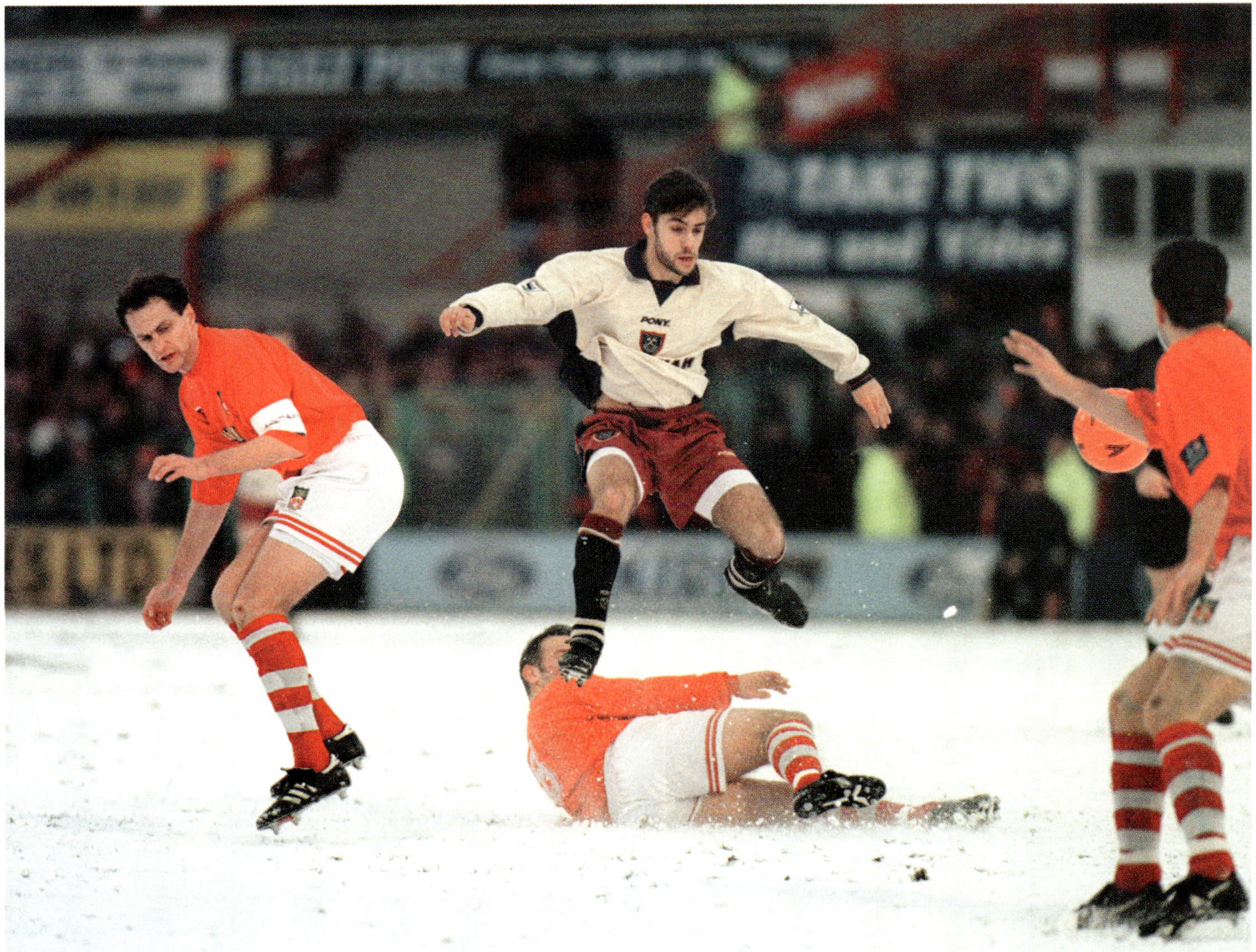

Slippery slope. Portuguese star Hugo Porfirio got his first sight of the white stuff when West Ham took on Wrexham at a snow-covered Racecourse Ground for their FA Cup third round tie in January 1997. Hugo saved the visitors' embarrassment by lobbing an equalising goal to force a replay, but not even he could save the Hammers in the replay as they went out 1–0 to a 90th-minute Russell goal.

Glorious mud. A torrential downpour just minutes before kick-off of the home match against Newcastle United in the 1996–97 season left the referee no option but to call the match off at the last moment. He took a ball out to see if it would roll on the wet surface and this was the end result.

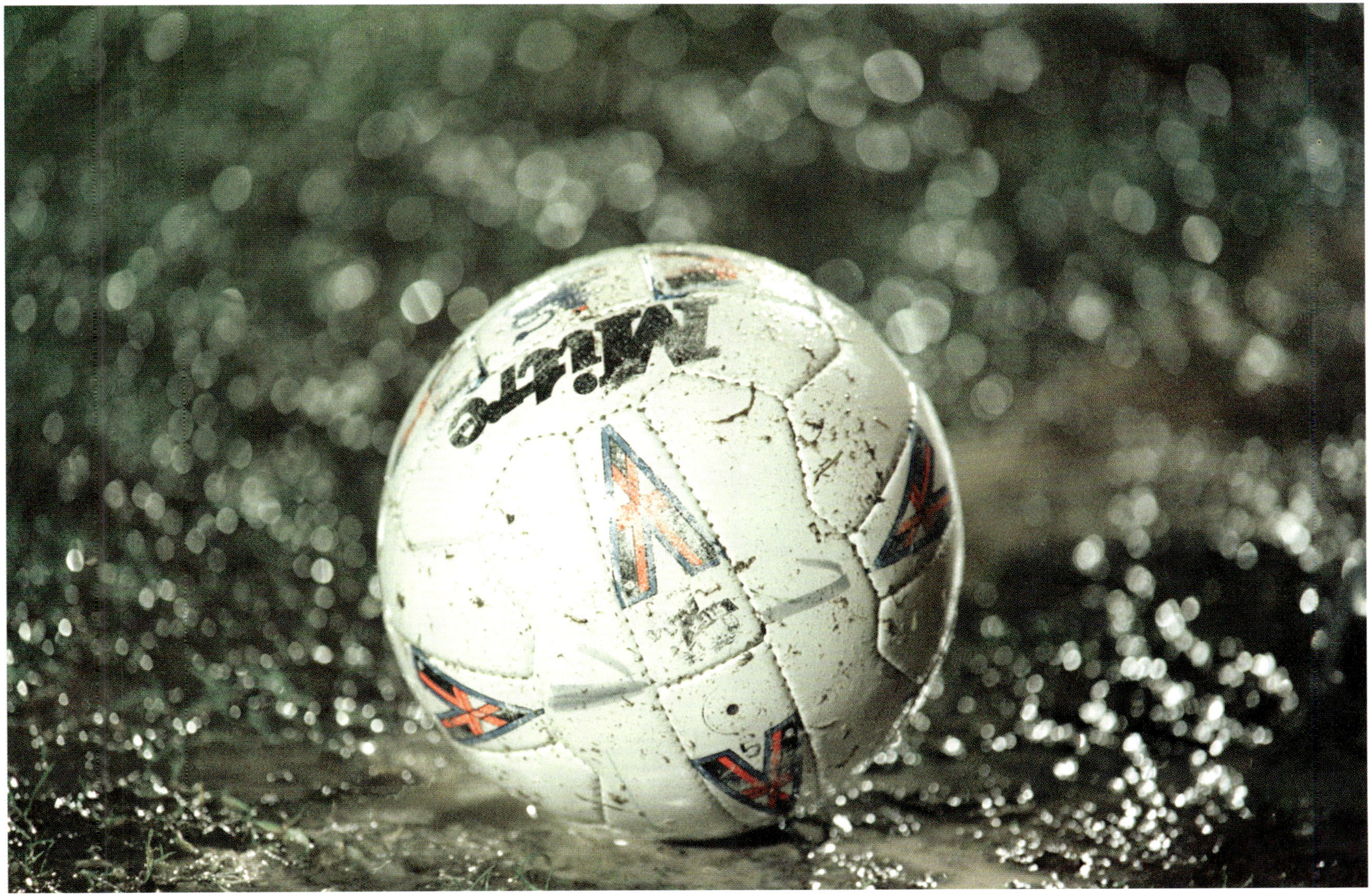

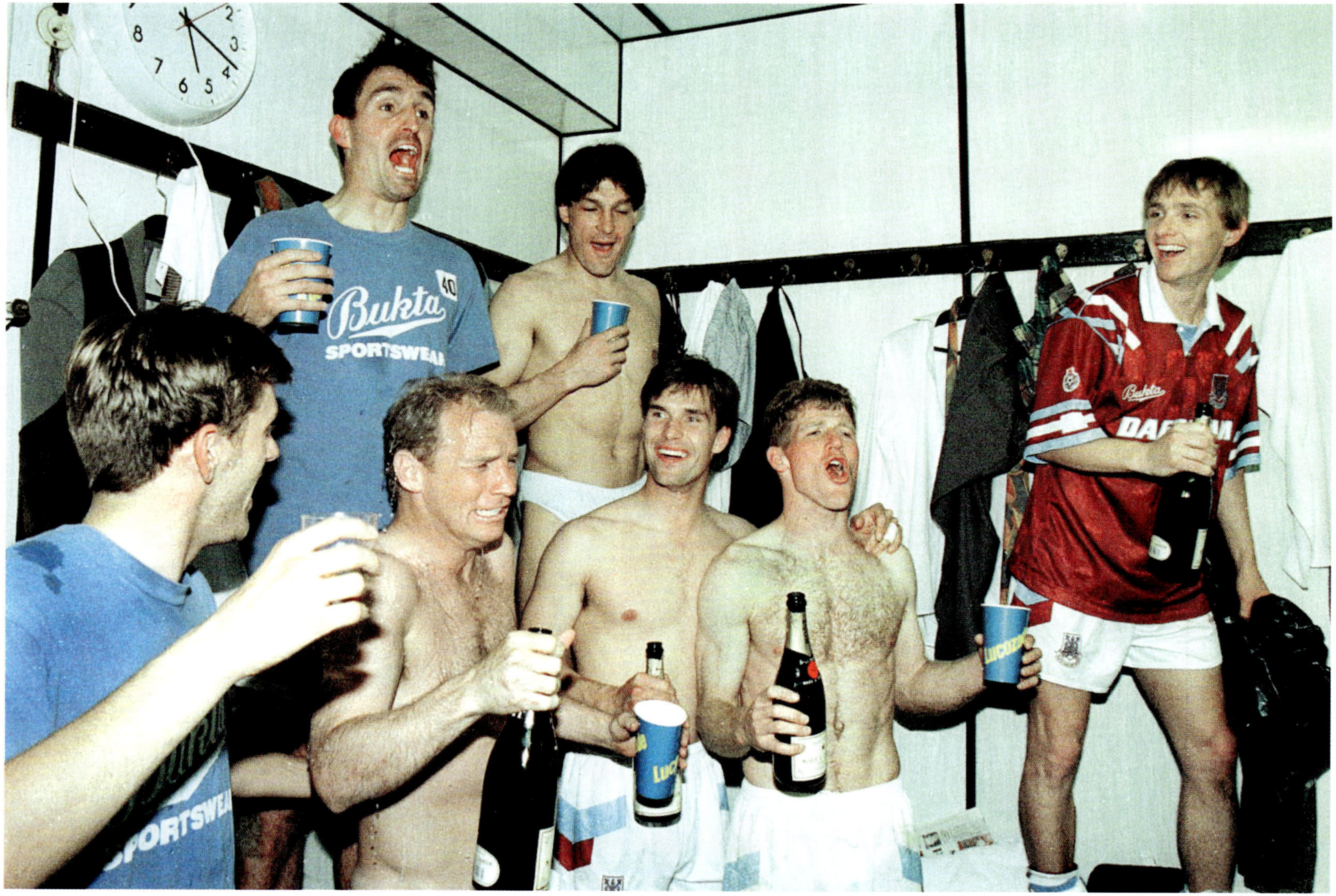
Bukta
SPORTSWEAR
40

Going up. 'Mad Dog' Martin Allen leads the vocals in the Upton Park dressing room as West Ham celebrate promotion to the Premiership in May 1993 after beating Cambridge United 2–0. Mark Robson, David Speedie, Peter Butler, Trevor Morley, Steve Potts and Kevin Keen toast success with champagne.

Dicks between the sticks. Julian Dicks was forced to don the goalkeeper's jersey at Goodison Park following the dismissal of Ludek Miklosko for a foul on Everton's Daniel Amokachi in December 1995. Future team-mate David Unsworth put the resulting penalty past Dicksie, and the Hammers lost the match 3–0.

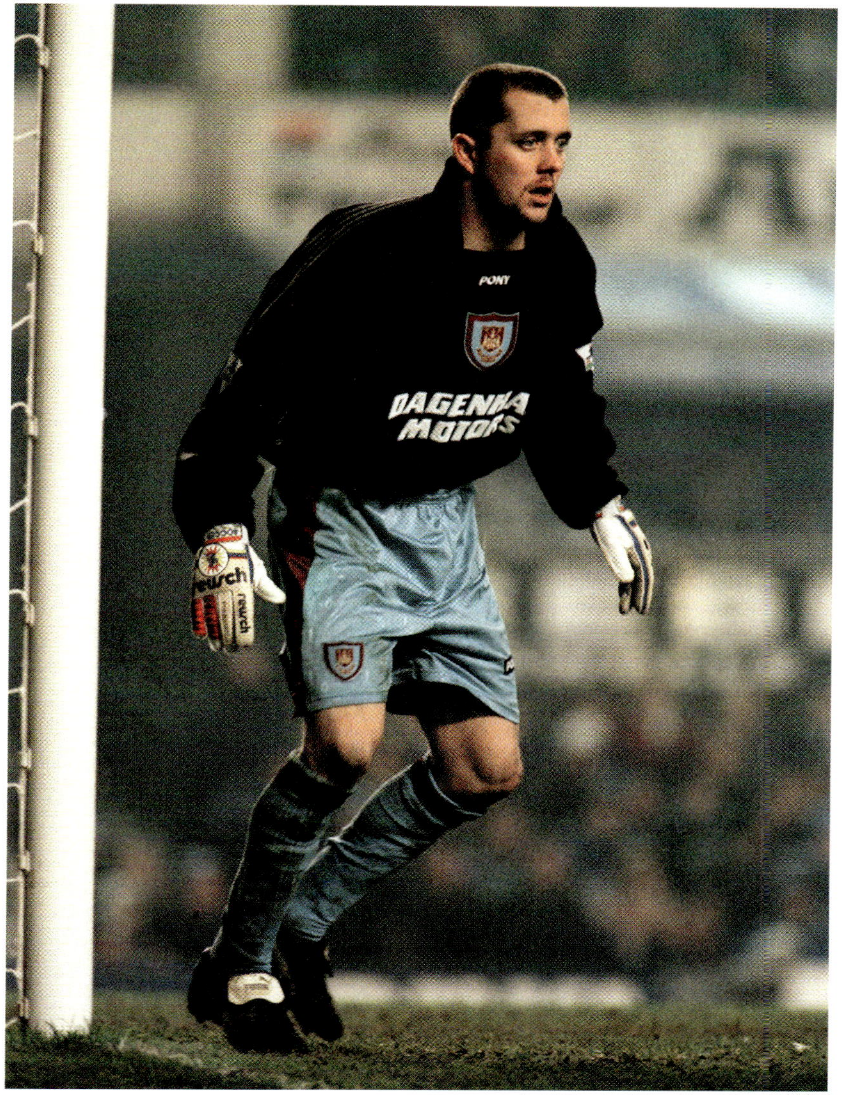

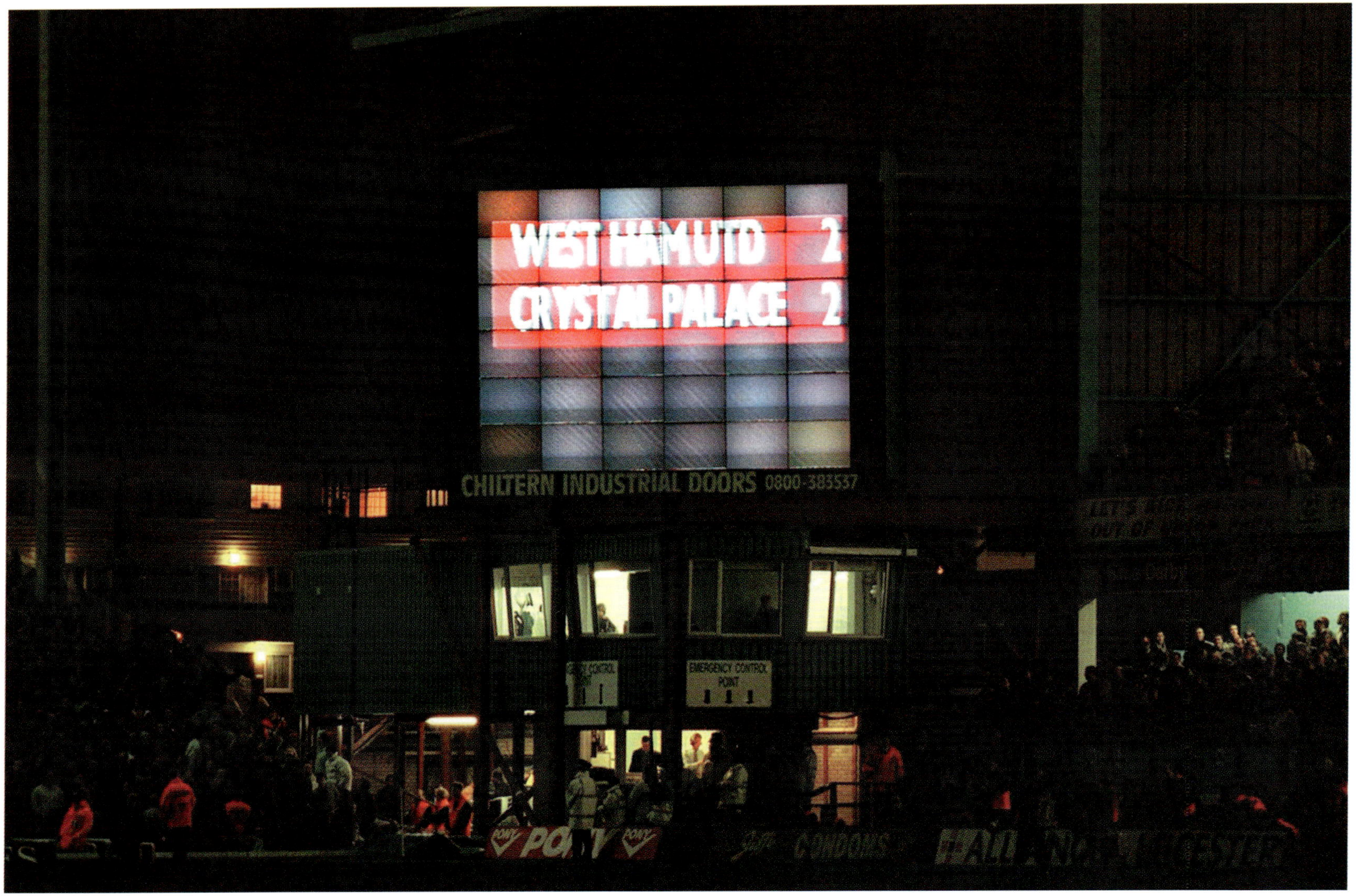
WEST HAM UTD 2
CRYSTAL PALACE 2
CHILTERN INDUSTRIAL DOORS 0800-383537
EMERGENCY CONTROL POINT
CONDOMS

Lights out. Upton Park was plunged into darkness as West Ham took on Crystal Palace during the 1997–98 season. The visitors were leading 2–0 at one stage before Hammers fought their way back to 2–2. But, just as Frank Lampard scored the second goal, the floodlight system blew and the game was postponed after some 45 minutes' delay. The rearranged fixture was won 4–1 by the Hammers, leaving Palace to rue their bad luck.

Goo'day at the office. Assistant manager Frank Lampard and managing director Peter Storrie have business to discuss during Hammers' Centenary Tour of Australia in 1995. And what better place to hold a meeting than on board a ferry-boat with a backdrop of the famous Sydney Harbour Bridge and Opera House?

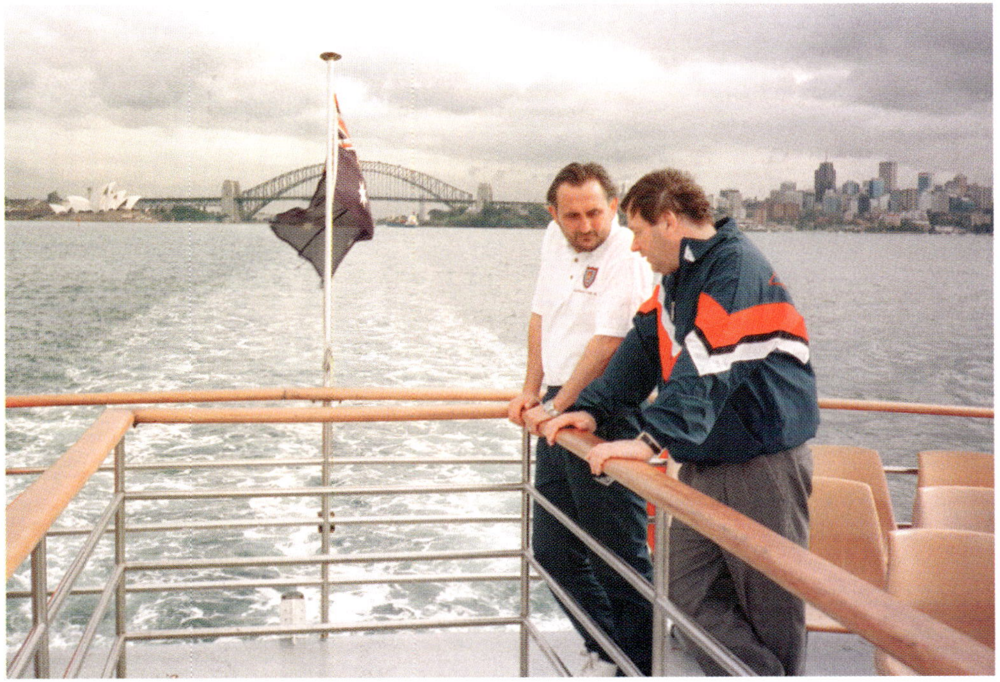

It's the way I cell 'em. Comedian Frank Carson was up to his old tricks on a visit to Upton Park but had his collar felt by police liaison officer Jeff Martin when he tried to infiltrate the West Ham dressing room.

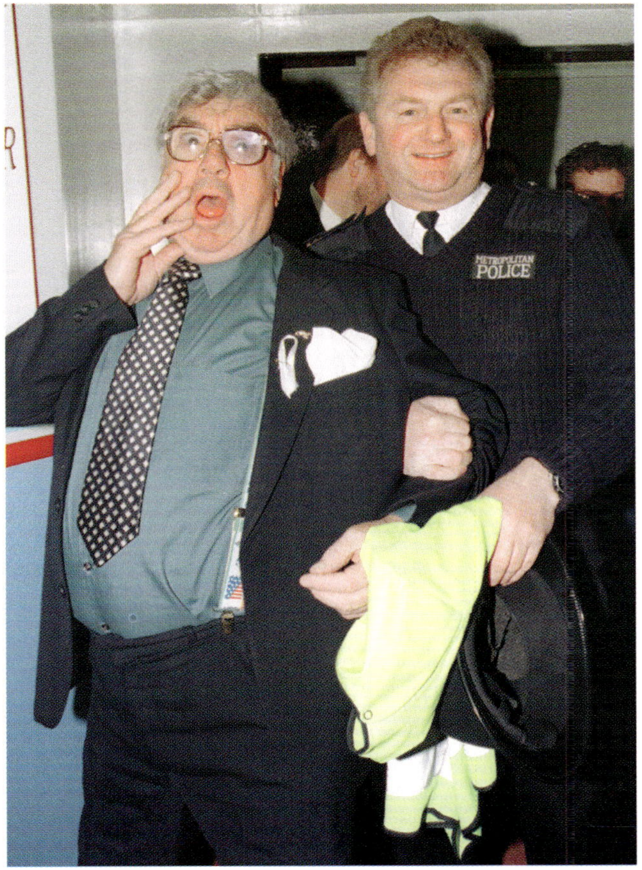

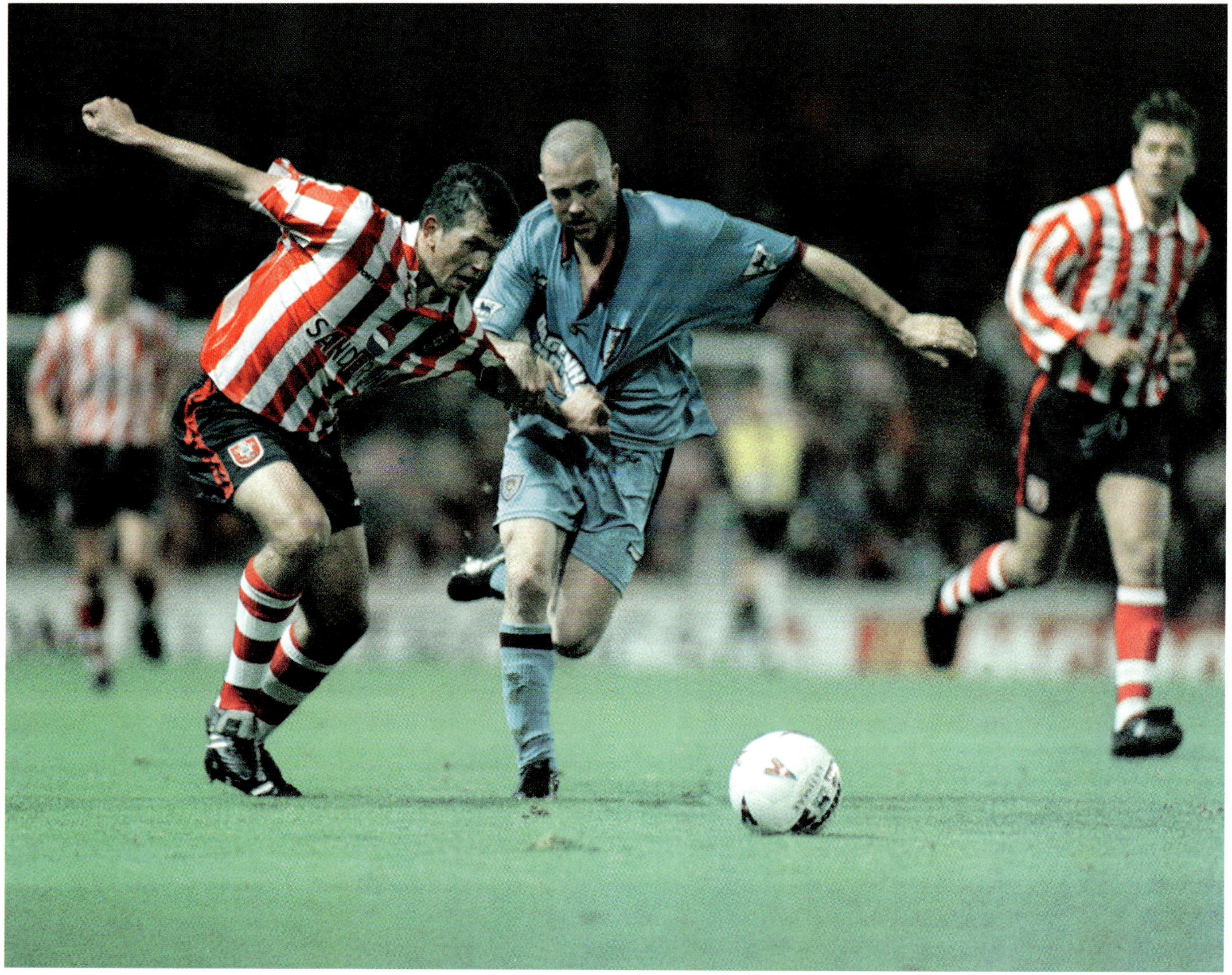

Get a grip. Southampton's Neil Heaney gets a grip on Julian Dicks as the pair tussle for possession as Hammers bow out of the Coca-Cola Cup at the Dell in October 1995.

Close marking. David Unsworth was all over Aston Villa's Savo Milosovic 'like a bad suit' when the two sides met at Villa Park in April 1998. Sadly for West Ham, they lost the game 2–0 as they pushed for a European place at the end of the season.

Spurred on. Israeli superstar Eyal Berkovic just cannot conceal his delight after scoring Hammers' second goal in a 2–1 win over Tottenham Hotspur in the first home game of the 1997–98 season. Eyal had previously been linked with Spurs and many of his countrymen thought he had chosen wrongly in opting for East London. So this goal must have been particularly sweet.

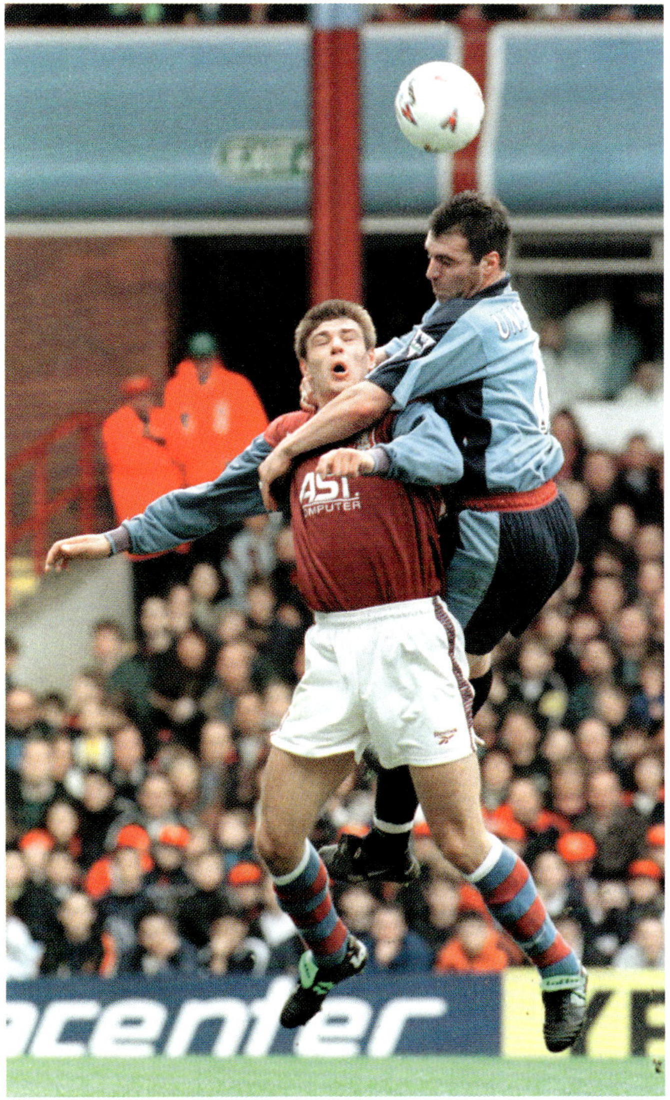

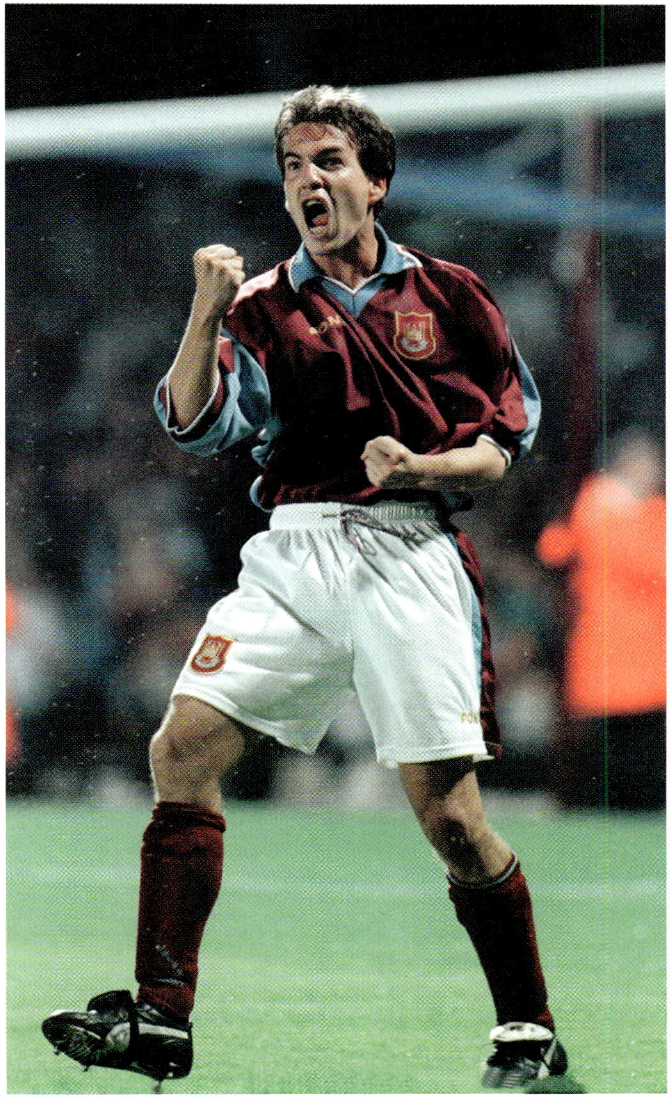

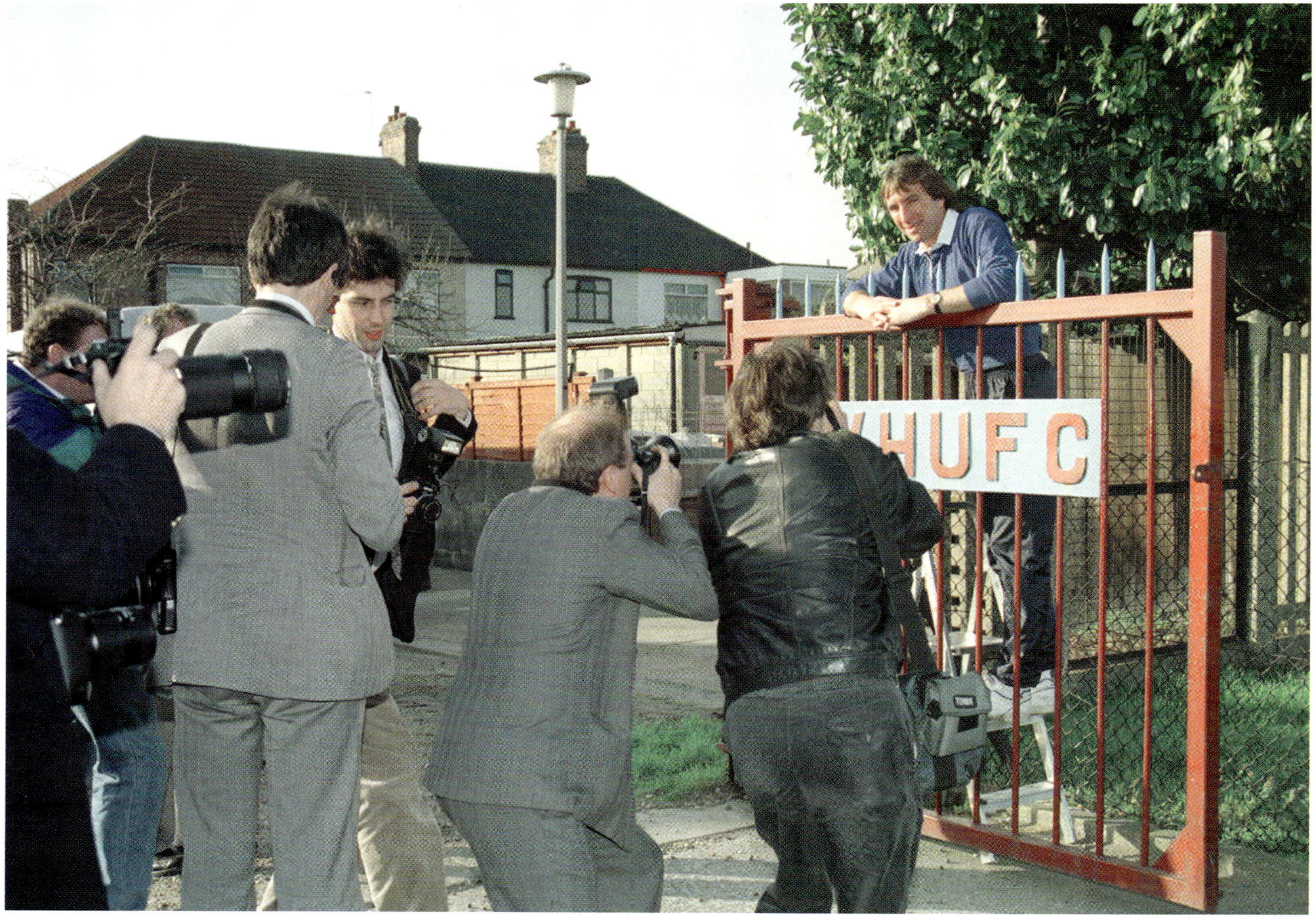

You're the boss. Billy Bonds poses for the photographers at the gate to Hammers' Chadwell Heath training HQ in February 1990, having just been installed as manager in succession to Lou Macari. Bonzo was never very happy in these situations but had to get used to it during his short reign as boss.

That's handy. After playing the whole of the 1997–98 campaign without a shirt sponsor, West Ham finally landed a deal with Dr Marten's in time for the start of the following season. The press conference coincided with the signing of goalkeeper Shaka Hislop from Newcastle so I, like every other photographer at the photo shoot, thought it would be a good idea to get a pair of DMs on the 'keeper's hands — clever, eh?

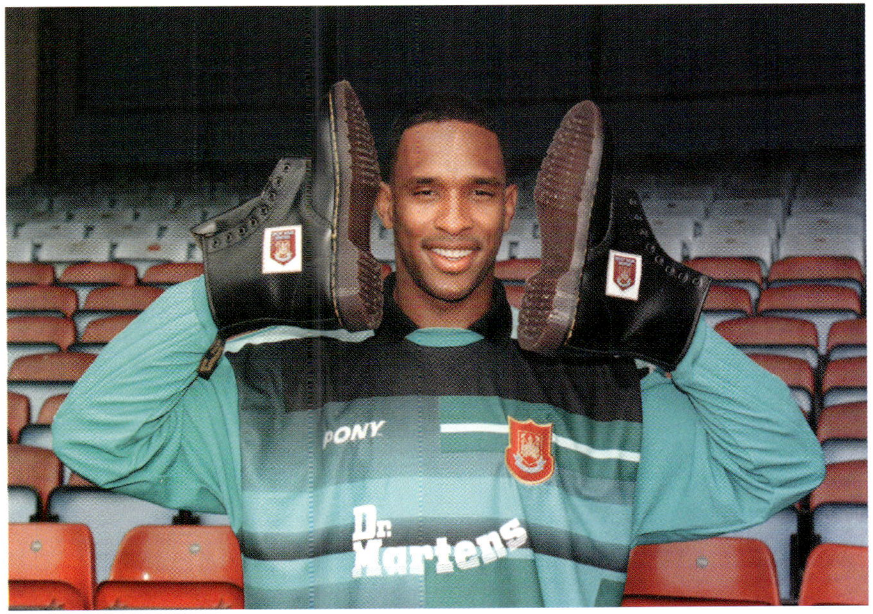

Wright on. Another summer 1998 signing was that of Ian Wright from Arsenal. Once again, silly props were to the fore and gentle persuasion got Ian to pose with some rather natty little fluffy hammers.

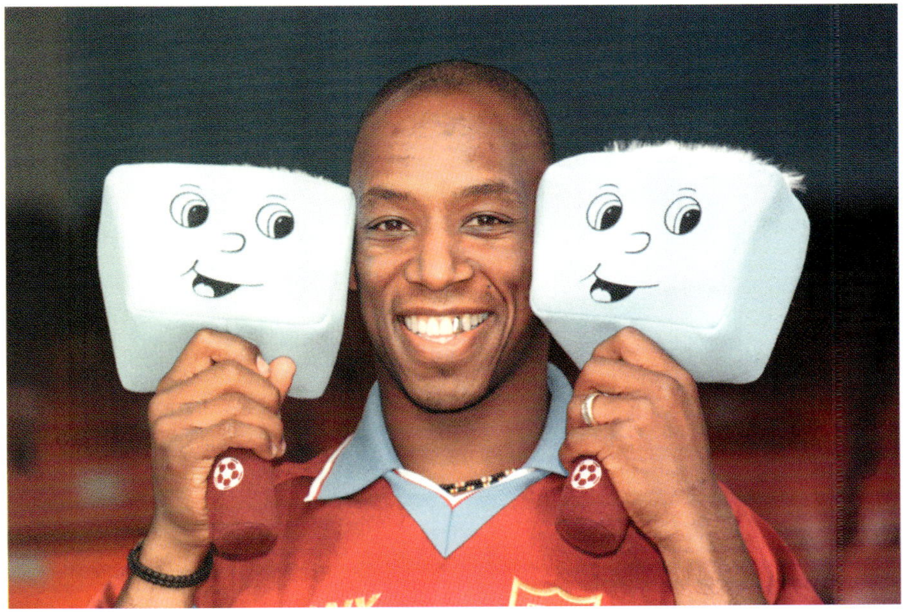

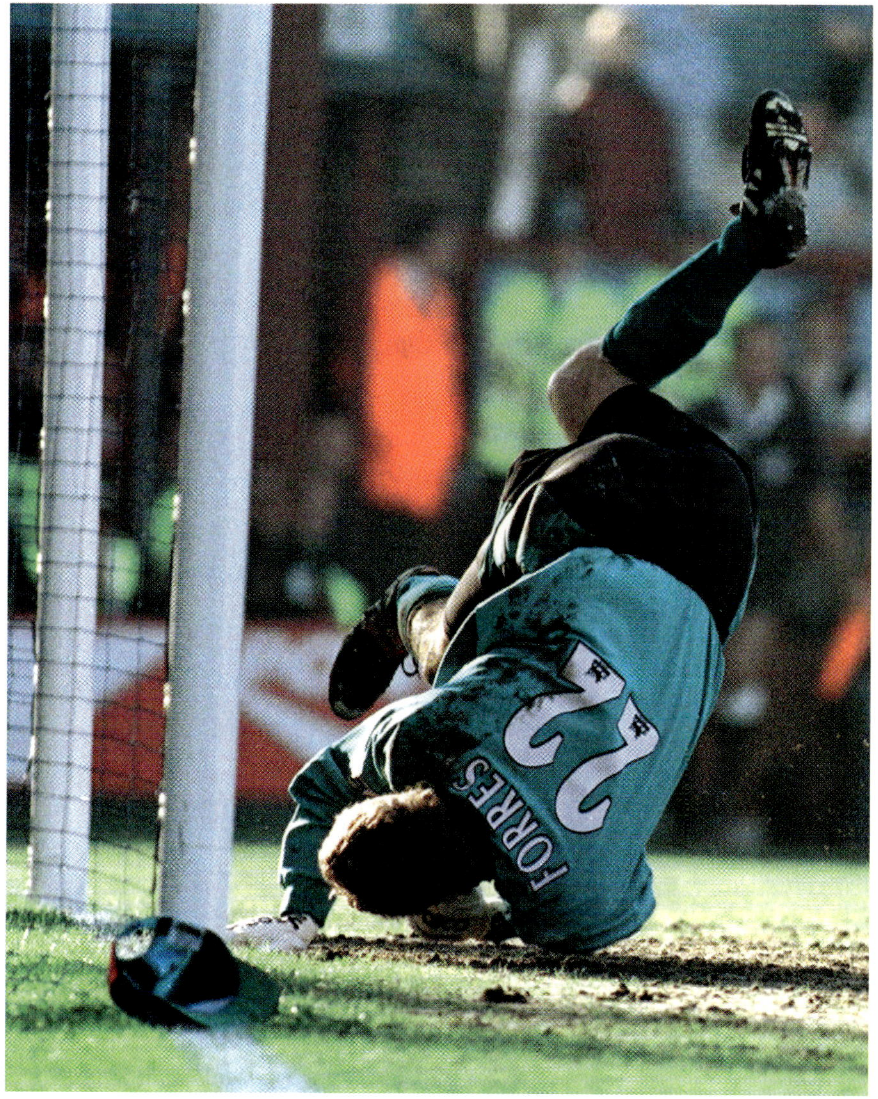

All ends upwards. Goalkeeper Craig Forrest is beaten by a first-minute goal in Hammers' FA Cup fifth round tie against Blackburn Rovers at Upton Park in February 1998. The match ended in a 2–2 draw, but Craig was to play a big part in the Ewood Park replay, saving a penalty in the shoot-out to help Hammers through to the next round.

Only the lonely. Harry Redknapp took over as manager on the eve of the 1994–95 season after Billy Bonds had sensationally quit the job. At the press conference I had to try to get Harry to pose for the photographers who were desperate for some kind of picture. He really didn't want to know, telling me that he was too upset by Billy's resignation. I think it shows in his face in the picture we set up.

Flying tonight. Hammers' marksman Tony Cottee is sent flying by this challenge in the opening game of the 1995–96 season against Leeds United at Upton Park. Despite a fifth-minute opener by Danny Williamson, West Ham lost the game 2–1 when Tony Yeboah netted twice in the second period.

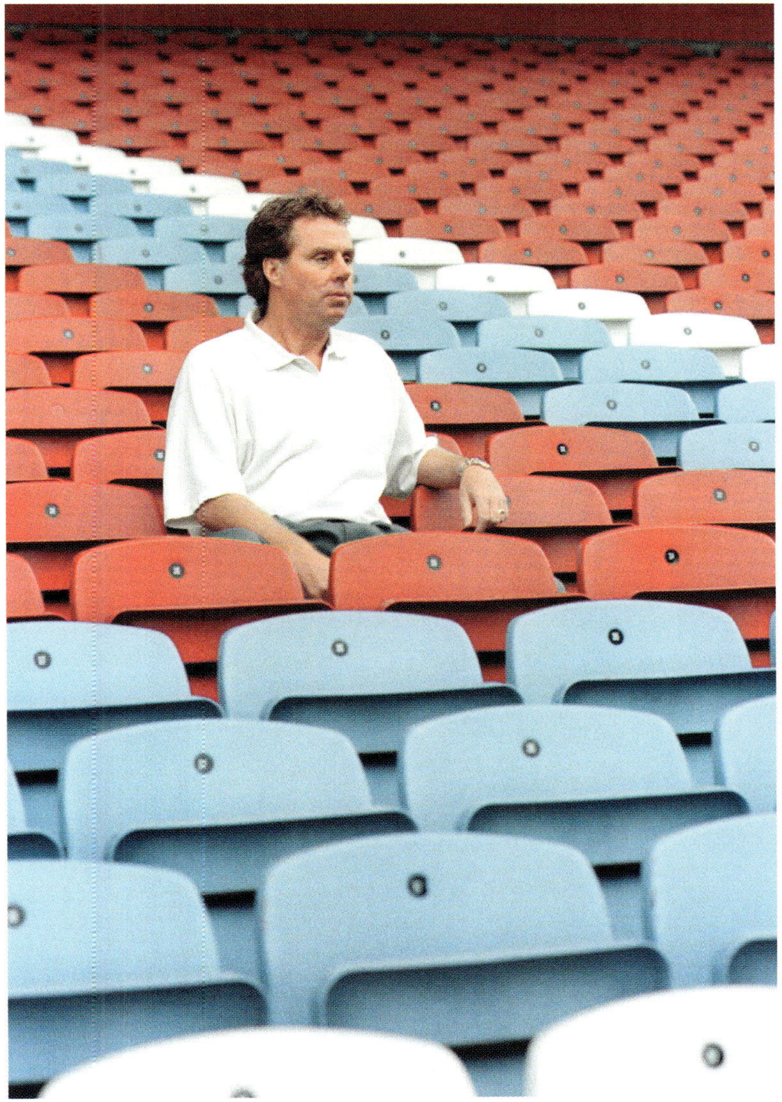

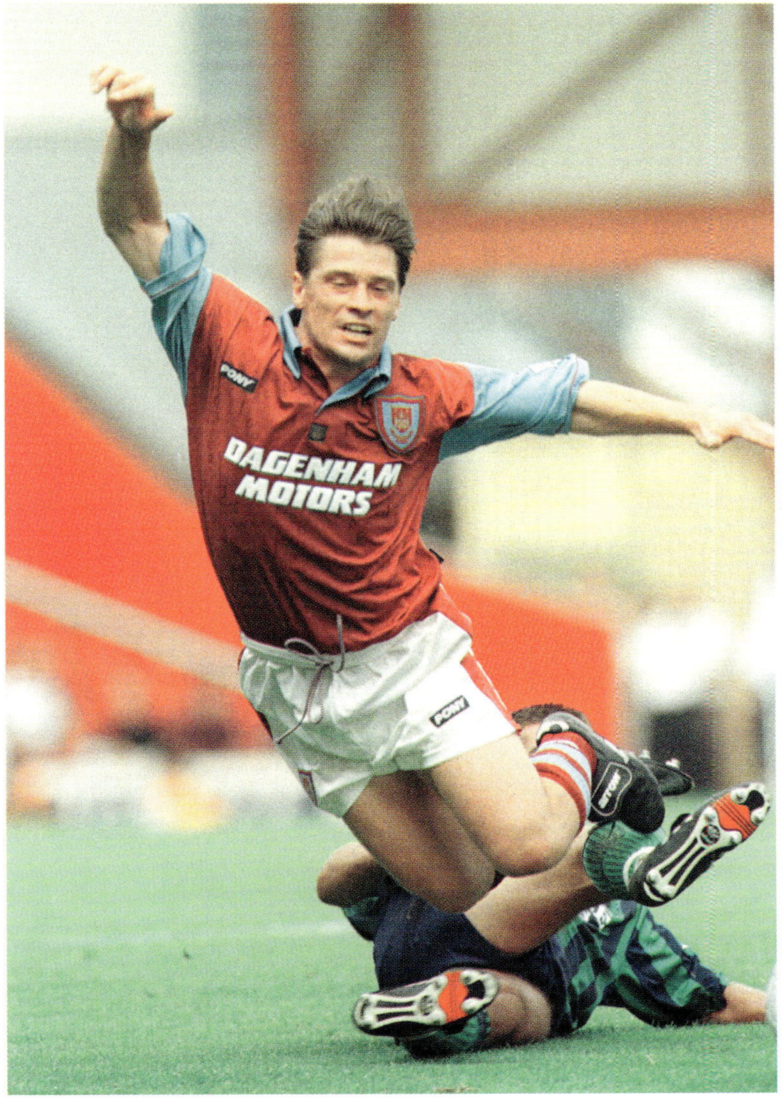
PONY
DAGENHAM
MOTORS

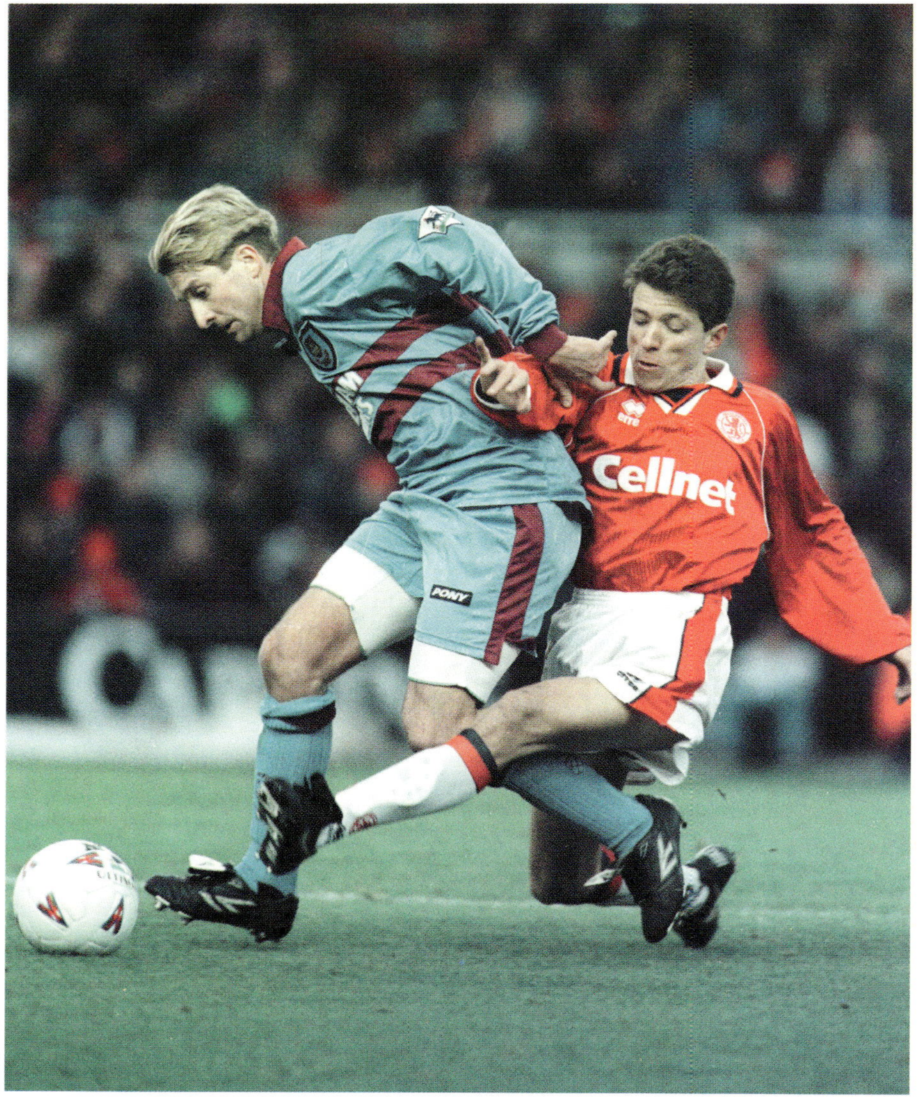

No Christmas cheer. John Moncur tries to shake off Middlesbrough's Brazilian wizard Juninho as the Hammers go down 4–2 in the Riverside Stadium just two days before Christmas 1995.

Generation game. This is one of Harry's favourite pictures, taken during the home match with Coventry City in January 1996. Frank Lampard Junior was about to make his West Ham debut as a substitute when City decided to put veteran Gordon Strachan on as well. Harry put his arms around both players and the three of them enjoyed a joke, even though the match was at a crucial stage.

Lomas lament. Ian Bishop rides this tackle by Manchester City's Steve Lomas as the two sides meet at Upton Park in March 1996. Hammers won this encounter 4–2 in the season that saw City relegated to the Nationwide League. Steve Lomas, destined to join West Ham a year later, was sent off for two bookable offences.

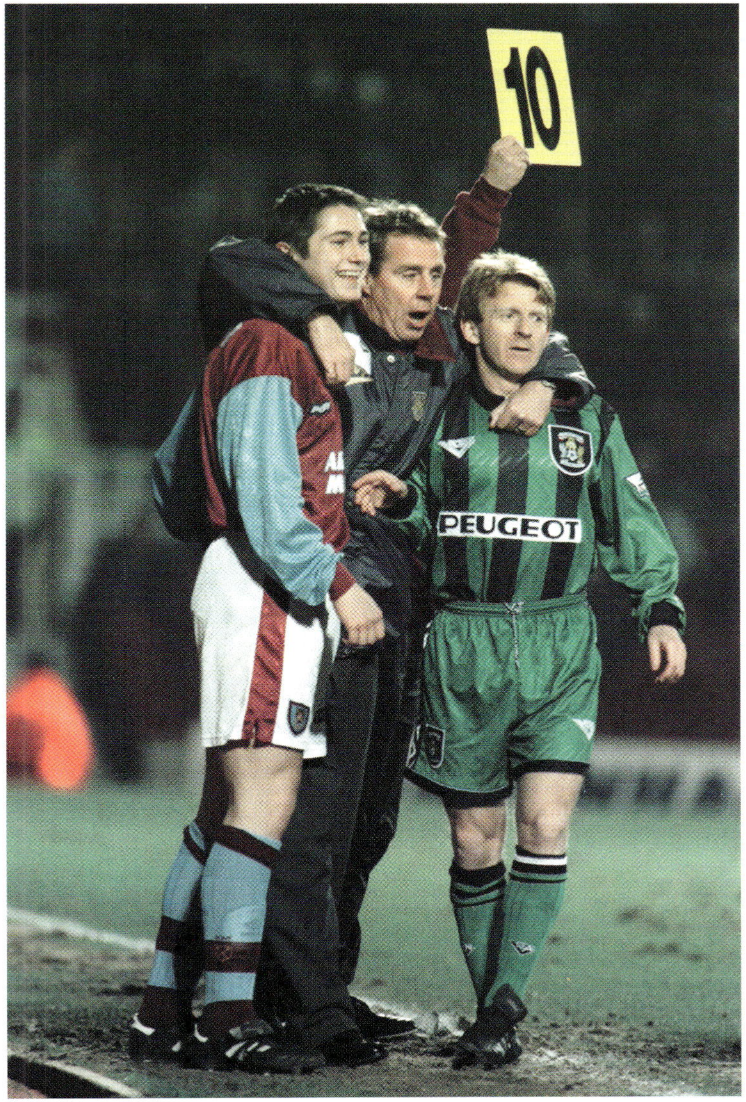
10
PEUGEOT

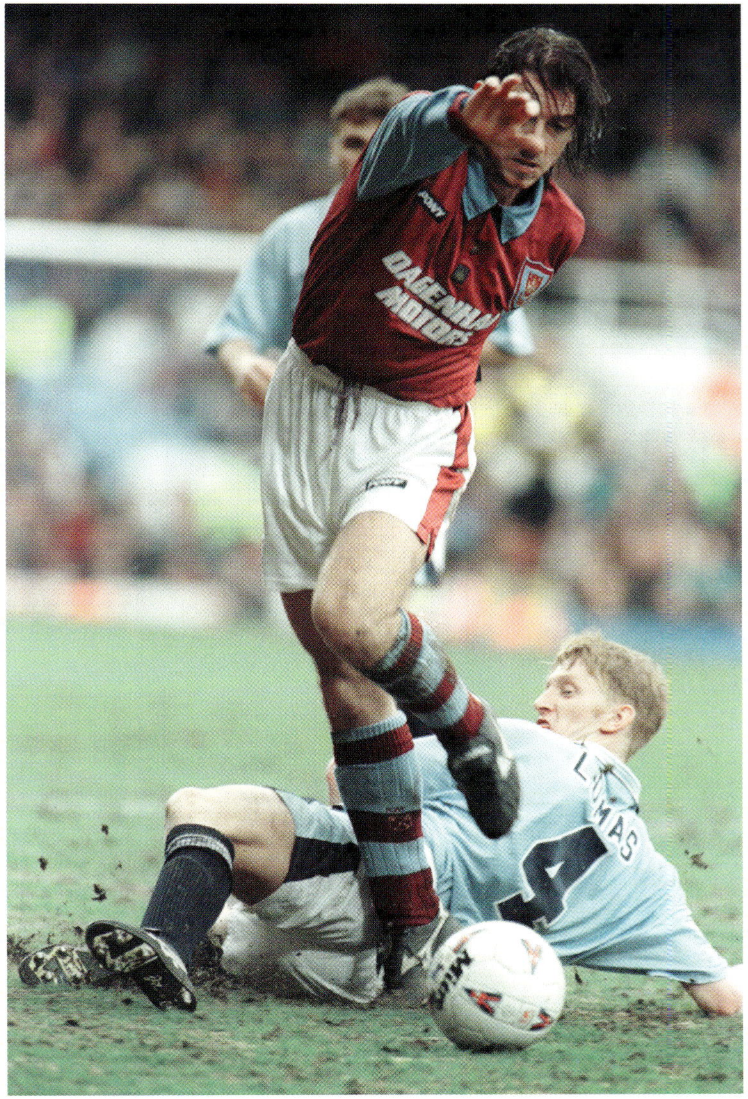
MOTORS

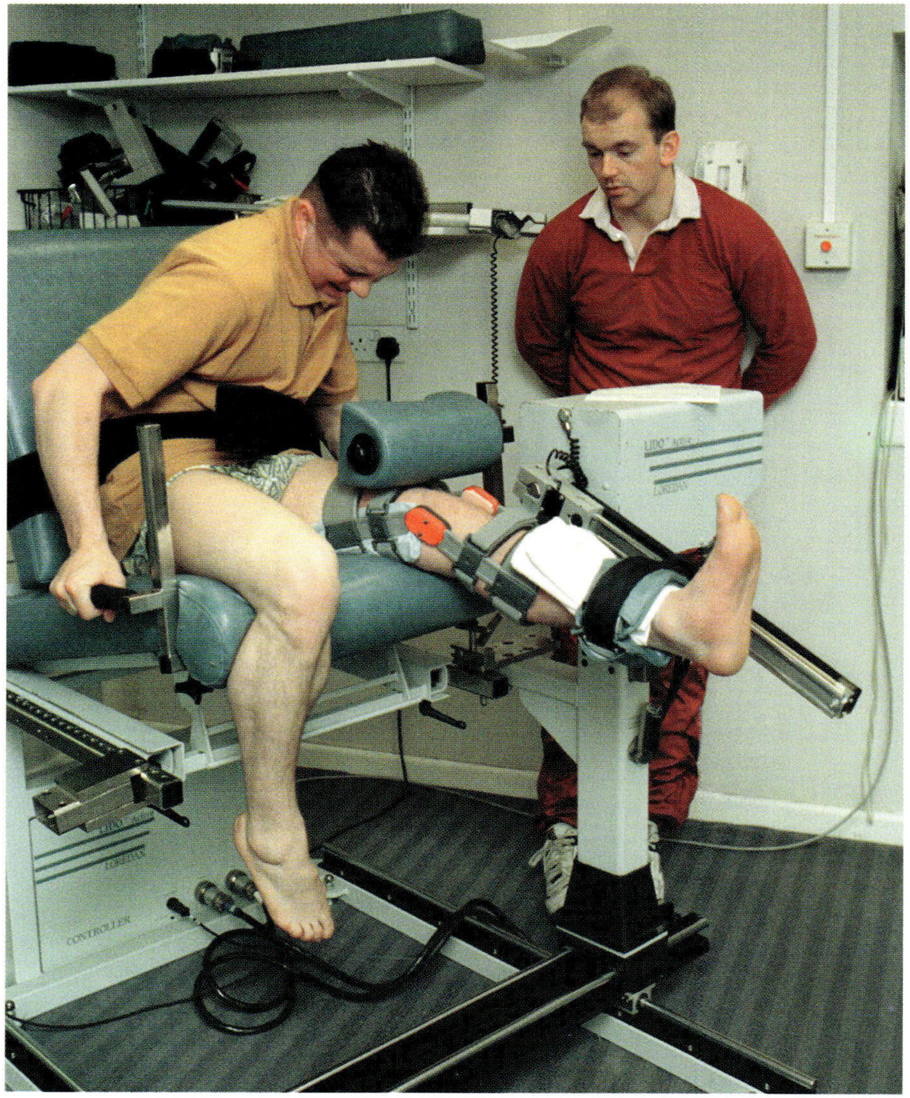

No pain; no gain. Julian Dicks shows the strain as he puts everything into his rehabilitation following knee surgery in January 1991. Physio John Green oversees the session at a Harley Street clinic which Dicksie visited several times a week. Julian did not return to first team action until December 1991 when he scored a penalty in the 1–1 draw at home to Sheffield United.

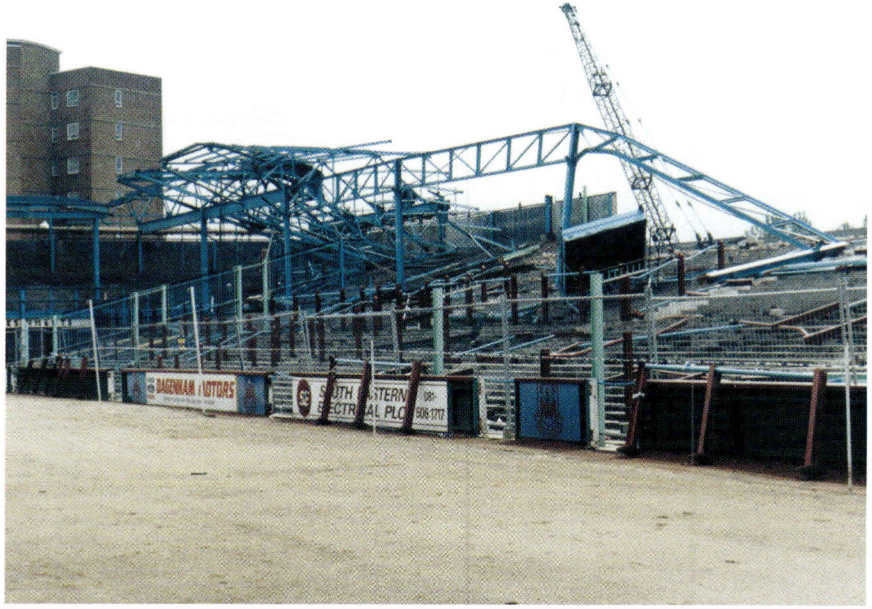

In memoriam. The Boleyn Ground saw major changes in the early nineties with new North and South stands erected. The demolition of the old South Bank was well under way when this picture was taken in May 1993. With the tragic, premature death of Bobby Moore on 24th February 1993, it was only natural that the new stand should bear the name of West Ham's greatest son when it was officially opened on Monday 7th March 1994.

Hart of gold. John Hartson cues the ball up nicely on his toe to score the second of his two goals against Sheffield Wednesday in the penultimate home game of the 1996–97 season, a resounding 5–1 victory. John and Paul Kitson had joined the club in February 1997, and the goals they grabbed between them made the difference between survival and relegation.

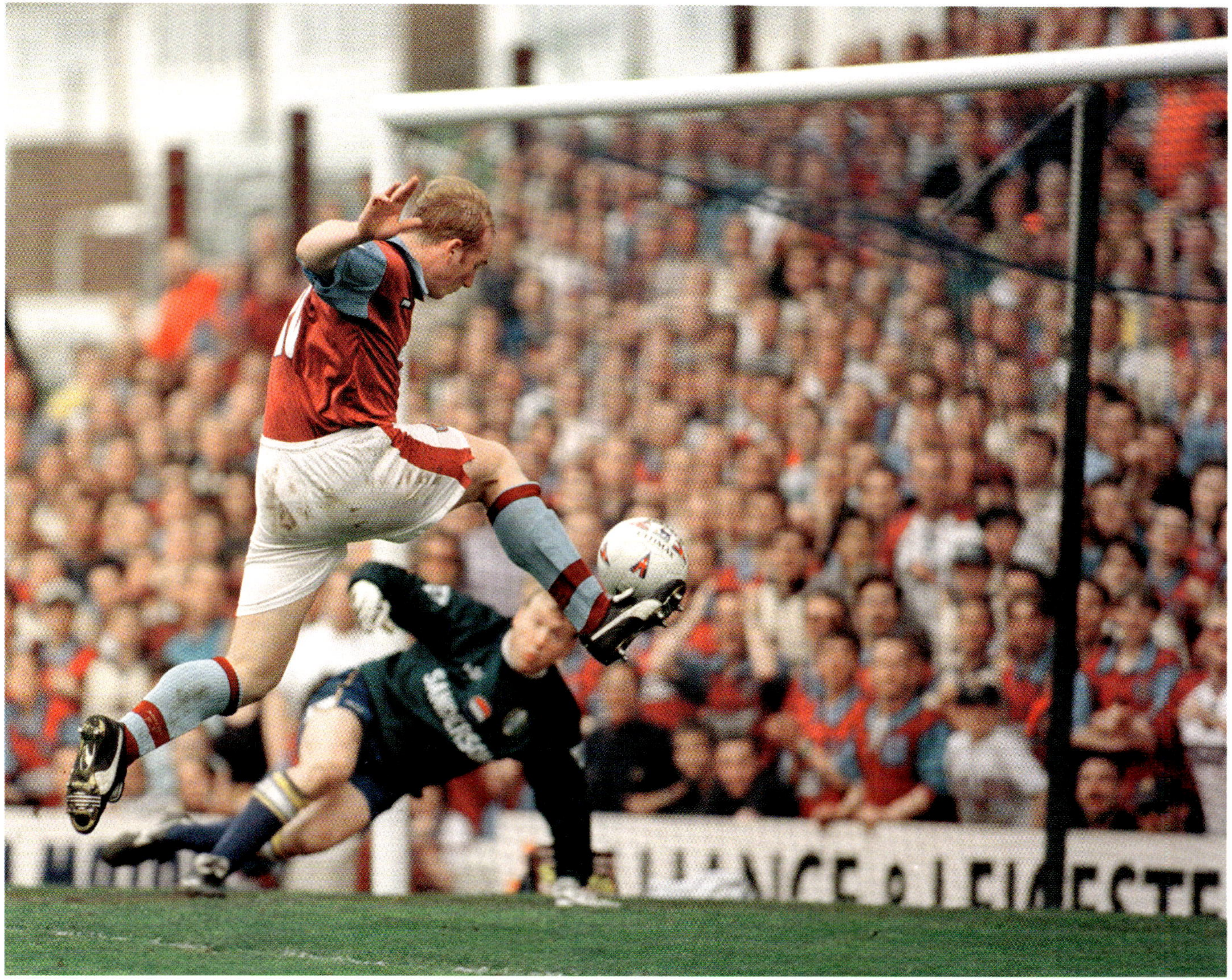

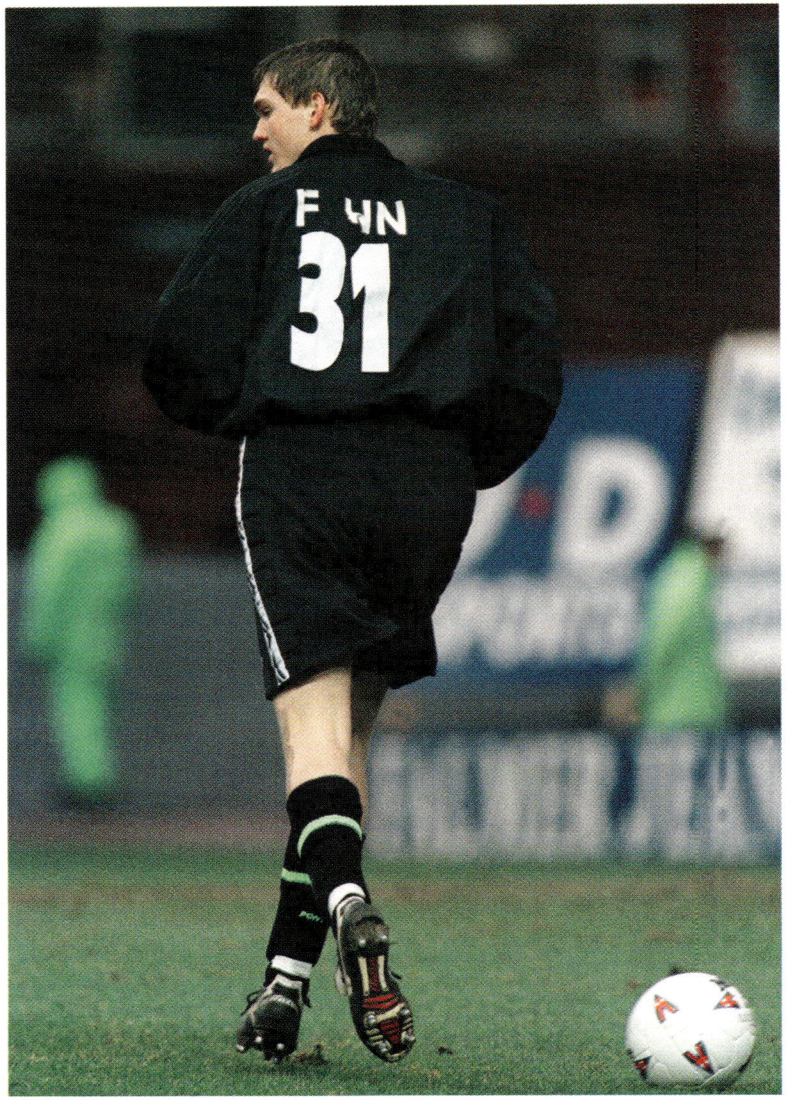

Got it taped. Young goalkeeper Neil Finn got an unexpected call-up into first-team action at Maine Road on the first day of 1996 when both Ludek Miklosko and Les Sealey suffered injury. It was such a late call that his number 31 jersey was only completed minutes before kick-off. Ludek's wife had sewn the number on the back but Neil's name was put on with strapping tape — which started peeling off just as the game began. Hammers lost the match 2–1.

Tributes: part of the massive display of floral tributes from fans of many clubs which grew daily outside the gates of Upton Park. I had gone to the club the night that the news of Bobby Moore's death broke and there were a few fans and flowers there at that time. I could not believe it when I returned the following morning and saw how the shrine to Hammers' favourite son had grown overnight.

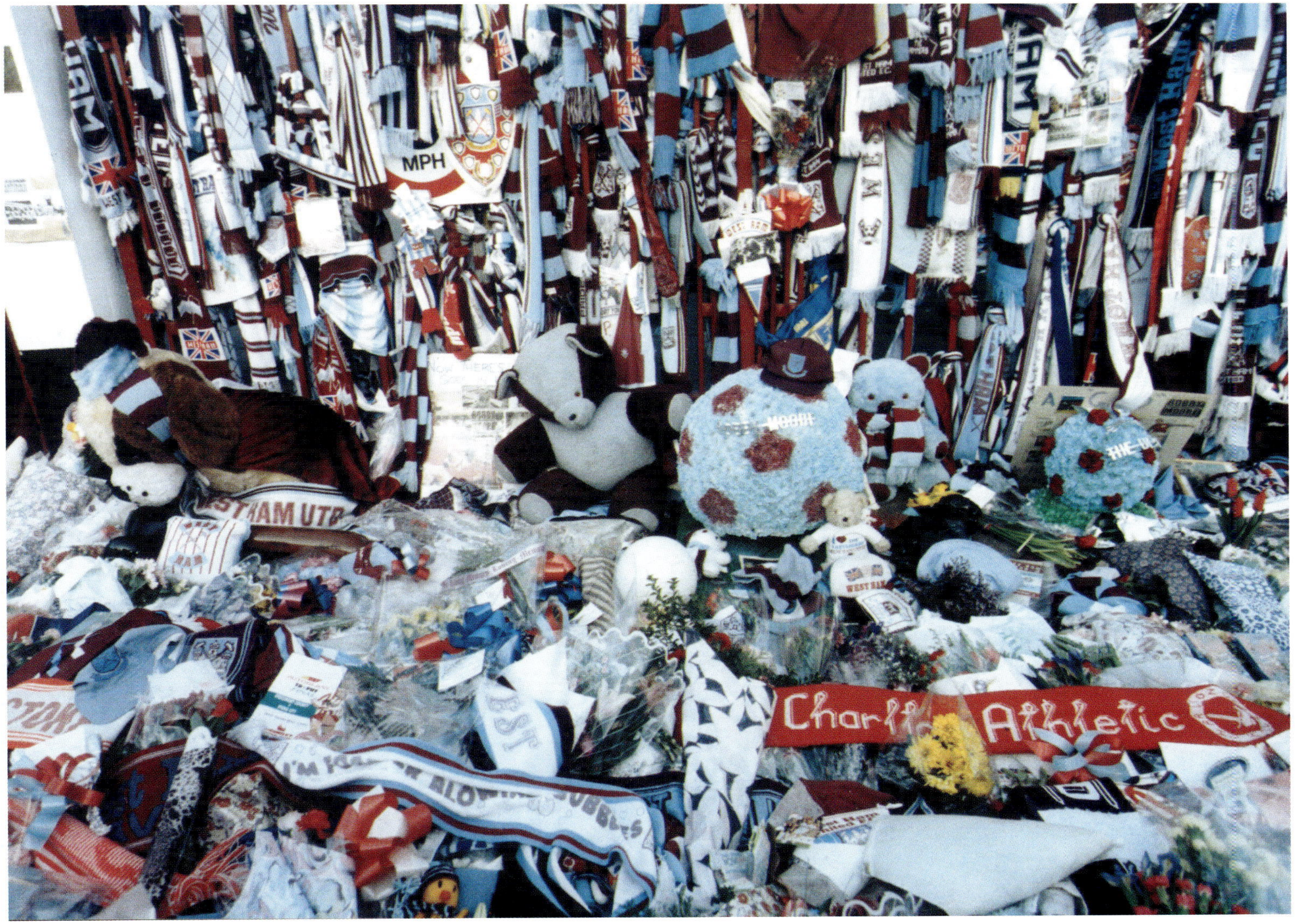
MPH
Athletic

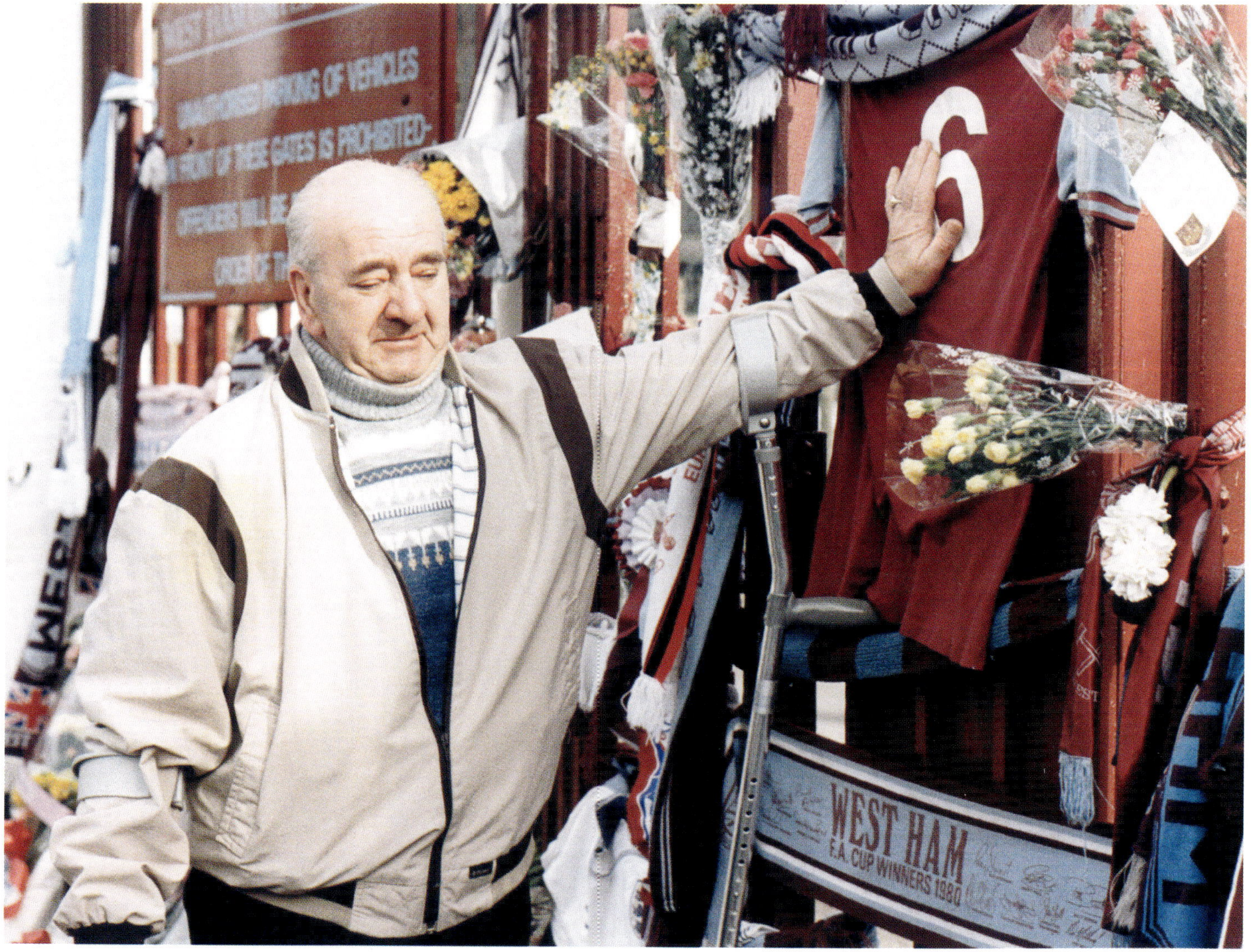

Tears. An elderly supporter lets his feelings show as he touches a number six shirt hung on the Upton Park gates by a Hammers' fan. Nobody who visited the ground at that time could fail to be caught up in the emotion of the moment. I know that I was no exception, even though I made many visits over the days after Bobby's death.

Six for the best. The first game at Upton Park following the death of Bobby Moore was against Wolverhampton Wanderers on Saturday 6th March 1993. Before the match, Bobby's old West Ham and England World Cup-winning team-mates, Martin Peters and Geoff Hurst, were joined by former manager Ron Greenwood to carry a giant number six shirt, made out of hundreds of flowers, into the middle of the pitch.

Silence is golden. The players of West Ham United and Wolverhampton Wanderers form a circle in the middle of the pitch as a minute's silence is observed in respect for Bobby Moore. This was the most immaculately held silence I have ever known and was a very emotional moment for me personally.

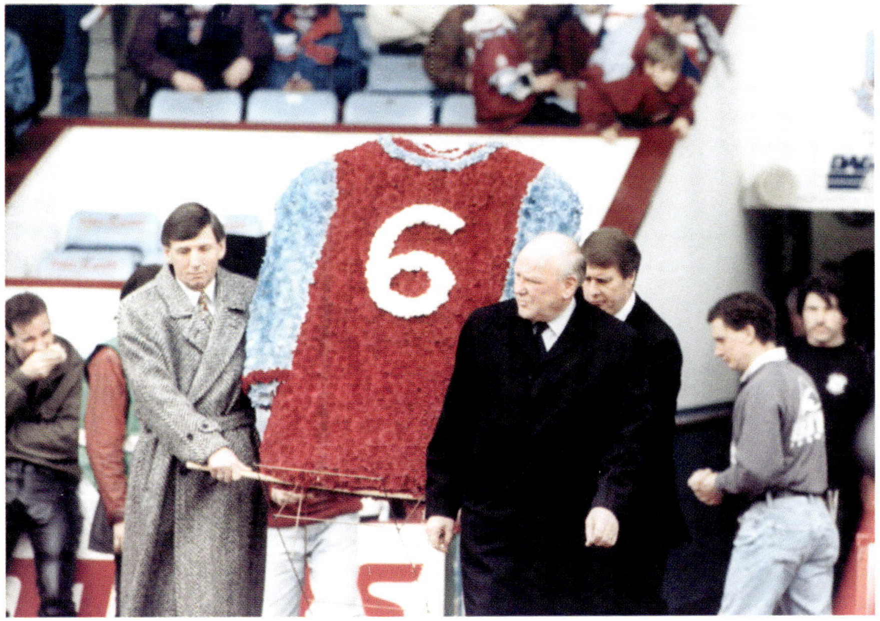

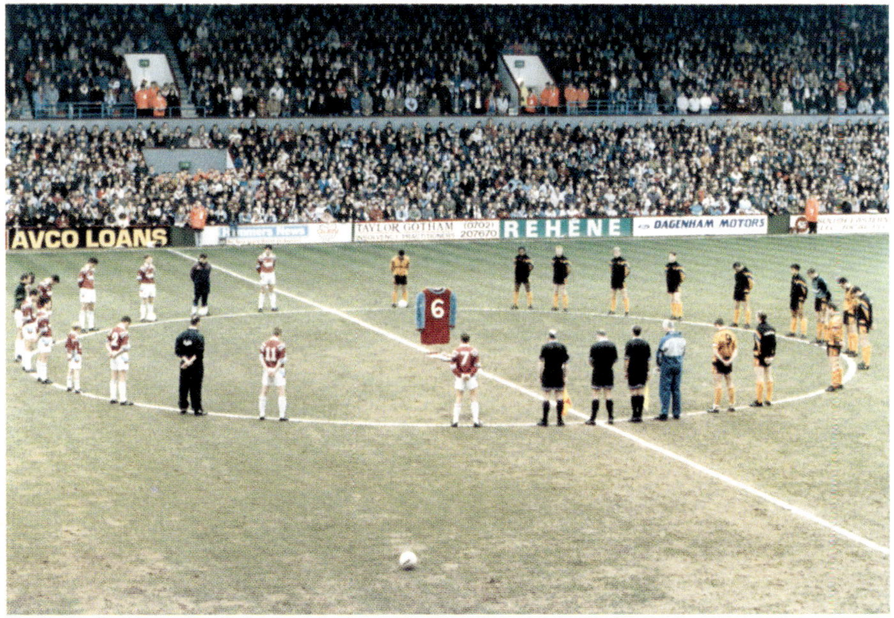

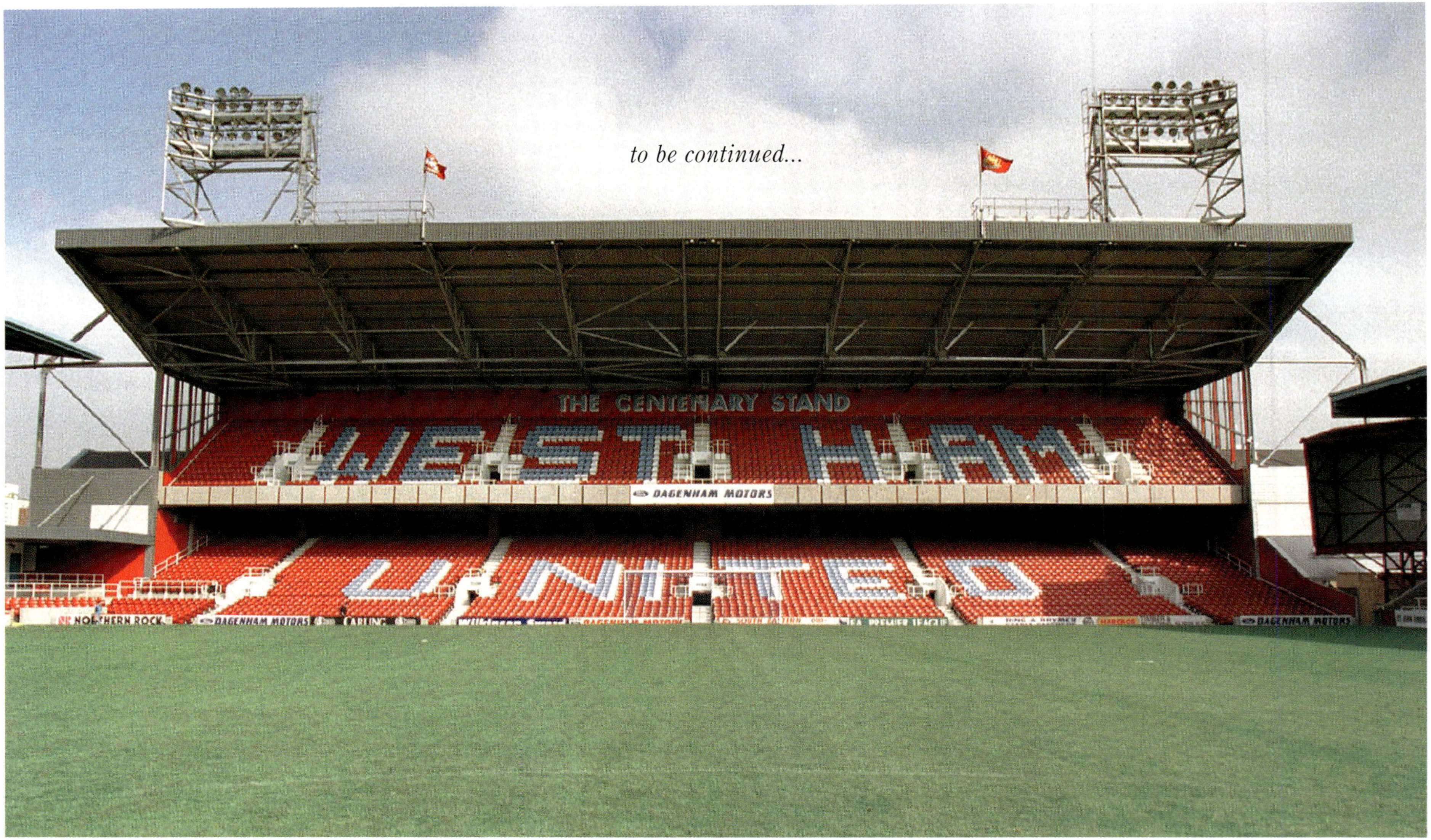

to be continued...